# Contents

# FOURTH EDITION

# ALL IN ONE

# Basic Writing Text, Workbook, and Reader

### LARAINE FERGENSON
### MARIE-LOUISE NICKERSON

**Bronx Community College**
**City University of New York**

*[handwritten: manner Pg. 100 read. 100-113 thru Exercise 11d, 11E]*

## PRENTICE HALL
Upper Saddle River, New Jersey 07458

Fergenson, Laraine.
    All in one : basic writing text, workbook, and reader / Laraine
Fergenson, Marie-Louise Nickerson. — 4th ed.
        p.    cm.
    Rev. ed. of: All in one / Marie-Louise Matthew [i.e. Marie-Louise
Nickerson]
    Includes index.
    ISBN 0-13-530940-9
    1. English language—Rhetoric.   2. English language—Grammar—
Problems, exercises, etc.   3. Report writing—Problems, exercises,
etc.   4. College readers.   I. Nickerson, Marie-Louise.
II. Nickerson, Marie-Louise. All in one.   III. Title.
PE1408.F446   1999
808'.0427—DC21                                      97-43263
                                                    CIP

Editor-in-Chief: *Charlyce Jones Owen*
Assistant Editor: *Maggie Barbieri*
Editorial Assistant: *Jean Polk*
Managing Editor: *Bonnie Biller*
Production Liaison: *Fran Russello*
Editorial/Production Supervision: *Publications Development Company of Texas*
Prepress and Manufacturing Buyer: *Mary Anne Gloriande*
Cover Director: *Jayne Conte*
Cover Designer: *Bruce Kenselaar*
Marketing Manager: *Rob Mejia*

This book was set in 10/12 point Century Schoolbook by Publications Development Company of Texas
and was printed and bound by R. R. Donnelley & Sons Company.
The cover was printed by Phoenix Color Corp.

Printed in the United States of America

10  9  8  7  6  5

ISBN 0-13-530940-9

Prentice-Hall International (UK) Limited, *London*
Prentice-Hall of Australia Pty. Limited, *Sydney*
Prentice-Hall of Canada, Inc., *Toronto*
Prentice-Hall Hispanoamericana, S. A., *Mexico*
Prentice-Hall of India Private Limited, *New Delhi*
Prentice-Hall of Japan, Inc., *Tokyo*
Pearson Education Asia Pte. Ltd., *Singapore*
Editora Prentice-Hall do Brasil, Ltda., *Rio de Janeiro*

*To the memory of Mina P. Shaughnessy*

PART TWO

# Reader with Study Questions and Vocabulary-Building Exercises  401

# Preface

**ALL IN ONE** is really three books in one. This edition, like the first three, is (1) a comprehensive writing skills handbook and workbook, (2) an anthology of acclaimed reading selections, edited and annotated for basic writing students, and (3) a vocabulary builder, with vocabulary exercises based on the words in the readings.

Along with new readings and exercises, this fourth edition features a rearrangement of the chapters in order to incorporate the material on editing and correcting into the first unit, which takes the "whole-paper" approach. The chapter on "The Double Correction Method," so popular with students and instructors because of its success in helping basic writers to learn from errors noted on their previous essays, is now in Unit One, since most instructors choose to teach it early and encourage students to use the method throughout the semester. Instructors may easily rearrange chapters to suit their individual methods because each chapter is self-contained, but the new chapter order provides a sequence that many instructors might want to follow.

This fourth edition of **ALL IN ONE** contains fifteen readings, five of which are different from those in the third edition. These readings, like those in previous editions, are works of enduring literary value. In addition to the works by William Shakespeare, Miguel de Cervantes, Henry Thoreau, Langston Hughes, and other great authors, we have added readings from Maya Angelou, Mohandas K. Gandhi, Antoine de Saint-Exupéry, Richard Wright, and Frank McCourt, recent winner of a Pulitzer prize for *Angela's Ashes*. Thus, we have included a mixture of writing ranging from the distant past to the contemporary scene.

Although we have concentrated on prose, we have also included some poetry and drama to introduce students to the richness and variety of literature. The readings in **ALL IN ONE** have been selected to challenge and interest students and to arouse, motivate, and inspire them by demonstrating what writing can do. By reading selections from writers as diverse as Cervantes, Thoreau, Martin Luther

King, Jr., Maya Angelou, and Frank McCourt, students can learn to appreciate the power of the written word. They see how literature can provide enjoyment, express inner feelings, and even help to create a better world.

This fourth edition retains the sample essays by students written in response to the study questions following the readings. The inclusion of these essays, all of which were written by Bronx Community College students, creates a greater integration between the two parts of the book. The essays, while providing peer prose models, link the workbook and rhetoric in Part One and the reading selections in Part Two. The questions and comments following the sample essays emphasize and clarify this link.

From previous editions we have retained two successful means of vocabulary building. The words defined with the readings are tested in the first vocabulary exercise following the reading. Most of the selections have an "Expanding Your Vocabulary" section that builds on these words, teaching different meanings and connotations of the words found in the text as well as new words related to them. Thus, **ALL IN ONE** offers two proven methods of vocabulary building: (1) natural encountering of new words through reading, and (2) building from root words.

Like the first three editions, this new **ALL IN ONE** provides extensive practice in sentence structure, verbs, diction, and writing mechanics for students who may not have heard standard English spoken very frequently and who may have had little previous opportunity to practice writing.

New to this fourth edition are sections designed to help students who approach English as a second language (ESL). We have added two chapters, "English Idioms for ESL Writers" and "Advice for ESL Writers," that will be particularly useful. We have retained from earlier editions the chapter "Articles: *The, A, An*," which many of our ESL students have found particularly valuable.

We have streamlined the approach to sentence structure, retaining those aspects of grammar that are essential to help students understand the basic syntax of the sentence, but shortening some grammatical explanations to provide more exercises that directly address some common problems—fragmented, run-on, or comma-splice sentences. We have also combined two chapters dealing with the past tense of verbs, incorporating the "confusing verb forms," that is, the principal parts of irregular verbs, into the chapter dealing with the past tense. We have retained and expanded sections of the book on proofreading strategies, especially on avoiding the problem of dropped word endings (*s, 's, s', and ed*), which previous users of this text have found very helpful. In short, we have aimed at retaining all that was valuable and helpful from previous editions while improving grammatical explanations wherever possible.

Because the varied reading, writing, and editing skills are best learned in conjunction with one another, **ALL IN ONE** embodies a comprehensive view of basic writing. At a stage when students are practicing subject-verb agreement, they can also be writing paragraphs or compositions, as well as reading examples of good literature. This book takes an all-in-one approach, offering exercises for practicing essential writing skills and a selection of stimulating readings with vocabulary exercises.

We are grateful to many people who helped during the writing and production of **ALL IN ONE.** Special thanks go to those who edited and contributed to the *Journal of Basic Writing* for their valuable insights and specific suggestions on the teaching of composition; to Irwin Berger of Bronx Community College for teaching us his version of the Double-Correction Method; to Susan Fawcett for her encouragement and practical advice; to classroom assistants David Elias, Louise Lord, and George Whitman for helping to test the exercises; to Oral Harrison, Martha Perez, and Ruth Rivers for allowing us to publish their essays; to Maggie Barbieri, our editor at Prentice Hall, and her assistant Joan Polk for their valuable help in preparing this book; to Fran Russello of Prentice Hall for guiding the book production; to Nancy Marcus Land and Pam Blackmon of Publications Development Company; to Ruth V. Anderson of Trident Technical College, Anne E. Cathey of Hartnell College, Colleen Corless of Saint Peters College, Richard H. Dodge of Santa Monica City College, Jane Haynes of Ball State University, Eric P. Hibbison of J. Sargeant Reynolds Community College, Deborah Israel of South Oklahoma City Junior College, Judith Longo of Ocean County College, Sarah MacMillan of John Jay College of Criminal Justice, Gail M. McDonald of Southern Vermont College, JoAnna Moore of State Technical Institute at Memphis, Terrence Morgan of Tidewater Community College, Carol A. Paskuly of Erie Community College, A. Rae Price of Penn Valley Community College, Jon T. Taylor of Florida Junior College, Dorothy Voyles of Parkland College, and Harvey Wiener of City University of New York, for thoughtful readings of our manuscript and valuable suggestions for its improvement; to our families for their understanding and patience; and, finally, to all our students—past, present, and future—who are the main reason for this book.

LARAINE FERGENSON

MARIE-LOUISE NICKERSON

# PART ONE

# Basic Writing Text and Workbook

# AN APPROACH TO WRITING

CHAPTER

# 1

# Introduction: Getting Started

## WHY WE WRITE

We live in a world of words. Language is the lifeblood of civilization. With language we can communicate our ideas, our discoveries, our hopes, and our fears. With language we can sell products. With language we can convince people to vote a certain way. With language we can make people see things as we see them. With language we can even change people's basic ideas. In short, language is a powerful tool. Mastery over language is *power*.

A student in a college English course once wrote, "The man who doesn't know the language of his society well is a lost and forgotten man." He was right. A mastery of the language is necessary for any man or woman who wants to play an important role in society, hold a responsible position, and earn a good salary. Most large companies want managers who can write clear letters and memos. Writing well is also essential for doctors and others in the medical field, lawyers, educators, newspaper reporters, radio announcers, and people in all the communications media including television.

## Writing Can Help You

- **Get through college with good grades.** Many tests are essay tests, and even in subjects other than English, compositions and research papers are required.
- **Find a good job.** Writing well is one of the really important skills for most well-paid jobs that offer a chance for advancement.
- **Take action to change things you don't like.** You might want to write a petition to give to the president of your college, a letter to your landlord asking for improved conditions in your apartment building, or a letter to your senator or representative about an issue that is important to you.
- **Express yourself to "get something off your chest."** Writing down your feelings can be a great relief. People who can express themselves well in writing have an emotional outlet.
- **Express your happy and positive feelings.** Did you ever feel so happy about something that you wanted everyone to know how you felt? Did you ever see something so beautiful that you wanted other people to know how beautiful it was? Did you ever meet a person who was so wonderful that you wanted to tell all your friends about him or her? Professional writers have these feelings, and they write them down. You can do so too.

## WHY WE ARE AFRAID TO WRITE

Although most people agree on the importance of writing, many students groan when they are asked to write a composition. Why?

Maybe they feel that writing is too difficult. So much is involved in writing. You have to think up ideas, put them in the right order, find the right words, and use correct grammar, spelling, and punctuation. It seems like so much to do at once. And there are so many possibilities for making errors. What can you do to eliminate, or at least reduce, the fear of writing?

First, you can learn to break down the complicated writing task. Good writing is a series of steps, which may include most or all of the following activities: brainstorming, freewriting, clustering, outlining, drafting, revising, and editing. You can learn these steps with the help of your instructor and the exercises in this book.

Sometimes beginning writers complain that they have "nothing to say." Actually everyone has ideas. It's a matter of learning how to turn on the tap and let your ideas flow. There are methods described in this book that will help you to do this.

Many people fear writing because they have not had much practice and because they are afraid of making mistakes, especially grammatical mistakes. First, we must remember that we write mainly to express ideas, and correct grammar simply helps us to make those ideas clear and comprehensible. Second, it is important to understand that making mistakes is part of the learning process. Third, experienced writers use the same techniques you will learn to use; they too, just like you, go through the process of thinking, writing, revising, and correcting. Even the greatest writers made mistakes when they were first learning. **No one is born knowing how to write.** Writing is a skill that is acquired through study and practice. So if you have ever felt afraid to write because you were worried about making errors, remember that making mistakes in writing is a stage that everyone passes through. The double-correction method, described in Chapter 9, will show you a way to learn from your mistakes, and as you continue writing and correcting your papers, you will make fewer and fewer errors.

To help overcome your fear, write as much as possible. Sometimes students are so afraid of making errors that they write very little. This is no solution. These students are like beginning skaters who avoid falling by taking small, halting steps. Such skaters don't fall down, but they don't learn how to skate well either. If they really want to skate, they have to move in big, sweeping steps. They may fall at times, but they can get up again—and in this way can learn how to skate with confidence. Similarly, people learning to write must not let their fear of making mistakes limit their progress. Writing often and writing down many ideas will help you to become a more confident writer.

## HOW TO START

Some beginning writers feel uncomfortable when writing on an assigned topic, and you may feel this way too. To begin with, you may enjoy "free" writing—with no limits on topic or length.

If you could write on any subject at all, what would it be? Here is a list of possible writing topics. If you like one of them, write about it. Or make up your own subject. Perhaps this list will give you ideas for other topics.

1. Write a description of yourself. You can begin with a physical description and then go on to describe your personality and character.

2. Write a short autobiography, the story of your life.

3. If you could go back to the past and change one decision that you made, what would it be?

4. Do you have a particular talent? Describe it and explain how you developed that talent.

5. Compare and contrast two of your friends or relatives.

6. Describe a person who has influenced or changed you in some way. Did that person change you for the better or for the worse?

7. Describe the happiest moment in your life, or the saddest.

8. Describe a movie, book, or television show you have enjoyed.

9. Describe the registration process at your college. Does it run smoothly, or is it difficult? How could it be improved?

10. Do you want to live to be 100 years old? Explain why or why not.

## KEEPING A JOURNAL

Some students find that keeping a journal, also known as a diary, can help them to get used to the idea of writing. The words *journal* and *diary* refer to daily writing (day is *jour* in French, *dia* in Spanish). In other words, a journal or diary is a place where a person can record a day's activities or the thoughts and feelings that occurred to him or her during the day.

You may keep a journal in order to help increase your writing fluency. If you write every day or nearly every day, you will find that it becomes easier and easier to think of things to write down. You may discuss the work you are doing in school, or you may write about your life in general. You may want to use your diary as a place to write down feelings that you might like to explore.

The form of a journal is generally quite simple. Each entry usually begins with the date. Then some people include a greeting, such as "Dear Diary," if they are considering their diary as a kind of friend to confide in. Some examples are shown on the following page.

*January 3, 1998*

Dear Diary,

Today I went back to school to take my math exam. It was not as hard as I expected, and I think I did pretty well in it. I finished the exam about twenty minutes before the time was up, so I had a chance to check over all of the problems.

As I was leaving the exam, a guy who is also in my French class started talking to me. He said he thought the exam was pretty fair. Then he asked me if I wanted to have some coffee with him, and we went to the cafeteria. His name is Johnny, and he seems very nice. He says I look like his sister. We are going to get together tomorrow to review for the French exam.

March 20, 1998

I saw a robin today, and then looked at the calendar and noticed that it is the first day of spring.

I wish I could write more today, but I have a ton of work to do.

*June 6, 1998*

My exams are over! I took chemistry today, my last one. I was so happy afterwards that I took my mother out to lunch to celebrate. Then we went shopping for some summer clothes.

*When we returned home, Eddie said that I had received a call from Mrs. Blackwell at the town's recreation office, but it was too late for me to call her back. I hope that I got the summer job at the day camp. I'll call her first thing tomorrow morning to find out.*

You can choose any of the forms illustrated above if you wish to keep a journal, or you can use one that your instructor recommends. You may write in a specially prepared diary with the dates pre-printed, or in a notebook, which gives you more flexibility in the length of your entries. If your instructor collects and reads diary entries, you may use a loose-leaf notebook so you can hand in just a few pages at a time.

By writing every day or as often as you can, you will become accustomed to putting your thoughts into written form.

CHAPTER

# 2

# What Is a Composition?

When your instructor assigns a composition on a certain subject, do you feel confident that you know what is wanted? Or do you wonder what the instructor expects of you? What actually is an English composition?

Sometimes looking at the parts of a word can reveal its meaning. The word "composition" breaks up into:

|  |  |  |
|---|---|---|
| *com* | and | *position* |

*Com* comes from the Latin word *cum,* meaning "with" (compare the Spanish *con*).

*Position* means where something has been put or placed. It comes from the Latin word *ponere,* meaning "to put or place."

Therefore, a composition is a number of things placed together.

Not all compositions are made with words. There are musical compositions made up of different sounds, and there are artistic compositions made up of different lines and colors. But when we speak of a composition in an English class, we mean an arrangement of words and sentences to express ideas clearly.

A composition consists of paragraphs. Each paragraph develops an idea. Paragraphs usually contain three or more related sentences; in the various kinds of assignments college students write, paragraphs may contain as few as three or as many as fifteen sentences. Paragraphs are indicated by an indentation of one inch or five typed spaces (notice the indentations in the sample essay below).

One way to think of a composition is in diagram form. Many compositions have an **introduction,** several **main-body paragraphs,** and a **conclusion.** The introduction and the conclusion may be separate paragraphs, or, in a short paper, the introduction may be combined with the first main-body paragraph, and the conclusion may be combined with the last main-body paragraph.

The composition below was written in response to an essay question asking the writer to discuss how technology has changed the average American house in the last forty years.

### The Modern American House

INTRODUCTION

Today the average American house is very different from the average house of forty years ago. Advances in technology have brought into our homes machines and appliances that offer us convenience, entertainment, and greater efficiency. In the kitchen, the family room, the home office, virtually every room in the house, we find objects rarely if ever seen forty years ago.

MAIN-BODY PARAGRAPH

In most modern households, out of economic necessity both partners work, and technology has supplied appliances that save time and effort in the kitchen. Coffeemakers can be filled the night before and programmed to have coffee ready when the family wakes up. Crockpots can be set to have dinner ready when family members get home from school and work. Ovens with built-in thermometers can shut themselves off when the food is fully cooked. Microwave ovens not only reheat leftovers but also cook many foods in a fraction of the time needed by conventional ovens.

MAIN-BODY PARAGRAPH

In the family room, and in fact throughout the house, technology has added greatly to the American family's entertainment. Some television sets allow viewers to watch one program and monitor another. VCRs can be programmed to record shows that people watch later, omitting the advertisements. Those same VCRs can show movies, either commercial ones that are bought or rented, or home movies shot on a video camera. Turntables still exist, but most home stereo systems include tape players and CD players. Many people also have portable tape or CD players.

An aspect of the home that has been greatly affected by technology is communication. Within the house, intercoms allow people in different rooms to talk to each other. Many parents use baby monitors in their infants' bedrooms. If the baby is crying, parents can respond at once. Technology has also made communicating with others from a home office easier and faster. Telephones now are equipped with call waiting, call forwarding, and the capacity to handle conference calls. Fax machines can send copies of documents in just seconds. Sending e-mail on a computer is much faster than the regular mail and usually much less expensive than a telephone conversation.

In many ways, the houses of today are very different from those in the past. Technology has changed the ways in which we cook, entertain ourselves, and communicate. If people from the 1950s could be transported by time machine (one invention technology has not given us yet!) into the present, they would be astonished by the variety and capacity of the machines that many of us take for granted.

MAIN-BODY PARAGRAPH

CONCLUSION

CHAPTER

# 3

# Planning Your Essay: The Thesis

## THESIS STATEMENT VS. TOPIC STATEMENT

A thesis is the main idea of an essay. It can often be expressed in a single sentence, which we call the **thesis sentence.**

When you begin to write, you will probably have a **topic.** A topic is the general subject. You may be able to choose your own, or the teacher may assign the topic. **However, your topic is *not* the same as a thesis.** A thesis must include your point of view, the specific idea about the topic that you want to prove. The teacher may assign the topic, but only *you* can supply your thesis.

Suppose, for example, that your instructor assigned a composition on child abuse. Child abuse is an important topic, but it is not a thesis. A thesis would express a definite point of view on child abuse.

For example:

> Parents who abuse their children should lose the right to keep their children.

or

> Parents who abuse their children need help and understanding, not punishment.

Notice that these two thesis statements take different points of view about the topic.

A thesis often appears early in an essay. The first paragraph, or **introduction,** is a good place for it. In the introductory paragraph you may first state your topic and then present your particular view on that topic. Here is a sample introduction from an essay on parents who smoke.

|  |  |
|---|---|
| *STATEMENT OF TOPIC:* | **Many parents who smoke wonder about the effect of this habit upon their children.** They certainly have reason to be concerned. **Parents who smoke may be harming their children both physically and psychologically, so they should seriously try to give up the habit.** |
| *THESIS STATEMENT:* | |

In the sample introduction above, the thesis statement is placed at the end of the paragraph. Placing the thesis as the last sentence in the first paragraph is an effective way to begin an essay.

Any topic may lead to many different thesis statements. For example:

| *Statement of Topic* | *Thesis* |
|---|---|
| You can hardly open up a newspaper or magazine lately without reading something about computers. | All children should be required to take a computer course. |
| or | or |
| Everyone today seems to be talking about computers. | Computers are changing our society for the worse. |
| or | or |
| People nowadays often ask: How will computers affect the future? | Computers can improve the way we live. |

| *Statement of Topic* | *Thesis* |
|---|---|
| Overpopulation is a topic of much interest these days. | To solve the problem of overpopulation, all families should have only one or two children. |
| or | or |
| Many people today are worried about overpopulation. | To fight overpopulation, birth control should be a legal requirement. |
| | or |
| | Overpopulation would not be an issue if the world's food and other resources were distributed equally. |

Remember that a thesis presents a specific point of view on a topic. Thus the thesis statement provides the focus of the essay.

Often it is not necessary to have a separate sentence to introduce a topic, especially in a short paper. An essay may be more interesting if the thesis statement itself introduces the topic. Introductions like "I would like to discuss . . ." and "The following essay will consider . . ." can often slow down the reading of a paper and make it boring. Occasionally such introductory statements may be necessary, but you should try to avoid them when possible.

**EXERCISE 3a**

*State whether each sentence is a thesis or a topic statement.*

EXAMPLES   *thesis*    **a.** Being famous has more disadvantages than advantages.

     *topic*    **b.** In this paper I will discuss the effects of fame.

_____ **1.** Many people are currently discussing the serious problem of crime.

_____ **2.** Everybody should learn to speak and read a second language.

_____ **3.** This paper will discuss the subject of pesticides.

_____ **4.** Fathers can take care of children as well as mothers can.

_____ **5.** I will compare country life and city life.

_____ **6.** Poverty is the main cause of crime.

_____ **7.** The law should require birth control clinics to tell parents when their teenage children receive contraceptives.

_____ **8.** Picasso is the most important figure in twentieth-century art.

_____ **9.** I will discuss the life and work of Pablo Picasso.

_____ **10.** Teenagers, just like adults, have a right to keep their birth control plans confidential.

_____ **11.** Without chemical pesticides, American agriculture would fail.

_____ **12.** Chemical pesticides are destroying our land, our food, and our health.

_____ **13.** The topic of this report is Sigmund Freud.

_____ **14.** In addition to being a civil rights leader, Martin Luther King, Jr., was an excellent writer.

_____ **15.** A controversial question these days is whether birth control clinics should be required to tell parents when their teenage children ask for contraceptives.

After you have completed the exercise, consider this question: Are the topic statements or the thesis statements more interesting and thought-provoking?

**EXERCISE 3b**   *Create two or more thesis statements for each topic listed below.*

*EXAMPLE*   Sex education

*1. All high schools should offer sex education courses.*

*2. A young person's sex education should be left up to his or her parents.*

**1.** Drug abuse

_____

_____

_____

**2.** Television

_____

_____

_____

**3.** Marriage during the teenage years

_____

_____

_____

## FORMULATING A THESIS IN RESPONSE TO TEST QUESTIONS

Students in college classes are often asked to write essays in re-sponse to particular questions, and very often these questions appear on tests. When you take an exam, you may be asked to write an essay on a particular issue. Sometimes the wording of the test question may help you to formulate your thesis. For example, you may be pre-sented with an idea on an issue and asked whether you agree or dis-agree with it. When you decide how you feel, you are beginning to formulate your thesis. Let's consider the following essay test question as an example:

> Children under the age of five need the care of their moth-ers. For that reason, women with preschool children should stay at home with them and postpone starting their careers until their children are older. Do you agree or disagree?

Since this paragraph expresses a clear point of view, it already has a thesis: "women with preschool children should stay at home with them and postpone starting their careers until their children are older." If you agree with this idea, you will be adopting the thesis ex-pressed in the test question. You may want to restate the thesis in your own words, and then you can begin to plan your essay by think-ing up reasons why you have taken up this point of view. On the other hand, if you disagree with this statement, you are formulating an-other thesis. You may feel that a mother has just as much right as a father to begin a career while her child is very young. This idea is a thesis too, a thesis that takes the opposite point of view from the one presented. When you are asked if you agree or disagree with a particular statement, do not hesitate to disagree if that is how you feel. Your essay will not be penalized for taking a point of view opposed to the statement in the test question. It will be judged on how well your thesis is supported.

**EXERCISE
3c**

*Formulate at least one thesis for each of the following "agree or disagree" statements. Try to formulate one thesis that agrees with the statement given and one that disagrees with it.*

1. Every year young people, often of college age, get hopelessly in debt by misusing their credit cards. Credit card companies and banks should realize that many young people are too irresponsible to use credit cards wisely and should stop issuing them to anyone under the age of 21. Do you agree or disagree?

   Thesis 1: _____

   _____

   _____

   Thesis 2: _____

   _____

   _____

2. Many families move into public emergency shelters when they could be living with relatives. The government should save money by refusing to place any family in a shelter if relatives live in the same city. Do you agree or disagree?

   Thesis 1: _____

   _____

   _____

   Thesis 2: _____

   _____

   _____

3. Since dogs require a great deal of attention and free space to run in, people who live in apartments and are away at work or school all day should not own a dog. Do you agree or disagree?

Thesis 1: _certain_ _____

_____

_____

Thesis 2: _____

_____

_____

## FORMULATING A THESIS IN RESPONSE TO ESSAY TOPICS THAT CALL FOR DISCUSSION

In many cases, directions that appear on essay tests do not suggest a thesis, but instead ask the student to "discuss" a certain issue. The test topic may present a brief quotation from a book or essay and ask the student to discuss the issues presented, for example:

> Marriage requires sacrifice and a certain level of compromise. Marriage partners must learn to give and take. Some of one's freedom and personal plans have to be changed or even given up for the value of marriage itself. Compromise is necessary to the survival of a marriage.
>
> The statement above tells us that compromise is part of a successful marriage. Discuss ways in which compromise can help a marriage to survive.

It may be more difficult to formulate a thesis in response to this kind of exam topic than to one that asks if you agree or disagree with a statement. Instead of an opinion thesis that focuses and controls the essay, you will need to develop a kind of essay organization based upon a **discussion thesis** (sometimes called a **directional thesis**). This type of thesis is not so obviously argumentative as the examples we have seen earlier in this chapter, but it does provide your essay with a general focus and point of view. For example, let us look again at the sample topic. If we read it carefully, we see that the key words are "compromise," "marriage," and "survive." We can ask questions about these words. For example, what does "compromise" mean? In the example, the word "compromise" is followed by a sentence telling us that marriage partners must "give and take," and this statement gives us a clue to the meaning of "compromise." Our next question might be: How does the give-and-take process contribute to the survival of a marriage? In response, you might say that compromise can help a marriage to survive by allowing both the husband and the wife to have their own way some of the time, but not all of the time. Now you have a thesis that will help you to organize your essay. You might then develop the essay by giving examples of the types of conflicts that might arise in a marriage and explaining how each type might be settled through compromise.

**EXERCISE 3d**  
*Formulate at least one thesis for each of the following essay questions. If necessary, look back at the example on marriage.*

1. The purpose of education is not simply to learn a body of facts or to learn how to perform specific tasks. Instead, education is a development of the whole person. It involves the shaping of the character as well as the mind.

   This passage suggests that education has many different goals. Discuss this view of education with relation to your own educational goals.

   Key words: _____

   Questions about key words: _____

   _____

   _____

   _____

   Discussion thesis: _____

   _____

   _____

2. Provided that they have the love of their parents, children who come from homes in which there is not much money are not badly off. In fact, these children may be better off than very rich children because at an early age they learn how to economize and how to make wise choices.

   This passage suggests that having a limited income may have certain advantages in forming the character of a child.

Discuss ways in which families without a great deal of money might have children of good character.

Key words: _____

Questions about key words: _____

_____

_____

_____

Discussion thesis: _____

_____

_____

3. Some sports programs in high school and college put great emphasis on teams and winning games. Some physical education instructors, however, emphasize life-long physical fitness and good health habits for everyone.

This passage suggests that some physical education instructors are trying to include all of the students in the benefits of sports and not just focusing on those who can help their teams win games. Discuss ways in which schools' physical education programs can benefit all of the students, not just star athletes.

Key words: _____

Questions about key words: _____

_____

_____

_____

Discussion thesis: _____

_____

_____

## STICKING TO YOUR THESIS

When you have learned how to formulate a thesis, you have gained a valuable skill, one that will help your writing enormously. A well-organized essay develops a thesis carefully, and it sticks to the thesis. In your paper, you give examples, illustrations, details, and explanations that support your thesis. If one of your ideas has nothing to do with the thesis, do not include that idea in your paper. You can think of your thesis as a kind of lighthouse guiding you through the writing of your essay. As you write, always remember the thesis you are trying to prove. Always keep your eye on the lighthouse.

**EXERCISE 3e** | *In the following essay, one of the paragraphs does not support the thesis, so it does not belong. Circle it. (Note: You will recognize the beginning of the essay from page 13. The thesis sentence is indicated.)*

## Parents Who Smoke

*THESIS→* Many parents who smoke wonder about the effect of this habit upon their children. They certainly have reason to be concerned. **Parents who smoke may be harming their children both physically and psychologically, so they should seriously try to give up the habit.**

When children live in a house with a smoker, they are frequently exposed to exhaled cigarette smoke. There is a growing body of evidence that such secondhand smoke may be harmful to those who inhale it. Recent studies have shown that children of parents who smoke miss more school days because of colds and suffer more throat irritations than children of nonsmoking parents.

But far more serious than missed school days and minor illnesses is the possibility that secondhand smoke may also be a cancer threat. The cancer-causing chemicals that endanger a smoker may also threaten those who passively breathe in the air the smoker has exhaled. It is known that the life expectancy for smokers is less than that of nonsmokers, and it seems likely that the life expectancy for those who live with a smoker is less than the life expectancy of those who do not. Thus, parents who smoke may be shortening not only their own lives, but also the lives of their children.

In addition to the physical dangers that parental smoking poses to children, there may also be psychological harm. When children learn about the dangers of smoking, they may begin to worry a great deal about the health of parents who smoke. They may also wonder why their parents continue to engage in such risky behavior. If parents lament their inability to stop smoking, the children may begin to regard them as weak. When parents seem to be saying, "Do as I say, not as I do," the children may become confused and may question the parents' judgment in many other areas.

People should also consider the negative effects of smoking on their attractiveness. As any heavy smoker can tell you, cigarettes may cause yellowed and stained teeth. They can also cause unpleasant "smoker's breath." Some studies have even suggested that smoking causes premature wrinkling of the skin.

Thus, parents who smoke may be harming their children emotionally and physically. People who wish to be good role models and to provide their children with a clean, unpolluted environment should not smoke. Even people who have been heavy smokers for many years should make every effort to quit when they become parents, if not for their own sake, then for the sake of their children.

**EXERCISE 3f** | *Go back to Exercise 3b and write an essay on one of the topics given. Use one of the thesis sentences you wrote. Remember that your essay should stick to the idea in the thesis sentence and should prove it.*

**Remember:** **As you write, think of your thesis sentence as a lighthouse. Keep your eye on the lighthouse.**

**EXERCISE 3g** | *Go back to Exercise 3c and write an essay on one of the topics given. Use one of the thesis sentences you wrote. Choose either thesis 1 or thesis 2 on one of the topics. You cannot choose both, because they express opposite points of view. Remember that your essay should stick to the idea in the thesis sentence and should support it consistently.*

**EXERCISE 3h** | *Go back to Exercise 3d and write an essay on one of the topics given. Use one of the discussion thesis sentences you wrote. Remember that your essay should stick to the idea in the thesis sentence, which will provide you with a focus for the whole composition.*

CHAPTER

# 4

# Planning Your Essay: Creating Ideas and Paragraphs

Beginning writers often take one look at the assigned topic, take out a clean sheet of paper, and immediately start to write their first sentence. The results are usually disappointing, for they are trying to handle several things at once—ideas, organization, and grammar. A paper written off the top of your head may have some good ideas, but those ideas will not be well arranged, and you will make some avoidable errors.

When you write, instead of trying to do everything at once, follow this series of steps:

1. **Create your ideas** first.
2. Next **organize** your ideas.
3. Then **write** your paper.
4. **Check** your work last.

How much time you spend on each step depends on how much time you have.

Let's consider how we might budget the time for essays written in various time allotments.

|  | 50-Minute Plan | 60-Minute Plan | 75-Minute Plan | 120-Minute Plan |
|---|---|---|---|---|
| Thinking up and arranging ideas (planning) | 10 | 10 | 15 | 20 |
| Writing the paper (drafting) | 30 | 35 | 40 | 75 |
| Checking the paper (editing) | 10 | 15 | 20 | 25 |

You might vary these time allotments according to your own needs.

## Brainstorming and Sorting Ideas

Think of a composition as a meal. You can't prepare a meal without ingredients. You can't write a paper without ideas. So the first step is to assemble ingredients. Get your ideas on paper.

One good way to get ideas is to **brainstorm** for a few minutes. For five or six minutes, write down, as fast as you can, any and all ideas relating to the topic. Let's look at an example of the process. A student was asked to write a paper about growing old, so for five minutes she wrote down every thought about the topic that popped into her head. Here are her notes:

*Growing Old*

*unable to go out*                   *burden others*
*finances*                                 *social security system weak*
*future—not pleasant*          *old people—pity*
*victim of crime*                     *losing friends and family*
*unable to get about*              *seeing others pass away*
*shut in at home*                    *loneliness, fear*
*not enough money*               *society should provide*
*no chance to work*                *improve conditions for the elderly*
*unable to defend myself*       *doctors' bills expensive*
*savings might not be enough*  *enjoying grandchildren*

Even though the student has many good ideas, she is not ready to write. First she has to organize. She takes five minutes to arrange her notes in groups. When she finds similar ideas, she groups them together. She notices that her groups of ideas concentrate on aspects of growing old that are frightening. Her feelings about the topic determine her title, "Fear of Growing Old." All the groups of ideas are related to her fearful attitude toward aging. (She has discarded one idea, "enjoying grandchildren," because it does not support the thesis of this essay.)

## Fear of Growing Old

shut in at home
victim of crime
unable to get about
unable to defend myself

finances
not enough money
savings not enough
doctors' bills expensive
social security system weak
burden on others

society should provide
change things
improve conditions

loneliness
seeing others pass away
losing friends and family
can't get out and make
    new friends

future not pleasant
old people—pity

Her ideas and examples are now arranged in groups. All the ideas on physical condition are together; so are her ideas on finances and those on loneliness. Each group of ideas will become a paragraph. **A paragraph is a series of sentences that all deal with one particular area of the general topic.** For example, in this essay on the fear of growing old, one paragraph will deal with loneliness, one with finances, and so on.

Now the student has prepared the material for five paragraphs. Is she ready to write? No. She has to create a thesis and decide which paragraph to put first, second, and so on. When she looks over her notes, she decides that a thesis might be "Our society allows most of the elderly to live in fear, loneliness, and poverty." This thesis will be placed in her first group. Then the student decides that her thoughts on society and the elderly would be a good conclusion, and the ideas about finances belong near the end, so now she numbers her groups.

*shut in at home*  ②
*victim of crime*
*unable to get about*
*unable to defend myself*

*finances*  ④
*not enough money*
*savings not enough*
*doctors' bills expensive*
*social security system weak*
*burden on others*

*society should provide*  ⑤
*change things*
*improve conditions*

*loneliness*  ③
*seeing others pass away*
*losing friends and family*
*can't get out and make*
   *new friends*

*future not pleasant*  ①
*old people—pity*
*thesis—Our society allows*
*most of the elderly to live in*
*fear, loneliness, and poverty.*

The student now has a thesis and plenty of ideas. The ideas, arranged in groups, are ready to become paragraphs. The idea groups are numbered in order. The student now writes her composition.

**Special Hint**

Do NOT write your composition on the same piece of paper you used for your notes. If you do, you will not be able to refer to them easily. You may write your notes on a separate piece of composition paper, or if you are writing an essay in an exam booklet, you may use the inside of the front cover for notes.

**NOTES**

**GROUPS**

**Note:** **Number the boxes after you have finished filling them. (This method for creating and arranging ideas will be helpful in writing on the suggested topics listed after each reading in Part II of this book.)**

## Other Ways to Create Ideas: Freewriting and Mapping

We have seen how brainstorming and then sorting ideas can help to plan an essay. But there are other methods to help writers generate (create) and organize their ideas. We'll discuss two: freewriting and mapping.

Freewriting is just what its name suggests: A writer writes freely everything that comes to mind. The writing is called "free" because in this very early stage of planning an essay, the writer is free from concern about correct sentence structure or paragraph organization. In many ways freewriting is similar to brainstorming, but a page of freewriting may look more like an ordinary essay because it usually takes the form of sentences rather than just phrases. This approach to generating ideas works well when the essay is based on a short passage that the writer is asked to discuss. For example, consider the following essay topic and the freewriting that follows it:

Exam

Read the following passage and write an essay based on topic A or B:

One day, late in the summer of 1895, Albert Einstein bought a ticket to Zurich and settled down in a small sparsely furnished room to study intensively for the entrance examinations to the Swiss Federal Polytechnic School. His dreams of the future took on a rosy hue, for he imagined himself to be the brightest student in all Zurich. And, being the most brilliant student, he would almost certainly have an easy time. Those dreams ended when he failed the entrance examination.

(Adapted from <u>Albert Einstein and the Theory of Relativity</u> by Herbert Kondo (New York: Franklin Watts, Inc., 1969), pp. 22–23)

Topic A. This passage shows us that even a brilliant person like Albert Einstein can fail at something important at one point in his life, but one failure does not mean that the person will not be successful later on. Discuss the importance of continuing to aim for success in the future despite a previous failure.

Topic B. This passage shows us that someone who is very confident of being successful may be surprised and even shocked to find that he has failed. Discuss the necessity to hope for the best but prepare for the worst.

**Freewriting**

*Wow! Einstein, even the brilliant Einstein could fail a test once in a while—even a very important test like an entrance exam. This reminds me of the time I failed some of the placement exams, but I'm in college anyway and I'm going to succeed, just the way Einstein finally did. The important thing is to be sure to continue and not get so discouraged that you drop out. I wonder how Einstein felt when he found out he failed. He must have been pretty surprised. I guess he was just so sure he'd pass that he didn't study enough. I'm not going to be overconfident when I take the final exams this semester. I'm really going to study all my subjects and ask the professors for extra help if I need it. In a way, it's odd, but reading about this makes me feel more confident. I mean if even Einstein could fail once in a while, that means that a person can fail a test and still be very intelligent. It doesn't mean a student is stupid or ignorant just because he failed a test. He might be very smart in other subjects. It just means he has to study harder and take the test again.*

Although the freewriting sample contains some good ideas, it is obviously not an essay. But the writer can take ideas from it and use them as the basis of an essay.

## Mapping

Another method a writer can use to help create ideas on a subject is called **mapping,** or creating a visual diagram of the thought process by which one idea leads to another. For example, you might start with an idea given in a test question. Write the idea in a circle and then branch off into the supporting ideas. Then ask yourself: "Where is all this leading me?" Answering the question and looking over the diagram you have created may provide you with a thesis.

Here is an example of this process at work:

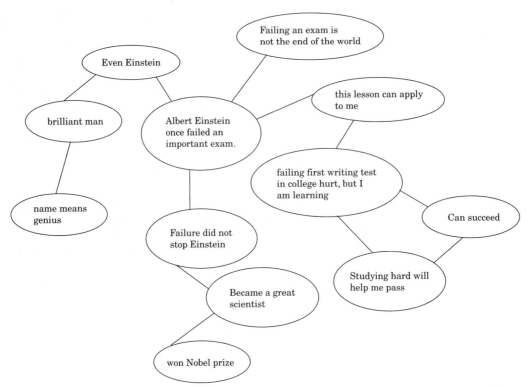

*Where is all of this leading me? Even Einstein failed once, so a failure is not the end of the world.*
*Thesis: Failure happens to everyone at times, but it doesn't have to be permanent.*

The following essay was based on the ideas created by the freewriting and mapping strategies.

## Success and Failure

We are all concerned with success in life. But just as everyone wishes for success, everyone fears failure. People should remember one important thing. Almost everyone fails at something at some point in life, but failure does not have to be permanent. If a person persists in trying to attain his or her goals and is willing to work hard, success is sure to follow.

As an example of what I mean when I say that everyone fails at least once in life, consider Albert Einstein. Certainly no one would consider him a failure. He was one of the most brilliant scientists of all times. His name means genius. When a person is described as really intelligent, he or she may be called an "Einstein." Nevertheless, this genius once failed an exam. Maybe he was overconfident and didn't study enough, but he certainly was not stupid or ignorant. The important thing is that he obviously did not let this one failure hold him back forever. He continued with his studies and succeeded.

When I first arrived at this college, I had been out of school for over five years, so I was not very well prepared for the placement exams I had to take. I failed the English exam because I was not used to writing an essay. Since then I have been studying and learning what I need to know, and I am sure I will pass that writing test the next time I take it. Thinking about how even a genius like Einstein could fail a test makes me feel a little better than I felt when I first found out my score. Now I know that anyone, even someone as brilliant as Einstein, can fail a test, but that does not make a person a failure. Failing a test is not the end of the world. A person can fail once and succeed the next time. That is just what I'm going to do. I am going to study very hard, and I will be sure to pass all of my exams. Success, here I come.

**EXERCISE
4b**

*From the list of topics given in Exercise 4a, choose one that you have not yet written on. Use either the freewriting or the mapping techniques to generate ideas on your subject, and turn these ideas into an essay.*

CHAPTER

# 5

# Improving Your Paragraphs

A paragraph, as we have seen, is a group of sentences developing one of the ideas in an essay. Although there may be paragraphs of one sentence, these are very rare. A good rule of thumb for the length of a paragraph is **more than a sentence, less than a page.** (This is a general rule; there are exceptions.)

A paragraph should be more than one sentence so it can develop or explain an idea. It is hard to say much in one sentence. When you make a statement, you should support it.

A paragraph should usually be less than one page (depending upon your handwriting) because it is supposed to stick to a single topic. Paragraphs that get too long may be going off the track.

Three qualities that are needed in good paragraphs are:

1.  Unity—sticking to a topic
2.  Development—working out, explaining, or proving the topic sentence of the paragraph
3.  Coherence—arranging the sentences of the paragraph in a clear, logical order.

## Paragraph Unity

Most paragraphs contain a **topic sentence,** which gives the main idea of the paragraph. It is often (but not always) the first sentence of the paragraph.

Can you find the **topic sentence** of the paragraph below?

A diet that emphasizes vegetables, beans, grains, and fruits can help protect against many serious diseases. Eating fruits and vegetables seems to lower the risk of getting smoking-related cancers and gastrointestinal cancers. Those foods also reduce the risk of stroke and heart disease. Certain foods, especially leafy greens, help prevent macular degeneration, a major cause of blindness in elderly people.

Did you pick out the first sentence as the topic sentence? Notice how all the sentences in the paragraph relate to the topic sentence. They all describe diseases that proper diet can help people avoid.

Not every paragraph will have a single, neat topic sentence. Some paragraphs may have an **implied** topic rather than one stated in sentence form. Other paragraphs may have a topic that is expressed in two of the paragraph's sentences. Many paragraphs, however, do have one clear topic sentence, and it will help you if you think in terms of a topic sentence for your own writing.

**EXERCISE 5a**

*Underline the topic sentence in each of the following paragraphs. Be prepared to explain how each sentence in the paragraph relates to the topic sentence.*

**1.**    My brother is crazy about baseball. He can tell you the names of all the players on every major league team, and he knows most of their batting averages also. He must have about a thousand baseball cards, which he is always studying—that is, when he isn't watching a game or reading the sports page.

**2.**    There are three major types of rock—igneous, metamorphic, and sedimentary. *Igneous,* a word related to the Latin for "fire," describes rock formed by volcanic action. *Metamorphic,* which means "relating to change," applies to rock produced by heat and pressure. Finally, *sedimentary* rock is formed by sediment, such as particles that settle to the bottom of a river bed.

**3.**    Punctuation can be compared to traffic signs and signals. A period is like a red light; the sentence comes to a full stop. A comma is similar to a caution sign, asking drivers to slow down before continuing. A semicolon is like a stop sign, indicating a full stop before proceeding.

If you wander from the topic of a paragraph, you will be destroying its unity. Look at the following example:

> I prefer summertime to the winter. In the summer there is no school, and I am not under the same pressures that I face in winter. The summer offers more opportunity for outdoor exercise—swimming, surfing, tennis, baseball, just to name a few summer sports. In the summertime, also, one can travel. I prefer to see America first. In short, I think of summer as a time for rest and recreation, while winter is a time for work.

In the paragraph above there are two possible topic sentences, the first and the last. Is there anything in the paragraph that does not relate to the topic? If so, underline it.

Did you underline *I prefer to see America first*? That sentence really does not relate to the topic.

**EXERCISE 5b**  | *In the following paragraphs underline the topic sentence and bracket any sentence that seems to destroy the paragraph unity. Every sentence in each paragraph should relate to the topic sentence. The first one is done as an example.*

**1.** <u>I would not like to be famous because celebrities never have any privacy.</u> Wherever they go, they are followed by crowds of photographers. They cannot even eat dinner in a restaurant without being approached by autograph-seekers. [Celebrities can afford to eat at very nice restaurants like the Golden Noodle.] Their lives and the lives of their families are constantly exposed to the public.

**2.** Beatriz has always been interested in science. When she was in high school, she took several advanced courses in biology and chemistry. In college, she was a lab assistant helping some of her professors with their research. In her spare time, she likes to play tennis and soccer. Now she is studying chemistry in graduate school.

**3.** Taking good notes in class requires several kinds of skills. First, a student must have good listening skills. Often, people who are simply classmates later become good friends. Another crucial skill is selection, knowing which points are the most important. Many successful note takers use abbreviations and symbols to help them take notes quickly. Later, after class, they review their notes and write the words out in full.

**4.** Computers are rapidly changing American business. Almost all major corporations now employ computers to keep track of inventory and the company's payroll. Word-processors with printers have replaced ordinary typewriters in most offices. Computers are used in homes as well, and most children love computer games. Any job applicant who is familiar with the use of computers has a better chance than one who is not.

**EXERCISE 5c**

*Go over your most recent composition looking for the topic sentence in each paragraph. See if other sentences in the paragraph are clearly related to the topic sentence.*

## Paragraph Development

A paragraph should **develop** an idea. It should explain or prove the statement made in the topic sentence. It should give examples, state facts, or in some way bring out the point being made.

Sometimes beginning writers make the mistake of simply putting forth a statement and then going on to something else. Look at the following example of a paragraph lacking unity and development.

> One reason I don't like living in a city is that people tend to be rude and unfriendly. I also dislike the noise and pollution of city life.

The paragraph above has several problems. The first sentence could be a topic sentence, but it isn't developed at all. Instead, the writer changes the topic and brings in a new idea that should be developed in its own paragraph. Before switching to the topic of noise and pollution, the writer should try to prove the point that city people tend to be rude and unfriendly. After all, why should a reader believe such a statement?

Here is a revision of the paragraph. Notice that it has been expanded into two paragraphs, each developing its own topic.

> One reason I don't like living in a city is that people tend to be rude and unfriendly. Nobody is even willing to give you the time of day. Yesterday I had to ask three people just to find out what time it was. The first two simply walked away from me. Perhaps city people are so cold because they live in constant fear of each other.

I also dislike the noise and pollution of city life. It's so noisy on the streets sometimes that you can't carry on a conversation as you walk with a friend. In addition, the streets are often dirty with the litter of so many people. The air is even worse than the streets. Cars give off their poisonous exhaust constantly; apartment houses burn trash, and the smoke goes into the air. It's really discouraging to turn on the radio and hear the announcement that the day's air quality is unacceptable.

The two paragraphs above are not perfect. You might still be unconvinced that city people tend to be rude and unfriendly, but at least the writer has given **some** evidence. The reader does not feel that he or she is being shifted from one subject to another before the first statement has been developed.

Paragraphs can be developed by stating facts, by giving specific details and examples, by telling a story to illustrate the topic sentence, or by stating the reason for something. We have seen some of these ways used above. In the first paragraph, the writer develops the topic with an account of what happened when she asked people the time. Then the writer further develops the topic by stating a reason. In the second paragraph, she uses specific details to demonstrate that cities have a noise and pollution problem.

Actually many paragraphs use a combination of methods to develop their topic. You do not have to label the techniques you use. The important thing is to be sure that you are developing your main idea and not just leaving it hanging.

**EXERCISE 5d**

*On separate paper write a paragraph on one or more of the topic sentences given below. Make sure that your paragraphs are developed and do not wander from your topic. The suggestions will help you.*

1. Ms. Florentino is a very helpful person.

   *Suggestion:* Develop the paragraph by giving several examples of her helpfulness, or tell a brief story that shows her helpfulness.

2. A woman on the checkout line at the grocery store seemed to be very agitated.

   *Suggestion:* Develop the paragraph by listing the signs of her agitation and perhaps by explaining why she was agitated.

**3.** Making a mistake can help people learn.

*Suggestion:* Develop the paragraph by describing a specific mistake that helped a person learn.

**4.** My grandmother was not rich, but she was still a generous woman.

*Suggestion:* Develop the paragraph by giving examples of her generosity, or by telling one brief story showing how generous she was.

**5.** Education should do more than just train a student for the job market.

*Suggestion:* Develop the paragraph by telling what else education should do.

## Paragraph Coherence

Coherence means "sticking together." If something is coherent, its parts are properly arranged and relate logically to each other. It is clear. In a coherent paragraph, each sentence follows logically from the one before and leads logically to the one after. A paragraph should not confuse the reader with awkward shifts and changes, nor should it bore the reader with awkward repetition. Most of all, it should not force the reader to sort things out and rearrange them mentally. The sorting and arranging of details in a paragraph should be done by the writer.

Consider the two paragraphs below. They contain the same topic sentence, and both are developed with the same details. The second, however, is far more coherent than the first. Can you see why?

*LACKING COHERENCE:* Jennie was very nervous. Her mouth was dry. She had never held a gun before, but now, not only was she holding one, she might have to use it. Her hands were moist. Her arms and legs trembled. Her hands were unsteady.

*IMPROVED:* Jennie was very nervous. Her mouth was dry; her hands were moist and unsteady. Her arms and legs trembled. She had never held a gun before, but now, not only was she holding one, she might have to use it.

What is the topic sentence in each paragraph? If you said the first, you are right. Notice how the paragraphs are developed. Details are given to illustrate Jennie's nervous state: her moist, unsteady hands, her dry mouth, her trembling arms and legs. In paragraph 2, by putting all the details together, the writer arranges or sorts things out for us. For example, he puts the information about her hands in one sentence, not in two separate places.

Both paragraphs are also developed by the writer's giving a reason for Jennie's nervous state. We learn that she is probably in some kind of danger. We do not have the whole explanation yet, but that can be given in another paragraph. By placing the details first and the reason last in paragraph 2, the writer has smoothed the way for a switch to the next paragraph.

Several methods can help you to write coherent paragraphs.

1. Sentences may follow **chronological order** (a time sequence).

> Writing an essay is not difficult if you follow a series of steps. Your first step is to brainstorm, that is, to think of ideas on your subject and formulate a thesis or main point. Next, organize your ideas, deciding what will come first, what next, and what last. Now you are ready to write your first draft. When you have written the essay, read it over, making changes and corrections. Finally, if you are writing the paper at home, recopy it neatly and proofread the final draft.

2. Sentences may follow **spatial order** (a sequence that describes things by moving from place to place in order, as a movie camera might pan a scene). This method is especially helpful when you are writing a descriptive paragraph.

> As I approached the old house, I noticed that its steep roof had several shingles missing. Below the roof some of the gutters needed repair, and one shutter on the upper floor had come loose and was banging in the wind. As my eye traveled down the house, I saw peeling paint and noticed that several boards were missing from the front porch. On the ground in front of the porch, the un-pruned shrubbery fought with the aggressive weeds, and crumbling bricks made the front walk an obstacle course. I wondered why this once fine house had become so dreary and decrepit.

*Hint:* Notice that this paragraph has its topic sentence last.

3.  Sentences may be arranged in **order of importance.** The most important idea may be in the first sentence, or it may be reserved for last.

> People should practice conservation of energy for several reasons. One reason is that by avoiding the waste of fuel at home and in the family car, people can save hundreds of dollars a year. Another, even more important reason for conservation is patriotism. By saving precious energy, Americans can help to make our nation less dependent on foreign oil and thus strengthen the position of the United States in the world. Finally, the most important reason for conservation today is that it helps to avoid shortages or even a total depletion of the world's sources of energy for future generations.

4.  Sentences in a paragraph may follow a **pattern set up by the topic sentence.** When items are listed in a certain order in the first sentence, they should be discussed in the same order.

> Three things that contribute to a person's success in life are inborn ability, hard work, and luck. The intelligence, strength, and positive personality traits that one is born with can certainly influence success. But natural ability alone is not enough; one must also work hard to succeed. Many people with great talent fail because they never work hard enough to fulfill their potential. A third important factor in success is luck. Being in the "right place at the right time" can make the difference between great success and just getting by, even for talented and hardworking people.

5.  **Signal words** may be used to help the reader understand the relationship between sentences. Examples of signal words are *first, second, next, one reason, another reason, however, but, in addition, furthermore, most important, finally,* and *last of all.* These words are usually used along with the other coherence patterns mentioned.

**EXERCISE**
**5e**

*Notice that the signal words in the paragraph above (number 5) have been underlined. Go back to paragraphs 1 through 4 and underline the signal words in them.*

**EXERCISE**
**5f**

*For each pair of paragraphs below, circle the one you think is **more coherent**. Be prepared to explain why.*

**1.  a.** I saw a really exciting movie last night. The hero is an explorer who has to replace a stolen ruby into the head of an ancient idol before a curse destroys a village of innocent people. Just as he swings across a pit of snakes, trying to reach the rocky shelf where the idol is, he sees a band of jewel thieves who are also after the ruby, but they want it for their own selfish purposes. They have been trying to keep him from getting there first, and they had him tied up and lowered into a den of hungry lions, but he manages to get away. First they follow him to find out where the jewel is, but once they know, they try to kill him. After he gets away, he goes back to the hiding place and gets the gem before they get there. Then he has to cross the snake pit to get to the place where the idol is. Just as he is swinging across, he sees the jewel thieves again. I won't spoil the ending for you.

**b.** I saw a really exciting movie last night. The hero is an explorer who has to replace a stolen ruby into the head of an ancient idol before a curse destroys a village of innocent people. As he tracks down the ruby, he is followed by a band of jewel thieves, who want the gem for their own selfish purposes. Once they find out where the jewel is hidden, they try to destroy the hero by tying him up and lowering him into a den of hungry lions. He manages to get away, gets back to the jewel before they do, and takes it to where the idol is. But

ol stands, he has to
swinging across, he
ut I do not want to

onesty, understand-
e relied upon to give
be someone who will
Above all, I expect a
k or side with others

**b.** Three qualities I value in a friend are honesty, understanding, and loyalty. Above all, I expect a friend to be loyal and never talk behind my back or side with others against me. I want a friend who can always be relied upon to give me her true and honest opinion. She should be someone who will really try to understand me if I confide in her.

**3.** **a.** There are many important reasons for earning a college degree. A good reason to earn a college degree is the social prestige of being educated. But the most important reason of all for completing your college education is to expand your knowledge, develop your intellect, and become a more fulfilled human being. The degree also gives you a definite advantage in the job market and will probably increase your lifetime earnings.

**b.** There are many important reasons for earning a college degree. One reason is the social prestige of being educated. Another, even more important reason is that a college degree gives you a definite advantage in the job market and will probably increase your lifetime earnings. But the most important reason of all for completing your college education is to expand your knowledge, develop your intellect, and become a more fulfilled human being.

**EXERCISE 5g** | *On a separate paper, rewrite the following paragraphs to improve coherence. You will have to rearrange sentences. You may also add signal words and make whatever changes you feel are necessary.*

**1.** Headaches can be caused by illness, a lack of sleep, or nervousness. Some people get headaches whenever they are in an unfamiliar situation. For some people a headache is the first sign of a cold. The fear of something new can make them nervous, bringing on an annoying headache. Other people develop headaches whenever they have less than seven hours of sleep. Whatever the cause, a headache is sure to be unpleasant. Some headaches can signal very serious medical problems.

**2.**   Lasagne is a delicious dish made with layers of pasta, sauce, and cheese. Usually you cover the bottom of the lasagne pan with some sauce, and then you add successive layers of pasta, sauce, and cheese. First, you have to make the sauce, grate the cheese, and cook the pasta. When you have finished layering the ingredients, bake the lasagne in the preheated oven. While you are preparing the sauce and pasta, the oven should be preheated.

**3.**   Organizing a composition is not difficult when you follow a series of steps. Be sure to proofread your paper before you hand it in so that you can correct the spelling, punctuation, and typographical errors. Before you start writing, think of lots of interesting ideas. Write the paper carefully, paying attention to sentence structure and grammar. Make sure that you organize your ideas so that your essay is coherent.

**4.**   Fred owns an unusual car, which he has customized himself. He has painted a strange design on the outside. Inside, there is leather upholstery. The body of the car has green vines and red flowers painted all over it. The seats have red suede headrests and gold and green seat belts. The vines are set off by lots of chrome. There are stereo speakers in both the front and the back of the car.

**EXERCISE 5h**   *Review your last composition. Check each paragraph for coherence, and rewrite any paragraphs that are not coherent.*

CHAPTER

# 6

# Essay Patterns

We have seen how brainstorming and sorting ideas can help you to create a well-organized essay. You can further improve your ability to organize your compositions by becoming familiar with certain essay patterns that can help you to structure your ideas. In this chapter you will find two suggestions, the **four-paragraph plan** and the **three-point-thesis plan.** You may want to change these plans slightly to fit your own needs, and always keep in mind that these are only two of many possible essay patterns. But by learning these two plans, you can learn strategies that will help you to feel confident about structuring various kinds of papers, including persuasive, descriptive, analytical, and compare-contrast essays.

## TYPES OF ESSAYS

Writing assignments are not all exactly alike. Some assignments may require a persuasive essay, asking students to express and defend an opinion about a controversial statement on a current issue. For example, a possible persuasive topic is: "Should the children of illegal immigrants be forbidden to go to public schools?"

Another type of assignment may ask for a description of a person, a place, or a process. For example, a possible descriptive topic is: "Describe a place that has significance for you." An analytical assignment asks students to break a topic down into several parts and to explain the meaning of each part. For example, a possible analytical topic is: "Analyze the effect that television has on the lives of average Americans." Another kind of assignment is the compare-contrast essay, asking for a discussion of the similarities and differences between two (or more) things, places, or people. For example, a possible compare-contrast topic is: "Compare and contrast the ideas of Malcolm X and Martin Luther King, Jr."

## THE FOUR-PARAGRAPH PLAN

The four-paragraph plan works well for most types of essay assignments, especially persuasive, descriptive, and compare-contrast topics. First, the introduction states the topic and presents your thesis—the main point that you are trying to prove in the essay (see Chapter 3). A thesis can be effective when it is the last sentence of the first paragraph, after you have worked into the topic.

Next, the two middle paragraphs, often called the main-body or support paragraphs, present the development of your ideas. In a persuasive essay, each main-body paragraph will state a reason for your thesis, and then that reason is illustrated with examples. In a descriptive essay, each main-body paragraph can concentrate on one particular area of your topic. In a compare-contrast essay, one main-body paragraph can discuss the similarities between two things, and the other main-body paragraph can discuss their differences.

Finally, in the last paragraph, you can summarize the ideas you presented in the two main-body paragraphs and restate your thesis. (Do not use the exact same words from the first paragraph.) The last paragraph is your conclusion.

Look at the following diagrams and notes for three essays using the four-paragraph plan. The first diagram gives notes for the descriptive topic: "Describe an experience that taught you something important." The second diagram gives notes for the compare-contrast topic: "Compare and contrast two of your relatives." The third diagram gives notes for the persuasive topic: "Should a person choose an interesting but risky job over a boring but secure job?" Finally, you will find a persuasive essay written from the notes in the third diagram.

# Diagram for an Essay on the Topic
# "Describe an experience that taught you something important."

INTRODUCTION

Lead into topic.
State thesis.

*tutoring—an experience
that taught me something*

*thesis—math tutoring helped
me as much as it helped my
students*

MAIN-BODY
PARAGRAPH

Give details of the situation.

*when in 10th grade, math tutor
for 8th graders*

*computation and algebra—
had to explain in simple words
strengthened my own math
understanding*

MAIN-BODY
PARAGRAPH

Explain results of situation.

*learned that teaching is not
easy.
8th graders didn't always
understand
had to repeat, explain in
different ways
more patient than before*

CONCLUSION

Summarize ideas and
restate thesis.

*became a tutor to help others*

*unexpectedly, helped me, too*

# Diagram for an Essay on the Topic
## "Compare and contrast two of your relatives."

INTRODUCTION     Lead into topic.
State thesis.

> *topic — compare two daughters,*
> *Myrna, Patricia*
> *some similarities, but*
> *differences are more interesting*

MAIN-BODY
PARAGRAPH     Discuss similarities.

> *Myrna, Patricia, physically*
> *similar, black hair, brown eyes*
> *both born in February*
> *both love animals*

MAIN-BODY
PARAGRAPH     Discuss differences.

> *temperaments very different.*
> *Myrna — noisy, very active,*
> *dramatic. Involved in basketball,*
> *chorus, and debate club at*
> *school.*
> *Patricia — quiet, observant, reads*
> *a lot. At school, likes science,*
> *languages. Thinks first, then acts*

CONCLUSION     Summarize ideas and
restate thesis.

> *Myrna and Patricia — physically*
> *similar, yet temperamentally*
> *different.*
> *personalities different yet both*
> *have strengths that make them*
> *interesting*

## Diagram for an Essay on the Topic
## "Should a person choose an interesting but
## risky job over a boring but secure job?"

INTRODUCTION
Lead into topic.
State thesis.

*topic—choice of risky, interesting job or boring, secure job to provide for family security thesis—interesting, risky job is wiser choice*

MAIN-BODY
PARAGRAPH
Introduce first reason for thesis.
Explain reason.

*boring job—hidden dangers example—factories, boredom, carelessness, accidents psychological damage low morale poor self-esteem hurts employees and families*

MAIN-BODY
PARAGRAPH
Give another reason for thesis.
Explain reason.

*advantages of exciting job— social—high salaries, prestige. example—high-level managers. educational—learning new skills, handling different situations psychological—morale, self-esteem, making contribution*

CONCLUSION
Summarize ideas and restate thesis.

*avoid dangers of boredom many advantages to interesting, risky job interesting, risky job is wiser and safer.*

## Choosing the Right Kind of Job

If people could be given a choice between a boring but secure job and an interesting but insecure job, many would choose the boring job. They worry about providing for their families, so the idea of lifetime security appeals to them. However, the interesting but insecure job is the wiser choice.

First, that boring job may seem safe, but there are hidden dangers. In factories and other work places, boredom with the job can lead to carelessness. In turn, carelessness can cause dangerous and even fatal accidents. Besides physical harm, a boring job can also result in psychological damage. People who do boring work sometimes feel depressed and worthless. When workers have low morale and poor self-esteem, they suffer psychologically. Eventually, their psychological problems will have harmful effects on their families. Thus, the boring but secure job harms rather than helps the employees and their families.

A second reason to choose the interesting job is that the choice can bring social, educational, and psychological advantages. High salaries and social prestige are often connected with professions that are both exciting and risky. For example, high-level managers do not have job security, but their salaries are impressive and their work is fulfilling. Next, working at different jobs is educational and therefore advantageous. People who switch jobs learn to cope with various situations, and they also have a chance to acquire new skills. Finally, people who hold interesting jobs have high morale and self-esteem. They feel that their work is important and that they are making a contribution. Rather than just jobs, they have careers.

In conclusion, people who dare to experiment and to look for interesting work avoid the hidden dangers of a boring job. They gain prestige, skills, and knowledge. Therefore, the interesting but insecure job is both the wiser and, in the long run, actually the safer choice.

---

**EXERCISE 6a**

*Choose one of the following topics. Use one of the four-paragraph models for your notes. Then, following your notes, write a four-paragraph essay.*

1. Should all students be required to study a second language?

2. Describe the best (or the worst) job you have ever had.

3. Compare and contrast two of your friends.

4. Describe your favorite hobby.

5. Compare and contrast two neighborhoods you are familiar with.

6. Describe the kinds of people who are the best role models for children.

7. How much help with homework should parents give their children?

8. Compare and contrast two books you have read.

## THE THREE-POINT-THESIS PLAN

Another method for structuring an essay is to include within the thesis statement a very brief reference to three major reasons for your point of view and to develop each of these reasons in the next three paragraphs. This type of essay will generally have five paragraphs: an introduction, three main-body paragraphs to develop the three points in the thesis, and a conclusion.

With this method, the thesis sentence becomes somewhat more complex than in the previous plan because in addition to simply stating a point of view, it reveals a little of the ideas that will follow. We may refer to the thesis sentence of an essay written this way as a **three-point thesis** because it includes a very brief statement of the three major points of the essay.

The three-point thesis is generally best for essays in which your main arguments can be summarized easily. This plan is especially useful for persuasive, compare-contrast, and analytical essays. Look at the thesis sentences for the following topics.

*TOPIC:* Should all children be taught to use computers?

*THESIS:* All children should be taught to use computers because these skills will eventually bring them personal, educational, and financial benefits.

*TOPIC:* Compare and contrast two jobs you have had.

*THESIS:* My two summer jobs had certain minor similarities, but they differed greatly in the amount of responsibility I was given, the attitude of my co-workers, and relevance to my future career.

TOPIC:    Analyze (or discuss) the ways in which parents can help their children do well in school.

THESIS:   Regardless of their own level of education, parents can help their children by making sure that they are physically, psychologically, and intellectually prepared for their school experience.

The essay below follows this three-point plan. Its points are developed following the order in which they are given in the thesis sentence to improve the organization of the essay and help the reader to understand it.

### Helping Children Succeed in School

INTRODUCTION

Leads into topic.

Almost all parents hope that their children will do well in school. Sometimes parents who were not successful students themselves and are consequently not well educated feel at a loss as to how to help their offspring become more successful than they were as school children. Actually, there is a great deal that they can do. Regardless of their own level of education, parents can help their children by making sure that they are physically, psychologically, and intellectually ready for their school experience.

States three-point thesis

MAIN-BODY PARAGRAPH

Develops first point of the thesis

One of the most important things parents can do is to make sure that their children are physically prepared to benefit from school. Parents should take their children for regular medical checkups, including all required immunizations and testing to make sure that hearing and vision are normal. Parents should also see that children establish a healthy daily routine. Children should be well rested, so parents must make sure that their children get to bed early when they have school the next morning. Also, they should eat a nourishing breakfast before leaving for school.

MAIN-BODY PARAGRAPH

Develops second point of the thesis

While ensuring that the children will arrive at school on time, parents should not pressure their youngsters, but should organize the household so that the early morning activities can take place in a calm, unhurried atmosphere in order to prepare the child psychologically for school. Simple measures such as setting out clothing, preparing school lunches, and signing all permission slips the evening before can avoid a frenzied rush in the morning. Moreover, the parents should take a friendly interest in the children's school activities, for example, by asking at breakfast what lessons will be held that day and by asking occasional questions about the children's favorite subjects and about their feelings regarding school. Parents should also show their children that they take an interest in their education by attending open-school nights, when they can meet with their children's teachers and learn about the curriculum.

MAIN-BODY
PARAGRAPH

Develops
third point
of the thesis

Even parents who are not highly educated themselves can help to prepare their children intellectually for schoolwork. They can take their children to the public library to borrow books. Parents can build upon children's natural curiosity about their world by taking them to science museums, especially those with "hands-on" exhibits. They can subscribe to popular magazines with eye appeal. Younger children will enjoy cutting out pictures from them, and older children who have begun to read may become interested in some of the articles. Concerned parents can monitor their children's television watching, making sure that the children finish their homework before watching television and that when they do watch, they choose good programs.

CONCLUSION

Summarizes ideas
and restates thesis

As we have seen, there are a great many ways that parents can help to prepare children for success in school if they are conscientious in meeting their children's physical, emotional, and intellectual needs.

**EXERCISE
6b**

*Choose one of the following topics. Use the five-paragraph model on page 55 for notes that will develop an essay with a three-point thesis. Then, using your notes, write the essay.*

1. Should children have pets? If yes, why? If no, why not?

2. Analyze (or discuss) some of the ways that the average citizen can help to care for the environment.

3. Should there be a mandatory retirement age for all workers in all kinds of jobs?

4. Analyze (or discuss) some of the benefits of having a small family of one or two children.

5. Compare and contrast your education with the education of your grandparents.

6. Discuss making a career change during middle age.

7. Should volunteer work in the community be a graduation requirement for a high school diploma?

8. Discuss the ways in which people can make a good impression at a job interview.

**NOTES**

INTRODUCTION
Lead into topic.

State three-
point thesis.  $\longrightarrow$

MAIN-BODY
PARAGRAPH

Develop first
point of the
thesis.

MAIN-BODY
PARAGRAPH

Develop second
point of the
thesis.

MAIN-BODY
PARAGRAPH

Develop third
point of the
thesis.

CONCLUSION

Summarize ideas
and restate
thesis.

CHAPTER

# 7

# Editing Your Writing

After you have completed writing an essay, your job is not done. You still have a very important part of the writing task before you— editing your paper. All writers on every level, from college freshmen to professional journalists, must go back over every piece of writing and read it critically, making necessary changes.

Sometimes these changes may be as routine as correcting misspelled words or punctuation errors, but sometimes editing can involve rewriting sentences or whole paragraphs, or moving material from one part of the essay to another. Sometimes you may feel, as you reread an essay, that it needs greater coherence, so you may supply signal words to help the reader follow your train of thought, and you may reorder ideas to produce a more logical arrangement.

Sometimes, you may drop a paragraph because you think that it does not really support your thesis, or you may rearrange the order of the main-body paragraphs so that the paper builds toward your strongest points. Occasionally, you may wish to rewrite your thesis because the main-body paragraphs do not support the original thesis.

On the other hand, you may be pleased with the organizational pattern of your essay, but you may find errors in grammar that you need to correct. You may also find that while writing your ideas down quickly, you have skipped over some important words or word endings. Thus, editing your paper is very important in order to make it as clear and correct as possible.

## DIFFERENCES BETWEEN EDITING AT HOME AND EDITING IN CLASS

When an essay is assigned for homework, you are not under as much time pressure as when you are writing in class. Therefore, you will be able to make a new copy of a paper after you reread it and make changes. When you are editing at home, what you write on the first copy of your essay, called your **rough draft,** will be indications to yourself of changes needed. Your instructor will expect you to hand in a neat final copy with a minimum of crossed-out words or additional words inserted above the line. (If you are composing on a word processor, you are lucky, because the changes can be made in the text on the screen and the printer will produce a neat copy.)

On the other hand, you will often be asked to write an essay in class. Your English teacher may routinely assign in-class essays, and in other courses, such as history or sociology, the examinations may include essay questions. Therefore, it is also necessary to develop strategies for editing in class when you will not have time to recopy your writing. In such cases, any changes or corrections you make when editing are not just notes to yourself but are designed to be read by your instructor. They must be very clear.

## EDITING STRATEGIES

Below is a list of editing strategies. As you will see, some of these strategies are better for writing at home, while others will work equally well at home or in class.

1. Read over your essay aloud.
2. After writing the first draft, wait a while before editing your essay.
3. To spot sentence-level errors, use your hands or two pieces of paper or cards to help focus on one sentence at a time.

4. To spot sentence-level errors, read over the essay backwards, sentence by sentence.

5. Reread the essay several times, each time looking for something different.

6. Read over the editing checklist on the inside back cover of this book just before rereading your essay.

7. Read over your instructor's comments on your previously corrected essays.

8. If your instructor permits, ask a friend to read your essay aloud and comment on it.

## Strategy #1: Read Over Your Essay Aloud

Sometimes errors that are not apparent during silent reading may be easier to spot when you read the essay aloud. Not only errors, but also awkward writing may be noted and corrected by this method. If you are writing in class, you will not be able to read your essay out loud, because doing so would disturb other students. You can, however, **subvocalize,** saying each word in your mind.

This method is especially helpful for spotting places where words have been accidentally omitted. Read aloud or use the subvocalization method as you do the next exercise.

**EXERCISE 7a**

*Some of the following sentences have a word or words missing while others do not. If the sentence is all right as it is, write a "c" on the line next to it. If you think that a word or words have been left out, write them in above the sentence, using a caret mark (∧) to show where they belong.*

*EXAMPLES* _____ **a.** Jean lost her wallet, but she did ∧ *not* notice that it was missing until she returned home.

_____ *c* **b.** At two o'clock in the morning, Arthur received a telephone call.

_____ **c.** Nancy ∧ *was* very happy because she received ∧ *a* scholarship to Cornell University.

_____ **1.** Some of the secretaries taking a special course.

_____ **2.** I have been to the movies in a year.

_____ **3.** Gun control is a controversial issue.

_____ **4.** The boss asked him to write report.

_____ **5.** Where the envelopes?

_____ **6.** The bridge is closed because it very weak.

_____ **7.** Is a good idea to review your class notes every day.

_____ **8.** The newspapers say that the governor going to resign.

_____ **9.** The McIntyres planning to visit China next year.

_____ **10.** Many television shows are rerun for years.

_____ **11.** Swimming good exercise for almost everyone.

_____ **12.** Is not a good idea to go out when lightning flashing.

## Strategy #2: After Writing the First Draft, Wait a While Before Editing Your Essay

When you are writing an essay at home, a good proofreading idea is to allow some time to pass between the writing of your essay and your editing. The amount of time can vary, but at least several hours is recommended. Overnight is even better. When you return to your essay after some time has passed, you can see it more objectively, more as your teacher or some other reader might see it.

This distancing is helpful. Often writers think they have expressed themselves clearly on paper only because they know what they want to say, but their ideas are not really clear to others. Has this ever happened to you? If you return to something many hours after you have written it, what you wanted to say is perhaps no longer so clearly written in your mind, so you will be better able to judge whether or not it is clearly written on paper.

Leaving a piece of writing for several hours or overnight before editing it and making a final copy is a method that many professional writers use. This method demands self-discipline and organization. You have to plan ahead and start your composition well before it is due. You cannot use this method if you do your assignment at the last minute.

Of course, you will not be able to use this method when writing in class. You can, however, do the following. After completing your essay, do not immediately begin rereading—unless, of course, you are running out of time. Instead, look up for a minute and try to clear your mind. Then return to the essay and reread it carefully, making changes where necessary.

### Strategy #3: To Spot Sentence-Level Errors, Use Your Hands or Two Pieces of Paper or Cards to Help Focus on One Sentence at a Time

When you are concentrating on the composition as a whole, you may not notice errors within sentences. Of course it is important to keep the whole essay in mind as you edit, but it is also important to try to correct as many sentence-level errors as possible. After rereading the whole essay for coherence, it is a good idea to go back over it sentence by sentence.

To understand why isolating each sentence helps, consider the following examples:

*INCORRECT:*    It is important to make reservations for a vacation. Especially during the busy summer months.

Now use your hands to cover all but the words "Especially during the busy summer months," because this unit begins with a capital letter and ends with a period. Now that you have isolated this group of words, you can see that it is not a complete sentence. It is really a sentence fragment since the words do not form a complete thought (see Chapter 11 for more about this). It should be linked to the preceding sentence with a comma, like this:

*CORRECTED:*    It is important to make reservations for a vacation, especially during the busy summer months.

When first reading the incorrect example above, you might not notice that the second "sentence" is really a sentence fragment, because the two parts together make sense. Therefore, isolating each sentence unit by blocking off all the words between the start of the sentence and the period will help you to notice if a sentence is not complete. This method will also help you to notice other sentence-level errors by concentrating your attention on one sentence unit at a time.

## Strategy #4: To Spot Sentence-Level Errors, Read Over the Essay Backwards, Sentence by Sentence

After you have read the essay as a whole from start to finish, read it again, but this time start from the last sentence. This method, like the one we just examined, helps you to deal with each sentence unit individually. You can ask yourself if each sentence you read is complete. Try it on the incorrect example below:

INCORRECT:    That book has many interesting stories. Which I really enjoyed reading.

While reading the two parts of the above example in the normal order, you may link the ideas together so that you may not notice that the words "Which I really enjoyed reading" are not a complete sentence. But when you read the words "Which I really enjoyed reading" first, it is easier to see that they do not form a true sentence. The example should read as follows:

CORRECTED:    That book has many interesting stories, which I really enjoyed reading.

## Strategy #5: Reread the Essay Several Times, Each Time Looking for Something Different

After giving your essay a general reading, you can go back over it looking for particular trouble spots. For example, if you know that you tend to write sentence fragments, you might read over the essay carefully just to make sure that each sentence is complete. If spelling is a particular problem, you might read over your essay just to look for spelling errors and then check any questionable spelling by looking the word up in a dictionary.

## Strategy #6: Read Over the Editing Checklist on the Inside Back Cover of This Book Just Before Rereading Your Essay

The editing checklist on the inside back cover of this book can help you to interpret the comments your instructor writes on your papers, and it can also remind you of what to look for in an essay that you are currently writing.

## Strategy #7: Read Over Your Instructor's Comments on Your Previously Corrected Essays

If you are writing at home, or if it is permitted in class, go over one or more of your earlier essays that have been returned to you by the instructor. Note carefully any comments or corrections that were made, and then return to the essay you are currently working on to see if any of those comments can help you with your present editing task. For example, if you misspelled a certain word on the previous paper, make sure that it is spelled correctly if it appears on the present one. If your instructor noted that your paragraphs were not sufficiently developed in your previous essay, ask yourself if the paragraphs in your present one have adequate development.

## Strategy #8: If Your Instructor Permits, Ask a Friend to Read Your Essay Aloud and Comment on It

If you are working at home, a friend or family member can be a great help as you edit your work. Someone else can give you an objective view of your writing. If your friend is puzzled over something in your essay, you may need to clarify the point. If you are writing a persuasive essay, ask your friend if your essay is convincing. If your instructor does not mind and your friend is knowledgeable, he or she might also point out places where spelling, grammar, and punctuation need correction.

This is a method that will usually be used at home, but occasionally two students in a class might exchange essays and help edit each other's work.

**EXERCISE 7b**  *Use at least four of the strategies above to edit an essay that you have written. Take notes on whatever changes you decide to make as a result of your editing, and then make a neat copy of the edited essay. Write a brief summary of the editing methods you used, stating which method or methods worked best for you.*

# 8

# The Appearance of Your Paper

Compositions, like people, are often judged by their appearance. Just as a person dressed in dirty, wrinkled clothing with uncombed hair and untied shoelaces may make a bad impression, so does an English composition that has many crossed-out words or erasures, is written on a torn and wrinkled piece of paper, and in general presents a sloppy appearance. The carelessly dressed person might actually be very interesting and intelligent and might have a truly nice personality, but many people may be so put off by the poor appearance of the person that they will not trouble themselves to find out any more. In the same way, a composition that presents a poor appearance may contain some good and original ideas that will never be fully appreciated because of the outward appearance of the paper. This is really a shame, because with just a little effort, anyone can produce work that is neat and easy to read.

When you write a paper at home, your instructor will expect you to make a neat final copy. Your main concern should be to make your paper legible (easy to read). Typing or word processing is always desirable, but if you cannot type or use a word processor, write your paper neatly by hand. If you skip every other line (just as you would double-space if you typed or word-processed), your instructor will have room above each line to make any necessary corrections. Another way to improve the appearance of your paper and to give your instructor room to make comments is to leave a one-inch margin at both sides of the paper and at the bottom. Leaving margins will also help you to proofread your paper easily.

When you write your paper in class, try to be as neat as possible, although your instructor will not expect the composition to look as clean as one written at home. Usually you will not have enough time in class to make a final copy of your composition, so your first draft will be the paper that you hand in. Naturally there will be some corrections made by erasing or crossing out. It would be almost impossible to write a perfect paper the first time through. On a paper written in class, crossed-out words or erasures are allowed. Just make sure that your paper is easy to read.

A composition should have a title centered in the middle of the line on the first page. You should capitalize the first letter of every important word in the title—that is, every word except for articles, prepositions, and conjunctions—and always capitalize the first letter of the first word in the title. (You can find out about articles, prepositions, and conjunctions in Chapter 19 of this book.) It is not necessary to underline the title of your composition or put it in quotation marks unless your title is also the title of an essay or book you have been asked to write about.

Here is a list of directions for handing in neat papers:

1. Write your composition on paper of standard size (8½ by 11 inches).

2. Do not use paper with torn edges.

3. Use only one side of a sheet of paper.

4. Type or word-process your composition or write neatly in ink.

5. If you type or word-process, double-space your composition; if you write by hand, skip every other line.

6. Leave a margin of one inch on both sides of the paper and at the bottom.

7. Number each page in the upper right-hand corner.

8. Clip or staple the pages at the upper left-hand corner.

9.  Make sure your name is on the first page, and follow any directions your instructor gives you about including the date, the course number, or other information.

10. Center the title at the top of the first page.

## A SPECIAL NOTE ON WORD PROCESSING

It is more and more common to find computer labs on college campuses, and many students are taking advantage of the word-processing programs available to them. Most professional writing is being done on word processors. It is far easier for writers to edit their work using a word processor. Editing requires adding, omitting, or changing words, sentences, or whole paragraphs. When an essay has been written on a word processor, making a change is easy. The writer can just make the necessary changes on the screen, and then reprint the revised version. Since the printer does the job quickly and neatly, there is no need for the writer to recopy or retype pages.

Some programs can even help writers to check their essays for correctness. Most word-processing programs will check the spelling of the words. Some word processors can even check grammar and usage. If you have access to a computer lab, you can ask your lab manager if such programs are available.

Even though computers can make the job of producing neat and legible essays easier, there are some important things to remember.

**1. Make sure that the margin settings are correct and that double spacing has been selected before you print your essay.** In some labs, the word processors are preset for double spacing, but in others they are not. Make sure to select double spacing for your essay before you print. Some writers like to compose their essays with a single-space setting so that more of the essay is visible on the computer monitor (screen). It is fine to follow this practice, but don't forget to change the whole essay to double space before printing. If you do not know how to do this, ask the lab manager for help. Be sure that your work has been "saved" before you change the format and print it.

Your printed essay should have margins of one inch at the left, right, top, and bottom. Usually the margins have been preset to ensure a correct print, but check your computer because a previous student may have altered the margins. If you need to reset the margins, consult your lab manager or a software manual that tells you how to use your word-processing program.

**2. Make sure that the paper is correctly aligned before you print.** Sometimes the margins have been set correctly in the word-processing program, but when you print, there is no bottom margin, or in some cases, no top margin. Such a situation might occur if the paper has not been properly set up in the printer. Ask your lab manager to help you reposition the paper if need be.

**3. If your printer uses computer paper with side sprockets, be sure to remove the "runners," the perforated parts of the paper with the holes, and separate the pages before handing in your essay.** Once the runners are removed, you should align all of the pages correctly, making sure they are right side up, and staple the pages at the upper left. Never hand in your paper folded over with the runners attached. This would be inconsiderate to your instructor.

**4. Since papers should have pages numbered, set your computer to number your pages at the upper right-hand corner.** If you do not know how to create a "header" with automatic page numbering, ask your lab manager for help or consult the software manual.

**5. When printing, select the "best" rather than the "draft" quality.** If the print is very light, even though "best" has been selected, or if it is smeared or streaked, ask your lab manager if the printer's ribbon or ink cartridge can be changed. Remember that your instructor has many essays to read, so do not hand in work with very light or blurry print.

**6. Preview your print on the screen to avoid "orphan lines."** By "scrolling" through your essay on the computer screen, you can tell if the last page will have only one line, often called an "orphan line." If it does, try to change the margins slightly to avoid this situation. If you cannot fit more of the essay on each page, then you can make your margins wider, so that the final page will have a few more lines rather than just one.

**7. Select a standard font (print type) and size.** Your essay should be easy to read, so avoid fancy fonts and very small or very large print. Select the standard 12-point size (usually pre-set on a computer).

CHAPTER

# 9

# The Double-Correction Method

After you have written a paper and handed it in, you are still not finished with it. As you know, your instructor will hand back the composition, probably sprinkled with comments, suggestions, and corrections. This chapter will give you a method of correction that will make your instructor's comments even more useful to you.

Students react in several ways to all those marks on compositions. One of the least helpful reactions is to ignore the corrections and look only to see what the grade is. Grades **are** important, but unfortunately, worrying about the grade will not improve the next composition. A better reaction is to glance through the paper to see what kinds of mistakes you have made.

When you look down the page, it may seem as if almost every sentence needs some correction. The instructor may have bracketed words and labeled them "sentence fragment" to indicate that they are not complete sentences (as we saw in Chapter 7 on editing). Some sentences may be labeled "run-on," indicating that two separate sentences have been run together, for example:

INCORRECT:   The main character in the story has no na*run-on*me he is a
strange person.

The comment "run-on" is meant to help you realize that a mark of separation (such as a period), or a joining word (such as *and*) is needed.

CORRECTED:   The main character in the story has no name. He is a
strange person.

or

CORRECTED:   The main character in the story has no name, and he is a
strange person.

We will learn more about run-on sentences and how to correct them in Chapter 12, but the double-correction method can provide a means of dealing with this error and learning from it immediately.

Another common problem is a lack of subject-verb agreement (see Chapter 14), which occurs when a verb does not match its subject—for example:

The two main ideas in the story *are* easy to spot.

Since the subject of the sentence is the plural *ideas,* we need the plural verb *are.*

During the course of the semester you will do many exercises designed to help you to avoid problems with verbs, sentence structure, and spelling, but right from the beginning you will probably be writing essays, and your instructor will no doubt make comments and corrections in order to help you to learn from any mistakes you happen to make. One good way to help yourself is to turn to the sections of this book dealing with your problem areas. (You can locate the pages by using the table of contents, the index, or the editing checklist on the inside back cover.) If you read the rules and examples and then do the exercises, you can reduce the number of errors in your essays.

You may still find that although you have studied hard and done your exercises carefully, you continue to make the same types of errors over and over. This experience can be very frustrating. You do your best, and yet your paper is returned with errors noted. Why does this happen? Why do the same errors pop up over and over again?

The answer is complex. First, there are no shortcuts to good writing. You don't acquire a great serve in your very first tennis lesson. Similarly, you don't learn writing rules in one lesson. Writing is a slow process that requires work and persistence.

Second, note our description of what you should do when you see an error. It is fine to do exercises in a workbook, but what about the actual composition you wrote? What are you doing with that? The error happened in a composition, in a paragraph, in a sentence. It did not happen in a grammar book.

One way to learn to avoid future errors is to rewrite your essay, making all of the improvements and corrections your instructor has suggested. However, completely rewriting every paper is a time-consuming process, and it is not the most efficient method of learning to avoid sentence-level errors. Another method is to focus on specific problem sentences and correct them. Actually if you use this method, you will correct each targeted sentence twice. That is why we call this the **double-correction method.**

Let's take a sample paragraph and follow it through all the steps of the double-correction method. Here is the paragraph, which has been corrected by the instructor.

FRAGMENT—PUT #1 AND 2 TOGETHER WITH A COMMA

[1][*Because my alarm clock did not go off this morning.*] [2] *I was late to work at the supermarket.*

WERE-VERB AGR.   N-SPELLING   PED-VERB

[3] *My problems⋀was just begining.* [4] *I drop* ⋀TENSE

S-PLURAL      ED-VERB TENSE

*six carton* ⋀*of eggs.* [5] *I knock* ⋀*over a display*

RUN ON CAP

*of spagetti sauce⊙ when I was cleaning it up, I got sick and had to go home early.*

[6] *I hope tomorrow is a better day.*

You will notice several things about this paragraph. First, the instructor has numbered each unit that starts with a capital letter and ends with a period. (Let's call them "units," not "sentences," because some of them are not really sentences.) Second, the instructor has pointed out each error, named it, and indicated how to correct it. (Your instructor will probably use abbreviations when correcting your work. For example, **fragment** might be written **frag.,** and

**run-on** might be written **r-o.**) Looking carefully, you see that there are errors in units 1, 3, 4, and 5. The student, when correcting this paper, will concentrate on those units that need improvement.

In order to do the double corrections, you will need two pens, each with a different color ink. You may use the blue ink for rewriting your sentences and green for the corrections. If your instructor uses red ink to correct your work, it is better that you use a different, distinguishing color. You also need a separate sheet of paper—**not** the back of the paper that was corrected.

Suppose the student who wrote the sample paragraph wants to use the double-correction method. On a separate sheet of paper, he or she first copies in pen the first unit that has an error. In our example, this is unit 1. So, in pen the student copies the original writing:

*1. Because my alarm clock did not go off this morning.*

Then the student uses a green pen to make corrections, just as the instructor has made corrections. The unit now looks like this:

FRAGMENT—PUT #1 AND 2 TOGETHER WITH A COMMA
*1. [Because my alarm clock did not go off this morning.]*

Notice that the instructor has pointed out that what the student thought was a sentence was really a fragment, and the instructor has told the student how to correct the fragment. So now the student **rewrites** the entire sentence, this time with no errors. The correction page now looks like this:

FRAGMENT—PUT #1 AND 2 TOGETHER WITH A COMMA
*1. [Because my alarm clock did not go off this morning.]*

*1. Because my alarm clock did not go off this morning, I was late to work at the supermarket.*

You can see why we call this the double-correction method. The student writes the sentence twice. First he or she **corrects** it, just as the instructor has done; second, the student **writes it correctly.**

In our example, the student has finished unit 1 and is ready to go on to the next unit that needs correcting. In this case, it is unit 3. So the student again goes through the steps:

1. Copy the sentence in blue ink and correct it in green ink.
2. Rewrite the sentence correctly in blue ink.

Our student's unit 3 will look like this:

WERE-VERB AGR.  N-SPELLING

3. *My problems was just begining.*

3. *My problems were just beginning.*

Then the student will go on to numbers 4 and 5. Unit 6 does not need to be double-corrected; it contains no errors. When the student has finished all the double corrections, the correction paper will look like this:

FRAGMENT—PUT #1 AND 2 TOGETHER WITH A COMMA

1. *[Because my alarm clock did not go off this morning.]*

1. *Because my alarm clock did not go off this morning, I was late to work at the supermarket.*

WERE-VERB AGR.   N-SPELLING

3. *My problems was just begining.*

3. *My problems were just beginning.*

PED-VERB TENSE
S-PLURAL

4. *I drop ∧ six carton ∧ of eggs.*

4. *I dropped six cartons of eggs.*

ED-VERB TENSE          RUN ON

5. *I knock ∧ over a display of spaghetti sauce.*
CAP
*when I was cleaning it up, I got sick and had to go home early.*

5. *I knocked over a display of spaghetti sauce. When I was cleaning it up, I got sick and had to go home early.*

Note these points about the double-correction method:

1. You do not rewrite the entire paper. You concentrate on those sentences that need work.
2. You first write and correct a sentence. Then you rewrite it.
3. The double process reinforces the correction.
4. You make the corrections in the sentences **you** wrote.

Each time you receive a corrected composition, you should double-correct it on a separate sheet of paper and clip the correction sheet to your original composition. You should save all of your compositions and correction sheets. You can study them before you write your next composition, and you will be pleased, in going back over them, to note the gradual improvement in your writing during the course of the semester.

In the beginning of the semester, the correction may be supplied for you. For example, in sentence unit 3 above, the instructor crossed out the word *was* and wrote in the correct word *were* for the student. As the weeks go by, you will be more and more on your own. Later on, if an error is made, the instructor may simply note the type of error on your paper. For example, he or she may write just "fragment" or "verb agreement" and expect you to know how to correct it.

## AN ALTERNATE NUMBERING SYSTEM FOR THE DOUBLE-CORRECTION METHOD

Here is a slight variation on the double-correction method. Some instructors do not number every sentence unit. They number only those sentence units that need to be corrected. Here is an example of a paragraph that has been double-corrected in this way:

Cats have played many roles throughout history.
                    CAP      WERE-VERB AGR.   ED
①In ancient egypt, they was consider∧ sacred.
During the Middle Ages they were thought to be
evil companions of witches. ②Today cats are not
        RUN ON   CAP
worshiped◦however, they are popular as

*pets. Most cats are neat and tidy. Some are*

SP IES

*very affectionate. ③ These qualitys make them*

SP PLURAL NOUN-ADD S

*so desireable as house guest∧ that people*

VERB-AGR

*spends millions of dollars on cat food each*

*year.*

Notice that in the paragraph on cats, the instructor has numbered only those sentences that need to be double-corrected. Of the seven sentence units in the paragraph, three are numbered. Those three are corrected below. Notice that the sentence with the corrections marked is given a letter "a," and the rewritten correct sentence has the letter "b," so that the correction paper will be numbered **1a, 1b, 2a, 2b,** and so on. The correction paper will look like this:

VERB AGR.

CAP WERE ED

1a. *In ancient egypt, they was consider∧ sacred.*

1b. *In ancient Egypt, they were considered sacred.*

RUN-ON CAP

2a. *Today cats are not worshiped however, they are popular as pets.*

2b. *Today cats are not worshiped. However, they are popular as pets.*

SP IES SP

3a. *These qualitys make them so desireable*

PLURAL NOUN-ADD S VERB AGR

*as house guests that people spends millions of dollars on cat food each year.*

3b. *These qualities make them so desirable as house guests that people spend millions of dollars on cat food each year.*

The most important feature about the double-correction method is that it works. When you get a composition back, double-correct it, and you will learn from your mistakes. No matter which method of numbering your instructor uses, you can really improve your writing by double-correcting every composition.

CHAPTER

# 10

# Building a Sentence

## WHAT IS A GOOD SENTENCE?

A good sentence has at least one subject, one verb, and one complete idea. The subject of a sentence is the person, thing, or idea that the sentence is about. The verb shows action or expresses a state of being. What do we mean when we say that a good sentence contains a complete idea? From the capital at the beginning to the period at the end, a good sentence gives information that a reader can understand; the good sentence has a comprehensible unit of information. Sometimes the information is very simple, and sometimes it is very detailed. Look at the following examples. Each one contains a complete idea. In each example, the <u>subject</u> is underlined once and the verb is underlined twice.

Six <u>people</u> <u>waited</u> at the bus stop.

My right <u>foot</u> <u>hurts</u>.

Somebody should close the window.

It was raining.

The math professor in the large classroom across the hall from my office speaks softly but emphatically.

There is no difference between these two cars.

Where were you last night?

That important letter should have been mailed yesterday.

One of these computers is broken and should be replaced.

Barking dogs and loud noises make him nervous.

**EXERCISE 10a** | *Some of the following sentences contain complete ideas, and some do not. Identify each idea as complete or not complete.*

EXAMPLES   *complete*    **a.** The bank is closed today.

*not complete*   **b.** As soon as you get home after work today.

_____   **1.** The movie ended at 10 P.M.

_____   **2.** The committee will have finished its report by next week.

_____   **3.** Not knowing what to do next.

_____   **4.** Even though he was relatively light and short for professional football.

_____   **5.** Whenever there is a really big snowstorm.

_____   **6.** The baby is beautiful.

_____   **7.** We were stuck in traffic for a long time during the morning rush hour.

_____   **8.** A person who always thinks people are laughing at him.

_____   **9.** Ms. Aponte works during the day and goes to school at night.

_____ **10.** The telephone rang once.

_____ **11.** There were long lines and long delays at registration.

_____ **12.** Where are you going?

_____ **13.** Whispering through the whole class to the person sitting next to him.

_____ **14.** Because Mr. Smith told the truth.

_____ **15.** The house really needs to be repainted.

## CLAUSES AND PHRASES

## What Is an Independent Clause?

A clause is a group of words that contains a subject and a verb. An **independent clause** (also called a main clause) has a subject and a verb and can stand by itself as a sentence. In the following examples of independent clauses, each sentence provides information that makes sense. Each subject is underlined once and each verb twice.

The streets were quiet and empty.

Heavy rain fell for hours.

The windows of the apartment held plants and flowers.

One of my children tends to get ear infections frequently.

## What Is a Subordinate Clause?

A **subordinate clause** (also called a dependent clause) has a subject and a verb, but it does not express a complete idea. We cannot put a subordinate clause by itself; if we do, we will have written a fragment (see Chapter 11). In the following examples, each subordinate clause provides partial information, but not a complete idea. Subjects are underlined once, verbs twice.

since the streets were quiet and empty

while heavy rain fell for hours

that the windows of the apartment held plants and flowers

because one of my children tends to get ear infections frequently

## What Is a Phrase?

A **phrase** is a group of words working together. Unlike a clause, a phrase does not contain a subject and a verb. A phrase can be part of a sentence, but it cannot stand alone as a sentence. Look at the following examples:

after the party

closing his eyes very tightly

to find a well-paying job

the first person to walk on the moon

having finished her speech

**EXERCISE 10b**

*Identify each group of words as an independent clause, a subordinate clause, or a phrase. In each clause, identify the subject and verb. If it is an independent clause, put a capital at the beginning and a period at the end.*

_independent clause_  **a.** The weather is hot

_subordinate clause_  **b.** as soon as you finish your report

_phrase_  **c.** swimming two miles every day

_____  **1.** you should always proofread your work

_____  **2.** she is very angry

_____  **3.** if students want to enter the nursing program

_____  **4.** at the end of the nineteenth century

_____  **5.** although he is very shy

_____  **6.** unless there is a very good reason for his absence

_____  **7.** that my parents would never agree with my plan

_____  **8.** until January 28 you can change your class schedule

_____  **9.** waiting for just the right moment to announce the winner

_____  **10.** before you use the microwave oven

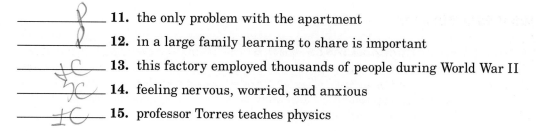

**11.** the only problem with the apartment

**12.** in a large family learning to share is important

**13.** this factory employed thousands of people during World War II

**14.** feeling nervous, worried, and anxious

**15.** professor Torres teaches physics

## BUILDING INTERESTING SENTENCES: SENTENCE COMBINING

Look at the following paragraph:

> Many parents worry about the behavior of their two-year-old children. The two-year-olds are often very stubborn. Their favorite word is "no." They won't obey their parents. They usually refuse to share their toys. Such behavior is totally normal. This stage is called the "terrible two's." It does not last forever. It may seem that way to some parents.

This paragraph has many ideas, and it is grammatically correct, but it is still not satisfactory. You will notice that each sentence contains just one independent clause and that all the sentences are approximately the same fairly short length. As a result, the paragraph sounds choppy and overly simple. In contrast, look at the next paragraph:

> Many parents worry about the behavior of their two-year-old children. Two-year-olds are often very stubborn, and their favorite word is "no." They won't obey their parents, and they usually refuse to share their toys. Such behavior is totally normal. Even though the stage called the "terrible two's" does not last forever, it may seem that way to some parents.

In this example, some of the short sentences have been combined. Several **joining words** have been used to show the relationships between the ideas in the paragraph. Instead of sounding overly simple and choppy, the paragraph sounds fluent and smooth. Compare the two paragraphs and underline the joining words that have been added in the second example.

There are two main ways to combine short, choppy sentences into longer, smoother sentences. Those two combining methods are called **coordination** and **subordination.**

## COORDINATION

### Joining Independent Clauses with a Coordinating Conjunction

Independent clauses may be joined with a coordinating conjunction. The coordinating conjunctions are:

| | | |
|---|---|---|
| and | for | yet |
| but | nor | so |
| | or | |

Look at the following examples showing how the coordinating conjunction are used:

The coordinating conjunction **and** simply adds one piece of information to another.

*SEPARATE:* The math exam is on Monday. The biology exam is on Tuesday.

*COMBINED:* The math exam is on Monday, **and** the biology exam is on Tuesday.

The words **but** and **yet** imply contradiction.

*SEPARATE:* Mr. Milfort wanted to mail a package. The post office was closed.

*COMBINED:* Mr. Milfort wanted to mail a package, **but** the post office was closed.

*SEPARATE:* Mr. Cory was very rich. He was not a happy person.

*COMBINED:* Mr. Cory was very rich, **yet** he was not a happy person.

The words **or** and **nor** indicate choices or different possibilities.

*SEPARATE:* Ms. Carole may go to graduate school. She may join the Peace Corps.

*COMBINED:* Ms. Carole may go to graduate school, **or** she may join the Peace Corps.

*SEPARATE:* The mayor will not attend the meeting. He will not send a representative.

*COMBINED:* The mayor will not attend the meeting, **nor** will he send a representative.

The word **for** explains why something happened.

*SEPARATE:* He was very happy. He had just won the lottery.

*COMBINED:* He was very happy, **for** he had just won the lottery.

The word **so** indicates cause and effect.

*SEPARATE:* Ms. Mauricio worked late last night. She is very tired this morning.

*COMBINED:* Ms. Mauricio worked late last night, **so** she is very tired this morning.

When a coordinating conjunction joins two clauses, the clauses are equal to each other; neither clause is subordinate to the other. Consider the following example:

Sally played her guitar, **and** her little brother did his homework.

In the sentence above, equal stress is placed on the actions of both Sally and her brother. In fact, a period could be placed after *guitar,* giving us:

Sally played her guitar. And her little brother did his homework.

**Note: Beginning a sentence with the word *and* or *but* is grammatically correct but should not be done often. It can be done once in a while for emphasis and sentence variety.**

**PUNCTUATION TIP**

Note that a comma is usually placed after the first independent clause, just before the coordinating conjunction.

The rain had stopped, and the sun was shining.

She was angry, but she did not admit it.

He had no money, nor did he have a place to live.

Notice in the last example that when **nor** is used, a helping verb (in this example, **did**) comes before the subject **(he).**

**EXERCISE 10c** | *Using the given coordinating conjunctions, join each pair of sentences.*

*EXAMPLE*   *yet*   Ms. Daley seemed quiet. She had strong opinions on many issues.

*Mrs. Daley seemed quiet, yet she had strong*
*opinions on many issues.*

*but*   **1.** I wanted to do some research. The library was closed.

*I wanted to do some research, the*
*library was closed,*

*so*   **2.** Alex needed to lose weight. He went on a diet.

*Alex need to lose weight, he*
*went on a date.*

*for*   **3.** Paulina has no trouble finding a job. She speaks five languages.

*Paulina has no trouble finding a*
*job, she speaks five languages.*

*nor*   **4.** Andrew did not miss his bus. He was not late for work.

*Andrew did not miss his bus, nor*
*he was not late for work.*

*and*   **5.** Ms. Randall wrote a memo. She made an important phone call.

*Ms. Randall wrote a memo and she*
*made an important phone call,*

*yet*   **6.** The box of books was small. It was extremely heavy.

_____

_____

*or*   **7.** The cavity must be filled. You will lose your tooth.

_____

_____

*for*   **8.** The concert was postponed. The auditorium had no heat.

_____

_____

*so*    **9.** A blackout hit the area. We could not use our electric appliances.

_____

_____

*yet*    **10.** She had never visited that city before. It seemed familiar.

_____

_____

## *Joining Independent Clauses with a Semicolon*

Two independent clauses can be combined in one sentence by using a semicolon (;). Look at the following sentence:

The book was exciting; he read it in a single night.

This sentence contains two independent clauses. Each clause could stand on its own as a sentence; that is, we could have written the following:

The book was exciting. He read it in a single night.

There is nothing wrong with writing the two clauses as separate sentences, but since they are closely related to each other, we may want to put them together in one sentence.

**Remember:    A comma alone cannot join two independent clauses. Use the semicolon.**

Here are more examples of sentences with a semicolon:

Robin Hood was an unusual thief; he robbed from the rich to give to the poor.

Jonathan loves to read; he goes to the library nearly every day.

The park was crowded; many people were strolling there.

The tenants' committee elected a new chairperson; Ms. Anderson will replace Ms. Brown.

Notice that the word after the semicolon is not capitalized unless it is a name. The word after the semicolon does not begin a new sentence.

Remember that when the semicolon is used, there is usually an independent clause—a grammatically complete idea—on each side of it. A diagram might help you to understand.

[independent clause]; [independent clause]

(The park was crowded); (many people were strolling there).

Be careful not to misuse the semicolon. It should **not** be placed after a subordinate clause. Remember this punctuation guideline:

In general, put a semicolon only where you could put a period.

**EXERCISE 10d** | *Combine the following pairs of sentences by using a semicolon.*

*EXAMPLE*   Heart disease is a serious problem. It is the leading cause of death in America.

*Heart disease is a serious problem; it is the leading cause of death in America.*

1. People can help themselves to stay healthy. A good diet and daily exercise are important.

2. The heart is a muscle. Its contractions pump blood through the body.

3. Sometimes blood vessels leading to the heart get clogged. Then a heart attack can occur.

4. Heart attacks cause a variety of symptoms. Pain is the most common one.

**5.** A heart attack is a medical emergency. A person with severe chest pain should get help immediately.

_____

_____

*Now make up your own sentence using a semicolon between the independent clauses. You may write about heart disease or another subject.*

**6.** _____

_____

_____

_____

**EXERCISE 10e** | *Using semicolons, join the following pairs of sentences.*

*EXAMPLE*  When a traffic light turns yellow, drivers approaching the intersection should stop. Trying to rush through it may cause an accident.

*When a traffic light turns yellow, drivers approaching the intersection should stop; trying to rush through it may cause an accident.*

**1.** A knowledge of history is important. Therefore, most colleges require students to take at least one history course.

_____

_____

**2.** Buying something that you did not plan to buy is called impulse buying. Most people do it occasionally.

_____

_____

_____

3. If the weather permits, the picnic will be held next Saturday. Otherwise, we will have it on Sunday.

_____

_____

_____

4. Because the biology professor had published two books and had appeared on television, she was quite well-known. Consequently, many students signed up for her class.

_____

_____

_____

*Now make up a sentence of your own, using the semicolon. You may use marriage as your topic, or, if you like, choose another subject.*

5. _____

_____

_____

## Connecting Adverbs

You may have noticed that some of the sentences in the previous exercises contained the words *consequently, otherwise,* and *therefore.* These words are **connecting adverbs.** Here is a list of common connecting adverbs.

| | |
|---|---|
| also | moreover |
| besides | nevertheless |
| consequently | otherwise |
| furthermore | still |
| however | then |
| instead | therefore |

The following phrases work as connecting adverbs to connect ideas:

| | |
|---|---|
| as a result | in fact |
| for example | in other words |
| in addition | on the other hand |

The words and phrases listed above are important for making connections between ideas in your compositions. They are good for transitions within and between paragraphs. As was noted in Chapter 5, they are sometimes called **signal words.**

Connecting adverbs can join ideas, but they do not work exactly the way the coordinating conjunctions do. Look at the following sentences and see if you notice the difference between them:

> John could run fast, but he was not on the track team.

> John could run fast; however, he was not on the track team.

Did you notice what happened when the word *however* (a connecting adverb) was used in place of *but* (a coordinating conjunction)? The punctuation changed. The words *however* and *but* both express opposition between ideas. However, when the coordinating conjunction *but* is used to introduce a new idea, we just place a comma after the first independent clause. When we use *however* to introduce a new independent clause in a sentence, we need the semicolon after the first independent clause.

Study the following pairs of sentences:

> The President promised to introduce a tax reform bill, **and** he promised to do it soon.

> The President promised to introduce a tax reform bill; **moreover,** he promised to do it soon.

> The message was in code, **so** only the intelligence officer could understand it.

> The message was in code; **therefore,** only the intelligence officer could understand it.

> The landlord promised to have our stove repaired, **and** he promised to have the apartment painted.

> The landlord promised to have our stove repaired; **furthermore,** he promised to have the apartment painted.

> The sentence is a basic unit of thought, **so** it is very important to understand sentence structure.

> The sentence is a basic unit of thought; **consequently,** it is very important to understand sentence structure.

Connecting adverbs are not true conjunctions because they do not always appear at the beginning of clauses. Connecting adverbs can be moved to almost any position in a clause. Look at the following examples:

The concert was supposed to begin at eight o'clock; **however,** it did not start until 8:30.

The concert was supposed to begin at eight o'clock; it did not start, **however,** until 8:30.

The concert was supposed to begin at eight o'clock; it did not, **however,** start until 8:30.

The concert was supposed to begin at eight o'clock; it did not start until 8:30, **however.**

Look at what happens when we use the true coordinating conjunction "but."

The concert was supposed to begin at eight o'clock, **but** it did not start until 8:30.

Notice in this last example that the word "but" cannot be moved to any other part of the sentence.

## PUNCTUATION TIP

Notice the comma that follows the connecting adverb in each sentence. This is the usual punctuation pattern when connecting adverbs are used between independent clauses:

Independent clause; connecting adverb, independent clause
semicolon————    comma—

The train broke down today; consequently, I was late to work.

A short word like **then** can sometimes be used without a comma after it.

I wrote a ten-page report; then I typed and mailed it.

If a connecting adverb is in the middle of a clause, put a comma before it and another comma after it.

independent clause    semicolon    independent clause

Frank's car would not start; he was, therefore, late to work.

comma    connecting adverb    comma

**EXERCISE 10f** | *Write sentences using semicolons and the given connecting adverbs.*

*EXAMPLE*   *however*        Suggested topic: a friend of yours

*Sonia is a good friend of mine; however, I get annoyed when she keeps me waiting.*

**1.** *therefore*        Suggested topic: a friend of yours

_____

_____

_____

**2.** *however*        Suggested topic: your college

_____

_____

_____

**3.** *nevertheless*        Suggested topic: getting a job

_____

_____

_____

## SUBORDINATION

### Joining Clauses with a Subordinating Conjunction

Another way to combine two clauses is to make one clause subordinate by adding a *subordinating conjunction*. Look at the following example:

Mrs. Smith is a good counselor. She is patient and sympathetic.

Instead of writing two choppy sentences, we can make one clause subordinate and then combine both clauses into one smooth sentence.

Ms. Smith is a good counselor **because** she is patient and sympathetic.

The sentence now contains one independent clause *(Ms. Smith is a good counselor)* and one subordinate clause *(because she is patient and sympathetic).* The subordinating conjunction *because* explains the relationship between the two ideas in the sentence.

Here is a list of the most common subordinating conjunctions:

| | | |
|---|---|---|
| after | how | unless |
| although | if | until |
| as | in order that | when |
| as if | since | whenever |
| as though | so that | where |
| because | that | while |
| before | though | |
| even though | | |

Some subordinating conjunctions express a time relationship:

| | | |
|---|---|---|
| after | until | while |
| before | when | |
| since | whenever | |

*EXAMPLE:*   **Before** television was invented, people read more books.

Some subordinating conjunctions express contradiction:

| | |
|---|---|
| although | though |
| even though | unless |

*EXAMPLE:*   She is a good basketball player **even though** she is short.

Some subordinating conjunctions express cause and effect:

because
since

*EXAMPLE:*   **Since** the radio was so loud, I did not hear the doorbell.

Note that the coordinating conjunction *since* has more than one function.

When you use a subordinating conjunction to combine two ideas, choose the conjunction that best explains the relationship between those ideas. The subordinating conjunction may be found in the middle of or at the beginning of the new sentence. Look at the following examples:

*SEPARATE:*   It was raining heavily. The highway was flooded.

*COMBINED:*   **Because** it was raining heavily, the highway was flooded.

*SEPARATE:*    Alex washed the dishes. Kelly vacuumed the living room.

*COMBINED:*    Alex washed the dishes **while** Kelly vacuumed the living room.

*SEPARATE:*    There is a thunderstorm. The dog starts trembling.

*COMBINED:*    **Whenever** there is a thunderstorm, the dog starts trembling.

---

**PUNCTUATION TIP**

When a subordinate clause **introduces** the sentence, a comma follows it.

When a subordinate clause **follows** a main clause, there is **usually** no need for a comma between the clauses. Consider the following examples.

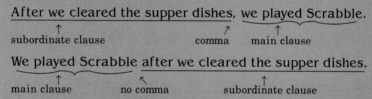

There are exceptions to this rule.

A comma may be placed before a subordinate clause when the subordinate clause provides contrast to the main clause. For example:

Ken plays the guitar well, although he has never taken

lessors.    ↑              ↑              ↑

      main clause        comma        subordinate clause

---

**EXERCISE 10g**

*In the following sentences underline the subordinate clauses and circle the independent clauses (the main clauses). Draw an extra line under the subordinating conjunctions.*

*EXAMPLES*    **a.** When the snow stops falling, people begin to shovel.

        **b.** John can lend money to his friends because he has a good job.

        **1.** Although the heat was on, the room felt cold.

        **2.** When the school bus lights were flashing, all traffic came to a stop.

3. Whenever there is thunder, my cats hide.

4. Before you use the microwave oven, you should read the directions.

5. He went to work even though he had a cold.

6. Although the pitcher gave up just one hit, his team lost the game.

7. While Tom did the laundry, Arlene balanced the checkbook.

8. Andrew demanded silence while he was studying.

9. The child waited patiently until it was her turn on the swings.

10. I felt tired all day because I got very little sleep last night.

11. The apartment looks bright and cheerful since we repainted it.

12. If you want to be a doctor, you will have to take many science courses.

13. Unless there is a blizzard tomorrow, all the usual parking regulations will be in effect.

14. After their first child was born, Mr. and Mrs. Sackey bought a house.

15. The suspect showed the police where he had buried the stolen property.

**EXERCISE 10h** | *Provide commas where necessary in the following paragraph. Be prepared to explain which clauses are subordinate and which are independent.*

Although being a working parent of small children is not easy, most parents do not have any other choice. The family must live on one income if one parent stays home to take care of the children. Because the costs of housing, food, and transportation are very high one income may not be enough to cover even the basic necessities for a family. When both parents work the family is more likely to have a higher standard of living.

## Joining Clauses with a Subordinating Relative Pronoun

Two clauses that mention the same person or thing can sometimes be joined by using a subordinating relative pronoun. A relative pronoun relates to or refers to a word in the first clause of a sentence. The following pronouns can introduce a subordinate clause:

| | | |
|---|---|---|
| that | wherever | whoever |
| what | which | whom |
| whatever | whichever | whomever |
| | who | whose |

When using a relative pronoun to combine two or more sentences, we must usually cross out one or more words or rearrange some words in the second sentence. In the following examples, the subordinating relative pronoun is in **boldface** and the entire subordinate clause is in *italics*.

*SEPARATE:*   Ms. Andes bought a new computer. It has more power and memory than her old one.

*COMBINED:*   Ms. Andes bought a new computer ***that*** *has more power and memory than her old one.*

*SEPARATE:*   I have a good friend. She lives in Boston.

*COMBINED:*   I have a good friend ***who*** *lives in Boston.*

*SEPARATE:*   Today the class reviewed DNA testing. It will be a major topic on the exam.

*COMBINED:*   Today the class reviewed DNA testing, ***which*** *will be a major topic on the exam.*

*SEPARATE:*   I had to call my cousin Frank. I borrowed his car yesterday.

*COMBINED:*   I had to call my cousin Frank, ***whose*** *car I borrowed yesterday.*

Sometimes the subordinate clause is placed in the middle of the independent clause. In the following examples, the subordinating pronoun is in **boldface,** and the entire subordinate clause is in *italics*.

The energy crisis, ***which*** *was widely discussed in the seventies,* is still a serious problem today.

The librarian ***whom*** *I asked to help me* was very informative.

Rose, ***whose*** *painting won first prize,* has been interested in art for many years.

My neighbor Walt, ***who*** *used to be a salesperson,* changed careers and became a chef.

**PUNCTUATION TIP**

Sometimes a subordinate clause that begins with **who** or **whom** is set off by commas and sometimes not. If you can drop the clause without changing the basic meaning of the sentence, you need commas around it. If you cannot drop the clause without distorting the sentence's meaning or making it impossible to understand, then do not use commas.

| Commas Needed | Commas Not Needed |
|---|---|
| Mrs. Baker, who has just been promoted to sales manager, has been with this company for three years. (The **who** clause is not needed to identify the woman because we know her name. The clause provides extra information and could be dropped from the sentence.) | The woman who has just been promoted to sales manager has been with this company for three years. (The **who** clause is needed to identify the woman.) |
| Jan hates her next-door neighbors, who are very cruel to their pets. | Jan hates people who are cruel to their pets. (Jan does not hate all people so the **who** clause is necessary to explain the sentence.) |
| George Washington, whom we call the father of his country, was our first president. | The man whom we call the father of his country was our first president. |

**Hint: Notice that in order to read the sentences clearly, you must pause where the commas are needed.**

**EXERCISE 10i**  *On separate paper, combine each group of sentences into one sentence using* who, whose, which, that, *and other subordinating pronouns listed on page 93.*

*EXAMPLES*  **a.** I spoke to the manager. She gave me an application.

*I spoke to the manager, who gave me an application.*

**b.** Here is my biology textbook. You may borrow it.

*Here is my biology textbook, which you may borrow.*

**c.** Julia's parents live in Italy. She speaks several languages.

*Julia, whose parents live in Italy, speaks several languages.*

**d.** The Guzmans have bought a new house. It is larger than their old one.

*The Guzmans have bought a new house, which is larger than their old one.*

1. The pediatrician examined the baby. She had an earache.
2. I have a good friend. Her name is Janice.
3. He is learning a new piano solo. It is very difficult.
4. We are returning these two library books. We found them very interesting.
5. Mr. Gregory works as a security guard. He is studying data processing.
6. The interviewer decided to hire Ms. Anderson. Her speaking and writing skills were quite impressive.
7. The actor recited the speech beginning "To be or not to be." It is a soliloquy from *Hamlet,* by William Shakespeare.
8. In the hamper was a large pile of clothing. It needed to be washed.
9. At the embassy I spoke to an official. She was very polite and helpful.
10. Herbert should return my lawn mower. He borrowed it a month ago.

## SUMMARY: FOUR TYPES OF CONNECTING WORDS

We have now discussed four types of connecting words.

1.  You can use a **coordinating conjunction.** *FAN BOY*
2.  You can use a **connecting adverb** after a **semicolon.**
3.  You can use a **subordinating conjunction.** *AC*
4.  You can use a **subordinating relative pronoun.** *AC*

Here is a brief list of words from each category. Let's see how they can all work to join clauses.

| *Coordinating Conjunctions* | *Connecting Adverbs* | *Subordinating Conjunctions* | *Subordinating Relative Pronouns* |
| --- | --- | --- | --- |
| but | however | although | who |
| so | therefore | because | whose |
| and | then | when | that |

Consider these two independent clauses.

Charles was very handsome. He was not popular.

When we write these two clauses as separate sentences, the result is choppy and unconnected. We need to join the ideas somehow. Let's see how we can use words from each list to join these two clauses. We might expect a handsome person to be popular. Since Charles is handsome but **not** popular, there is opposition between the two ideas. The following words from each category express opposition: *but, however, although.* Let's use each one in turn to join the clauses.

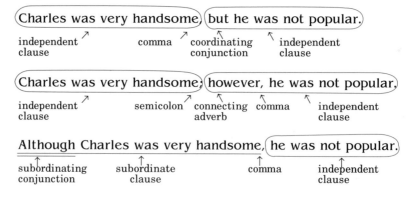

We can also use the subordinating relative pronoun "who" to combine the independent clauses. To emphasize the opposition between the two clauses, we can add the signal word "nevertheless."

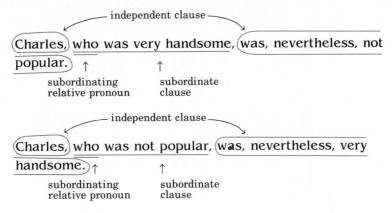

Let's consider two more clauses:

> There was a bad storm. Many towns lost electric power for two days.

Here the relationship between the clauses is one of cause and effect. The joining words from each category that we can use are *so, therefore, because,* and *which.* Notice that when we combine with *which,* we must change a few words.

> There was a bad storm, **so** many towns lost electric power for two days.

> There was a bad storm; **therefore,** many towns lost electric power for two days.

> **Because** there was a bad storm, many towns lost electric power for two days.

> There was a bad storm, **which** caused many towns to lose electric power for two days.

**EXERCISE 10j**

*Combine the following sets of clauses as many ways as you can by using coordinating conjunctions, subordinating conjunctions, connecting adverbs, and subordinating relative pronouns. You may have to rearrange some words. Use separate paper.*

EXAMPLES    **a.** Our natural environment is precious. We should protect it.

*(1) Because our natural environment is precious, we should protect it.*

*(2) Our natural environment is precious, so we should protect it.*

*(3) Our natural environment is precious; therefore, we should protect it.*

*(4) We should protect our natural environment, which is precious.*

**b.** Mr. Adams works fifty hours a week. He finds time to coach a Little League baseball team.

*(1) Although Mr. Adams works fifty hours a week, he finds time to coach a Little League baseball team.*

*(2) Mr. Adams works fifty hours a week, but he finds time to coach a Little League baseball team.*

*(3) Mr. Adams works fifty hours a week; nevertheless, he finds time to coach a Little League baseball team.*

*(4) Mr. Adams, who works fifty hours a week, finds time to coach a Little League baseball team.*

1. Einstein was a great genius. He was very modest.

2. Some people are careless with medicines. Thousands of children are poisoned every year.

3. My brother is always dieting. He never seems to lose weight.

4. Many colleges are teaching computer skills. These skills are very important in the modern world.

5. The brains of infants are stimulated by speech. Parents should speak to their babies often.

**EXERCISE 10k**  | *On separate paper, combine the following sets of clauses using the method that seems most appropriate for each. More than one method may be possible.*

*EXAMPLES*  **a.** A new store recently opened on Main Street. It is doing very well.

*A new store that recently opened on Main Street is doing very well.*

**b.** The runner did not win the race. She was still happy with her performance.

*Even though the runner did not win the race, she was still happy with her performance.*

**c.** Getting a flu shot is a good idea. The shot does not totally protect people against new kinds of flu virus.

*Getting a flu shot is a good idea; however, the shot does not totally protect people against new kinds of flu virus.*

**d.** It was a cold winter. Our heating bill was very high.

*It was a cold winter, so our heating bill was very high.*

1. Britain usually has mild winters. The Gulf Stream keeps the British Isles warm.    *The Gulf Stream Keeps the British Isles warm.*
2. Japan's subways are very crowded. They are very clean.
3. The Smiths installed a new furnace. It works more efficiently than the old one.    *nor Anyone*
4. I have had no mail this week. No one has telephoned me.
5. Many young people dream of becoming professional athletes. Only a very few succeed in professional sports.
6. The museum is having an exhibition of American quilts. The quilts were made in the early nineteenth century.
7. The car was not very expensive. It runs well.    *so*
8. Oil has been discovered in Chesterfield County. Land values have soared.
9. Dr. Nichols dislikes flying. She is driving to Chicago this week.
10. Sherry grew up in the country. She had never been in an elevator until age twelve.

CHAPTER

# 11

# How to Avoid Sentence Fragments

In most college writing assignments, every sentence should be complete; you should avoid sentence fragments. A sentence fragment is only a piece of a sentence, a part of an idea. A fragment does **not** present a complete idea that can stand on its own. Remember that a good sentence must have the following:

1.  **A verb:** Verbs may show action or a state of being. Verbs are essential; trying to write without verbs is like trying to make bread without flour.

2.  **A subject:** To find a subject, ask who or what is doing the action shown in the verb; who or what is being discussed.

3.  **A complete idea:** From the capital letter at the start to the period at the end, the sentence must be able to stand on its own. (In other words, every sentence must have at least one independent clause. See Chapter 10, p. 77.)

If any of these three elements is missing, the result is a sentence **fragment,** not a true sentence. Do not judge by length. A very short group of words may be a complete sentence, and a very long group of words may be a fragment. Let's look at different kinds of fragments and various ways to turn them into good sentences.

## MAKE SURE YOUR SENTENCE HAS A COMPLETE VERB

Verbs are basic elements of a sentence. A sentence is not complete if it has no verb or only part of a verb. In the following paired examples, the first has no verb or only a partial verb, and the second is complete.

*FRAGMENT:*   Shakespeare a poet and a playwright.
*(NO VERB)*

*COMPLETE:*   Shakespeare **was** a poet and a playwright.

*FRAGMENT:*   Ms. Andes very knowledgeable about diet and nutrition.
*(NO VERB)*

*COMPLETE:*   Ms. Andes **is** very knowledgeable about diet and nutrition.

*FRAGMENT:*   Janice **watching** a special program about air pollution.
*(PARTIAL VERB)*

*COMPLETE:*   Janice **was watching** a special program about air pollution.

*FRAGMENT:*   Bill **spilling** ink all over his math notebook.
*(PARTIAL VERB)*

*COMPLETE:*   Bill **is spilling** ink all over his math notebook.

When we write very fast or under pressure, our ideas may come faster than our pens can move. Under such conditions, it is possible to leave out a verb or part of a verb, especially short verb forms like *is, am, are, was, were, has, have,* and *had.* After you finish an assignment, proofread it carefully and make sure that each sentence has a complete verb.

> **BRIEF PRACTICE 11.1**   *Write in the missing verbs. The first is done as an example.*
>
> **1.** The dog $\overset{was}{\wedge}$ barking most of the night.
>
> **2.** Mr. Jackson an enthusiastic teacher.
>
> **3.** Nobody in the classroom or in the writing lab.
>
> **4.** The post office not open on Sunday.

## MAKE SURE YOUR SENTENCE HAS A SUBJECT

Sometimes a fragment occurs because the writer has forgotten to give the sentence a subject. In the following paired examples, the first is a fragment lacking a subject, and the second is a complete sentence.

*FRAGMENT:*
*(NO SUBJECT)*   Received her engineering education from Columbia University.

*COMPLETE:*   **She** received her engineering education from Columbia University.

*FRAGMENT:*
*(NO SUBJECT)*   For several years worked in a day-care center.

*COMPLETE:*   For several years **Mr. Yates** worked in a day-care center.

*FRAGMENT:*
*(NO SUBJECT)*   Never knew the results of the test.

*COMPLETE:*   **They** never knew the results of the test.

Fragments with no subjects sometimes occur because many sentences in the same paragraph may discuss the same person or thing, and the writer does not want to repeat the same words too often. Look at the following brief paragraph:

Ms. McCarthy had finished a long, hard day at work. She had taken care of all of the patients on her ward, and she had counseled the distressed relatives of a particularly ill patient. When she got home, she was really tired. **Instead of starting to cook dinner, just sat down to rest for while.**

The last sentence in the paragraph is a fragment. From reading the previous sentences, we understand *who* sat down to rest for a while, but remember that each sentence must make sense by itself. To be complete, the last sentence needs a subject: *Instead of starting to cook dinner, **she** just sat down to rest for a while.*

---

**BRIEF PRACTICE 11.2**    *Find and correct the fragment in this paragraph.*

Roger was very excited about his first job interview. He had his hair cut, and he carefully chose the clothes he would wear. Really wanted to make a good impression. On the day of the interview, he got up early because he didn't want to be late.

---

**EXERCISE 11a**    *Add the missing verbs and/or subjects to these fragments.*

*EXAMPLES*    **a.** Really wanted to do well on the physics exam.

*She really wanted to do well on the physics exam.*

**b.** The glass broken into six or seven pieces.

*The glass had broken into six or seven pieces.*

1. The movie very exciting but a little too violent.

_____

_____

2. It been a long time since our last meeting.

_____

_____

3. Angrily shouted at everyone to leave him alone.

_____

_____

**4.** Nervous and irritable the whole day.

_____

_____

**5.** They hoping to move to a bigger place after the birth of their first child.

_____

_____

**6.** Luckily found another job right away.

_____

_____

**7.** Decided to major in both business and secretarial studies.

_____

_____

**8.** Everything going perfectly all day and all evening.

_____

_____

**9.** Is never a good idea to drink and drive.

_____

_____

**10.** Usually in his office at the this time of the day.

_____

_____

## MAKE SURE YOUR SENTENCE HAS A COMPLETE IDEA

A group of words may have a verb and a subject and still not be a complete sentence. Look at the following fragments:

**1.** Since he began working the night shift.
         ↑         ↑
      subject   verb

**2.** Because the photo is not clear.
              ↑      ↑
          subject  verb

**3.** Whenever the doctor prescribes penicillin.
    ↑              ↑
    subject        verb

**4.** After heavy rains had flooded the area.
       ↑              ↑
       subject        verb

**5.** Mrs. Jacobs, who is head nurse at Valley Stream
       Hospital.          ↑     ↑
                   subject     verb

All these examples have verbs and subjects, but they do not have complete ideas. Each example is a **subordinate clause** (see Chapter 10). A subordinate clause should never stand by itself because it has only a partial idea and leaves the reader wondering. Look at Example 4: *After heavy rains had flooded the area*—what happened as a result? Example 4 does not say what happens, and so it is a fragment. These examples are not independent clauses and should not be standing by themselves.

## HOW TO FIX SUBORDINATE CLAUSE FRAGMENTS

There are several ways to fix subordinate clause fragments. Each method has its own advantages.

### Fixing Fragments by Removing the Subordinating Word

One method of fixing this kind of fragment is to remove the subordinating word, the word that makes the idea incomplete. (See Chapter 10, pp. 90 and 93 for lists of subordinating words.) In the following examples, each fragment has been corrected by removing the subordinating word.

subordinating word
↓
*FRAGMENT:*    **Since** he began working the night shift.

*COMPLETE:*    He began working the night shift.

subordinating word
↓
*FRAGMENT:*    **Because** the photo is not clear.

*COMPLETE:*    The photo is not clear.

subordinating word
↓
*FRAGMENT:* **Whenever** the doctor prescribes penicillin.

*COMPLETE:* The doctor prescribes penicillin.

subordinating word
↓
*FRAGMENT:* **After** heavy rains had flooded the area.

*COMPLETE:* Heavy rains had flooded the area.

subordinating word
↓
*FRAGMENT:* Mrs. Jacobs, **who** is head nurse at Valley Stream Hospital.

*COMPLETE:* Mrs. Jacobs is head nurse at Valley Stream Hospital.

---

**BRIEF PRACTICE 11.3**   *Correct each fragment by crossing out the subordinating word. You may need to change capitalization. The first two are done as examples.*

A
1. ~~When a~~ blizzard dropped twenty inches of snow over the entire area.

2. Mr. Holder, ~~who~~ is a medical lab technician.

3. Because the tree fell, knocking down a telephone pole.

4. Ms. Elumeze, who is originally from Nigeria.

5. Since I cannot remember my new neighbor's name.

---

The chief advantage of this method is that it is fast. If you are under time pressure, it takes only a few moments to cross out the subordinating word and (in most cases) change a small letter to a capital. If you use this method too often, however, you will end up with short, choppy sentences that have no logical connections between them. The writing will be overly simple, and readers will not see relationships between your ideas.

*CORRECT BUT*
*CHOPPY:* I cannot identify the suspect. The photo is not clear.

## Placing a Subordinate Clause Fragment with Another Sentence

A good method of fixing an incomplete idea is to see if you can place the fragment with another sentence in the composition. The fragment may actually be related to the idea in the previous sentence *or* in the next sentence. Look at the following examples. In the first example, the fragment fits well with the sentence just before it. In the second example, the fragment goes logically with the sentence after it.

independent clause (complete idea)     subordinate clause (fragment)

*INCORRECT:*   I cannot identify the suspect. Because the photo is not clear.

*CORRECTED:*   I cannot identify the suspect because the photo is not clear.

subordinate clause           independent clause
(fragment)                  (complete idea)

*INCORRECT:*   After heavy rains had flooded the area. Many roads were closed.

*CORRECTED:*   After heavy rains had flooded the area, many roads were closed.

Notice the punctuation in the corrected examples. If the independent clause is first and the subordinate clause second, usually no comma is needed. If the subordinate clause is first, it is marked off with a comma, and then the independent clause follows. (See the Punctuation Tip on p. 91 of Chapter 10.)

This linking method has several advantages. First, it does not take much time. Second, it allows you to show clearly the relationships between various ideas in your paper. This method works very well to eliminate many (but not all) fragments.

**BRIEF PRACTICE 11.4** *Correct each fragment by placing it with a complete sentence. The first one is done as an example.*

1. Because Ella wants to be a doctor, ~~S~~he is taking many science courses.

2. I get a bad allergic reaction. Whenever a cat comes near me.

3. The manager wants to see you. Right after you have finished your work shift.

4. Even though the weather was warm and sunny. Nobody was in the park.

## Adding New Material to Fragments

Another method of fixing incomplete ideas is to add new material that finishes the idea. Usually you have to write a new independent clause, which can be added before or after the fragment. In the following examples, the new words are in **boldface.**

*FRAGMENT:* Mr. Washington, finally getting home after a hard day at work.

*CORRECTED:* **As I looked out the window, I noticed** Mr. Washington, finally getting home after a hard day at work.

*FRAGMENT:* Many nations from different parts of the world.

*CORRECTED:* Many nations from different parts of the world **discuss international matters at the United Nations.**

Adding new words is a good way to fix a fragment, but it takes time. Sometimes, however, it is the only method that will allow a sentence to make sense.

## Adding New Material to "Who" Fragments

Make sure to finish the ideas in sentences containing the words *who, which,* or *that.* Look at the following example:

*FRAGMENT:* Ms. Ames, **who** is a bilingual secretary and works on Wall Street.

To correct this fragment, we can add new material about Ms. Ames. The new words can be placed either before or after the fragment. Look at the corrected examples below:

*CORRECTED:* **I recently met** Ms. Ames, who is a bilingual secretary and works on Wall Street.

*CORRECTED:* Ms. Ames, who is a bilingual secretary and works on Wall Street, **graduated from this college.**

In addition to the method shown above, we can also fix this fragment by eliminating the word "and."

*FRAGMENT:* Ms. Ames, who is a bilingual secretary and works on Wall Street.

*CORRECTING THE FRAGMENT:* Ms. Ames, who is a bilingual secretary ~~and~~ works on Wall Street.

*CORRECTED:* Ms. Ames, who is a bilingual secretary, works on Wall Street.
↑
new comma

---

**BRIEF PRACTICE 11.5**   *Correct each fragment by adding new words. The first one is done as an example.*

**1.** My neighbor who lives in the apartment upstairs.

*My neighbor who lives in the apartment upstairs has two cats.*

**2.** Ms. Carter, who is an interior decorator and the mother of three children.

_____

_____

**3.** Nobody who knows Mr. Soto really well.

_____

_____

**4.** Mr. Hart, who manages a factory.

_____

_____

## REVIEW OF WAYS TO FIX FRAGMENTS

When you find a fragment in your writing, you have a choice of ways to correct it:

1.  Remove the subordinating word.
2.  Place the fragment with another sentence in the composition.
3.  Add new material to complete the idea.

Do not judge whether an example is a good sentence or a fragment by length. Instead, judge by whether the idea is complete or incomplete. Judge by whether the example makes sense or leaves the reader wondering where the rest of the idea is.

## PROOFREADING FOR FRAGMENTS

Fragments are not always easy to spot. In fact, finding a fragment is usually more difficult than fixing it. Remember: If you cannot find it, you cannot fix it. An excellent way to recognize fragments is to use proofreading strategies 3 and 4 described in Chapter 7.

**EXERCISE 11b** | *Some of the following examples are fragments, and others are good sentences. If the example is a good sentence, make no changes. If the example is a fragment, correct it using any method you wish.*

*EXAMPLES*   **a.** Because many Americans worry about their weight.

*Diet books are popular because many Americans worry about their weight.*

**b.** The coffee tasted bitter.

_____

_____

**c.** After she got a computer.

*After she got a computer, she used it to write her term papers.*

**1.** Mr. Olsen, who is the bank manager.

_____

_____

**2.** Because a new car would be very expensive.

_____

_____

**3.** The Spanish and Italian languages have many similar words.

_____

_____

**4.** Always worrying about his health.

_____

_____

**5.** An interesting job, which she could not turn down.

_____

_____

**6.** Whenever the weather is really hot.

_____

_____

**7.** As soon as I finish this book.

_____

_____

**8.** The death penalty, a controversial topic.

_____

_____

**9.** I am very tired.

_____

_____

**10.** Saved money by planting a vegetable garden.

_____

_____

**11.** At age 19, Mozart wrote an opera.

_____

_____

**EXERCISE 11c**  *Some of the following examples are good sentences, and some are fragments. If an example is a good sentence, make no changes. If it is a fragment, correct it using any method.*

*EXAMPLES*  **a.** Know very little about nutrition and health.

*Many people know very little about nutrition and health.*

**b.** The accident occurred at 10 p.m.

_____

**1.** Studied computer technology while in the Army.

_____

_____

**2.** Because he is very shy.

_____

_____

**3.** After work he goes to night school.

_____

_____

**4.** Even though I can't remember his name.

_____

_____

**5.** While Mr. Diaz filled out the application.

_____

_____

**6.** The hairstyles that were popular in the 1940s.

_____

_____

**7.** A garden fence, which they built themselves.

_____

_____

**8.** A vaccine for measles is available.

_____

_____

**9.** Although we met only one month ago.

_____

_____

**10.** She took a special course in finance.

_____

_____

**EXERCISE 11d** _Some of the following examples contain two complete sentences. Others contain one or two fragments. Rewrite the examples that contain fragments so that every sentence is complete._

**EXAMPLE** William Wordsworth was an English poet. Who died in 1850.

_William Wordsworth was an English poet who died in 1850._

**1.** _Birth of a Nation,_ one of the first movies. Is very controversial.

*[handwritten margin note: Nonrestrictive Fragment!]*

_Birth of a Nation, one of the first movies, ~~that~~ is very controversial._

**2.** While the store owner was closing up for the evening. A robbery occurred.

*[handwritten note: Can't change it!]*

_While the store owner was closing up for the evening, a robbery occurred._

**3.** Several movies have been made recently based on Jane Austen's novels. One example is _Persuasion._

_Several movies have been made recently based on Jane Austen's novels; one example is Persuasion._

**4.** Many great books were published in the nineteenth century. For example, *The Scarlet Letter* and *Moby Dick*.

_Many great book were published in the 19th century, for example, The Scarlet letter_

**5.** Some people are so afraid of snakes. That they hardly ever go outside.

_restrictive_ _Some people are so afraid of snakes That they hardly ever go outside._

**6.** Researchers who study sleep patterns. Claim that most people do not get enough sleep.

_Researchers who study sleep patterns claim that most people don't get enough sleep._

**7.** Two-year-old children are often stubborn. They are behaving normally for their age.

_2 y. old children are often stubborn they are behaving normally for their age_

**8.** Mr. and Mrs. Villa have bought a new house. Which has enough room for their growing family.

_Mr. and Mrs. Villa have bought a new house, which has enough room for their growing fa_

**9.** We should not judge others by their appearance. Unfortunately, many people do judge others in this way.

_We should not judge others by their appearance unfortunately many people do judge this way_

**10.** Whether we like it or not. Life is sure to be different in the twenty-first century.

_Whether we like it or not, life is sure to be different in the 21 century._

**EXERCISE**
**11e**

*Some of the following examples contain two complete sentences. Others contain one or more fragments. Rewrite the examples that contain fragments so that every sentence is complete.*

*EXAMPLE*   Many colleges have evening classes. For people who work during the day.

*Many colleges have evening classes for people who work during the day.*

1. Some people get asthma attacks. When the weather is very cold.

   *Some people get asthma attacks when the weather is very cold.*

2. Baseball is extremely popular in many foreign countries. Especially Japan and Mexico.

   *Baseball is extremely popular in many foreign countries, especially Japan & Mexico.*

3. Soybeans can be made into many products. For example, tofu and soy milk.

   *Soybeans can be made into many products that are tofu and soy milk.*

4. Quilting and knitting are very popular. Many people enjoy these handicrafts.

   *Quilting and knitting are very popular many people in these handicrafts.*

5. Many great opera singers are African-American. For example, Leontyne Price, Kathleen Battle, Jessye Norman, and Denyce Graves.

   *Many great opera singers are African American*

6. Although the runner stumbled and nearly fell. She recovered and finished the race.

   *Although the runner stumbled*

**7.** The writer Mark Twain once lived in the Bronx in a large house. That overlooked the Hudson River.

_The writer Mark Twain once lived in the Bronx in a large house that overlooked the Hudson River_

**8.** Very small toys could be swallowed. Therefore, baby toys must be carefully designed.

_____

_____

**9.** When LaToya ~~was~~ in high school, She went to Spain with a school group. _LaToya._

_____

_____

**10.** Pessimists see a water glass as half empty. Optimists see the glass as half full.

_____

_____

<table>
<tr><td>EXERCISE<br>11f</td><td>_In the following examples, there are some fragments. Correct the fragments in the book, or rewrite the examples on separate paper._</td></tr>
</table>

**1.** Anne Tyler, a writer of novels. Published her first book when she was in her early twenties. Her novels often feature large families with interesting problems.

**2.** Smoking cigarettes for an extended period of time. Can cause various problems, including lung cancer and emphysema. In addition to these serious diseases. Smoking also yellows the teeth and wrinkles the skin.

**3.** Although sugar cane was the chief product of Puerto Rico for a long time. The island no longer has a one-crop economy. Machinery manufacturing, chemical production, and oil refining are now among the major industries.

**4.** Some of the games that children play. Have not changed very much for perhaps centuries. For example, hop scotch and jump rope.

**5.** Seiji Ozawa, a world-famous musician. Was the first Japanese conductor to gain fame and recognition in the West. He has been director of many orchestras. Including the Toronto Symphony Orchestra, the San Francisco Symphony Orchestra, and the Boston Symphony Orchestra.

**6.**    Although most professional hockey players used to be Canadian, Today players come from all over the world. Including the United States, Sweden, and Russia.

**7.**    Children learn more than academic subjects at school. For example, young children in the early grades learn how to get along with others. A valuable and necessary social skill.

**8.**    Technology usually makes inventions smaller, less expensive, and easier to use. The first computers, which were very complicated. Took up the space of an entire room. Today's portable computers are easy to use and weigh only a few pounds.

**9.**    America's greatest contribution to music is jazz. Jazz, which first developed late in the nineteenth century. Is a product of African-American culture.

**10.**    Coffee plants are small evergreen trees. While coffee trees can grow at sea level. The best coffee is produced at an elevation above 1500 feet.

---

**EXERCISE 11g**    *In the following examples, there are some fragments. Correct the fragments in the book, or rewrite the examples on separate paper.*

**1.**    America has sometimes been called a nation of immigrants. Because people from so many different countries have come to the United States. Bringing their special traditions, foods, clothing, and rituals.

**2.**    Because joggers do not need a lot of expensive equipment. Jogging has become very popular. However, to avoid foot and leg injuries, which can be very painful. Joggers should buy the right kind of running shoes.

**3.**    Ms. Miller will not use certain pesticides in her garden. Because they kill the bees, which pollinate many plants. If plants are not pollinated. They will not produce fruit.

**4.**    When the suffix of a word is changed. The word may change from a verb to a noun or even to an adjective. For example, *observe, observer, observant.*

**5.**    India, a republic in South Asia. Is a nation with the second highest population in the world. The republic, whose capital is New Delhi. Is divided into twenty-five states.

6.   The names of many American towns are colorful. And very descriptive. For example, Wounded Knee, Broken Arrow, Salt Lake City, Yellowstone, and Little Rock.

7.   Ralph Bunche, who was born in Detroit in 1904. Received his doctorate from Harvard in 1934. After teaching political science for a number of years. He entered government service. He was the first African American to be head of a division of the Department of State.

8.   In ancient Greek mythology, Mentor was a sensible and intelligent friend of the hero Odysseus. Today, the word *mentor* is used to describe a wise and faithful adviser. A person who gives advice and guidance.

9.   If a kitchen is poorly planned, It can cause the cook extra work. For example, if the refrigerator and the counter are far apart. The cook will waste time walking back and forth between them.

10.   The word *landlocked* means being surrounded on all sides by land. Not bordered by any large seas or oceans. An example of a landlocked nation is Chad. A country in the central part of North Africa.

CHAPTER

# 12

# How to Avoid Run-Ons and Comma Splices

Sentence structure must be clear and correct. Running two or more complete ideas together produces run-ons and comma splices, which are serious sentence-structure errors.

## WHAT IS A RUN-ON?

Look at the following example:

RUN-ON:    John fell down he hurt his knee.

Why is this example a run-on? It contains two complete ideas (independent clauses) without any separation or connection.

independent clause     independent clause

*RUN-ON:*   John fell down he hurt his knee.

↑

no separation or connection
between two independent clauses

## WHAT IS A COMMA SPLICE?

Suppose we placed a comma after the word *down* in the example above. Would the sentence be correct? No. We would still have an error in sentence structure called a comma splice.

independent clause     independent clause

*COMMA SPLICE:*   John fell down, he hurt his knee.

↑

not the proper separation
between two independent clauses

A comma alone is not strong enough punctuation to separate two independent clauses.

## EDITING TO AVOID CONFUSION

Run-ons and comma splices can confuse your reader. Look at the following example:

> Ms. Willis got a job as a salesperson in a department store when she proved that she had intelligence and common sense she was promoted to assistant buyer.

This sentence could be read two different ways. Did Ms. Willis's intelligence and common sense win her the job, or did they help her get the promotion? We really cannot tell. The run-on sentence has made the writer's ideas unclear and confusing. It is not the reader's job to *guess* what the sentence is saying; it is the writer's job to make each sentence clear. Look at the corrected example:

> Ms. Willis got a job as a salesperson in a department store. When she proved that she had intelligence and common sense, she was promoted to assistant buyer.

Now the writer's ideas are clear. The run-on in the first example is long, but when editing, you cannot always judge whether a sentence is a run-on or a comma splice by its length. A long sentence may have only one independent clause. On the other hand, a fairly short sentence may be a run-on or a comma splice. Look at the following example:

independent clause      independent clause

*RUN ON:*  My mother married young she was only eighteen.

↑
no separation or connection
between two independent clauses

independent clause      independent clause

*COMMA SPLICE:*  My mother married young, she was only eighteen.

↑
improper use of comma
between two independent clauses

A comma alone is not strong enough punctuation to separate two independent clauses. Instead of a comma, we can use several other methods to fix run-ons and comma splices.

## CORRECTING RUN-ONS AND COMMA SPLICES

### Correcting Run-Ons with a Period

One way to fix run-ons and comma splices is to **separate** the complete ideas from each other by putting each complete idea in its own sentence. Put a **period** at the end of the first complete idea. Start the next sentence with a **capital letter.** Look at the next examples:

*RUN-ON:*  My mother married young she was only eighteen.

*CORRECTED:*  My mother married young. She was only eighteen.

*COMMA SPLICE:*  My mother married young, she was only eighteen.

*CORRECTED:*  My mother married young. She was only eighteen.

The advantage of the separation method is that it takes very little time, so it is a good way to correct run-ons if you are writing under pressure in class or during an exam. If you have time, however, you may want to put two or more ideas in the same sentence. In those cases, you can use one of the following joining methods.

## Correcting Run-Ons with a Coordinating Conjunction

If the two ideas in a run-on are of equal importance, you can use a **coordinating conjunction** to join them. (See Chapter 10.) The coordinating conjunctions are *and, or, but, for, nor, yet, so.* When you join two independent clauses with one of these words, put a comma just before the coordinating conjunction. Look at how the following run-ons have been corrected with coordinating conjunctions:

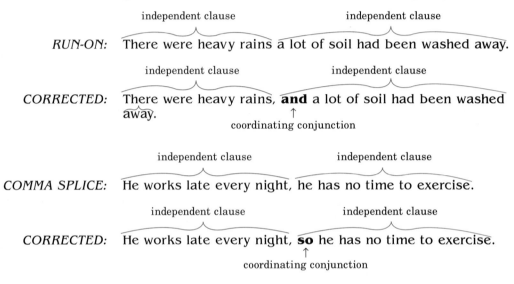

*RUN-ON:*  There were heavy rains a lot of soil had been washed away.

*CORRECTED:*  There were heavy rains, **and** a lot of soil had been washed away.

*COMMA SPLICE:*  He works late every night, he has no time to exercise.

*CORRECTED:*  He works late every night, **so** he has no time to exercise.

## Correcting Run-Ons with a Semicolon

Another way to correct a run-on or a comma splice is to put a **semicolon (;)** between the two complete ideas. Be careful. The semicolon *looks* like a fancy comma, but it functions more as a period does. Look at the following examples:

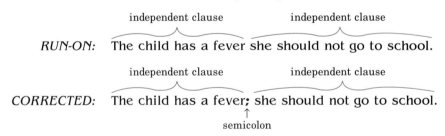

*RUN-ON:*  The child has a fever she should not go to school.

*CORRECTED:*  The child has a fever; she should not go to school.

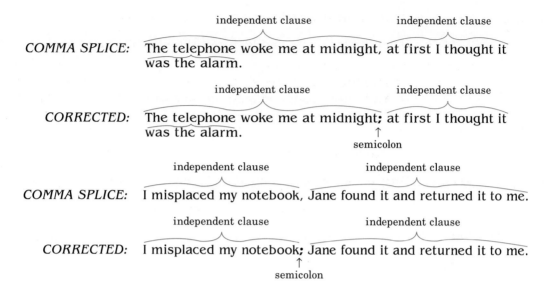

In these examples, the semicolon marks the end of one complete idea and the beginning of another complete idea. When we use a semicolon, the second independent clause starts with a lower-case letter, unless the first word would be capitalized in any position (as in the last example where the name *Jane* is the first word after the semicolon).

Remember that a semicolon is usually placed only where a period might appear. A semicolon is used when the independent clauses are closely related. If they are not related, use a period and a capital to make two complete sentences.

## Correcting Run-Ons with a Subordinating Word

Another way to correct run-ons and comma splices is to join two clauses with a **subordinating conjunction,** such as *because, if, when, since, although,* or with a **subordinating relative pronoun** such as *who, which, that.* (For more complete lists of subordinating words, see Chapter 10.) The new sentence will then have one independent clause and one subordinate clause. In the following examples, notice that the subordinating word is sometimes in the middle of the new sentence and sometimes at the beginning of the new sentence.

*RUN-ON:*    Helen Keller wrote and lectured she was blind and deaf.

*independent clause*        *independent clause*

*CORRECTED:*    Helen Keller wrote and lectured **although** she was blind and deaf.

*independent clause*        *subordinate clause*

↑
*subordinating word*

*COMMA SPLICE:*    High cholesterol is dangerous, many people eat a low-fat diet.

*independent clause*        *independent clause*

*CORRECTED:*    **Because** high cholesterol is dangerous, many people eat a low-fat diet.

*subordinate clause*        *independent clause*

↑
*subordinating word*

*COMMA SLICE:*    Every week I write to my mother, she lives in Mexico City.

*independent clause*        *independent clause*

*CORRECTED:*    Every week I write to my mother, **who** lives in Mexico City.

*independent clause*        *subordinate clause*

↑
*subordinating word*

## WATCH OUT FOR CONNECTING ADVERBS

Sometimes people write run-on and comma-splice sentences because they use connecting adverbs incorrectly. Look at the following examples:

*RUN-ON:*    The train broke down therefore I missed the meeting.

*independent clause*        *independent clause*

*COMMA SPLICE:*    She finished her paper, however, she did not have time to check it.

*independent clause*        *independent clause*

These examples are incorrect because *therefore* and *however* are not true conjunctions. They are **connecting adverbs.** Such words can show relationships between ideas in an essay, but they cannot make grammatical connections between two clauses. Here is a list of the most commonly used connecting adverbs and connecting phrases. A more complete list is on page 86.

| | |
|---|---|
| also | moreover |
| furthermore | nevertheless |
| however | on the other hand |
| in addition | then |
| in fact | therefore |

These are useful signal words. They explain the relationships between various ideas. They help the reader understand the link between one thought and another. But be careful. Connecting adverbs can cause run-ons and comma splices if they are mistaken for true conjunctions.

## How to Use Connecting Adverbs

If you use a connecting adverb to introduce a new clause, you have two choices: (1) start a new sentence with the connecting adverb; or (2) place a semicolon before the connecting adverb to start a new complete thought in the same sentence. Look at the following examples:

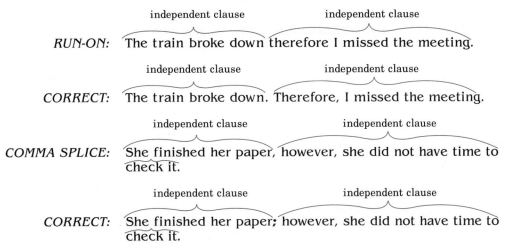

Sometimes when people mistakenly join clauses with words like *therefore,* they are confusing these words with the coordinating conjunctions: *and, but, for, nor, or, yet, so.* Coordinating conjunctions are **true** joining words. You can use them with a comma between two independent clauses. Look at the following examples:

*COMMA SPLICE:*

independent clause        independent clause

I missed the bus, therefore I was late to class.

comma    connecting adverb

*CORRECT:*

independent clause        independent clause

I missed the bus, so I was late to class.

comma    coordinating conjunction

There are two easy ways to know the difference between connecting adverbs and true conjunctions. One way is to memorize the seven coordinating conjunctions. A second way is to ask yourself if the connecting word could be moved around in the sentence. True coordinating conjunctions, which really link clauses grammatically, must be placed *between* the two clauses that they link. Connecting adverbs do not have one fixed location; they can be moved to different places in the clause. Look at the following examples:

*CORRECT:*    The bell rang, **but** there was no one at the door.

comma    coordinating conjunction

*CORRECT:*    The bell rang; **however,** there was no one at the door.

semicolon  connecting adverb

*CORRECT:*    The bell rang; there was, **however,** no one at the door.

semicolon        connecting adverb

*CORRECT:*    The bell rang; there was no one at the door, **however.**

semicolon                connecting adverb

The position of the word *but* is fixed. On the other hand, the connecting adverb *however* can be moved within its clause. It is important to understand the difference between true conjunctions and connecting adverbs in order to avoid run-ons and comma splices.

## SUMMARY: FOUR WAYS TO CORRECT RUN-ON SENTENCES AND COMMA SPLICES

Let's see how many different ways we can correct the following run-on and comma splice.

*RUN ON:*   The library was closed I could not return the books.

*COMMA SPLICE:*   The library was closed, I could not return the books.

1. We can create two separate sentences by placing a period after the word *closed*.

> The library was closed**.** I could not return the books.
>
> Since the period ends the first sentence and the word *I* starts a new sentence, we now have two sentences.

2. Another way to correct a run-on or a comma splice is to join the ideas (clauses) together properly. We can use a coordinating conjunction.

> The library was closed**, so** I could not return the books.
>
> Now we have one correct sentence.

3. We can use the semicolon to separate the two independent clauses.

> The library was closed**;** I could not return the books.
>
> Now the semicolon properly separates the two independent clauses, but it does not make them into separate sentences.

4. We can also join the clauses with a subordinating conjunction.

> **Because** the library was closed, I could not return the books.
>
> Again the two clauses have been joined into one correct sentence.

**EXERCISE
12a**

*Identify each example as a run-on, a comma splice, or a correct sentence.*

EXAMPLES    *run-on*    **a.** We should hurry the bus leaves in five minutes.

*correct*    **b.** It is sunny, but the temperature is very low.

*comma splice*   **c.** I can't find my textbook, it may be in my locker.

_____C_____ **1.** It is a national holiday, so all the banks are closed.

_____RO____ **2.** We forgot to turn off the lights they were on all night.

_____C_____ **3.** Although the crime rate has decreased, many people are afraid to go out at night.

_____CS____ **4.** Jan completed the work, however, she did not have time to check it.

_____CS____ **5.** Jan completed the work, but she did not have time to check it.

_____CS____ **6.** He has the flu, therefore, he has to stay home.

_____C_____ **7.** She had not finished her report, so she stayed late at the office.

_____C_____ **8.** We could not drive into town because twenty inches of snow had fallen.

_____CS____ **9.** It is raining hard, but it will be clear tomorrow.

_____CS____ **10.** The senator is intelligent, furthermore, she has experience.

_____RO____ **11.** Ms. Parker is a biology teacher she is an expert on flatworms.

_____CS____ **12.** He was a good baseball player, and now he is a fine coach.

_____CS____ **13.** The movie was great, I saw it twice.

_____C_____ **14.** I need to speak to Mr. Eng, the guidance counselor, he is very patient and understanding.

_____RO C___ **15.** Ever since Mark was a little boy, he has been interested in dinosaurs.

**EXERCISE 12b**    *Correct the following run-ons and comma splices. Use any method.*

*EXAMPLE*    Some people think novels are a waste of time others find them educational.

*Some people think novels are a waste of time while others find them educational.*

1. She would like to join the Navy, however, she is too young.

   *She would like to join the Navy; however, she is too young.*

2. Many young people would like to be professional athletes very few realize their dreams.

   *Many young people would like to be professional ath*

3. The tenor Placido Domingo is Spanish he lived in Mexico in his youth.

4. Smoking and drinking can harm a fetus, pregnant women should avoid cigarettes and alcohol.

5. Some people are allergic to wool they must check the labels carefully when buying clothing.

6. A tanker spilled oil in the waters near Alaska, cleaning up the oil took months.

   *A tank*

**7.** Rosa puts lavender on the pillows, she says lavender prevents colds.

*Rosa who puts lavender on the pillows says that lavender prevents colds.*

**8.** Dogs are often affectionate and friendly, but cats tend to be more independent.

**9.** Mr. Williams wants to change careers, he is thinking of going to law school.  ; however,

**10.** A little anxiety before an exam is normal, although too much anxiety can prevent a student from doing well.

**EXERCISE 12c**  *Some of the following examples are incorrect. If an example is correct, make no changes. If it is a run-on or a comma splice, correct it with any method.*

*EXAMPLE*  There were long lines at the checkout counter one of the cash registers was broken.

*There were long lines at the checkout counter because one of the cash registers was broken.*

**1.** Satellite dishes allow television viewers to watch programs in many languages they may see shows in English, Spanish, Italian, Portuguese, and Russian.

**2.** Movie stars are often recognized in public; they have very little privacy.

**3.** I like the new neighbors, they are friendly and considerate.

_____

_____

**4.** Children seem to outgrow their clothing quickly, they need new clothes every few months.

_____

_____

**5.** The word "bow" is pronounced two different ways, one way rhymes with "low," the other rhymes with "now."

_____

_____

**6.** Years ago a left-handed child was usually forced to use his or her right hand, but nowadays this practice is rare.

_____

_____

**7.** A house is the biggest investment of most Americans, a car is the next largest investment.

_____

_____

**8.** Solar power is an alternative to oil, windmills can also be used as a source of energy.

_____

_____

**9.** Laura bought cotton sheets they are more comfortable than sheets made of polyester.

_____

_____

**10.** Some children can read fluently in first grade, others acquire good reading skills a year or two later.

_____

_____

**EXERCISE
12d**

*Correct each of the following run-ons and comma splices in at least two ways.*

*EXAMPLE*   That car has a bad safety record Alice won't buy it.

*That car has a bad safety record. Alice won't buy it.*

*That car has a bad safety record, so Alice won't buy it.*

*That car has a bad safety record; therefore, Alice won't buy it.*

*Because that car has a bad safety record, Alice won't buy it.*

1. December and January are summer months in Australia many people go swimming on New Year's Day.

   _____

   _____

   _____

   _____

2. Ms. Cuevas was a nurse, she served in Vietnam.

   _____

   _____

   _____

   _____

3. There is no school on Thanksgiving it is a national holiday.

   _____

   _____

   _____

   _____

4. Many great books are made into movies, however, seeing a movie is not the same as reading a book.

   _____

   _____

   _____

   _____

**EXERCISE 12e** | *Fix each run-on or comma splice in at least two different ways.*

*EXAMPLES*    **a.**  The experiment has begun, the scientists are working hard.

*The experiment has begun, and the scientists are working hard.*

*The experiment has begun; the scientists are working hard.*

**b.**  It had been an interesting evening we were sorry when it ended.

*It had been an interesting evening, so we were sorry when it ended.*

*Because it had been an interesting evening, we were sorry when it ended.*

**1.**  There was a drought, the crops suffered.

_____

_____

_____

_____

**2.**  Aesop's fables are entertaining stories, they teach moral lessons.

_____

_____

_____

_____

**3.**  Professional ice skaters make skating look effortless and easy it is actually very difficult.

_____

_____

_____

_____

**4.** The baby was born a few weeks prematurely he is normal and healthy.

_____

_____

_____

_____

*Edit the following paragraphs to correct the run-ons and comma splices. Write your revised paragraphs on separate paper.*

*EXAMPLE*    My next door neighbor, Ms. Goines, is a writer, she has written a novel and two volumes of poetry. Her novel, which was published two years ago, is about three generations of one big family. It was a long book I enjoyed reading it very much.

*My next door neighbor, Mrs. Goines, is a writer who has written a novel and two volumes of poetry. Her novel, which was published two years ago, is about three generations of a big family. Although it was a long book, I enjoyed reading it very much.*

**1.**    Aleksandr Pushkin was born in 1799 and died in 1837, he wrote both poetry and prose. He came from an old and aristocratic family his maternal greatgrandfather was Abram Hannibal, the black general of Tsar Peter the Great. Pushkin died after a duel with a French nobleman.

**2.**    Grafting is a process by which parts of two plants are put together to grow as one usually only two plants that are closely related can be successfully grafted. It has been done for centuries, as far back as ancient Roman times. Grafting is done for many reasons, one is to add more buds to a fruit tree to increase its productivity.

**3.**    Linen is a fabric made from the flax plant, linen has been used by people for thousands of years. It is stronger than cotton, however, cotton is easier to use in commercial power looms. Today, Ireland is the largest producer of linen.

**4.**    Latin was the language of ancient Rome. In the third century B.C., two different forms of the language began to emerge. One form was classical Latin, which was used for literature, the other was Vulgar Latin, from which the various Romance languages are descended.

**5.**    There are cities named Worcester in England, South Africa, and the United States. The American Worcester is in central Massachusetts, it was first settled in 1673. Several notable events in American history happened in Worcester, one example is Shay's Rebellion (1786).

CHAPTER

# 13

# Sentence Style: Clarity, Coherence, and Grace

In order to communicate clearly to a reader, your sentences should flow smoothly and gracefully. Sentences are clear and pleasing to read when their parts create a pattern that the reader can follow. We can say that such sentences have **coherence,** or a clear and logical order.

Sometimes your ear can be your guide to developing a clear and graceful style. For example, in the following section on parallel structure, you will learn that you probably have a natural sense of this important sentence pattern.

## PARALLEL STRUCTURE

Look at the following pair of sentences. Which sentence do you like better?

**1.** During my vacation, I went bowling, skating, and hiked a lot.

**2.** During my vacation, I went bowling, skating, and hiking.

Most people choose sentence 2 because it sounds smoother. The first sentence goes off the track. Where does this happen? If you say "at the word *hiked*," you are right.

What is wrong with the word *hiked* in sentence 1? It does not match the other words, *bowling* and *skating*. *Hiked* breaks the pattern. In sentence 2 the words *bowling, skating,* and *hiking* match. This matched pattern is called **parallel structure.** In sentence 1 a pattern is started, but then it is broken. This breaking of the pattern is called **faulty parallelism.**

Here are some parallel patterns:

| *Infinitives* | *"ing" Words* | *Nouns* |
|---|---|---|
| to dance | dancing | dancer |
| to sing | singing | singer |
| to write | writing | writer |

| *Present Tense* | *Past Tense* |
|---|---|
| dances | danced |
| sings | sang |
| writes | wrote |

Let's see how we can use them:

*CORRECT:* My cousin likes to dance, to sing, and to write.

My cousin likes dancing, singing, and writing.

My cousin is a dancer, a singer, and a writer.

What is wrong with the following sentences? Can you correct them?

*INCORRECT:* My cousin likes to dance, to sing, and writing.

My cousin dances, sings, and wrote.

There are other patterns. Look at these examples:

CORRECT:    Myra has grace, intelligence, and strength. (series of nouns)

Myra is graceful, intelligent, and strong. (series of adjectives)

**EXERCISE 13a**

*Circle the item in each group that is not parallel to the others. Then rewrite it so that it is parallel. Then write a sentence using the three parallel phrases.*

EXAMPLE    mowing the lawn        *pruning the bushes*

(to prune the bushes)

raking the leaves

*On a lovely October day, Mr. Jones was busy mowing the lawn, raking the leaves, and pruning the bushes.*

1. to listen carefully
   paying attention
   to take accurate notes

   _____

2. answered the mail
   wrote a memo
   makes a telephone call

   _____

3. cleaning the oven
   vacuuming the rugs
   to dust the furniture

   _____

4. to change beds
   feeding patients
   taking blood pressure

   _____

**5.** persistence    _____
intelligence
ambitious

_____

_____

**6.** a fine manager    _____
does volunteer work willingly
a loving parent

_____

_____

**EXERCISE 13b**    *Rewrite the sentences so they have parallel structure.*

*EXAMPLE*    She enjoys sewing and knitting, but not to mend rips.

*She enjoys sewing and knitting, but not mending rips.*

**1.** He enjoys teaching small children because they are imaginative, creative, and intelligence.

_____

_____

**2.** At age two, many children are contradictory, rebellious, and stubbornness.

_____

_____

**3.** She will have happiness, security, and satisfied.

_____

_____

**4.** The course will include how to use your textbooks, how to increase your vocabulary, and writing a term paper.

_____

_____

**5.** Tennis players must have speed, mobility, and be strong.

_____

_____

6. School should help children develop mentally, physical, and socially.

_____

_____

7. Parents' responsibilities include providing their children with food and clothing, caring for their health, and to give them a good education.

_____

_____

8. He was promoted for three reasons—for always being prompt, for showing good judgment, and he took good care of the equipment.

_____

_____

9. The old man taught his sons the value of hard work and how to be responsible.

_____

_____

10. In his lifetime Mr. Wright overcame poverty, ignorance, and being discriminated against on the basis of race.

_____

_____

11. The requirements for the job are good word-processing skills and you must be able to communicate well.

_____

_____

12. The character in the novel had to choose between living a comfortable but controlled life or to live in poverty as a free man.

_____

_____

## SENTENCE COHERENCE: AVOID CONFUSING SHIFTS OF VIEWPOINT

To maintain sentence coherence, always keep to a particular point of view within each sentence. For example, if you are writing from the third-person (*he, she, it,* or *they*) viewpoint, avoid a sudden switch to *"you."* This shift might confuse your reader. Consider the following sentences:

*CONFUSING:*    If students want to improve their vocabulary, you should read a great deal.

*CLEAR:*    If students want to improve their vocabulary, they should read a great deal.

*CLEAR:*    Students who want to improve their vocabulary should read a great deal.

*CLEAR:*    If you want to improve your vocabulary, you should read a great deal.

A sentence that starts out with one point of focus and then switches to another is **awkward** and confusing. A **graceful** sentence maintains its focus. Consider this example:

*AWKWARD:*    When running for public office, the voters have a right to know everything about a person's past.

*MORE GRACEFUL:*    The voters have the right to know everything about the past of a person running for public office.

The awkward sentence above misleads the reader. The first words of the sentence seem to refer to a person seeking office, but then the sentence shifts its focus to the voters. In the more graceful sentence, the focus begins with the voters and does not shift away from them.

Let's look at another example and see how it can be revised:

*AWKWARD:*    If you want to get your car fixed, a garage can be found on the next block.

*MORE GRACEFUL:*    If you want to get your car fixed, you can find a garage on the next block.

The awkward sentence above shifts its focus from the subject "you" to "a garage."

**EXERCISE**
**13c**

*Rewrite the following sentences to make them clearer and more graceful.*

1. A person can make a small business grow if you work hard.

_____

_____

2. If you see any errors, a student should correct them before the paper is handed in.

_____

_____

3. While batting in the third inning, the ball hit the player.

_____

_____

4. Polite people always wait until everyone else is served before you begin to eat.

_____

_____

5. If a student is not sure about how to do an assignment, you ought to ask the instructor to explain it.

_____

_____

6. When one reads the works of Martin Luther King, Jr., he is an inspiring writer.

_____

_____

7. If you need a doctor in a certain medical field, specialists can be found in the guide supplied by your insurance company.

_____

_____

8. Many people have discovered that happiness is often right before your eyes.

_____

_____

## SENTENCE COHERENCE: MAINTAIN SENTENCE SENSE AND LOGIC

**Coherence** means *a clear and logical order.* This idea comes from the root or basic meaning of "coherence," which is "sticking together." When elements *cohere,* they fit together nicely, and their parts are clearly related to each other. Coherent sentences are graceful and easy to read. Above all, coherent sentences make sense.

If a sentence lacks coherence, it may have parts that do not match other parts of the sentence. It may misdirect a reader and cause confusion. Consider the following example:

*INCOHERENT:*    By working hard in this society can help you succeed.

The problem with the sentence above is that its construction changes in the middle. It starts going in one direction, but then it veers off in another so that the reader has trouble following the thought. It can be corrected by being rewritten in several ways.

*IMPROVED:*    By working hard in this society, you can succeed.

*IMPROVED:*    By working hard you can help yourself to succeed in this society.

*IMPROVED:*    Working hard in this society can help you succeed.

Sometimes a sentence sounds illogical because important words have been omitted or misplaced. Consider the following:

*INCOHERENT:*    Thoreau was a great man who had the courage to stand up and protest against injustice and what he believed in.

This sentence starts out fine, but when it gets to the phrase "what he believed in," there is a problem because it seems to relate to the verb "protest against." Obviously, Thoreau did not want to protest against something he believed in. Here is a revision:

*COHERENT:*    Thoreau was a great man who had the courage to protest against injustice and stand up for what he believed in.

When you edit your essays, always ask yourself if every sentence sounds smooth and logical. Reading aloud may help because it is easier to notice if a sentence has a problem when you hear it. Reading aloud to a friend or to an editing partner in class can also be very useful. If your instructor permits it, read your compositions to your friends and ask them to tell you if something sounds awkward or unclear.

**EXERCISE
13d**  | *The following sentences are unclear because they lack coherence.
Rewrite them for clarity.*

1. By writing compositions every day improved Kenny's skill.

   _____

   _____

2. Jennifer recognized the importance of telling the truth and to
   always stick to it.

   _____

   _____

3. The topic for today's essay is: Should all schools, both public and
   private, be required to wear uniforms?

   _____

   _____

4. Though she was poor, Mrs. Smith was an excellent mother; even
   though her children's clothes were old, they all received good
   grades in school.

   _____

   _____

5. By pleading guilty, he will serve 99 years in prison instead of
   the electric chair.

   _____

   _____

6. Gandhi was a great man who had the courage to take a stand
   against injustice and what he believed in.

   _____

   _____

7. This report on AIDS is something I have really put a lot of time
   and effort into this concept of AIDS.

   _____

   _____

**8.** If we had more police to protect our city streets, many crimes might be prevented and made safe for our children.

---

## AVOID AWKWARD REPETITION AND REDUNDANCY

Some repetition can be graceful and helpful. For example, consider Abraham Lincoln's famous phrase "government of the people, by the people, and for the people." This sentence contains the word "people" three times, but no one would object to this type of repetition for emphasis. On the other hand, repetition is sometimes jarring to a reader, as in this example: "In our nation, the people must follow the laws, which are made by the people for all the people to follow." When you reread your paper to edit it, if you notice that there is awkward repetition, try to rephrase your sentence to avoid it. You may choose another word that means something similar to one you have overused. You may also cut unnecessary words from your sentence. Study the following examples:

*AWKWARD:*   In our apartment building nearly every tenant in the apartment building participates in the tenants' association.

*BETTER:*   Nearly every resident in our apartment building participates in the tenants' association.

*AWKWARD:*   Matthew has been a volunteer in the Big Brothers Club for five years, and for the last five years he has been very active in the Big Brothers Club.

*BETTER:*   For the last five years Matthew has been a very active volunteer in the Big Brothers Club.

## Redundancy

Like repetition, redundancy means saying the same thing more than once. When a sentence is redundant, however, it employs different words to say the same thing over again.

Like repetition, redundancy may confuse the reader and make the writing awkward. Consider the following redundant sentence:

REDUNDANT:    Mary did all she could to help her team that she was on win the game.

This sentence is redundant because the phrase "that she was on" means the same as "her." *Her* team is the team *that she was on.* Here is a revised version of the sentence:

IMPROVED:    Mary did all she could to help her team win the game.

**EXERCISE 13e** | *The following sentences contain awkward repetition or redundancy. Rewrite them.*

1. A careful driver always drives carefully and courteously, watching the road carefully, especially at intersections where extra care is needed.

   _____

   _____

2. Michael was extremely proud of his new hat that he had just bought.

   _____

   _____

3. The students were instructed by their instructor to follow all of the instructions.

   _____

   _____

4. Responsible executives must try to attempt to establish a foundation that is based upon trust among the employees who work in their departments that they lead.

   _____

   _____

5. Another week will be sufficient and enough time to allow me to finish the completion of the project.

   _____

   _____

**6.** The results of the project will result in a new way of utilizing and using magnetized metal magnets.

_____

_____

**7.** Some people take drugs or drink alcohol whenever they don't want to deal with something they don't understand or don't want to deal with.

_____

_____

**8.** In January 1776, John the minuteman incurred a fatal injury, which led to his death.

_____

_____

**9.** Conditions are so bad now that they can only get better through improvement.

_____

_____

**10.** In the world of tomorrow's future, scientists will make many new discoveries of things that are as yet undiscovered.

_____

_____

CHAPTER

# 14

# Subject-Verb Agreement

## WHAT IS SUBJECT-VERB AGREEMENT?

Remember that every sentence must have a subject and a verb. (See Chapter 10.) Subject-verb agreement means matching the right verb form with each subject. **Singular subjects take singular verb forms; plural subjects take plural verb forms.**

How do you know which verb forms are singular and which verb forms are plural? In the present tense, most English verbs follow these rules:

1. If the subject is a singular pronoun such as *he, she,* or *it,* or *a singular noun,* then the verb should end in **s** or **es.** (We will call any verb ending in **s** a singular verb.)

2. If the subject is *I, you, we, they,* or *a plural noun,* then the verb should not end in **s.** (Exceptions: verbs ending in double **s** such as boss, confess, and dress.)

Look at the following sets of examples:

| Singular Subjects | Singular Verb Forms (ending in **s**) |
|---|---|
| She | think**s** |
| He | wish**es** (Notice in this case, **es** is added.) |
| It | happen**s** |
| Nobody | know**s** |
| Mr. Franklin | work**s** |
| The college | offer**s** |

| Plural Subjects | Plural Verbs (not ending in **s**) |
|---|---|
| We | expect |
| They | study |
| He and she | talk |
| Some students | worry |
| Mistakes | happen |

**Note:  In verbs the letter *s* is a sign of the singular; in nouns the letter *s* is a sign of plural. Compare:**

**One student write_s_.**

**Two student_s_ write.**

The pronoun "I" always refers to one person, and the pronoun "you" can refer to one person or more. To keep your subjects and verbs in agreement, remember that with *I* and *you* present-tense verbs do not add the **s.**

There is another way to know which verb forms end in **s** and which do not. You can refer to a conjugation chart, a chart that gives all forms of the verb in one tense (time).

Conjugation Chart of the Verb "To Work" (present tense)

| | Singular | Plural |
|---|---|---|
| first person | I work | we work |
| second person | you work | you work |
| third person | he | they work |
| | she } **works** | |
| | it | |

Notice this **s** ending.

The present tense describes action in the present time. It may refer to something that always happens or that usually happens. Most subject-verb agreement problems occur with present-tense verbs because in the present tense the third-person singular verb is different from the other verb forms. *In the third-person singular, the verb has the s ending.* Therefore, in most of this chapter, we are going to concentrate on the present tense.

### Conjugation Chart of the Verb "To Explain" (present tense)

|               | Singular    | Plural       |
|---------------|-------------|--------------|
| first person  | I explain   | we explain   |
| second person | you explain | you explain  |
| third person  | he          | they explain |
|               | she   **explains** |  |
|               | it          |              |

Notice this **s** ending.

**Note:** <u>To explain</u> is the *infinitive* form of the verb. <u>To</u> plus a basic verb is an infinitive. It is called an infinitive because it is not *limited* to a particular person or tense.

### Conjugation of the Verb "To Say" (present tense)

|               | Singular | Plural   |
|---------------|----------|----------|
| first person  | I say    | we say   |
| second person | you say  | you say  |
| third person  | he       | they say |
|               | she   **says** |  |
|               | it       |          |

Notice this **s** ending.

**BRIEF PRACTICE 14.1** *Fill in the blanks to complete the conjugation chart for the verb "to help" (present tense):*

|  | Singular | Plural |
|---|---|---|
| first person | I ___*help*___ | we _____ |
| second person | you _____ | you _____ |
| third person | he _____ | they _____ |
|  | she _____ |  |
|  | it _____ |  |

In the next set of examples, notice the pattern of agreement between each subject and verb.

**1.** Every *child* **needs** love and attention.

    ↑       ↑

  singular subject  singular verb (ending in s)

**2.** In the autumn the *leaves* **turn** red, yellow, and orange.

       ↑     ↑

    plural subject    plural verb (no s)

**3.** *Mr. Jackson* **works** in Omaha.

  ↑       ↑

  singular subject    singular verb (ending in s)

**4.** Several *customers* **want** their money back.

   ↑     ↑

  plural subject   plural verb (no s)

The subject and the verb must agree even when they are separated by a word.

*EXAMPLE:* He always works in the lab.

**EXERCISE 14a**

*Choose the correct verb form for each sentence.*

EXAMPLES   **a.** (works, work)     He _*works*_ at the post office.

              **b.** (talks, talk)      They _*talk*_ very fast.

              **c.** (enjoys, enjoy)   I _*enjoy*_ roller skating.

1. (knows, know)  Most people _____ how to swim.

2. (keeps, keep)  He always _____ his money under the mattress.

3. (organizes, organize)  They _____ their work efficiently.

4. (expects, expect)  Ms. Jackson _____ us to arrive promptly.

5. (hopes, hope)  I _____ that it does not rain today.

6. (wants, want)  These customers _____ to talk to the manager.

7. (chooses, choose)  All second-year students _____ a major.

8. (prefers, prefer)  She usually _____ to study in the library.

9. (arrives, arrive)  You _____ early almost every day.

10. (explains, explain)  This article _____ how to choose a good doctor.

11. (supervises, supervise)  Mr. Rios _____ the personnel department.

12. (understands, understand)  We _____ German but don't speak it.

13. (rains, rain)  Some people feel blue whenever it

_____ .

14. (blooms, bloom)  I like this plant because it

_____ in winter.

15. (irritates, irritate)  Loud noises often _____ me.

16. (says, say)  Mr. Gray _____ that the stock market will rise.

**EXERCISE 14b** | *On separate paper, write a sentence using each suggested subject and verb.*

*EXAMPLE*   he looks

*He looks very happy whenever he is playing baseball with his friends.*

1. I know
2. you understand
3. Ms. Benson believes
4. we hope
5. they accept
6. the professor wants
7. it happens
8. she says
9. small children behave
10. he works

## IMPORTANT VERBS: *TO HAVE, TO DO,* AND *TO BE*

*To have, to do,* and *to be* are important verbs. These three verbs are often used in writing, both by themselves and as helping verbs. Therefore, it is necessary to know their various forms.

In the following conjugation chart for the present tense of *to have,* notice the **s ending** on the verb with a third-person singular subject.

### To Have (present tense)

|  | Singular | Plural |
|---|---|---|
| first person | I have | we have |
| second person | you have | you have |
| third person | he she it } **has** | they have |

↑
Notice the **s** ending.

In the following conjugation chart for the present tense of the verb *to do,* you see that a third-person singular subject takes a verb with the **s ending.**

### To Do (present tense)

|              | Singular | Plural  |
| ------------ | -------- | ------- |
| first person | I do     | we do   |
| second person | you do  | you do  |
| third person | he       | they do |
|              | she } **does** |   |
|              | it       ↑ |       |

Notice the **es** ending.

The next conjugation chart is for the present tense of the verb *to be.* *To be* is an *irregular verb;* its forms do not look like the word "be" and do not follow a regular pattern.

### To Be (present tense)

|              | Singular | Plural  |
| ------------ | -------- | ------- |
| first person | I am     | we are  |
| second person | you are | you are |
| third person | he       | they are |
|              | she } **is** |     |
|              | it     ↑ |         |

Notice the **s** ending.

The s-ending rule does not apply to verbs in the past tense, with one exception—the past tense of *to be.*

### To Be (past tense)

|              | Singular | Plural  |
| ------------ | -------- | ------- |
| first person | I **was** | we were |
| second person | you were | you were |
| third person | he       | they were |
|              | she } **was** |    |
|              | it      ↑ |        |

Notice the **s** ending.

**BRIEF PRACTICE 14.2**    *Fill in the conjugation charts with the correct verb forms.*

**1.** To Have (present tense)

I _have_        we _____
you _____      you _____
he _____       they _____
she _____
it _____

**2.** To Do (present tense)

I _____        we _____
you _do_         you _____
he _____       they _____
she _____
it _____

**3.** To Be (present tense)

I _____        we _are_
you _____      you _____
he _____       they _____
she _____
it _____

**4.** To Be (past tense)

I _____        we _____
you _____      you _____
he _____       they _were_
she _____
it _____

**BRIEF PRACTICE 14.3**    *Fill in the blank with* was *or* were. *The first one is done for you.*

**1.** You _were_ here on time.

**2.** They _____ late.

**3.** We _____ glad that he _____ here.

**4.** You _____ happy when you _____ promoted.

**5.** I _____ born in Seattle, but my sister _____ born in Rome.

**6.** It _____ a pity that you _____ not here last night.

### *To Have, To Do,* and *To Be* as Helping Verbs

The verb forms of *to have, to do,* and *to be* may be used alone in sentences, or they may be used as helping verbs. In every sentence, each verb must agree with its subject. Look at the following examples:

| *To have, to do, to be* used alone | *To have, to do, to be* used as helping verbs |
| --- | --- |
| Ms. Santiago **has** an interesting job at the U.N. | She **has *finished*** her work. |
| All these children **have** their coats and boots on. | They **have *decided*** which movie to see. |
| He **does** his chores very fast. | It **does *rain*** frequently here. |
| My daughters **do** their hair in braids. | The computers **do *break*** down sometimes. |
| Ms. Briggs **is** not here. | It **is *snowing*** now. |
| Several customers **are** in the store. | The Andersons **are *planning*** a vacation in Mexico. |
| It **was** a rainy day. | He **was *laughing*** at my jokes. |
| You **were** very polite to him. | They **were *terrified*** by the violence in that movie. |

When a verb needs an s-ending, put the **s** only on the first word in the verb. Do not put an *s* on any other word in the verb. In the following examples, the verbs (in **boldface**) have two or three words. Notice that the s-ending is found *only on the first word in each verb.*

She **does speak** very slowly.
↑　　　　↑
**s** on first word　　no **s**
of verb

He **has been working** very hard.
↑　　↑　　　↑
**s** on first word　no **s**　　no **s**
of verb

The house **is being painted** green.
↑　　↑　　　↑
**s** on first word　no **s**　　no **s**
of verb

**EXERCISE 14c**   *On separate paper, write a sentence using each suggested verb.*

*EXAMPLE*   are helping

*Some of the neighbors are helping the Jacksons paint their house.*

1. has been canceled
2. have seen
3. do know
4. am calling
5. was required
6. are satisfied
7. were hoping
8. does need
9. is explaining
10. was being honored

## NEGATIVES AND NEGATIVE CONTRACTIONS

To make a verb negative, we use a negative word such as *not*.

He is **not** here.

Notice that the verb has two words, and the negative word is placed in between them:

He does **not** like ham.

Sometimes the negative word *not* is shortened into the contraction *n't,* and this contraction is placed at the end of the first word in the verb:

He does**n't** like ham.

Making a verb negative does not change the subject-verb agreement rule; a singular subject must have a singular verb form, and a plural subject must have a plural verb form. In the following examples, the verbs are in *italics,* and the negative words (or contractions) are in **boldface.** Notice the placement of the negative words and the negative contractions:

The classrooms *do* **not** *have* windows.

The classrooms *don't have* windows.

We *are* **not** absent.

We *aren't* absent.

She *has* **not** *answered* my letter.

She *hasn't answered* my letter.

They *have* **not** *arrived* yet.

They *haven't arrived* yet.

---

**BRIEF PRACTICE 14.4**   *Rewrite each sentence, changing* n't *to not.*

1. High-fat food isn't always nutritious.

   *High-fat food is not always nutritious.*

2. You weren't home when I called you.

   _____

3. I wanted to leave a message, but your answering machine wasn't on.

   _____

4. The work hasn't been completed yet.

   _____

5. I may miss the bus, but it doesn't matter.

   _____

**BRIEF PRACTICE 14.5**   *In each blank, write* doesn't *or* don't. *The first one is done as an example.*

1. If it *doesn't* rain soon, the plants will die.

2. Mr. Manley _____ have time to see us today.

3. I can't call her because I _____ know her number.

4. Ms. Tam _____ leave work until 7 P.M.

5. If you can't pick me up after work, it _____ really matter.

6. Some of these students _____ have their final schedules yet.

7. That old house _____ have air conditioning.

8. These taxis _____ have very comfortable seats.

**EXERCISE 14d**   *Choose the correct verb form for each sentence.*

*EXAMPLES*  a. (has, have)   This classroom *has* twenty desks.

b. (doesn't, don't)   These people *don't* want to leave.

c. (is, are)   One person *is* standing outside in the hall.

d. (was, were)   I thought that you *were* going to be late.

1. (is, are)   Six students _____ waiting to see their adviser.

2. (wasn't, weren't)   I needed to check out some books, but the library _____ open when I got there.

3. (has, have)   Our next-door neighbors _____ planted a large vegetable garden.

4. (does, do)   Those people _____ not work here anymore.

5. (hasn't, haven't)   Mr. Long _____ given us his opinion of this issue.

**6.** (am, is, are)    As soon as possible, I _____ going on vacation.

**7.** (isn't, aren't)   That car model _____ very popular with young people.

**8.** (does, do)    Ms. Mercado says that the bank _____ require two forms of identification to open an account.

**9.** (was, were)    I was worried because I did not know where you _____.

**10.** (doesn't, don't)    Mr. Rios is upset because his computer _____ work.

**11.** (am, is, are)    The children feel hungry, and they _____ getting restless.

**12.** (has, have)    We want to visit Alaska because we _____ never seen a glacier.

**13.** (am, is, are)    I am sure that you _____ going to like your new job.

**14.** (was, were)    The car hit a pothole, and the left front wheel _____ bent.

**15.** (wasn't, weren't)    Ms. Reid was sure she had put her shoes in the closet, but when she looked for them, they _____ there.

## TRICKY *S* VERB FORMS

At the end of some verbs, instead of adding just the **s,** we add **es.** With the verbs *to do* and *to go,* we add **es** to make the third-person singular form: *he does, she does, it does, he goes, she goes, it goes.* Verbs that end in **ch, sh, ss,** or **x** also need to add **es.**

He wash**es** the clothes.

She catch**es** the ball.

His bad behavior tax**es** my patience.

She brush**es** her teeth.

He boss**es** everyone around.

With some verbs that end in y, we form the third-person singular by changing **y** to **i** and then adding **es.** (See Chapter 29 for more about this spelling change.)

He worri**es** too much.

She stud**ies** diligently.

He hurri**es** every morning to catch the bus.

Verbs that end in *st, sk, ct,* or *sp* add only an **s** in the third-person singular form, but they may be difficult to pronounce.

She insist**s** on leaving early.

This exam test**s** our knowledge of biology.

He ask**s** many interesting questions.

She suspect**s** that something is wrong.

He usually grasp**s** what I am saying right away.

**EXERCISE 14e**    *Fill in each blank with the correct verb form.*

*EXAMPLES*    **a.** (watches, watch)    He _watches_ too much television.

**b.** (bosses, boss)    Those two boys _boss_ all the other ones around.

**1.** (insists, insist)    He _____ on having his own way all the time.

**2.** (scratches, scratch)    This wool sweater _____ my skin.

**3.** (copies, copy)    Children _____ the way their parents talk and act.

**4.** (catches, catch)    She _____ an early train every morning.

**5.** (goes, go)    He _____ to school at night.

**6.** (interrupts, interrupt)    He _____ other people all the time.

**7.** (finishes, finish)    My classmates _____ their work before I do.

8. (envies, envy)    Bob _____ his friend Fred because Fred is rich.

9. (asks, ask)    We always help Ana when she _____ for a favor.

10. (consists, consist)    This exam _____ of three parts.

11. (studies, study)    She _____ x-ray technology at the local college.

12. (carries, carry)    He _____ his books in a brown shopping bag.

13. (washes, wash)    They _____ their car every weekend.

14. (suspects, suspect)    She _____ that something is seriously wrong.

15. (matches, match)    This color _____ the rug in the living room.

**EXERCISE 14f** | *On separate paper, write a sentence using each set of subjects and verbs.*

*EXAMPLE*   the counselor suggests

*The counselor suggests taking chemistry next semester, but I am not sure about it.*

1. he catches
2. they study
3. the child bosses
4. she studies
5. she possesses
6. we envy
7. nobody suspects
8. he asks
9. they accept
10. he rejects

## SUBJECTS THAT ARE ALWAYS SINGULAR

### Indefinite Singular Pronouns

The words on the following list are called **indefinite singular pronouns.** They are *indefinite* because they do not refer to any specific person. They are singular because each word designates just one person or thing at a time:

| | | | | |
|---|---|---|---|---|
| everybody | somebody | anybody | nobody | each |
| everyone | someone | anyone | no one | either |
| everything | something | anything | nothing | neither |

To some people, these words *feel* plural, but grammatically each word is singular. Keep in mind that "everybody" means "every single person one at a time." In the following examples, notice that each indefinite singular pronoun is matched with a singular verb ending in **s.**

*Nobody* **was** in the classroom. (Not one person wa**s** in the classroom.)

*Everybody* **has** a favorite food. (Every single person ha**s** a favorite food.)

*Somebody* **is** in the computer lab. (Some person i**s** in the computer lab.)

*Neither* of us **is** ready to go. (Neither one of us i**s** ready to go.)

*Everyone* **likes** to be appreciated. (Every single person like**s** to be appreciated.)

I will check to see if *anyone* **is** in the lobby. (I will check to see if any single person i**s** in the lobby.)

No *one* **knows** what the future will bring. (Not one single person know**s** what the future will bring.)

**BRIEF PRACTICE 14.6**   *Choose the correct verb form for each subject.*

**1.** (expects, expect)   No one _expects_ a snowstorm in July.

**2.** (hopes, hope)   All students _____ to do well on the exam.

**3.** (has, have)   Everyone _____ a secret fear.

**4.** (was, were)   Somebody _____ knocking at the door.

**5.** (am, is, are)   These people _____ not ready to leave.

## Collective Nouns

Words that mean groups of people or things are called **collective nouns.** Each of these nouns is called collective because it names a *collection* of people or things. In American English, a collective noun is usually considered singular because even though there are many members in the group, there is just *one group.* Here are some examples:

| | | | |
|---|---|---|---|
| audience | family | team | class |
| tribe | club | jury | troop |
| committee | pack | group | |

Note that the following group of nouns refers to collections of things, not people. (In some languages, the equivalent words are plural.)

| | | |
|---|---|---|
| furniture | information | luggage |
| homework | jewelry | |

When a collective noun is the subject, it usually takes a singular verb. In the following examples, notice the **s** ending on each verb.

The *committee* **meets** every week.

The *family* **takes** a vacation each year.

This *furniture* **is** new.

That *audience* **was** really enthusiastic.

---

**BRIEF PRACTICE 14.7**   *Choose the correct verb form for each sentence.*

    **1.** (chooses, choose)    A jury *chooses* a foreman.

    **2.** (goes, go)    The girl scout troop _____ on camping trips.

    **3.** (wants, want)    All these people _____ application forms.

    **4.** (discusses, discuss)    Our class _____ short stories and novels.

    **5.** (am, is, are)    This homework _____ difficult but interesting.

---

## Activity Nouns

A verb form that ends in **ing** can be the name of an activity. This type of **ing** word can be a noun. Some examples are:

swimming    running    helping    cooking    studying

Since an activity noun names only *one* activity, it is singular. In each of the following sentences, notice that each activity-noun subject has a singular verb ending in **s.**

    **Swimming is** good exercise.

    **Knitting was** my grandmother's hobby.

    **Exercising helps** us lose weight.

Activity nouns often work with other words. These other words can sometimes make it difficult to know whether we need a singular verb form (with **s**) or a plural verb form (no **s**). A single activity noun is always a singular subject, even if it introduces a phrase containing plural words. Look at the following examples:

**Swimming** *two miles a day* **is** good exercise.

↑                ⌣               ↖
singular subject    not the main subject    singular verb

**Knitting** *socks for her sons* **was** Jan's hobby.

↑                ⌣              ↖
singular subject    not the main subject    singular verb

**Exercising** *three times a week* **helps** us lose weight.

↑                ⌣               ↑
singular subject    not the main subject    singular verb

---

**BRIEF PRACTICE 14.8**    *Choose the correct verb form for each sentence.*

1. (am, is, are)    Smoking *is* not good for athletes or anyone else.

2. (am, is, are)    Smoking cigarettes _____ a very harmful habit.

3. (makes, make)    Roller skating _____ me feel relaxed and free.

4. (was, were)    Cooking nutritious meals _____ important to my mother.

5. (am, is, are)    Studying class notes every night _____ a good way to remember the material.

---

**EXERCISE 14g**    *Fill in each blank with the correct verb.*

EXAMPLES
a. (wants, want)    Nobody *wants* to fail a course.
b. (enjoys, enjoy)    Some people *enjoy* silly jokes.
c. (am, is, are)    Your jewelry *is* beautiful.
d. (was, were)    Moving all those boxes *was* exhausting.

1. (meets, meet)    The committee _____ once a month.
2. (has, have)    Nobody _____ enough money.

**3.** (asks, ask)     Intelligent children _____ a lot of questions.

**4.** (am, is, are)     Accepting defeat _____ never easy.

**5.** (needs, need)     The furniture _____ to be moved before we paint.

**6.** (was, were)     My family _____ planning a picnic.

**7.** (does, do)     Each person _____ what he or she can to help.

**8.** (has, have)     The employees _____ asked for a new contract.

**9.** (am, is, are)     Word processing _____ usually neater than handwriting.

**10.** (am, is, are)     Everyone _____ hoping to have a happy and successful year.


**EXERCISE 14h**     *Fill in each blank with the correct verb.*

*EXAMPLES*     **a.** (treats, treat)     Nobody _treats_ him fairly.

    **b.** (am, is, are)     All the leaves _are_ turning red and orange.

    **c.** (was, were)     The club _was_ meeting in the Student Center.

    **d.** (does, do)     Worrying _does_ not help to improve anything.

**1.** (was, were)     All her jewelry _____ stolen in a burglary.

**2.** (am, is, are)     The homework _____ due next Friday.

**3.** (doesn't, don't)     Lifting weights _____ always strengthen the heart.

**4.** (has, have)     Someone _____ been calling me and then hanging up.

**5.** (volunteers, volunteer)     Many retired people _____ to tutor children.

**6.** (am, is, are)     Telling jokes _____ a way to reduce tension.

**7.** (camps, camp)  The scout troop _____ in the mountains every summer.

**8.** (suggests, suggest)  All my professors _____ that I should study more.

**9.** (knows, know)  Nobody _____ the exact location where Amelia Earhart's plane crashed.

**10.** (am, is, are)  Jogging _____ a sport that almost anybody can do.

**EXERCISE 14i** | *Using each set of suggested words, write a brief paragraph on a separate piece of paper.*

*EXAMPLE*   everybody, studying, students

*Everybody is getting a bit nervous because final exams are getting nearer. Studying for exams takes a lot of time. Students who wait until the last minute to study are really worried. They should be worried! The time to start studying for finals is during the first week of the semester.*

**1.** family, furniture, nobody

**2.** all my friends, working at two jobs, everyone

**3.** money, buying, credit cards

**4.** jewelry, knowledge, choosing

**5.** somebody, knowing the right answer, information

## COMPOUND SUBJECTS

Compound subjects are two subjects joined by *and, or,* or *nor.* When two nouns or two pronouns are joined by the word *and,* they become a plural subject and therefore need a plural verb form.

*SINGULAR:*   Ms. Williams **is** here.

Mr. Reed **is** here.

*PLURAL:*   Ms. Williams and Mr. Reed **are** here.

*SINGULAR:*   Money **does** not guarantee happiness.

Fame **does** not guarantee happiness.

*PLURAL:*   Money and fame **do** not guarantee happiness.

When two parts of a compound subject are joined by *or* or *nor,* the verb must agree with the *closer* of the two subjects.

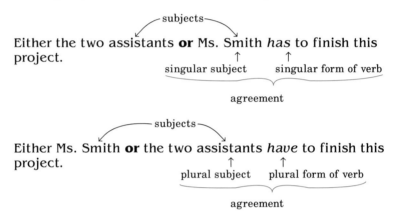

When a compound subject has one singular subject and one plural subject, as in the examples, it usually sounds better to put the plural subject second and therefore to use a plural verb form.

**EXERCISE 14j**

*Fill in the blank with the correct verb.*

*EXAMPLES*   **a.** (wants, want)   Mary and Fred _want_ to move to the country.

**b.** (likes, like)   Neither he nor she _likes_ spinach.

**c.** (am, is, are)   Either Ms. James or Ms. Andes _is_ on duty tonight.

**1.** (has, have)   Both Alex and Ramon _____ the same hobby.

**2.** (attends, attend)   Either the dean or two faculty members _____ the honors ceremony every year.

**3.** (picks, pick)  Either Kim or Jan _____ the children up after school.

**4.** (wants, want)  Neither Tim nor Francis _____ that assignment.

**5.** (was, were)  The office manager and the accountant

_____ having a conference.

**6.** (knows, know)  Neither the passengers nor the conductors

_____ why the train has stopped.

**7.** (has, have)  Both Ms. Tineo and Mr. Kirby _____ degrees in marketing.

**8.** (belongs, belong)  Either these books or those magazines

_____ on the top shelf.

**9.** (am, is, are)  Neither Mr. Rose nor his two assistants

_____ available to speak to you now.

**10.** (was, were)  A small child and a large dog _____ walking along the street.

## SUBJECTS THAT CAN BE SINGULAR OR PLURAL

### Some, Most, All, None

The words *some, most, all,* and *none* can be either singular or plural. The context, the rest of the sentence, is the clue. In the following examples, each verb is underlined.

| Singular | Plural |
| --- | --- |
| Some of the bread <u>is</u> stale. | Some of the rolls <u>are</u> stale. |
| Most of the pie <u>has</u> been eaten. | Most of the cookies <u>have</u> been eaten. |
| All of the wood <u>has</u> been burned. | All of the logs <u>have</u> been burned. |
| None of the fruit <u>is</u> ripe. | None of the bananas <u>are</u> ripe. |

**BRIEF PRACTICE 14.9**　*Write the correct form of the verb in each blank.*

1. All of the crackers _____ cracked.
   is, are

2. Some of the cheese _____ mold on it.
   has, have

3. Most of the bank's employees _____ their banking here.
   does, do

4. Some of the students _____ questions.
   asks, ask

5. All of the books _____ rebinding.
   needs, need

6. Some of the information _____ inaccurate.
   seems, seem

7. Some of those statements _____ false.
   seems, seem

## Who, Which, That

The words *who, which,* and *that* can be either singular or plural. To know if you need a singular or plural verb form, you must look at the whole sentence. If *who, which,* or *that* refers to one person, place, or thing, choose a singular verb form. If one of these words refers to a plural noun, choose a plural verb form.

　　　　singular　　singular verb form
　　　　　↓　　　　　↓
I met a woman **who *works*** in the bank on Main Street.

　　　　plural　　plural verb form
　　　　　↓　　　　↓
I met two women **who *work*** in the bank on Main Street.

　　　　singular　　singular verb form
　　　　　↓　　　　　↓
He sold his motorcycle, **which *was*** always breaking down.

　　　　plural　　　plural verb form
　　　　　↓　　　　　↓
He sold both his motorcycles, **which *were*** always breaking down.

singular       singular verb form<br>↓          ↓

Jean does not buy food **that *is*** high in fat.

plural   plural verb form<br>↓       ↓

Jean does not buy foods **that *are*** high in fat.

**EXERCISE 14k**

*For each sentence, choose the correct verb form.*

*EXAMPLES*

**a.** (am, is, are)       Some of the customers *are* impatient.

**b.** (was, were)       Some of the fruit *was* not washed.

**c.** (has, have)       I like a person who *has* self-confidence.

**d.** (does, do)       I like people who *do* not criticize others.

**1.** (tries, try)       The team needs players who _____ hard.

**2.** (demands, demand)       Tim is the kind of person who _____ attention all the time.

**3.** (am, is, are)       All of the rolls _____ stale.

**4.** (was, were)       Most of their money _____ stolen.

**5.** (blooms, bloom)       I bought a plant that _____ in winter.

**6.** (insists, insist)       Mike is the kind of person who _____ that he is always right.

**7.** (has, have)       None of these students _____ chosen a major yet.

**8.** (needs, need)       The clothes that _____ to be dry cleaned are in the hall closet.

**9.** (am, is, are)       None of this jewelry _____ expensive.

**10.** (wants, want)       Most of the customers _____ their money back.

**11.** (was, were)   These books, which _____
                                published in the late eighteenth century,
                                are very valuable.

**12.** (works, work)   Some of my neighbors _____ at
                                the local hospital.

## WHEN SUBJECTS ARE DIFFICULT TO FIND

When it is difficult to find the subject of a sentence, it is also hard to choose the right verb form. This problem occurs often with the following cases:

- Questions
- Inverted (turned-around) sentences
- Separated subjects and verbs

### Questions

In a question, the verb usually (but not always) has two words, and the subject is placed in between those two words. In the following examples, notice the placement of subjects and verbs in statements and then in questions.

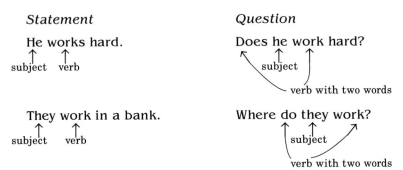

*Statement*                        *Question*

He works hard.                  Does he work hard?

They work in a bank.        Where do they work?

In questions, just as in other sentences, the subject and the verb must agree. When a verb has two words, the *first* word of the verb agrees with the subject. Look at the following examples:

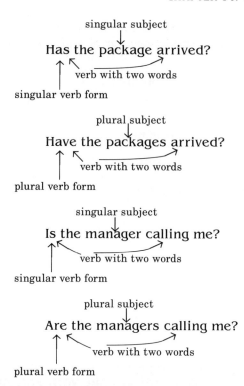

singular subject

Has the package arrived?

verb with two words

singular verb form

plural subject

Have the packages arrived?

verb with two words

plural verb form

singular subject

Is the manager calling me?

verb with two words

singular verb form

plural subject

Are the managers calling me?

verb with two words

plural verb form

---

**BRIEF PRACTICE 14.10**   *Underline the subject once and the verb twice. Write* **sing.** *above the subject if it is singular, and write* **pl.** *above the subject if it is plural. The first one is done as an example.*

*pl.*
1. <u>Are</u> the <u>others</u> <u>waiting</u> for me?

2. Where has he gone?

3. Do these students have their ID photos?

4. Was the movie good?

5. Has anybody seen my umbrella?

---

## Inverted (Turned-Around) Sentences

In an inverted sentence, the normal subject-verb order is turned around. The verb appears first, and the subject comes later. The changed position does not change the verb agreement rule: a singular subject must have a singular verb form, and a plural subject must have a plural verb form.

There is an ambulance outside.
　↑　　　　　　↑
singular verb　　singular subject

There are fifty-two cards here.
　↑　　　　↑
plural verb　plural subject

Under the bed was my watch.
　　　　　　↑　　　　↑
　　　singular verb　singular subject

Under the dresser were a dirty comb and a curler.
　　　　　　　↑　　　　　　↑　　　↑
　　　　plural verb　　　plural subject

Many (not all) inverted sentences begin with the word **there**. The word **there** is never the subject of an inverted sentence; the subject will be found after the verb. Also, remember that the word **there** does *not* contain a hidden verb.

**Note: Some people mistakenly think that the letters *re* at the end of *there* represent the verb *are,* and so they forget the verb. Look at the following examples:**

*INCORRECT:*　　There thirty people in the class.

*CORRECT:*　　There *are* thirty people in the class.

---

**BRIEF PRACTICE 14.11**　*Underline the subject once and the verb twice. If the subject is singular, write "sing." above it. If the subject is plural, write "pl." above it. The first one is done as an example.*

　　　　　　　　　　*pl.*
1. There <u>are</u> my <u>brothers</u>.

2. Under the chair were two cats.

3. Here are your presents.

4. There were three computers in the office.

5. There is only one answer to this problem.

## Separated Subjects and Verbs

Subjects and verbs are not always right next to each other in a sentence. Even when separated by other words, subjects and verbs must agree.

One of my children has a cold.

Who has a cold? Is it all of the children, or just one? Just one! **One** is the subject. Don't let the words between the subject and the verb mislead you.

**One** of my children **has** a cold.
  ↑                        ↑
singular subject      singular verb

In the following examples, the subjects and verbs are separated but still agree.

The **editor,** along with two reporters, **reviews** every story.
       ↑                                         ↑
  singular subject                        singular verb form

The **books** that I gave to Jen **are** by Alice Walker.
         ↑                          ↑
   plural subject            plural verb form

**One** of these police officers **was** attending law school.
  ↑                                  ↑
singular subject              singular verb form

Six **people** at the bus stop **were** sneezing.
         ↑                          ↑
   plural subject            plural verb form

**BRIEF PRACTICE 14.12**  *In each sentence, underline the subject once and the verb twice. Identify each subject and verb as singular or plural. The first one is done as an example.*

  *singular*              *singular*
**1.** One of these children needs some help.

**2.** The main reason for all those accidents was the bad weather.

**3.** The chairs in this room are not very comfortable.

**4.** One of these roads goes to Masonville.

**5.** The joggers in my neighborhood run even in the rain.

Before doing the next exercises, review the material on subject-verb agreement in questions, in inverted sentences, and in sentences in which the subject and verb are separated.

**EXERCISE 141** | *Choose the correct verb for each sentence.*

*EXAMPLES*  **a.** (am, is, are)  One of my daughters *is* a lawyer.

**b.** (Has, Have)  *Have* you seen my chemistry notebook?

**c.** (was, were)  There *were* no people on the street at 2 A.M.

1. (has, have)  One of these trees _____ to be cut down.

2. (does, do)  Where _____ these books and papers belong?

3. (is, are)  I am not sure if there _____ a phone booth at the train station.

4. (has, have)  There _____ been two accidents at the corner this week.

5. (Was, Were)  _____ you waiting here for me very long?

6. (isn't, aren't)  There _____ any reason to worry.

7. (has, have)  Two of the people on the jury _____ become ill.

8. (owns, own)  Several people on my block _____ large dogs.

9. (is, are)  There _____ at least two different ways to solve this math problem.

10. (Has, Have)  _____ the baby had her nap yet?

**EXERCISE 14m** | *Choose the correct verb for each sentence.*

*EXAMPLE*    (is, are)    There _is_ never a parking space when you really need one fast.

**1.** (has, have)    One of these nurses _____ asked for a transfer to another floor in the hospital.

**2.** (is, are)    Two of the twenty-three houses on my block _____ for sale.

**3.** (Doesn't, Don't)    _____ this bus go to Yankee Stadium?

**4.** (wasn't, weren't)    It is overcast now, but when I got up this morning, there _____ a cloud in the sky.

**5.** (Has, Have)    _____ you applied for financial aid for next semester?

**6.** (is, are)    There _____ two baseballs, a small doll, and a crayon under the kitchen table.

**7.** (does, do)    Where _____ your daughter, Laura, go to school?

**8.** (was, were)    A bright green envelope with my name printed in large red letters _____ lying on my desk.

**9.** (is, are)    When _____ the right time to plant string beans?

**10.** (has, have)    How long _____ you been feeling pain in your back?

**EXERCISE 14n** | *Finish each sentence. Use separate paper.*

*EXAMPLE*   One of my classmates *is writing a paper about the poet William Wordsworth.*

1. There wasn't . . .
2. Six people in line at the bus stop . . .
3. Is there a . . .
4. I could see that there were . . .
5. When does . . .
6. How long have . . .
7. One of my notebooks . . .
8. The manager says that there is . . .
9. Two police officers from the local precinct . . .
10. One cause of many traffic accidents . . .

## VERBS THAT NEVER TAKE *S*

Most verbs follow the third-person singular **s** pattern, but there are exceptions. The following verbs do *not* add the **s** endings:

| | |
|---|---|
| can | He *can* drive a car. |
| could | She *could* sing very well. |
| shall | It *shall* not happen again. |
| should | She *should* return the book. |
| will | It *will* be sunny tomorrow. |
| would | He *would* be very angry. |
| may | It *may* snow. |
| might | She *might* get here a little late. |
| must | He *must* answer this letter. |
| ought | He *ought* to know better. |

**EXERCISE 14o**   *On separate paper, write a sentence using each suggested verb.*

*EXAMPLE*   ought to apply

*I think Ms. Mais ought to apply for a college scholarship.*

1. may be promoted
2. can speak
3. ought to call
4. should have finished
5. must hand in

## PROOFREADING STRATEGIES FOR SUBJECT-VERB AGREEMENT

Making subjects and verbs agree is not always easy, especially in difficult cases such as inverted sentences or questions. It would be very hard to memorize a long list of rules for all the situations covered in this chapter. Since the basic problem with verb agreement is deciding when to use **s** and when not to use **s** on verbs, it may be helpful to memorize the following guidelines:

• verb plus **s** = singular verb for *he, she, it*
• verb minus **s** = plural verb for *we, you, they*
• no **s** with *I* except *I was*

You can check your sentences to see if the verbs follow these guidelines using strategies from Chapter 7, "Editing Your Writing." Proofread your paper backwards, one sentence at a time, using two blank index cards to isolate each sentence. These strategies help you focus and concentrate on your grammar. If it is permitted, just before you proofread, you could write down the verb guidelines, from memory, on a piece of scrap paper. Place this scrap paper next to each sentence to see if your verbs follow the correct patterns.

**EXERCISE 14p**  |  *In the following examples, some of the verbs are correct and some are incorrect. Proofread the examples and make corrections.*

*EXAMPLE*   One of my daughters ~~want~~ *wants* to go to medical school. Her grades in high school ~~was~~ *were* really excellent, and her college grades are also high, so her chances of getting into medical school ~~is~~ *are* very good.

1.   I volunteer at a day care center one morning every week. There is five groups of children, who has been assigned to the groups according to their age. I am usually assigned to the group of two-year-olds. Working with two-year-old children are not always easy, but it is certainly challenging.

2.   Is it always wrong to tell a lie? Is telling lies ever acceptable? Answering these questions are very difficult. Justina, who is one of my closest friends, say that everyone must always tell the truth. However, I believe that sometimes there is situations when not telling the whole truth is necessary.

3.   What would you do if you suddenly won a million dollars? On many people's lists of things to buy is fashionable clothes, a fancy car, and an elegant mansion. A mansion cost a lot of money to buy, and a lot more money to take care of. Every year, the owner have to pay for insurance, security, cleaning, and so on. There are also real estate taxes to pay every year. Maybe even a million dollars would not be enough.

## VERBS

### CHAPTER

# 15

# The Past Tense

## THE PAST TENSE OF REGULAR VERBS: THE *ED* Ending

The past tense shows action or state of being that belongs to a time before the present. For example,

Last night at ten o'clock my sister arrived. She seemed tired from her journey.
                                ↑         ↑
                           past action   past state of being

Look at the following examples:

| Past Tense | Present Tense |
| --- | --- |
| Yesterday I help<u>ed</u> at the picnic. | I always help at the picnic. |
| You remember<u>ed</u> my birthday! | You always remember my birthday. |
| They chang<u>ed</u> the rules last month. | They change the rules too often. |
| We notic<u>ed</u> a new car in the lot yesterday. | We often notice new cars in the lot. |

| Past Tense | Present Tense |
|---|---|
| She studi<u>ed</u> every night last week. | She studies every night. |
| The ghost appear<u>ed</u> at midnight. | The ghost appears every night. |
| Maggie seem<u>ed</u> very happy. | Maggie always seems happy. |

**Note:**
- **In most of these examples, the past tense is formed by the addition of the *ed* ending.**
- **If the present-tense verb ends in *e*, only a *d* is added.**
- **Because the basic verb form does not change, we call these verbs *regular*. (But notice that in the verb *studied*, the past tense of *study*, the *y* has changed to *i*. See Chapter 29 for more about this spelling change.)**

**EXERCISE 15a**  |  *Change the present tense verbs to the past tense. The first has been done for you. (If you are not sure of the spelling of the past tense verb, check your dictionary.)*

| *PRESENT* | *PAST* |
|---|---|
| 1. He arrives | He  *arrived* |
| 2. It changes | It _____ |
| 3. They review | They _____ |
| 4. You call | You _____ |
| 5. She hopes | She _____ |
| 6. They cry | They _____ |
| 7. It happens | It _____ |
| 8. They disappear | They _____ |
| 9. He adores | He _____ |
| 10. She rejoices | She _____ |
| 11. They celebrate | They _____ |
| 12. The people applaud | The people _____ |

13. She contemplates          She _____

14. They experiment           They _____

15. They seem                 They _____

16. We regret                 We _____

17. She excuses               She _____

18. They greet                They _____

---

**BRIEF PRACTICE 15.1**    *Change the following sentences from the present tense to the past. One has been done for you.*

1. Present:  We always park our car at the end of the driveway.

   Past:  *We always parked our car at the end of the driveway.*

2. Present:  The President often appears sad.

   Past:  _____

3. Present:  She seems to enjoy writing essays.

   Past:  _____

4. Present:  We always lock the door.

   Past:  _____

5. Present:  Henry adores foreign films.

   Past:  _____

6. Present:  Mr. Frederick receives a package every week.

   Past:  _____

---

**Note: When changing tense, do not change verbs that are in the infinitive form. They do not express the main action or time in a sentence. For example:**

**Carol likes to walk in the park.**
    ↑       ↑
present tense    infinitive

**Carol liked to walk in the park.**
    ↑      ↑
past tense    infinitive

**EXERCISE 15b** | *Change the present tense sentences to the past tense. (If you are not sure of the spelling of the past tense verb, check your dictionary.)*

*EXAMPLE* He wants to be an X-ray technician.

*He wanted to be an X-ray technician.*

**1.** Juana receives high marks in math.

_____

_____

**2.** Spring arrives in the third week of March.

_____

_____

**3.** Some students change their programs in September.

_____

_____

**4.** June greets each guest with a smile.

_____

_____

**5.** Greta insists that she wants to be alone.

_____

_____

**6.** Ralph always remains at attention while the sergeant talks.

_____

_____

**7.** The writer remembers and describes her childhood.

_____

_____

**8.** The curator inspects the museum's exhibits regularly.

_____

_____

**EXERCISE
15c**

*The following examples are written in the present tense. On separate paper, rewrite them changing all the main verbs to the past tense. (If you are not sure of the spelling of the past tense verb, check your dictionary.)*

*EXAMPLE*   Laura studies ballet and attends an advanced ballet class three times a week. Her teacher considers her to be very talented. Laura hopes to be a professional dancer, although she realizes that years of hard work remain ahead of her.

> *Laura studied ballet and attended an advanced ballet class three times a week. Her teacher considered her to be very talented. Laura hoped to be a professional dancer, although she realized that years of hard work remained ahead of her.*

**1.**   Mrs. Pryor works in a dress shop. She helps customers and orders merchandise. She receives a fairly good salary and enjoys the pleasant atmosphere at her workplace.

**2.**   The factory never closes down. It remains open at all times because three shifts use the workplace. When one group of workers finishes a shift, another group arrives to begin the next shift.

**3.**   Professor Jones believes that maintaining her good health depends on regular exercise. Every day she uses the fitness center. Some days she works out with light weights and walks rapidly around the indoor track. Sometimes she plays handball or squash.

**4.**   Many girls and boys join the Young Inventors Club. The club encourages young people to think creatively. Students attend monthly meetings of the club and share their ideas. Every year the club offers a prize to the student who invents the most useful and original item.

## THE PAST TENSE OF IRREGULAR VERBS

Many verbs, including some of the most common ones, do not add an **ed** or a **d** to form the past tense. Instead, these verbs change their basic form. Since these verbs form the past tense in many different ways, they are called *irregular*.

Look at the following examples:

| Past Tense | Present Tense |
| --- | --- |
| Yesterday I <u>wrote</u> an essay. | I write an essay every week. |
| You <u>spoke</u> very well at the meeting. | You always speak well. |
| They <u>broke</u> the rules last month. | They break the rules too often. |
| We <u>saw</u> a new car in the lot yesterday. | We often see new cars in the lot. |
| She <u>thought</u> about her son. | She always thinks about her son. |
| The drama class <u>went</u> to a play. | The drama class often goes to plays. |
| Jan <u>kept</u> her money hidden. | Jan always keeps her money hidden. |
| She <u>taught</u> us all about verbs last year. | She always teaches us about verbs. |

A few irregular verbs look the same in the past and the present. Here are some examples:

| Past Tense | Present Tense |
| --- | --- |
| Yesterday I <u>hurt</u> my knee. | I often hurt my knee when I run. |
| You <u>cut</u> the lawn two days ago. | You often cut the lawn on Friday. |
| Those shoes <u>cost</u> $30 last year. | This year the shoes cost $32. |
| I <u>put</u> my book on the desk. | I always put my book on the desk. |

If you are not sure how to form a verb in the past tense, you can look up the word in a dictionary, which will give you several forms, like this:

go        went        gone        going

The first form is the basic present tense. Put the pronoun **I** in front of it, and you have **I go.** The second form is the past tense form, as in **I went.** The third form is the past participle, which is used for forming other tenses, such as **I have gone** or **I had gone.** (See Chapter 16 for more information.) The last form is the present participle used to form the progressive tenses such as **I am going** and **I was going.** (See Chapter 17.) These forms are called the *principal parts* of verbs.

**Tip:**    **To form the fourth principal part, just add *ing* to the basic verb form. Thus, *think* becomes *thinking.* You must sometimes double a final consonant before adding *ing*, so *bet* becomes *betting.* Usually you must drop silent *e* before *ing*, so *write* becomes *writing.* (See Chapter 29 on these spelling rules.)**

The following list of the first three principal parts of common irregular verbs can serve as a reference chart. Experienced writers are familiar with most of them.

Irregular Verbs

| Present | Past | Past Participle |
| --- | --- | --- |
| am, are, is | was, were | been |
| bear | bore | borne |
| become | became | become |
| begin | began | begun |
| bet | bet | bet |
| bite | bit | bitten |
| blow | blew | blown |
| break | broke | broken |
| bring | brought | brought |
| build | built | built |
| burst | burst | burst |
| buy | bought | bought |
| catch | caught | caught |
| choose | chose | chosen |
| cling | clung | clung |
| come | came | come |
| cost | cost | cost |
| cut | cut | cut |
| deal | dealt | dealt |
| dig | dug | dug |
| do | did | done |
| draw | drew | drawn |
| drink | drank | drunk |
| drive | drove | driven |

*(continued)*

| Present | Past | Past Participle |
|---|---|---|
| eat | ate | eaten |
| fall | fell | fallen |
| feed | fed | fed |
| feel | felt | felt |
| fight | fought | fought |
| find | found | found |
| fling | flung | flung |
| fly | flew | flown |
| forbid | forbade | forbidden |
| forget | forgot | forgotten |
| forgive | forgave | forgiven |
| freeze | froze | frozen |
| get | got | gotten *or* got |
| give | gave | given |
| go | went | gone |
| grow | grew | grown |
| have | had | had |
| hear | heard | heard |
| hide | hid | hidden |
| hit | hit | hit |
| hold | held | held |
| hurt | hurt | hurt |
| keep | kept | kept |
| know | knew | known |
| lay (put down) | laid | laid |
| lead | led | led |
| leave | left | left |
| let | let | let |
| lie (recline) | lay | lain |
| lose | lost | lost |
| make | made | made |
| mean | meant | meant |
| meet | met | met |
| pay | paid | paid |
| put | put | put |
| quit | quit | quit |
| read | read | read |
| ride | rode | ridden |
| ring | rang | rung |
| rise | rose | risen |
| run | ran | run |
| say | said | said |
| see | saw | seen |
| seek | sought | sought |

*(continued)*

| Present | Past | Past Participle |
|---|---|---|
| sell | sold | sold |
| send | sent | sent |
| set | set | set |
| shake | shook | shaken |
| shine | shone *or* shined | shone *or* shined |
| shoot | shot | shot |
| show | showed | shown *or* showed |
| shrink | shrank *or* shrunk | shrunk |
| sing | sang | sung |
| sink | sank | sunk |
| sit | sat | sat |
| sleep | slept | slept |
| slide | slid | slid |
| speak | spoke | spoken |
| spend | spent | spent |
| spring | sprang *or* sprung | sprung |
| stand | stood | stood |
| steal | stole | stolen |
| sting | stung | stung |
| strike | struck | struck |
| swear | swore | sworn |
| sweep | swept | swept |
| swim | swam | swum |
| swing | swung | swung |
| take | took | taken |
| teach | taught | taught |
| tear | tore | torn |
| tell | told | told |
| think | thought | thought |
| throw | threw | thrown |
| understand | understood | understood |
| wake | woke *or* waked | woken *or* waked |
| wear | wore | worn |
| win | won | won |
| wind | wound | wound |
| write | wrote | written |

It may help you to remember these irregular verb forms if you notice that there are certain patterns that some verbs follow, for example:

| | | |
|---|---|---|
| sell | sold | sold |
| tell | told | told |

We also find the following pattern:

| grow  | grew  | grown  |
|-------|-------|--------|
| know  | knew  | known  |
| throw | threw | thrown |

And there is the **i—a—u** pattern:

| begin | began | begun |
|-------|-------|-------|
| ring  | rang  | rung  |
| sing  | sang  | sung  |
| swim  | swam  | swum  |

But be careful not to be misled by patterns. The past tense of **fling** is **flung,** as in the sentence, **The batter <u>flung</u> the bat and had to leave the game.** The word **bring** is also tricky. Although it rhymes with **ring** and **sing,** it does not follow the **i—a—u** pattern. It is part of the following group:

| bring | brought | brought |
|-------|---------|---------|
| buy   | bought  | bought  |
| seek  | sought  | sought  |

Do not get confused by other sound-alikes. For example, **thought,** the past tense of **think,** should not be confused with **taught,** the past tense of **teach.** The best way to get to know these verb forms is to read widely and practice using them in your own writing.

**EXERCISE 15d**

*Fill in the blanks with the past tense verbs.*

|    | *PRESENT* | *PAST* |
|----|-----------|--------|
| **1.** | buy   | _____ |
| **2.** | lead  | _____ |
| **3.** | run   | _____ |
| **4.** | show  | _____ |
| **5.** | cost  | _____ |
| **6.** | begin | _____ |
| **7.** | bring | _____ |

    **8.** hurt            _____

    **9.** keep            _____

   **10.** choose        _____

   **11.** think          _____

   **12.** throw          _____

   **13.** put             _____

   **14.** leave          _____

**EXERCISE 15e**

*Rewrite the following present tense sentences in the past tense. Some of the verbs are regular while others are irregular. Check the verb chart or your dictionary if necessary.*

*EXAMPLE*    When the pitcher throws the ball, the first baseman catches it.

*When the pitcher threw the ball, the first baseman caught it.*

   **1.** Dr. Bronstein teaches biology.

_____

_____

   **2.** When she speaks, everyone listens.

_____

_____

   **3.** Sometimes the wind blows fiercely.

_____

_____

   **4.** Everyone who knows him respects him.

_____

_____

   **5.** The batter becomes angry when he strikes out.

_____

_____

**6.** Karen tells her children stories every night.

_____

_____

**7.** Each spring brings new hope to the people in the valley.

_____

_____

**8.** Every time we meet, I feel happy.

_____

_____

**9.** Michael often receives good advice from his brother, but he seldom follows it.

_____

_____

**10.** Jackie sees her sister often, and the two of them speak on the telephone nearly every day.

_____

_____

**11.** Eva buys most of her clothing at discount shops and takes pride in the bargains she finds.

_____

_____

**12.** Jerry skates well, but he fears trying any difficult moves because he feels foolish whenever he falls down.

_____

_____

**13.** George always hopes for the best but prepares for the worst.

_____

_____

**14.** Tina swims very well; every year she breaks another record and wins another race.

_____

_____

**EXERCISE
15f**

*Insert verbs from the list below in the correct places in the paragraph.
Use every verb, but use each one only once.*

arrested      freed        fought      influenced
joined        led          lived       meant
organized     persuaded    set         suffered
used

Mahandas K. Gandhi, who _____ from 1869 to 1948,

_____ India, his native land, from control by Great Britain.

Gandhi _____ a method he called *satyagraha,* which literally

_____ "firmness in the truth." Using this method, he

_____ for freedom by nonviolent means. For example, he

_____ boycotts against British goods and _____

many mass demonstrations. The British authorities _____

him many times, and Gandhi _____ from deprivation while in

prison. He _____ such a strong example of sacrifice that many

people _____ his movement. Eventually he _____ the

British to grant self-government to the Indian people. Gandhi's ideas

and methods _____ Martin Luther King, Jr., in the United

States.

## CHAPTER

# 16

# The Past Participle: When to Use It and When Not To

## THE PAST PARTICIPLE

The past participle is a verb form with many uses. Even though this verb form is called the *past* participle, it is used in many different tenses, including the present and the future. Here are some examples of past participles:

| Past Participles | Used in Phrases |
| --- | --- |
| known | I have **known** |
| graduated | he has not **graduated** |
| informed | you will be **informed** |
| said | it is **said** |
| seen | she has **seen** |
| married | a **married** man |

You already know the past participles of many verbs. If you do not know a verb's past participle, look it up in your dictionary. For example, if you don't know the past participle of the verb **sing,** look it up in the dictionary. The entry will look like this:

sing            sang            sung            singing

The third form is the **past participle.**
See also the list of irregular verbs in Chapter 15.

## FORMS OF THE PAST PARTICIPLE

Some past participles have *ed* at the end and look exactly like the past tense of their verbs, for example:

walked          discovered
informed        related

Some past participles are spelled quite differently from the basic verb but still look like the past tense, for example:

taught    (past participle of *teach)*

felt      (past participle of *feel*)

Some past participles have their own special form, for example:

been            done            gone

These special forms should *never* be put by themselves as the whole verb:

I ∧ **been** to see my parents. *(have)*

I ∧ **done** the work. *(have)*

Mr. Ames ∧ **gone** for the day. *(is)*

As we have seen in Chapter 15, verbs that add *ed* for the past tense and for the past participle are called *regular verbs*. Verbs that change their spelling for past tense and the past participle are called *irregular verbs*. Some writers have little trouble with irregular verbs, but sometimes they are not familiar with the *ed* ending on regular past participles. Therefore, this chapter concentrates on the participle that needs the *ed* ending.

> **BRIEF PRACTICE 16.1**   *Write the past participle of each of the following verbs. The first is done as an example.*
>
> 1. discover  *discovered*
>
> 2. change _____
>
> 3. expect _____
>
> 4. dress _____
>
> 5. finish _____

## THE PAST PARTICIPLE AFTER FORMS OF *TO HAVE*

Look at the following list of subjects and verbs. All of the examples have subjects, and they all have past participles. What else do they have in common?

I have noticed it.

He has discovered it.

You could have answered.

They had realized the truth.

He has arrived.

I should have insisted.

She has entered the room.

They have returned.

It might have happened.

We had considered leaving.

Before each past participle there is a form of the verb *to have*. Notice that adding the word *not* makes no difference in the verb form. This is also true of other interrupters.

I have received

I have not received

I have often received

I have never received

Use the past participle when the verb contains a form of *to have*. The forms of *to have* are:

has
have
had
having

---

**BRIEF PRACTICE 16.2**  *Underline the form of* have *and the past participle. The first one is done as an example.*

1. She <u>has</u> not <u>filled</u> that prescription.

2. By next year, they will have graduated.

3. I have returned that book.

4. They had purchased a new car.

5. You never could have finished the work in time.

6. Having finished her work, Ms. Smith left the office.

---

**EXERCISE 16a**  *Fill in the blank with the correct verb form. If you find a form of* have, *choose the past participle. If you do not find a form of* have, *choose the basic verb form.*

*EXAMPLES*  **a.** She has __*received*__ my letter.
receive, received

**b.** They did not __*answer*__ their phone.
answer, answered

1. I have never _____ a car before.
purchase, purchased

2. The mechanic has _____ the lawn mower.
repair, repaired

3. He did not _____ the dishwasher properly.
fix, fixed

4. The bus could have _____ the last stop by now.
reach, reached

**5.** Nobody could _____ his address.
    <u>remember, remembered</u>

**6.** The mall had _____ early that day.
    <u>open, opened</u>

**7.** Having _____ the window, she drew the curtains.
    <u>close, closed</u>

**8.** Ms. Fenton has _____ computer programming.
    <u>study, studied</u>

**9.** You should have _____ his invitation.
    <u>accept, accepted</u>

**10.** They might have _____ to Florida.
    <u>move, moved</u>

**11.** You may not _____ a dictionary during the exam.
    <u>use, used</u>

**12.** The student orchestra has _____ at graduation every
    year.    <u>perform, performed</u>

**EXERCISE
16b**

*In the following examples, circle the correct verb form.*

*EXAMPLE*   Mrs. Brown did not (expect, expected) a frost in September. She had
(plan, planned) to continue her garden until Thanksgiving. However,
one morning she found that an early frost had (kill, killed) many of
her plants.

**1.**   Having (finish, finished) my work for the day, I had (decide, decided) that I should (rest, rested). I had just (prepare, prepared) a
snack when suddenly there was a loud crash. The cat had (knock,
knocked) a lamp off the table in the living room.

**2.**   The governor may soon (appoint, appointed) several new state
judges. If he continues in the path he has (follow, followed) before,
the public can (expect, expected) some excellent choices.

**3.**   The Smiths have always (enjoy, enjoyed) hiking. They have
(hike, hiked) in Colorado, Vermont, and Canada. Even their youngest
child can easily (spot, spotted) trail markers.

**4.**    For years, people have (debate, debated) whether violence on television causes real violence. Some researchers have (point, pointed) out that as television violence has (escalate, escalated), so has violence in society. Other people, however, do not (believe, believed) that there is a direct relationship between the two.

## THE PAST PARTICIPLE AFTER FORMS OF *TO BE* AND VERBS OF BEING

The following examples illustrate another pattern of use for the past participle.

| Past Participle after Forms of to Be | Past Participle after Other Verbs of Being |
|---|---|
| They should **be** informed. | She **got** married. |
| The jewel **was** discovered. | I **became** tired. |
| I have not **been** notified. | You **felt** exhausted. |
| She **is** irritated. | He **seems** delighted. |
| They **were** enrolled. | They **look** amazed. |
| It will **be** photographed. | She often **gets** tired. |
| The road **was** paved. | |
| Your hair has to **be** trimmed. | |
| I **am** pleased. | |
| You **are** worried. | |

Before the past participle in each example, there is a form of the verb *to be* or another *verb of being*. Notice that using a negative makes no difference in the verb form.

Oil was discovered there.

Oil was not discovered there.

Use the past participle when the verb contains a form of *to be* or another verb of being.
The forms of the verb *to be* are:

| | | |
|---|---|---|
| am | was | be |
| is | were | being |
| are | | been |

Other verbs of *being* are:

| feel | become | look |
|------|--------|------|
| seem | get | appear |

---

**BRIEF PRACTICE 16.3**   *Underline the form of* to be *or other verb of being and the past participle. The first one has been done for you.*

1. This film has <u>been</u> <u>exposed</u>.

2. The work will be finished soon.

3. He felt pleased after the audition.

4. I am delighted with the new house.

5. They got married last month.

6. They were frightened by that movie.

---

## Passive-Voice Sentences

When the subject is acted upon instead of performing the action, its verb is in the passive voice. The verb in a passive-voice sentence contains a form of *to be* plus the past participle. For example:

She will **be invited.**

They have **been invited.**

You **are invited.**

Changing sentences from the active to the passive voice is a good way to practice using the past participle.

*ACTIVE:*   Volunteers **planted** flowers in the park.

*PASSIVE:*   Flowers **were planted** in the park by volunteers.

*ACTIVE:*   They **close** Loveland Pass each winter.

*PASSIVE:*   Loveland Pass **is closed** each winter.

**Note: The passive voice is preferable if you do not know who performed the action.**

**BRIEF PRACTICE 16.4**    *Change the following sentences to the passive voice.*

1. They resurface the road every two years.
   The road is _____

2. The scout troop will clean the beach tomorrow.
   The beach _____

3. Scientists have not yet discovered a cure for cancer.
   A cure _____

4. You should cover containers placed in the refrigerator.
   Containers _____

5. You should place the forks to the left of each plate.
   The forks _____

**EXERCISE 16c**    *Fill in the blank with the correct verb form. Use the past participle if you find a form of the verb* to be *or another verb of being. Otherwise, choose the basic verb.*

*EXAMPLES*

a. Children are often ___*frightened*___ by violent movies.
   <u>frighten, frightened</u>

b. The service station did not ___*open*___ until nine o'clock.
   <u>open, opened</u>

1. The exam schedule will be _____ tomorrow.
   <u>post, posted</u>

2. Loud noise might _____ a person's hearing.
   <u>damage, damaged</u>

3. The ceremony was _____ by a professional film maker.
   <u>tape, taped</u>

4. The new school building has not been _____ .
   <u>finish, finished</u>

**5.** We must _____ off the old paint before repainting.
<br>scrape, scraped

**6.** The city buses must be _____ often.
<br>inspect, inspected

**7.** Major Jones was _____ to Florida.
<br>transfer, transferred

**8.** They seem _____ of spiders.
<br>terrify, terrified

**9.** You did not _____ your mail yet.
<br>open, opened

**10.** A car was _____ illegally by a fire hydrant.
<br>park, parked

**11.** Your application for a credit card is being _____ now.
<br>process, processed

**12.** I am _____ to meet my cousin for dinner.
<br>suppose, supposed

**EXERCISE 16d**

*In the following examples, circle the correct verb form.*

*EXAMPLE*  A word is (include, (included)) in dictionaries when it is (use, (used)) by many people. "Ain't" is not standard English, yet many dictionaries do ((list,) listed) it.

**1.**  Many diseases cannot be (cure, cured) but they can be (prevent, prevented). With others, like Hansen's disease, the symptoms can be (halt, halted) but not (reverse, reversed).

**2.**  A skill like swimming is (learn, learned) by doing, not by watching. Looking at a good swimmer may (help, helped) a bit, but swimming will be (master, mastered) only by practicing.

**3.**  A poem that is (translate, translated) into another language will not (retain, retained) all of its original meaning. Each language has its own sayings that cannot be (express, expressed) in another language.

**4.**  Any person who works, goes to college, and has a family must be very (organize, organized). A parent who does not (plan, planned) carefully will soon be (overwhelm, overwhelmed). In the Johnson household, two weeks' worth of meals are (cook, cooked) and frozen so that they can be (defrost, defrosted) quickly. Chores are (assign, assigned) to everyone on a rotating basis.

## THE PAST PARTICIPLE AS AN ADJECTIVE

Look at the following sentences. The underlined words are used in a certain way. What is it?

The <u>horrified</u> spectators tried to leave the stadium.

We live in the <u>United</u> States of America.

They enjoy reading *Sports* <u>*Illustrated.*</u>

She seems <u>worried</u>.

The baseball fell right into the glove of a <u>surprised</u> child sitting in the stands.

Two <u>enraged</u> people were screaming at each other.

A customer <u>satisfied</u> with the merchandise will return to the store, but a <u>disappointed</u> customer will not.

The underlined words in these examples are all past participles used as **adjectives** describing nouns or pronouns. In the first example, the word *horrified* is not a verb; the *ed* ending changes the verb *horrify* into an adjective so it can describe "spectator." In the last example, the *ed* ending changes the verb *satisfy* into an adjective so that it can describe "customer."

We can call this use of the past participle a *verb adjective,* a name indicating that the verb has been turned into an adjective. Notice in the previous examples that these verb adjectives may come before *or* after the nouns that they describe.

**Note: Some adjectives are past participles with negative prefixes:**

**<u>unpaid</u> bills**

**<u>unannounced</u> tests**

**<u>dissatisfied</u> people**

**BRIEF PRACTICE 16.5**   *Underline the word that is being used to describe a noun. Circle that noun. The first is done as an example.*

1. Some <u>unopened</u> (letters) were on the desk.

2. She made a design with colored paper.

3. He donated to a home for abandoned dogs.

4. Her boss, irritated by her lateness, fired her.

5. The professor gave an unannounced quiz.

6. His sister, married ten years ago, has two children.

**EXERCISE 16e**   *Fill in the blank with the correct word. Choose the past participle if the word is used as an adjective. Otherwise, choose the basic verb form.*

**EXAMPLES**   **a.** The *delighted* children laughed at the clowns.
delight, delighted

**b.** Fine china will *shatter* if it is dropped.
shatter, shattered

1. Prolonged cloudy weather can _____ people.
depress, depressed

2. I always save my _____ checks.
cancel, canceled

3. This mill, _____ in 1820, is now a museum.
construct, constructed

4. They checked the list of ingredients _____ on the label.
print, printed

5. A _____ or _____ letter looks better
type, typed    word-process, word-processed
than a handwritten one.

6. Tension _____ by stress can be exhausting.
cause, caused

7. Rain will _____ suede clothing.
ruin, ruined

8. He took in an _____ cat.
   abandon, abandoned

9. Some _____ patrons asked to see the manager.
   dissatisfy, dissatisfied

10. Her _____ wrist will be better soon.
    sprain, sprained

11. A pack of _____ dogs wanders in the park.
    abandon, abandoned

12. Reading to your children every day can actually _____ their curiosity and intelligence.
    stimulate, stimulated

## WHEN <u>NOT</u> TO USE THE PAST PARTICIPLE

There are some cases when the past participle is not necessary; instead the ordinary verb is used.

1. Never use the *ed* form directly after the word *to*. The word *to* plus a verb is an infinitive, which does not change.

   I ought **to pay** my rent.

   He was never able **to guess** the answer.

**Note: Watch out for hidden infinitives.**

**Tom helped Jan (to) bake a cake.**

**↑**

**hidden infinitives**

**↓**

**He made me work hard. (Compare: He forced me to work hard.)**

2. When the verb comes after one of the following words, do **not** add *ed*. Use the basic verb form.

| | | |
|---|---|---|
| can | does (does not, doesn't) | shall |
| could | may | should |
| did | might | will |
| do (do not, don't) | must | would |

The doctor did not **answer** his telephone.

We knew we could **finish** the project.

They may **announce** their engagement tomorrow.

Notice, in these examples, that there are **no** forms of *to have* or *to be.* If forms of *to have* or *to be* are used after one of the words above, we use the past participle.

> I should **have** studi**ed.**
>
> I should study.
>
> I will finish the work.
>
> We will **have** finish**ed** the work by Monday.
>
> The work will **be** finish**ed.**

In the following examples, adding an extra word like *never* or *always* makes no difference to this rule. If the verb has a form of *to have* or *to be,* use the past participle; if the verb does not have those forms, do not add the *ed.*

> She will always **receive** company.
>
> You will never **finish** your paper at that rate.

3. Do **not** add *ed* to irregular verbs. Irregular verbs form the past tense and the past participle by making major spelling changes, and therefore they do not need the *ed.*

> I have not **kept** your letters.
>                ↑
>        irregular verb—no *ed*
>
> The lost necklace was not **found.**
>                              ↑
>                      irregular verb—no *ed*

4. Do **not** add *ed* to words that are not verbs; nouns and ordinary adjectives should not end in *ed.*

> His behavior was bizarre, almost **insane.**
>                                     ↑
>                   ordinary adjective, not a verb, no *ed*
>
> She has had a lot of **experience** working with small children.           ↑
>                                  noun, not a verb, no *ed*

(See Chapter 19 for material on the parts of speech, and for hints on using verbs, adjectives, and nouns.)

Before you do the next set of exercises, review all the material in this chapter. Keep in mind the three uses of the past participle, and review the rules for when not to use the past participle.

**EXERCISE 16f**  *Fill in the blank with the correct word.*

*EXAMPLES*  **a.** Nobody can ___*predict*___ the rate of inflation.
predict, predicted

**b.** The security guard has ___*checked*___ those doors.
check, checked

**1.** Computers have _____ the way many jobs are done.
change, changed

**2.** The brakes on his car need to be _____.
repair, repaired

**3.** Nurses have to _____ their patients carefully.
watch, watched

**4.** She has _____ her address book.
misplace, misplaced

**5.** Alicia gets _____ when Alvin tries to
annoy, annoyed
_____ her _____ the checkbook.
help, helped    balance, balanced

**6.** He was _____ by a misleading advertisement.
fool, fooled

**7.** Ballet dancers _____ in Russia have their own style.
train, trained

**8.** Gardeners should not _____ certain plants too often
water, watered
or they will become _____.
waterlog, waterlogged

**9.** Frank has to _____ which college to attend.
decide, decided

**10.** The town should have _____ a street light at that
intersection.   install, installed

**11.** The city will probably _____ that _____
building.   condemn, condemned    ruin, ruined

**12.** _____ by all their children and grandchildren, the
Surround, Surrounded
Del Vecchios celebrated their fiftieth wedding anniversary.

**13.** I didn't _____ this movie; we should have _____
like, liked    rent, rented
the other one.

14. The museum and the performing arts center are _____ in downtown Newark.
<br>locate, located

15. New diseases appear because viruses can _____ into different forms.
<br>mutate, mutated

**EXERCISE 16g**

*Circle the correct word.*

*EXAMPLE*  Both the movie and the television show (call, (called)) *MASH* were (base, (based)) on a book. The author was a doctor who had (serve, (served)) in Korea. The Korean War did not ((last,) lasted) as long as the television show.

1. Many people do not (want, wanted) to have credit cards. They are (worry, worried) that they will be (tempt, tempted) to (waste, wasted) too much money. People must (realize, realized) that credit cards are convenient if they are not (misuse, misused).

2. Because Dolores had (listen, listened) to the weather forecast, which had (predict, predicted) cold weather, she had (dress, dressed) herself in warm clothing. However, the weather had (change, changed) suddenly, and she felt (overdress, overdressed).

3. The energy crisis has (cause, caused) people to look for new kinds of housing that will not (use, used) much oil or electricity. Some have (experiment, experimented) with houses (bury, buried) partly in the earth. Earth does not (change, changed) its temperature much, so an earth-(cover, covered) house is well (insulate, insulated).

4. There are many things that can be done to (increase, increased) gas mileage. Tires should be (fill, filled) to the correct air pressure. Oil must be (check, checked) periodically. A well-(tune, tuned) engine will get better mileage than one not in tune.

**EXERCISE**
**16h**

*On a separate paper, write a short paragraph using each group of suggested phrases.*

*EXAMPLE*   the estimated cost        had to decide
            had received              felt relieved

*When Mrs. Sears had received a letter from the repair shop stating the estimated cost of fixing her sewing machine, she had to decide whether to have the work done. She said yes and felt relieved that it would not cost more.*

1. they have been notified            a complicated problem
                                       did not realize

2. several delighted children         have enjoyed
                                       were entertained

3. felt frightened                    had to stop
   could not continue                 seemed relieved

4. a renovated apartment              newly painted walls
   had rented                         could be purchased

5. a used car                         had decided
   was worried                        could not have afforded

CHAPTER

# 17

# Progressive Tenses: Present and Past

## PRESENT PROGRESSIVE TENSE

There is more than one way to show that action is happening in the present. In Chapter 14 the verb models show the simple present tense. Examples are *I walk, you think, she feels,* and so on. Another way of expressing these actions is to use the ***progressive*** form, for example:

I am walking

you are thinking

she is feeling

The **simple present tense** is commonly used to express action that happens habitually. The **present progressive tense** is used to express action that is happening at the present moment or will happen in the near future.

| Present Tense | Present Progressive |
| --- | --- |
| Mr. Vernon drives to work every day. | Mr. Vernon is driving to work right now. |
| | Mr. Vernon is driving to New York next week. |

Here is a conjugation chart of the present progressive tense:

| | Singular | Plural |
| --- | --- | --- |
| first person | I am driving | we are driving |
| second person | you are driving | you are driving |
| third person | he<br>she } is driving<br>it | they are driving |

The present progressive tense has two parts:
(1) the present tense of *to be* + (2) the present participle of the main verb.

| | |
| --- | --- |
| I am | driving |
| you are | driving |
| she is | driving |

The present participle is easy to form. In most cases, you simply take the verb and add *ing* to it.

| *verb* | + | *ing* | = | *present participle* |
| --- | --- | --- | --- | --- |
| walk | + | ing | = | walking |
| reveal | + | ing | = | revealing |
| think | + | ing | = | thinking |

**SPELLING TIPS**

There are some exceptions that affect the spelling of the present participle.

1. If the verb ends in silent **e,** drop the **e** before adding **ing.**

| *Verb* | *Present Participle* |
|---|---|
| take | taking |
| relate | relating |
| joke | joking |

2. In some cases, the consonant must be doubled before **ing** is added. (See Chapter 29.)

| run | running |
|---|---|
| rob | robbing |

Note: If the verb ends in **y,** keep the **y** when adding **ing.**

| study | studying |
|---|---|
| worry | worrying |

If you are unsure about the spelling of a verb's present participle, use your dictionary.

## Negative Progressive Verbs

If you wish to make your sentence negative, put the negative word between the two parts of the present progressive verb.

I am not going.

You are not trying.

She is not working.

Note:  **The present participle by itself is not a complete verb.**

Mrs. Jones $\overset{\text{is}}{\wedge}$ driving to Austin tomorrow.

We $\overset{\text{are}}{\wedge}$ studying data processing.

**EXERCISE 17a**

*Change the present tense verbs to present progressive.*

*EXAMPLE*   **Present tense:** I have a party for my daughter every year.

**Present progressive:** I *am having* a party for my daughter tomorrow.

1. He works hard on every assignment.

   He _____ very hard on this project.

2. The baby usually sleeps in the early afternoon.

   The baby _____ right now.

3. It often rains in April.

   It _____ this evening.

4. Our microwave oven works well.

   Our oven _____ better now that it has been fixed.

5. He cleans the oven once a week.

   He _____ it right now.

6. They watch every basketball game on television.

   Tonight they _____ the Knicks–Celtics game.

7. The pilot checks her parachute before each flight.

   She _____ the parachute now.

**EXERCISE 17b**

*Answer each question using the present progressive tense.*

*EXAMPLES*   **a.** Where are John and Joe working?

*John and Joe are working at the library.*

**b.** What are you doing?

*I am writing in my journal.*

1. What is she reading?

   _____

**2.** Where are they going?

_____

**3.** What is she watching?

_____

**4.** When is the plane leaving?

_____

**5.** When are you getting married?

_____

**6.** What is he washing?

_____

**7.** Where are the Giants playing tonight?

_____

**8.** Where are they taking the children?

_____

**9.** What is irritating Marge?

_____

**10.** What is he studying?

_____

## PAST PROGRESSIVE TENSE

The **simple past tense** shows action that happened at a particular time in the past. The **past progressive** shows action that continued for a while and is now finished.

| Past Tense | Past Progressive |
| --- | --- |
| I received a letter yesterday. | I was receiving my mail at the post office for several weeks. |
| Jan walked to work yesterday. | When Jan was walking to work yesterday, she met an old friend. |

Here is a model of the past progressive tense:

|  | Singular | Plural |
|---|---|---|
| first person | I was walking | we were walking |
| second person | you were walking | you were walking |
| third person | he<br>she   } was walking<br>it | they were walking |

The past progressive tense has two parts:
(1) the past tense of *to be* + (2) the present participle of the main verb.

I was          walking

you were       walking

she was        walking

**EXERCISE
17c**

*Change the past tense verbs to past progressive.*

*EXAMPLE:*   **Past tense:** We walked to the park last night.

**Past progressive:** While we *were walking*, we saw an accident.

1. He mowed the lawn yesterday.

   He _____ it all morning.

2. Fred played basketball well.

   He _____ for his college team when it won the division title.

3. He practiced the clarinet daily.

   He _____ for the spring concert.

4. I am glad you enjoyed the movie.

   You looked as if you _____ yourself.

**5.** The child cried when she fell down.

She _____ while the nurse was bandaging her knee.

**6.** I am glad that they studied hard for the test.

They _____ when I called last night.

**7.** It snowed a great deal last winter.

It _____ when I came home from work.

**8.** The kittens followed their mother everywhere.

They _____ their mother around the backyard.

**EXERCISE 17d**    *Answer each question using the past progressive tense.*

*EXAMPLES*    **a.** What was she drinking?

_She was drinking milk._

**b.** What were the children playing?

_They were playing tag._

**1.** What were the men arguing about?

_____

**2.** Where were the children skating?

_____

**3.** What was she checking in her car?

_____

**4.** What were the senators discussing?

_____

**5.** What was Flora planting in the garden?

_____

**6.** When was he cutting wood?

_____

**7.** Where was Mrs. MacArthur staying?

_____

**8.** What was Lucy reading?

_____


## THE PRESENT PERFECT PROGRESSIVE TENSE

In addition to the simple present and the simple past, verbs that are progressive may represent the present perfect tense, for example:

present perfect tense:    Sandra has received a good grade
(nonprogressive)      in English.

                         She has worked hard.

present perfect tense:    Sandra has been receiving good
(progressive)         grades in English recently.

                         She has been working hard.

The use of the progressive form of the present perfect extends the action, showing that it has been taking place over a period of time. Notice the way the progressive verb is formed and how it differs from the nonprogressive verb.

Formation of the present perfect tense:

| Nonprogressive | | Progressive | | |
|---|---|---|---|---|
| present tense of "have" + | past participle | present tense of "have" + | past participle of "to be" + | present participle |
| ↓ | ↓ | ↓ | ↓ | ↓ |
| has | received | has | been | receiving |
| has | worked | has | been | working |

**BRIEF PRACTICE 17.1**   *Change the verbs in the following examples from the nonprogressive form of the present perfect tense to the progressive form. The first one is done as an example. Be prepared to explain how the progressive tense changes the meaning.*

1. Carol has done well on her project.

   Carol *has been doing* well on her project.

2. Jorge has helped his father with the gardening.

   Jorge _____ his father with the gardening.

3. My niece has visited me recently.

   My niece _____ me recently.

4. Estella and Louisa have written to their grandmother.

   Estella and Louisa _____ to their grandmother.

## THE PAST PERFECT PROGRESSIVE TENSE

We use the past perfect tense to show action that has been completed earlier than the simple past tense, as in the following example:

Mark <u>told</u> us that the products he <u>had tested</u> <u>were</u> effective.
    ↑                                    ↑           ↑
 past tense                    past perfect tense   past tense

In this sentence, the past perfect tense verb *had tested* indicates that this action took place earlier than the main action of the sentence; thus, Mark had tested the products before he told us about them. See how we can make this verb progressive:

Mark <u>told</u> us that the products he <u>had been testing</u> <u>were</u>
    ↑                                    ↑           ↑
 past tense                    past perfect tense   past tense

effective.

Now compare the use of the two tenses:

past perfect tense:      Mark told us that the products he
(nonprogressive)       **had tested** were effective.

past perfect tense:      Mark told us that the products he
(progressive)         **had been testing** were effective.

The use of the progressive form extends the action. It suggests that the testing took place over a period of time. Notice the way it is formed and how it differs from the nonprogressive verb.
Formation of the past perfect tense:

### nonprogressive

past tense of "have" + past participle
    ↓                   ↓
   had               tested

### progressive

past tense of "have" + past partic. of "to be" + pres. participle
    ↓               ↓                ↓
   had            been         testing

**BRIEF PRACTICE 17.2**    *Change the verbs in the following examples from the nonprogressive form of the past perfect tense to the progressive form. The first one is done as an example. Be prepared to explain how the progressive tense changes the meaning.*

**1.** Carol knew she had done well on her project.

Carol knew that she __*had been doing*__ well on her project.

**2.** Jorge felt tired because he had helped his father with the gardening.

Jorge felt tired because he _____ his father with the gardening.

**3.** The cat had acted strangely before the vet diagnosed the feline flu.

The cat _____ strangely before the vet diagnosed the feline flu.

**4.** Before the plan to move was announced, the president had said that the company might relocate.

Before the plan to move was announced, the president _____ that the company might relocate.

## THE PROGRESSIVE TENSES AND ENGLISH AS A SECOND LANGUAGE (ESL)

Since the use of the progressive tense in English differs from the verb use in other languages, if your first language is not English, you should pay special attention to these verb forms. Remember that progressive verbs, no matter what their tense, show action that occurs over time.

Consider the difference in meaning between the following sentences using different verb forms:

| | |
|---|---|
| present (nonprogressive) | Jan reads a great deal. |
| present progressive | Jan is reading a great deal this summer. |

The first sentence (using the nonprogressive present tense) is making a general statement about something Jan does all the time. The second sentence, which uses the present progressive verb, says that Jan is currently involved in reading (this summer), but it does not say that she always reads. She may or may not read a great deal in general.

| | |
|---|---|
| present perfect (nonprogressive) | Jan has read that book. |
| present perfect (progressive) | Jan has been reading that book. |

The first sentence tells us that Jan has already read a certain book, but she is no longer reading it. In the second sentence, which employs the present perfect progressive, the reading of the book is still in progress.

| | |
|---|---|
| past perfect (nonprogressive) | Jan had studied English before coming to the United States. |
| past perfect progressive | Jan had been studying English before coming to the United States. |

The sentence using the progressive implies that the process of studying English extended for a while and was still in progress when Jan left for the United States. Note that in many sentences, both the regular tense and the progressive form can be correct, but they have slightly different meanings.

**EXERCISE
17e**  | *Change each of the following sentences so that a progressive verb form is used in place of the underlined verb. Be prepared to explain the difference in meaning that the rewritten sentence conveys.*

*EXAMPLES*  **a.** Xavier <u>has written</u> a song.

*Xavier has been writing a song.*

**b.** Betsy <u>had hoped</u> her parents would give her a puppy for her birthday.

*Betsy had been hoping her parents would give her a puppy for her birthday.*

**1.** The new foreman <u>has tried</u> to implement certain changes at the factory.

_____

_____

**2.** I <u>have read</u> *War and Peace* this summer.

_____

_____

**3.** <u>Have</u> you <u>watched</u> the new television sitcom about a space station?

_____

_____

**4.** My cousin Flora <u>has received</u> some wonderful letters from her daughter in Mexico.

_____

_____

**5.** Martin <u>had worried</u> so much about the weather that he did not enjoy the picnic.

_____

_____

**6.** Ethel <u>has studied</u> her driver's manual every night this week, so she <u>feels</u> confident about the driving test.

_____

_____

**7.** That actor <u>has played</u> the lead in *Hamlet* during the summer Shakespeare festival.

_____

_____

**8.** Laura <u>had hoped</u> to receive the good news about the promotion before her anniversary.

_____

_____

**9.** Felix <u>has changed</u> his views on many subjects since he <u>has attended</u> the university.

_____

_____

**10.** Our art class <u>has visited</u> many museums and galleries.

_____

_____

## WHEN TO USE THE PROGRESSIVE FORM OF THE VERB AND WHEN NOT TO

So far we have been examining the different uses of the progressive verb forms, and we have seen many examples in which both the progressive and the nonprogressive verbs would work equally well, although they would mean slightly different things. But there are certain situations that require *only* the progressive and other situations that require only the nonprogressive form of the verb.

**1. In sentences that express general rules or conditions, the nonprogressive form of the verb is necessary.**

*EXAMPLE:*    Many Americans vote only during Presidential elections.
(The progressive verb, "are voting" would not work here because the sentence is making a general statement.)

*EXAMPLE:*     It always rains after you wash your car.

(The progressive verb "is raining" would not work here because the sentence is making a statement that sets up a general rule or condition.)

2.   **In the case of a specific action that extends over time, the progressive form of the verb is needed.** For example, as we saw earlier, in answer to the question "What is he doing?" we must use a progressive verb.

*EXAMPLES:*     Jon is studying to be a doctor.

The students are writing essays now.

3.   **Certain verbs that express a wish or need rarely use the present progressive form.**

*EXAMPLES:*     The cats <u>want</u> me to feed them now.

I <u>want</u> to rest first.

That child <u>needs</u> help at this moment.

You <u>need</u> to help the child now.

The customers <u>desire</u> assistance.

Learning <u>requires</u> dedication.

I <u>require</u> absolute silence when I study.

I <u>require</u> absolute silence when I am studying.

4.   **Some verbs of being rarely use the progressive form.**

*EXAMPLES:*     Cathy <u>seems</u> depressed today.

The children <u>appeared</u> happy.

**Note:  The verb "appear" may be used in the progressive when it is an action verb. For example,**

**The actor is appearing on Broadway now.**

EXERCISE
17f

*Look at the following pairs of sentences and place a "C" next to the one that correctly employs the progressive or nonprogressive form of the verb. Be prepared to explain your choice.*

EXAMPLE _____ Mark studies to be an eye doctor.

_____*C*_____ Mark is studying to be an eye doctor.

_____ 1. Some people are blaming others for their problems.

_____ Some people blame others for their problems.

_____ 2. The cat wants me to feed him now.

_____ The cat is wanting me to feed him now.

_____ 3. The poetry class attracts many students whenever the college offers it.

_____ The poetry class is attracting many students whenever the college is offering it.

_____ 4. The college is offering a special advanced math class this semester.

_____ The college offers a special advanced math class this semester.

_____ 5. The defendant was appearing tense and nervous during the trial.

_____ The defendant appeared tense and nervous during the trial.

_____ 6. Tourists find many interesting bookstores in Copenhagen.

_____ Tourists are finding many interesting bookstores in Copenhagen.

_____ 7. Certain plants, like azaleas, require acid soil.

_____ Certain plants, like azaleas, are requiring acid soil.

_____ 8. Mr. Cornwall gets impatient when students come late to class.

_____ Mr. Cornwall is getting impatient when students are coming late to class.

_____ 9. Vanessa is studying for the bar exam now.

_____ Vanessa studies for the bar exam now.

_____ 10. The bus is fifteen minutes late now, and I am getting impatient.

_____ The bus is fifteen minutes late now, and I get impatient.

CHAPTER

# 18

# Tense Consistency

## AVOIDING NEEDLESS TENSE SHIFTS

**Don't shift tenses needlessly.** If you begin in the present tense, stay with it. Don't shift into the past, unless it is logical to do so.

I **am working** in a grocery store, but I **don't like it.** There **is** too much work to do, and I **have** no time to catch my breath.

The boldface verbs in the paragraph above are all in the present tense.

Similarly, if you begin in the past tense, stay in the past. Don't switch to the present, unless it is logical to do so.

The little boy **looked** out the door and then quietly **stepped** outside. When he **was** a few yards away from the house, he **began** to run. He **called** out, "Here I **come!**"

In this second example, all the actions are over; therefore, it is logical to use the past tense. Notice, however, that verbs in quotation marks do not have to match the rest of the verbs. Words inside quotation marks should be written exactly as the speaker says them.

Sometimes tense shifts are logical and necessary, as in the following example:

*LOGICAL TENSE*
*SHIFTS:*

I **am working** in a grocery store, but I **don't like** it. I
    (present)                                        (present)

**liked** my last job much better. A few months ago, I
(past)

**was working** in a pet shop, but I **lost** that job when the
    (past)                                    (past)

store **went** out of business.
        (past)

In the next example, the writer needlessly switches back and forth between past and present. See how confusing these tense shifts are:

*CONFUSING*
*TENSE SHIFTS:*

Orwell **discovers** that he **did** not **like** being a policeman
        (present)                (past)

in Burma. He **shot** that elephant because the crowd
                (past)

**expects** him to and because he **was** afraid of losing the
(present)                            (past)

respect of the natives. He really **does** not **want** to destroy
                                            (present)

the valuable animal.

The paragraph should be written in the present **or** the past, but not in a mixture. Here it is with the verbs all in the present:

*TENSES*
*CONSISTENT:*

Orwell **discovers** that he **does** not **like** being a policeman in Burma. He **shoots** that elephant because the crowd **expects** him to and because he **is** afraid of losing the respect of the natives. He really **does** not **want** to destroy the valuable animal.

It is permissible to use the present tense even when writing about authors who are dead because their works still exist.

Here is the paragraph with all the verbs in the past tense:

*TENSES*
*CONSISTENT:*

Orwell **discovered** that he **did** not **like** being a policeman in Burma. He **shot** that elephant because the crowd **expected** him to and because he **was** afraid of losing the respect of the natives. He really **did** not **want** to destroy the valuable animal.

**EXERCISE
18a**
*Underline all the verbs in the following sentences. Where neces-
sary, change the verbs to the past or past perfect to make the tenses
consistent.*

*EXAMPLE*    She <u>saw</u> her friend and ~~says~~ *said* "Hello."

1. He was riding down the street when he hit a pothole and falls off his skateboard.

2. The child looked at the chimpanzees, who seem to be looking at him.

3. The rice boils over, so I had to clean the stove top.

4. When he dropped the dish, it breaks, and he realizes that he has been careless.

5. When the baby started to choke, his father slaps him on the back.

6. The quarterback took several steps backward, and then he passes the football.

7. The guard checked all the doors, turned on the alarm system, and patrols the yard.

8. While I was riding the bus to work, I see a minor traffic accident.

9. He kept looking over his shoulder to see if anyone is following him.

10. Mandy does not want to see that movie because she had seen it before.

## TENSE PATTERNS

As we saw earlier, sometimes it is logical to shift tenses because one action happened in the present and one action happened in the past. Sometimes it is necessary to shift tenses because one action happened in the past and another action had already happened before that. Look at these tense patterns:

**1.** He **says** he **has been waiting** here for an hour.
<br>       ↑              ↑
<br>   present      present perfect

He **said** he **had been waiting** here for an hour.
<br>      ↑          ↑
<br>   past      past perfect

**2.** She **thinks** she **has completed** the work.
<br>     ↑          ↑
<br>   present     present perfect

She **thought** she **had completed** the work.
<br>    ↑        ↑
<br>   past     past perfect

Notice the difference between these tenses:

present perfect tense
<br>↓

Carol **has lived** in Chicago for five years. (She is still living in Chicago.)

     past tense
<br>     ↓

Carol **lived** in Chicago for five years. (She is not living in Chicago now.)

    past perfect tense
<br>    ↓

Carol **had lived** in Chicago for five years before she saw Sears Tower.

(She may or may not be living in Chicago now. She moved there five years before seeing Sears Tower.)

**Reminder:** **The present perfect tense is formed with the *present* tense of *to have* as a helping word. The past perfect tense is formed with the *past* tense of *to have* as a helping word.**

**BRIEF PRACTICE 18.1**    *Fill in each blank with the correct verb.*

1. Mrs. Stevens _____ always admired this sweater, so
   <br>has, had
   she is knitting one like it.

2. In 1939 the British were sorry they _____ ignored
   <br>have, had
   Churchill's warnings about the German military buildup.

3. All week Mike _____ had a bad cold, and he plans to
   <br>has, had
   rest this weekend.

4. Before Juan got pneumonia, he _____ had a cold for
   <br>has, had
   two weeks.

5. For years, Gladys _____ wanted to learn German, so
   <br>has, had
   she finally signed up for a course.

**Note: When changing tense, do not change verbs that are in the infinitive form. They do not express the main action or time in a sentence. For example:**

**Mr. Jones wants to *sell* some stock.**
<br>↑            ↑
<br>present tense    infinitive

**Mr. Jones wanted to *sell* some stock.**
<br>↑            ↑
<br>past tense    infinitive

The following pairs of sentences are examples of some tricky tense patterns:

1. He **thinks** he **can** swim.

   He **thought** he **could** swim.

2. She **says** she **will** help.

   She **said** she **would** help.

3. If I **win** the lottery, I **will** be rich.

   If I **won** the lottery, I **would** be rich.

Each sentence has two verbs and illustrates a particular tense pattern. If you begin with one pattern, you should stick with it. Do not change patterns in midsentence.

---

**BRIEF PRACTICE 18.2**    *Fill in each blank with the correct form.*

EXAMPLES    If I inherit a fortune, I ____*will*____ buy a boat.
                    will, would

If I inherited a fortune, I ____*would*____ buy a boat.
                    will, would

1. Janice says that she _____ speak French.
                    can, could

2. If we seriously try, we _____ complete the project by next week.
                    will, would

3. Lincoln said he _____ free the slaves.
                    will, would

4. If we worked harder, we _____ accomplish more.
                    can, could

---

**EXERCISE 18b**    *There are confusing tense shifts in the following sentences. Where necessary, change the verbs to the present to make the tenses consistent.*

                                        *admire*
EXAMPLE    The person I ~~admired~~ most is my mother, who is a wonderful human being.

1. They always try to follow directions, but sometimes they did not understand them.

2. Now she believed that she wants to go to law school.

3. Katie says that she could speak Korean well.

4. The supervisor insisted on punctuality, and she usually gets it.

5. The curtains moved when the windows are open.

6. As people looked ahead, they wonder what they will be doing in twenty years.

7. She is never late to work; in fact, she was usually early.

8. Jerry thought he is a karate expert.

9. I admired my current supervisor because she is very efficient.

10. Whenever my daughter telephones me, I felt happy.

|  |  |
|---|---|
| **EXERCISE**<br>**18c** | *The following sentences contain shifts in tense. Change some of the verbs to avoid confusing tense shifts.* |

*EXAMPLE*    Sam thinks he ~~could~~ *can* skate better than his brother.

OR

Sam ~~thinks~~ *thought* he could skate better than his brother.

1. The woman was pleased with the apartment I am showing her.

2. As the bus approaches the intersection, it did not slow down.

3. My father says we could go to Disney World next year.

4. The child was examined by the doctor as the parents wait nervously.

5. The singer says that he could sing over two hundred songs.

6. The men charged him ten dollars after they repair his radio.

7. I was worried about the baby, who had a slight fever, was sneezing, and refuses to eat.

8. When the river overflowed and flooded the town, all the residents have to be evacuated.

9. Mr. Roper did not realize that he forgets to lock the front door.

10. If I did not finish my work, I cannot go on vacation.

**EXERCISE 18d** | *The following paragraphs contain tense errors. Correct them.*

**1.** Juana and her sister receive a letter every day from their mother, who was visiting a sick cousin in Puerto Rico. Because this cousin is elderly and had no one to help her, Juana's mother has gone to be at her bedside until she recovered.

**2.** The students at Paloma State College really enjoyed the home economics class. They learn how to prepare specific recipes, and they were also taught basic cooking skills. For example, the teacher explains how to chop, dice, and blend different foods. But the best part is after each lesson ends, when the students could eat what they have prepared.

**3.** The incident starts on a quiet Saturday evening in front of the Corner Sweet Shop, where a lot of young people gathered to talk, drink beer, and horse around. One young man took offense at a remark and pushes another young man, who pushes back. Soon the street is filled with brawling teenagers, and the police arrived to break up the fight. They make twenty arrests.

**4.** Every year on the spring weekend when daylight savings time begins, many people forgot to set their clocks ahead one hour on Saturday night. As a result, they are confused on Sunday morning when the news announcer said it was was ten o'clock while their clocks say 9 o'clock. Some people even arrived late to work on Monday because they do not know about daylight savings time.

**5.** When George Orwell's novel *Nineteen Eighty-Four* was published in 1949, people are frightened by what it predicted and wonder whether the predictions will come true. Now that the year 1984 has come and gone, people are still debating whether or not Orwell's predictions had come true.

CHAPTER

# 19

# Using the Correct Part of Speech

## A REVIEW OF THE PARTS OF SPEECH

Words are catalogued into different types. Each type is called a *part of speech*. There are eight parts of speech in English:

1. nouns          5. adverbs
2. pronouns       6. conjunctions
3. verbs          7. prepositions
4. adjectives     8. interjections

### Nouns

A **noun** is the name of something, somebody, some place, or some quality. Here are some nouns:

| | | |
|---|---|---|
| chair | Lehman College | tree |
| college | luck | truth |

| | | |
|---|---|---|
| hat | Mrs. Jones | Wednesday |
| John | picture | wind |
| justice | Ruth | woman |

Notice that names of particular people, places, or days are capitalized. These are called *proper nouns*. Write your own list of nouns on the lines below. If you include any proper nouns, remember to capitalize them.

_____    _____    _____

_____    _____    _____

_____    _____    _____

## Pronouns

A **pronoun** is a word that can replace a noun in a sentence. Look at the following sentence.

Nancy is the captain of the basketball team because **she** is the best player and everyone respects **her.**

In this sentence the words *she* and *her* are pronouns; they replace the noun *Nancy.* For more information on pronouns, see Chapter 25.

## Verbs

A **verb** expresses action or state of being in a sentence. See Chapters 14 through 18.

## Adjectives

An **adjective** describes a noun or a pronoun. Note the adjectives *pretty* and *smart* in the following sentence:

Mary is **pretty** and **smart.**

Here are some other adjectives:

| | | |
|---|---|---|
| adorable | earnest | icy |
| brave | full | jolly |
| clever | graceful | loud |
| dear | hopeful | mysterious |

| noisy | pale | rude |
|-------|-------|------|
| open | quiet | silly |

Make your own list of adjectives:

_____    _____    _____

_____    _____    _____

_____    _____    _____

For more information on adjectives, see Chapter 27.

**Note:  There is a special subgroup of adjectives that contains only three words: *a, an,* and *the.* These words are called *articles.* (See the next chapter.)**

## Adverbs

An **adverb** modifies a verb. It answers the question "how?" "how much?" "when?" or "where?" Look at the following sentences:

Susan writes **beautifully.**

How does she write? *Beautifully* is the adverb that tells how.

Jack telephones his parents **often.**

*Often* is the adverb that answers the question "how much?"
An **adverb** can also modify an adjective or another adverb. The word *very* is a common adverb used in this way.

Susan is **very** smart.

How smart? *Very* smart.

Susan writes **very** beautifully.

How beautifully? *Very* beautifully.
Here are some other adverbs:

| adorably | foolishly | luckily |
|----------|-----------|---------|
| better | gracefully | merrily |
| carefully | hastily | nicely |
| dearly | innocently | openly |
| easily | justly | possibly |

Did you notice that many adverbs end with the letters *ly?*

Make a list of some other adverbs:

_____    _____    _____

_____    _____    _____

_____    _____    _____

For more information about adverbs, see Chapter 27.

## Conjunctions

**Conjunctions** are joining words. They connect elements of a sentence. Some common conjunctions are:

| | | |
|---|---|---|
| and | but | or |

Other common conjunctions are:

| | |
|---|---|
| although | if |
| because | when |

Here are some examples of conjunctions working in sentences:

Sally **and** her sister went shopping.

Dan likes to bake, **and** his brother enjoys hunting.

**If** it snows tomorrow, there will be no school.

For more information on conjunctions, see Chapters 10 and 12.

## Prepositions

**Prepositions** show how words in a sentence are related to each other. Some common prepositions are:

| | | |
|---|---|---|
| around | during | on |
| at | for | over |
| behind | from | to |
| by | in | toward |
| down | of | under |

Here are some examples of prepositions working in sentences:

Sally works **in** a drugstore.

Henry hung his coat **on** a hook.

The family took shelter **during** the storm.

## Interjections

**Interjections** are exclamations. They are added to the sentence for emphasis. Some common interjections are:

Wow!                    Gosh!                    Oh!

Interjections are easily recognized in sentences and do not cause grammatical problems.

## IDENTIFYING PARTS OF SPEECH

Of the eight parts of speech, it is the nouns, verbs, adjectives, and adverbs that create most vocabulary problems. We will concentrate on recognizing these parts of speech in sentences.

**EXERCISE 19a** | *Underline every noun in the following paragraph.*

Dentistry, the care of the teeth, has a very interesting history. Even ancient people, such as the Egyptians and Babylonians, practiced dentistry. From ancient to modern times, dentists have repaired or replaced damaged teeth. For centuries gold has been used for these purposes because of its durability. George Washington, the first American President, wore dentures made of gold and ivory. In modern dentistry, however, lightweight plastics are generally used to form false teeth. Although modern dentures are much more comfortable than the false teeth of years ago, most people would prefer to avoid the necessity of dentures, and they can do so by visiting their dentist regularly, by practicing good oral hygiene, and by eating a healthful diet.

## PARTS OF SPEECH IN DIFFERENT CONTEXTS

Sometimes the same word may be used as either a noun or a verb without changing form. Consider the word *kiss,* for example.

David gave his mother a **kiss.**

In the example above, *kiss* is a noun, a thing. Now consider the next example:

> The kindergarten children **kiss** their teacher every day when they leave school.

Here *kiss* is the verb in the sentence; it tells what the children do. When a word can be used as either a noun or a verb, the **context** (the rest of the sentence) will tell you how the word is being used.

Look at how the word *experience* is being used in the following sentence:

> Many children's first **experience** of being separated from their parents is the first day of school.

In the previous example, the word *experience* is used as a noun. An *experience* is something. But consider the following sentence:

> Many children **experience** their first separation from their parents on the first day of school.

In this sentence, the word *experience* is a verb. It tells something the children do. Now consider another example:

> Most employers prefer to hire **experienced** workers.

In this sentence, the word *experienced* is an adjective modifying *workers.* What kind of workers? *Experienced* workers. (Notice the **d** ending on this adjective. See Chapter 16.)

Thus, the context of a word is important in telling us what part of speech the word is. For example, consider the following words:

> run          house

Most people, seeing these words out of context (not in a sentence), would say that *house* is a noun and *run* is a verb. But look at the following sentences:

> The oak tree **housed** dozens of squirrels.
>
> Jenny has just hit a home **run.**

In the first sentence, the word *housed* is a verb. It tells what the tree did. In the second sentence, *run* is a noun. A *run* is a thing.

So you can see the importance of a word's context in telling what part of speech it is.

**EXERCISE
19b** | *On the line at the left of each sentence, write the part of speech of the boldface word.*

EXAMPLES  ___*noun*___  **a.** It is your **turn** to bat.

___*verb*___  **b.** He **telephoned** his wife that night.

___*adjective*___  **c.** Mr. Gray was a very **experienced** worker.

_____  **1.** She can **jump** easily over the hurdles.

_____  **2.** Her high **jump** won the meet.

_____  **3.** He **cut** his hand badly on a piece of metal.

_____  **4.** A doctor stitched up the **cut.**

_____  **5.** Her sales **experience** is extensive.

_____  **6.** She is an **experienced** sales manager.

_____  **7.** They gathered **sticks** for kindling.

_____  **8.** Chewing gum **sticks** to almost anything.

_____  **9.** I lost my shopping **list.**

_____  **10.** She **listed** her family's weekly expenses.

_____  **11.** He likes to collect foreign **stamps.**

_____  **12.** The horses **stamped** and snorted.

_____  **13.** The **stamped** envelopes are ready to mail.

## CHOOSING THE CORRECT PART OF SPEECH

Sometimes related words that are different parts of speech can be confusing. For example, consider the following words:

belief (noun)      believe (verb)      believable (adjective)

Look at the following sentences illustrating the use of these words:

John has a strong **belief** in God.
*Belief,* the noun, is used. A *belief* is something that John has.

**John believes strongly in God.**

    A form of the verb *to believe* is used. The verb *believes* tells what John does.

**The story was believable.**

    The adjective *believable* describes the story.

Consider the following words and the way they are used in sentences:

    probable (adjective)    probably (adverb)

**The story James told is possible, but not probable.**

In this sentence, the word *probable,* like *possible,* is an adjective. It modifies the noun *story.* Now consider the following sentence:

**Our team will probably win the game.**

In this sentence, the adverb *probably* modifies the verb *will win.*

---

**BRIEF PRACTICE 19.1**    *In the sentences below, fill in one of the following:* belief, believe, probable, *or* probably.

1. It will _____ rain later.

2. My parents _____ in the golden rule.

3. Jen has a _____ in the basic goodness of people.

4. His story was not at all _____ .

---

**EXERCISE 19c**    *Below are sets of words. In each set the words are related, but they are different parts of speech and so have slightly different meanings. Each group of words is followed by a list of sentences. The first few sentences show how the words should be used, and the rest of the sentences have blanks to be filled in with the correct word from each group.*

Group I
ignorance (noun)
ignorant (adjective)

1. Frederick Douglass felt that **ignorance** was terrible.

2. **Ignorant** voters cannot make good choices.

**3.** Ed was _____ of current events.

**4.** She was _____ , yet eager to learn.

**5.** His _____ did not stop him from judging others.

Group II
independent (adjective)
independence (noun)
independently (adverb)

**1.** She is very **independent** person.

**2.** America won its **independence** in the eighteenth century.

**3.** The scientists were working **independently.**

**4.** Most young people want to be _____ .

**5.** People are not really mature unless they can think _____ .

**6.** Schoolchildren used to memorize the Declaration of _____ .

Group III
lose (verb)
loss (noun)
lost (adjective or past tense of verb)

**1.** He hates to **lose** a game.

**2.** She reported the **loss** of her wallet.

**3.** Searchers finally found the **lost** hikers.

**4.** We **lost** the game.

**5.** He never recovered from the _____ of his wife.

**6.** I saw a _____ dog in the park.

**7.** He _____ all his money gambling.

**8.** If you leave, you will _____ your place in line.

Group IV
prejudice (noun)
prejudiced (adjective)

**1.** Martin Luther King, Jr., struggled against **prejudice.**

**2. Prejudiced** people judge others without knowing them.

**3.** A _____ person is very often ignorant.

**4.** Most Americans agree that _____ is a problem.

Group V
probable (adjective)
probably (adverb)
probability (noun)

1. It is **probable** that it will rain today, and it will **probably** rain tomorrow too.

2. There is a strong **probability** that it will rain next week.

3. That movie will _____ win an Oscar.

4. They discussed the _____ of finding a parking space downtown.

5. The excuse Jack gave was possible, but not _____.

Group VI
truth (noun)
true (adjective)
truly (adverb)

1. The witness was not telling the **truth.**

2. Nonfiction is said to be **true.**

3. I am **truly** sorry for my mistake.

4. Do you _____ want to be a nurse?

5. Small children cannot always tell the difference between _____ and fantasy.

6. It isn't _____ that all opera singers are fat.

Group VII
weigh (verb)
weight (noun)

1. The baby **weighs** fifteen pounds.

2. Wrestlers worry about their **weight.**

3. She and her sister _____ the same.

4. The _____ of the carton made it impossible for me to lift.

**EXERCISE
19d**

*Underneath each blank are several word forms. Decide whether a noun, verb, adjective, or adverb is needed in that space and choose the correct form.*

1. It takes great _____ to be a good fisherman.
   patient (adj.)
   patience (noun)

2. He relaxed in the _____ and solitude of the country.
   peaceful (adj.)
   peace (noun)
   peacefully (adv.)

3. Some people claim that scenes of _____ in the media
   violence (noun)
   violent (adj.)

   cause _____ behavior.
   violence (noun)
   violent (adj.)

4. They demonstrated for _____ rights.
   equal (adj.)
   equally (adv.)
   equality (noun)

5. She has a lot of _____ working with deaf children.
   experienced (adj.)
   experience (noun)

6. You _____ finished painting the living room.
   final (adj.)
   finally (adv.)

7. He is quite jealous and _____.
   possess (verb)
   possession (noun)
   possessive (adj.)

8. Their new house is _____ large.
   real (adj.)
   really (adv.)

9. _____ is not the most _____ thing to
   Obedience (noun)              importance (noun)
   Obedient (adj.)               important (adj.)

   _____ in rearing children.
   emphasis (noun)
   emphasize (verb)
   emphatic (adj.)

10. Joyce was a perfectionist who insisted on _____.
    excellence (noun)
    excellent (adj.)

11. The _____ of Van Gogh's paintings overwhelmed me.
    beautiful (adj.)
    beautifully (adv.)
    beauty (noun)

**12.** An awed _____ filled the hall after the great
silence (noun)
silent (adj.)
silently (adv.)

performance.

**EXERCISE
19e**    *Beneath each blank are several word forms. Decide whether a noun,
verb, adjective, or adverb is needed in that space and choose the right
form.*

**1.** My co-worker wanted to consult me on a matter of
_____ .
importance (noun)
important (adj.)

**2.** He did _____ on the civil service test.
poor (adj.)
poorly (adv.)

**3.** She had an _____ look on her face.
innocence (noun)
innocent (adj.)
innocently (adv.)

**4.** You seem very _____ about child development.
knowledgeably (adv.)
knowledgeable (adj.)
knowledge (noun)

**5.** The _____ between Tom and Jane is that Tom is too
difference (noun)
different (adj.)

_____ on his parents.
dependence (noun)
dependent (adj.)

**6.** The crime and trial got a lot of _____ .
publicly (adv.)
publicity (noun)
publicize (verb)

**7.** Sally used to be very _____ , but since she
confidence (noun)
confident (adj.)

_____ the championship, she has suffered from
loss (noun)
lost (verb)

a _____ of _____ .
loss (noun)          confidence (noun)
lost (verb or adj.)  confident (adj.)

8. The _____ of the land has risen.
   valuable (adj.)
   valuably (adv.)
   value (noun)

9. A _____ breakfast for him is ham and eggs.
   typical (adj.)
   typically (adv.)

**EXERCISE 19f** | *Write in the related forms of each word. Then write a sentence using each form correctly. If necessary, use your dictionary.*

*EXAMPLE*   adj.   eager _____   *She is eager to see New Orleans.*

   adv.   *eagerly*   *She waited eagerly for the plane to arrive.*

   noun   *eagerness*   *Her face revealed her eagerness.*

1. adj.   intelligent _____

   adv.   _____   _____

   noun   _____   _____

2. noun   difference _____

   adj.   _____   _____

   adv.   _____   _____

3. adj.   prejudiced _____

   noun   _____   _____

**4.** noun   importance _____

_____

    adj.   _____   _____

_____

**5.** noun   patience _____

_____

    adj.   _____   _____

_____

**6.** adj.   sincere _____

_____

    adv.   _____   _____

_____

    noun   _____   _____

_____

## DICTION: USING THE RIGHT WORD

# 20

# Articles:
# *The, A, An*

The words *a, an*, and **the** are a special group of adjectives called *articles*.

## THE USE OF *THE*

*The* can be used in front of both singular and plural nouns:

the child (singular)

the children (plural)

Using an adjective before the noun does not change the use of *the:*

The happy child (singular)

the happy children (plural)

Use *the* when you write about **specific** things, for example:

I went to **the** corner grocery store to buy bread.

*The* is used because it is one specific store.

**The** students in Mrs. Crews' biology class are taking a test.

*The* is used because those particular students are taking the test, not just students anywhere or students in general.

**The** town where I was born is very small.

*The* is used because a particular town (the town where I was born) is being discussed.

**The** essays in **the** textbook are interesting.

The word *the* is used in order to show that we are discussing specific essays in a specific book.

## WHEN NOT TO USE *THE*

Look at the following sentence:

As I drove along Main Street, I saw children playing, so I slowed down.

In this sentence, we are talking about some children, but not specific children, so the noun *children* is not preceded by *the*.

If the subject is general or abstract, omit *the*. Look at these examples:

Honor and duty motivated her behavior.

*Honor* and *duty* are general ideas. *The* is not necessary.

Children love bright colors.

This means children everywhere, and bright colors in general. Compare:

The children in the day-care center love the bright colors that decorate its walls.

CHAPTER 20: ARTICLES: *THE, A, AN*   **251**

Now we are talking about a certain group of children (the children in the day-care center) and certain bright colors (the ones that decorate the day-care center's walls).

**EXERCISE 20a**   *Write the word <u>the</u> in the blank if it is needed. Cross out the word <u>the</u> if it is not needed. Remember to capitalize words at the start of a sentence.*

*EXAMPLES*   **a.** Most children love ⸻ ~~the~~ candy.

**b.** *The* daughter of my best friend loved *the* candy I bought for her.
   The                                          the

1. Gwen loves ⸻ literature; now she is studying ⸻
   the                                              the
   literature of modern Spain.

2. ⸻ United States is a nation where
   The
   ⸻ equality and ⸻ justice are valued.
   the                    the

3. Kim loves ⸻ music, so for his birthday I bought
   the
   him a tape by ⸻ rock group he likes best.
   the

4. During ⸻ French Revolution in 1789, many people
   the
   spoke of ⸻ liberty, ⸻ fraternity,
   the              the
   and ⸻ equality.
   the

5. Christopher refused to join ⸻ first fraternity that
   the
   accepted him because he found out that it was known for
   ⸻ snobbishness.
   the

6. Many people who do not usually read ⸻ poetry
   the
   enjoy ⸻ poetry of Rod McKuen.
   the

7. We learn about _____ gods of Greek, Roman, and Norse
_the_

mythology; some played _____ tricks on each other.
_the_

8. Susan likes to read _____ novels, but she has not read
_the_

_____ novel *Tom Jones.*
_the_

9. _____ French professor told _____ class about a
_The_                                    _the_

field trip to _____ best French restaurant in
_the_

_____ town where _____ high school was located.
_the_                        _the_

10. Nathaniel Hawthorne, who is considered one of _____ classic
_the_

American writers, is known for his stories that concern

_____ power of love, _____ search for
_the_                        _the_

knowledge, and _____ attempt to understand _____ nature
_the_                                          _the_

of _____ good and _____ evil.
_the_                _the_

---

**EXERCISE
20b**
| *Write <u>the</u> in each blank if it is needed. Cross out <u>the</u> if it is not needed.*
*Capitalize where necessary.*

1. _____ founding fathers who wrote _____
_The_                                        _the_

American Constitution believed in _____ freedom.
_the_

2. _____ good parents know that _____
_The_                                    _the_

children need _____ books, _____ trips
_the_                    _the_

to museums, and _____ interesting toys.
_the_

3. One of _____ best books I ever read on geology was
_the_

written by _____ professor I studied with at
_the_

_____ college I attended.
_the_

**4.** Dr. Black is ___the___ most intelligent person I know.

**5.** We attended ___the___ groundbreaking of

___the___ new library, which was to be dedicated to

___the___ founder of ___the___ college, a man

who had done much for ___the___ excellence in education.

**6.** ___The___ worst fire in ___the___ history of

London occurred in ___the___ year 1666.

**7.** ___The___ tennis ball rolled under ___the___ desk.

**8.** People should be taught from ___the___ childhood to value

___the___ honesty, and they should be taught to try to do

___the___ right thing in every situation.

**9.** ___The___ quilt-making is a hobby that many women enjoy

because it gives them a chance to display ___the___ originality

and ___the___ skill as they create something that has

___the___ practical value as well as ___the___ beauty.


## THE USE OF *A* AND *AN*

*A* and *an* mean much the same thing as **one** and so should be used only in front of a **singular** noun.

To use *a* and *an* correctly, you must know what vowels and consonants are. All the letters in the alphabet are consonants except:

**a   e   i   o   u** (vowels)

(Sometimes the letter *y* is a vowel, but never at the start of a word, so we do not have to be concerned with *y* here.)

Use the word *a* before words beginning with a consonant. Use the word *an* before words beginning with a vowel. Following is a list of examples:

| | |
|---|---|
| a **b**anana | an **a**pple |
| a **r**otten apple | an **o**ld banana |
| a **d**og | an **e**lephant |
| a **c**lumsy elephant | an **o**ld dog |
| a **p**eninsula | an **i**sland |
| a **s**quare | an **o**val |
| a **r**aincoat | an **u**mbrella |

Watch out for exceptions. There are a few words that start with a vowel but the first **sound** is of a consonant. So we say:

a European
a universe
a union
a united country
a one-man band

The letters *f, h, l, m, n, r, s,* and *x,* although consonants, need the word *an* before them when they are written as letters by themselves, because the first sound is of a vowel. For example:

The word "wrong" begins with a "w," not **an** "r."

That is **an** X-rated movie.

Dolores has **an** R.N. and **an** M.B.A., so she can get a job in nursing or business.

**Note: Watch out for words that start with *h*. Use *a* if the *h* is pronounced. Use *an* if the *h* is not pronounced. So we say:**

| | |
|---|---|
| **an hour** | **a humid day** |
| **an honorable man** | **a hammock** |

**EXERCISE 20c** | *Write* a *or* an *in each blank.*

1. We went to see _____ award-winning play.

2. Ms. Gray is _____ elderly woman with _____ good memory.

3. Felicia is _____ altruistic person.

4. _____ essay by a student won _____ prize.

5. Twana has just bought _____ car.

6. It is _____ honor to present _____ award to such _____ honest and brave person.

7. _____ Academy Award was won by _____ European movie.

8. Dr. Green had to wait _____ hour for a table at _____ expensive restaurant.

9. Jackie found _____ hundred-dollar bill lying in _____ alley.

10. Mr. Kelly is _____ experienced plumber.

11. You have become _____ valuable asset to this firm.

12. Brutus was _____ honorable man.

13. "Politics and the English Language" is _____ excellent essay.

14. We have just completed _____ year of unparalleled growth.

15. It is _____ advantage to speak several languages.

CHAPTER

# 21

# Confusing Words

Some words are confusing because they look and sound alike. With practice you can learn the particular meanings and uses of all of the following words:

accept, except, expect
advice, advise
affect, effect
all ready, already
an, and
being, been
have, of
is, it's
its, it's
loose, lose, losing
loss, lost
no, know

passed, past
quiet, quite
than, then
their, there, they're
these, this
though, thought
to, too
weather, whether
went, when
were, where
whose, who's
your, you're

## ACCEPT, EXCEPT, EXPECT

*Accept* is a verb meaning "to take," "to say yes to."

Grace **accepted** Larry's invitation to the dance.

*Except* is usually not a verb. It means "not including," "all but."

We visited all the South American countries **except** Peru.

*Expect* is a verb meaning "to wait for," "to hope."

I **expect** to do well on the exam.

**EXERCISE 21a** | *Fill in each blank with the correct word.*

1. I intend to _____ that job offer.
2. Anna has brought all her children _____ Tom.
3. It is difficult to _____ a compliment.
4. The Joneses _____ a new baby in May.
5. No one _____ Harry knows the secret.
6. Most editors will not _____ handwritten manuscripts.
7. That professor will not _____ late assignments _____ under certain conditions.
8. Mr. and Mrs. Roper _____ to move to Oklahoma in late August.
9. The actor said, "I am happy to _____ this award, which I did not _____ to receive."
10. I hope that you will _____ my apology for being late.

## ADVICE, ADVISE

*Advice* is a noun meaning "a recommendation, words of wisdom."

**I will give you some good advice.**

*Advise* is a verb meaning "to recommend or suggest."

**My counselor advised me to take calculus.**

**A person who advises a friend is giving advice to that friend.**

**EXERCISE 21b** | *Fill in each blank with the correct word.*

1. Most people like to _____ others more than they like to take _____ .

2. Take my _____ and get rid of that old car.

3. When I want your _____ , I'll ask for it.

4. _____ may be free or very expensive.

5. Doctors often _____ patients to quit smoking.

6. "I _____ you to lose some weight," said Dr. Kantor.

7. Ruth never listened to her mother's _____ .

8. Your counselor can _____ you about applying for financial aid.

9. Antia gave me some _____ about how to handle the job interview.

10. My friends always _____ me to think before I speak, but sometimes I don't.

## AFFECT, EFFECT

*Affect* is usually a verb. It means "to influence or to change."

Will the cold weather **affect** the traffic?

*Effect* is usually a noun meaning "a result." Also, *effect* may sometimes be a verb meaning "to cause."

The **effect** of the cyclone was disastrous.

The new president wanted to **effect** many changes in the company.

**EXERCISE 21c**

*Fill in each blank with the correct word. Add verb endings if necessary.*

1. Brian's excessive smoking may adversely _____ his health.

2. The sad play _____ us all deeply.

3. Losing fifty pounds had a wonderful _____ on Mark's self-image.

4. The _____ of large doses of that chemical is unknown.

5. Unfortunately, education does not always have a lasting _____s___ on a person.

6. Those three beers will probably _____ your ability to play tennis.

7. The senators want to _____ great changes in the health care system.

8. This disastrous flood will certainly _____ our town's economy.

9. Has that new fertilizer had a good _____ on your tomato plants?

## ALL READY, ALREADY

*All ready* is a two-word phrase meaning "completely prepared."

The Girl Scouts were **all ready** for the camping trip.

*Already* is an adverb meaning "previously, before." Notice that it is spelled with one *l*.

We have **already** seen that movie.

**EXERCISE 21d** | *Fill in each blank with the correct word or phrase.*

1. The room was _____ for the guests.

2. Everything was _____ for the experiment in the science lab.

3. Haven't you done your work _____?

4. Are you _____ for the dance?

5. Michelle says that she has _____ written her essay.

6. That scientist has _____ received the Nobel Prize.

7. The team was _____ for the game, but it was canceled.

8. Marva has _____ taken chemistry and biology, but not her social sciences requirement.

9. I called you at the office in the late afternoon, but you had _____ left.

## AN, AND

*An* is an article used before words starting with a vowel. (See Chapter 20.)

For breakfast he ate **an** egg.

*And* is a connecting word, a conjunction. (See Chapter 10.)

Hannah **and** Abigail are twins.

**EXERCISE 21e**

*Fill in each blank with the correct word.*

1. Greg put _____ apple, _____ orange, _____ some grapes into the fruit salad.

2. Math _____ science are related fields.

3. It is interesting to study the history _____ the literature of a country at the same time.

4. John was handsome _____ intelligent.

5. You _____ I have been friends for a long time.

6. Do you have _____ old towel _____ a washcloth to lend me?

7. James has eaten nothing all day except for _____ apple _____ _____ olive.

8. The words *an* _____ *and* can be confusing.

9. The radiator was making _____ irritating noise.

10. He is _____ expert in both judo _____ karate.

## BEING, BEEN

*Being* is a form of *to be*. It can be used as a noun, as in "human being" or the phrase "being honest." When found in verbs, it follows another form of *to be (am, are, is, was,* or *were).*

He is **being** stubborn.

The lions in the zoo are **being** fed now.

He stressed the importance of **being** accurate.

*Been* is the past participle of *to be*. When found in verbs, it follows a form of *to have (has, have,* or *had).*

She has **been** very helpful.

The clue had **been** hidden.

**EXERCISE 21f** | *Fill in each blank with the correct word. Capitalize where needed.*

1. Carol has not _____ to the last four meetings of the club.

2. Sandy is not _____ very cooperative.

3. Imelda has _____ searching for meaning in life, seeking a reason for _____ .

4. This course has _____ interesting.

5. Rest assured that your case is _____ examined; you have not _____ forgotten.

6. If you had not _____ there, I don't know what the outcome would have _____ .

7. _____ unemployed for a long time is very depressing.

8. Ms. Canela has _____ thinking about majoring in business management.

9. Customers were angry because they had not _____ notified about the increase in the telephone rates.

10. The street has _____ closed while parts of the roadway are _____ repaired.

## HAVE, OF

*Have* is a verb or a part of a verb.

I should **have** gone home.

*Of* is a preposition and never part of a verb.

One **of** the students is here.

**EXERCISE 21g**

*Fill in each blank with the correct word.*

1. Surely you should _____ finished all _____ the work by now.

2. Gerry must _____ been ill last week.

3. I would _____ called you if I had known your number.

4. The check must _____ been with one _____ the cards I threw away.

5. You really ought to _____ returned that blouse.

6. One _____ these toys must _____ been broken.

7. You should _____ applied for that job; you are more qualified than all _____ the people who did apply.

8. One _____ the boys should _____ walked the dog after school.

9. One _____ these books is overdue; it should _____ been returned last week.

10. You should not _____ been surprised when I lent you money; you _____ always been one _____ my closest friends.

## IS, IT'S

*Is* is a verb, present tense of *to be,* used with third-person singular subjects.

> She **is** a computer programmer.

*Is* does **not** begin a sentence, unless the sentence is a question.

> It **is** raining.
>
> **Is** it raining?

*It's* is a contraction of *it is* or *it has.*

> **It's** too bad you lost your ring. (**It is** too bad. . . .)
>
> **It's** a sunny day. (**It is** a. . . .)
>
> **It's** been ten days since John's party. (**It has** been ten. . . .)

**EXERCISE 21h**

*Fill in each blank with the correct word. Capitalize where needed.*

1.  Hugh says _____ possible that _____ going to rain tomorrow.

2.  _____ it true that Friday _____ your last day here?

3.  When you wake up in the summer, _____ already light outside.

4.  Maria wants to know if _____ been snowing for a long time.

5.  _____ too bad that _____ too late to sign up for the course because everyone says _____ very interesting.

6.  The mountain we are climbing _____ the highest in the state, and _____ been described as the most difficult to climb.

7.  The counselor says that _____ not wise to drop a required course, especially if _____ late in the semester.

8.  The class _____ full, and _____ not possible to register for it.

## ITS, IT'S

*Its* is a possessive word, used for singular, neuter words (not masculine or feminine). It means "belonging to it."

The company is rearranging **its** offices.

Remember that the possessive *its,* like *his* and *hers,* has no apostrophe.

*It's* is a contraction for *it is* or *it has.*

I know **it's** too late to catch that train. (. . . **it is** too late. . . .)

**It's** been a hot day. (**It has** been. . . .)

**EXERCISE 21i**

*Fill in each blank with the correct word. Capitalize where needed.*

1. _____ an old saying that a tiger cannot change

   _____ stripes.

2. When _____ noon in Washington, D.C., _____ nine A.M. in San Francisco, California.

3. My calculator was not working properly because _____ battery was wearing out.

4. The corporation moved _____ headquarters to New Jersey.

5. _____ been a long time since the company had

   _____ merchandise catalog revised.

6. The ship was in drydock, having _____ hull repaired.

7. The college may change _____ registration procedures.

8. The building may be old, but _____ in very good shape

   and _____ heating system is very efficient.

9. The prosecution lost because it did not present _____ case very well.

## LOOSE, LOSE, LOSING

*Loose* is usually an adjective, a word used to describe nouns and pronouns. It means the opposite of "tight" or "confined."

The bull got **loose.**

My shoelace is **loose.**

*Lose* is a verb. It may mean "to misplace" or "fail to win." The word *losing* is a form of this verb.

People often **lose** pencils.

Children dislike **losing** at games.

**EXERCISE 21j**

*Fill in each blank with the correct word. Capitalize where needed.*

1. No business wants to _____ money; _____ money is not the purpose of a business.

2. The present mayor does not want to _____ the next election.

3. Win or _____, you must play by the rules.

4. After _____ ten pounds, Marge said, "This dress is too _____; I don't want to _____ any more weight."

5. Two shutters on our house are _____, and they bang in the wind.

6. My six-year-old daughter has a _____ tooth.

7. _____ his athletic scholarship meant that Nicholas had to drop out of college.

8. You can _____ control of your car if one of the wheels is _____.

9. The dog got _____ by digging under the fence.

## LOSS, LOST

*Loss* is a noun. You can say "a loss" or "the loss." (It rhymes with *boss*.)

I reported the **loss** of my purse to the police.

*Lost* is a form of the verb *to lose*. It may also be an adjective. Don't forget the *t* on *lost*. It rhymes with *frost*.)

They were **lost** in the woods.

He **lost** his keys.

The **lost** child cried.

**EXERCISE 21k**

*Fill in each blank with the correct word.*

1. I _____ my warmest gloves.

2. Gladys was overjoyed when she recovered her _____ wallet.

3. Despite hard luck, Ernie has never _____ his sense of humor.

4. Cora did not regret the _____ of her old sweater.

5. Mr. Edwards _____ some money gambling; he was reluctant to tell his wife about his _____.

6. The soccer team's record is three wins and one _____.

7. This year's profits may make up for last year's _____.

8. He has _____ his credit cards; he must report the _____ immediately.

9. The volleyball team's only _____ was to last year's championship team.

10. Those hikers got _____ because they left the marked trail.

## NO, KNOW

*No* is a negative word, not a verb.

There are **no** pencils in the box.

*Know* is a verb meaning "to understand" or "to be acquainted with."

Do you **know** where the hammer is?

**EXERCISE 211** | *Fill in each blank with the correct word.*

1. He has _____ problems now.

2. Do you _____ anyone who has _____ problems at all?

3. How many people _____ the answer?

4. There is _____ way to _____ if he got your letter.

5. Few people think they _____ the secret of happiness.

6. We did not _____ you were coming; _____ one told us.

7. In high altitudes, _____ large trees can grow.

8. Many people do not _____ the names of their senators or congressional representatives.

9. The movie will be shown with _____ commercial interruptions.

10. Does anyone _____ whether the library is open this weekend?

## PASSED, PAST

*Passed* is the past tense or past participle of the verb *to pass.*

> I have **passed** the test.
>
> The speeding car **passed** the others.
>
> Time **passed** quickly because we were busy.

The word *past* has several meanings:

*Past* as a noun means "a time gone by."

> The American Revolution is in the **past.**

*Past* as an adjective means "finished, ended, in the past."

> My **past** life has been exciting.

*Past* as a preposition means "by" or "beyond."

> He walked **past** the desk.
>
> The gas station is just **past** the intersection.

**EXERCISE 21m**

*Fill in each blank with the correct word.*

1. In the _____ , most lawyers _____ the bar exam.

2. The quarter miler _____ the other runners on the track.

3. The driver went _____ his exit.

4. We cannot live in the _____ .

5. The _____ year has been a very happy and exciting one.

6. For the _____ three years, most motorists have _____ the road test.

7. In the _____ week, she took five exams and _____ all of them.

8. On the New Jersey Turnpike we _____ six cars with Nebraska license plates.

9. He has made a lot of foolish mistakes in his _____ life.

## QUIET, QUITE

*Quiet* has two syllables. It means "not noisy."

**Laura is quiet.**

*Quite* is one syllable. (It rhymes with *bite.*) It means "completely" or "very."

**Are you quite finished with your work?**

**EXERCISE 21n** | *Fill in each blank with the correct word.*

1. Children who are always _____ are not always happy.

2. He was _____ alarmed when his brakes failed.

3. Mrs. Jones works in a _____ but efficient way.

4. After working in the barn all day, Don was _____ tired.

5. The downtown section of the city is never _____ .

6. Cows are usually _____ animals.

7. This house is spacious and lovely, but _____ expensive.

8. Mr. Joseph is usually _____ , but he can be _____ vocal when he is angry.

9. The cake layers are not _____ done; they need to bake about seven more minutes.

10. To my surprise, Ms. Wilson's behavior was _____ rude.

## THAN, THEN

*Than* is used in comparisons of two or more things.

She is older **than** I am.

*Then* usually means "next," "in those days," or "at that time."

The baby tripped and **then** fell down.

**EXERCISE 21o**

*Fill in each blank with the correct word.*

1. Napoleon lived longer _____ Alexander the Great did.

2. To me, novels are more interesting _____ poetry.

3. The dentist took X-rays and _____ studied them.

4. Years ago, people had big families. _____, it was not unusual to have seven or more children.

5. To Gail, roller blading is more fun _____ skiing.

## THEIR, THERE, THEY'RE

*Their* is a possessive word meaning "belonging to them"; it is found with a noun.

The Steins have sold **their** house.

*There* means "in that place" or "to that place." *There* may also start a sentence.

Put the books right **there.**

**There** are six apples in the bag.

*They're* is a contraction for *they are.*

Sandy and Joe don't know where **they're** going next.
(. . . where **they are** going next.)

**Note: Contractions often lead to mistakes. Avoid using contractions in your writing, especially if you are unsure of their spelling.**

**EXERCISE
21p** | *Fill in each blank with* their, there, *or* they're. *Capitalize where
needed.*

1. _____ building an addition to _____ house.

2. _____ are some parents who worry constantly about
   _____ children.

3. _____ is a first-aid kit on the shelf.

4. Opera singers must take care of _____ throats.

5. _____ has been an accident on the highway.

6. The Martins say _____ planning to go to Europe.

7. Mr. and Mrs. Olsen are going to sell _____ house.

8. Some people jog while _____ walking _____ dogs.

9. _____ are no houses on that road.

10. She put the keys right _____ on the desk.

11. Fred likes cats because _____ very independent.

12. Is _____ any reason that fathers can't be good parents?

13. I told the children that _____ could be an accident if
    they left _____ roller skates on the stairs.

14. All employees are required to show _____ ID cards at the
    gate.

15. Some people can't sleep when _____ worried.

16. It is difficult to read lists of food ingredients on labels when
    _____ printed in very small type.

17. Sometimes voters wonder if _____ votes really make a
    difference.

18. _____ are two stores and a church on that block.

## THESE, THIS

*These* is plural. It rhymes with *bees*.

**These** people are waiting for a train.

*This* is singular. It rhymes with *miss*.

**This** person wants to ask a question.

**EXERCISE 21q** | *Fill in each blank with the correct word. Capitalize where needed.*

1. All _____ books were written by James Baldwin.

2. One of _____ boxes is empty.

3. He could not solve _____ problems.

4. He knows _____ is our last meeting.

5. We discussed the material in _____ chapters.

6. _____ coat is extremely expensive.

7. The sports news in _____ newspaper is always well written.

8. You should put _____ vegetables in the refrigerator.

9. Because of a computer problem, I will have to do all of _____ work over again.

10. All _____ cold weather is not good for _____ plants.

## THOUGH, THOUGHT

*Though* is a subordinating conjunction. (See Chapter 10.) It means the same as *although* or *in spite of the fact that. Though* sometimes follows the word *even.*

**Though** Henry was tall, he couldn't play basketball.

I felt cold even **though** the heat was on.

*Thought,* as a verb, is the past tense and past participle of *to think.* As a noun, *thought* means "idea."

She **thought** about rearranging the living room.

That is an interesting **thought.**

**EXERCISE 21r** | *Fill in each blank with the correct word. Capitalize where needed.*

1. _____ he spoke softly, everyone could understand him.

2. Mr. Chin _____ his new play would be a success.

3. Joseph Conrad wrote well in English even _____ it was not his first language.

4. In 1948, Dewey _____ he had beaten Truman for the presidency.

5. Even _____ obesity and illness are related, many heavy people remain healthy.

6. Mrs. Holmes _____ she heard a burglar.

7. The _____ of running for student government president had never occurred to him.

8. I didn't call you because I _____ you were out.

9. The soccer players had tried hard, so the coach was pleased even _____ they lost the game.

## TO, TOO

*To* is used to form the infinitive of verbs, for example, *to* see, *to* think. *To* is also a preposition, showing location or direction.

I ran down **to** the corner.

He mailed a package **to** his fiancée.

*Too* can mean "also" or "in addition." *Too* can also mean "excessively" or "overly."

I want to go **too.**

He is **too** noisy.

**EXERCISE 21s**

*Fill in each blank with the correct word.*

1. She wants _____ practice her part _____ make sure she knows it well.

2. Do you want _____ see this movie _____?

3. She speaks _____ softly _____ be heard.

4. He is _____ noisy and aggressive.

5. He asked her _____ sing, but she didn't want _____.

6. Send a copy of this letter _____ the dean and a copy _____ the president _____.

7. Roy got _____ little sleep last night, and so he was _____ tired _____ pay close attention _____ his work.

8. The doorbell is ringing, and the phone is _____.

## WEATHER, WHETHER

*Weather* refers to rain, sun, fog, snow, sleet, and so on.

The **weather** is fine today.

*Whether* is a decision word, showing a choice between one thing and another.

I can't decide **whether** to go to college or to join the Navy.

**EXERCISE 21t**

*Fill in each blank with the correct word. Capitalize where needed.*

1. Rainy _____ has caused a lot of flooding.

2. We listened to the _____ forecast.

3. He can't decide _____ to apply for that job.

4. The _____ can affect people's moods.

5. _____ we like it or not, we all grow older.

6. The forecaster is not certain _____ it will rain or snow tonight.

7. The _____ looked stormy for opening day of the baseball season.

8. He had to decide _____ to go to school full-time or part-time.

9. I have to decide _____ to take my vacation now or during the summer.

10. We were discussing _____ it is better to be a dreamer or a realist.

## WENT, WHEN

*Went* is the past tense of *to go*. It rhymes with *sent*.

I **went** to a friend's house.

*When* means "at the time" or "at what time?" It rhymes with *pen*.

**When** do you get up in the morning?

I cry **when** I slice onions.

**EXERCISE
21u**

*Fill in each blank with the correct word. Capitalize where needed.*

1. He lived in Egypt _____ he was a child.

2. Before she _____ out, she set the burglar alarm.

3. _____ is your next appointment with the dentist?

4. _____ she was young, she _____ to ballet classes.

5. He _____ to the library yesterday.

6. Harriet _____ to her aunt's house.

7. _____ people drink and drive, they endanger many lives.

8. _____ the factory closed, many people lost their jobs.

9. Last summer, we _____ to the beach almost every day.

10. _____ the car alarm _____ off at 3 A.M., it woke us up.

## WERE, WHERE

*Were* is the past tense of the verb *to be*. It rhymes with *fur*.

They **were** late for work.

*Where* means "in what place?" It rhymes with *there*, which means "in that place."

**Where** should I park my car—here or there?

**EXERCISE 21v** | *Fill in each blank with the correct word. Capitalize where needed.*

1.  I put the report down _____ I wouldn't lose it.

2.  No one knew _____ the new books _____ .

3.  Several tape cassettes _____ lying on the table.

4.  Those buildings _____ renovated last year.

5.  Huge snow drifts _____ blocking the road.

6.  Put the hammer back _____ you found it.

7.  Sacks of coffee beans _____ piled in the warehouse.

8.  _____ _____ you last night?

9.  Two cats _____ fighting in the alley.

10. Several newspapers _____ lying near the front door.

11. My brother and I _____ hoping to see Edwina, but she wasn't home, and we didn't know _____ she had gone.

## WHOSE, WHO'S

*Whose* is used to show possession, ownership.

Here comes the poet **whose** book won a prize.

*Who's* is a contraction for *who is* or *who has.*

I met the woman **who's** going to be the next college president. (**who is** going. . . .)

**Who's** been invited to the party? (**Who has** been. . . .)

**EXERCISE 21w**

*Fill in each blank with* whose *or* who's. *Capitalize where needed.*

1. The neighbor _____ lawn mower you borrowed wants it back.

2. I admire Van Gogh, _____ paintings are magnificent.

3. _____ going to speak first?

4. Gandhi, _____ ideas on nonviolence are very important, was influenced by Thoreau.

5. She is a counselor _____ always been honest, yet tactful.

6. Martin, _____ usually quiet, surprised us today.

7. A person _____ not willing to work hard will not last long in this job.

8. _____ umbrella is lying on the desk?

9. Any person _____ taken care of small children knows that child-care givers need energy and patience.

10. Jackie Robinson, _____ major league baseball career started in 1947, had served in the armed forces in World War II.

## YOUR, YOU'RE

*Your* is a possessive and is followed by a noun. It means "belonging to you."

I found **your** socks.

What is **your** schedule like?

*You're* is always a contraction of *you are.*

**You're** late again. (**You are** late. . . .)

Where do you think **you're** going? (. . . think **you are** going?)

**EXERCISE 21x** | *Fill in each blank with the correct word. Capitalize where needed.*

1. If _____ interested in medicine, you should take science courses.

2. _____ family is protected if _____ insured.

3. He is pleased with _____ work.

4. When _____ feet hurt, _____ not comfortable.

5. Do you get nervous when _____ going to speak in public?

6. _____ almost as tall as _____ brother.

7. I can always tell when _____ not telling the truth.

8. Do you use an accountant, or do you fill out _____ income tax forms yourself?

9. You can take the driving test any time you feel that _____ ready.

10. The dentist wants to know if _____ willing to reschedule _____ appointment.

**EXERCISE
21y**

*Fill in each blank with the correct word.*

EXAMPLE    You should ___*have*___ called me as soon as you were ___*all ready*___ to go.
<br>have, of <br> all ready, alréady

1. _____ you like it or not, _____ staying here so
<br>Weather, Whether <br> your, you're

   that we can have a _____ evening at home.
   <br>quiet, quite

2. My _____ was to study harder, _____ you should
<br>advice, advise <br> an, and

   _____ listened to me, but _____ much _____
   <br>have, of <br> is, its, it's <br> to, too

   late now.

3. It is _____ five o'clock; it has _____ a busy day,
<br>all ready, already <br> been, being

   but it has _____ quickly.
   <br>passed, past

4. A warning light in the car _____ on because
<br>went, when

   _____ was a _____ wire in the engine.
   <br>their, there, they're <br> loose, lose, losing

5. _____ people _____ sleeping _____ the fire
<br>These, This <br> were, where <br> went, when

   alarm rang.

6. Mr. Adler was _____ worried because he _____
<br>quiet, quite <br> though, thought

   that he had _____ his wallet.
   <br>loss, lost

7. Ms. Smith did not _____ that bad _____ was
<br>know, no <br> weather, whether

   predicted, and so she did not take _____ umbrella to
   <br>an, and

   work.

8. Because crime has a negative _____ on business,
<br>affect, effect

   merchants want the city to increase _____ police force.
   <br>its, it's

**9.** A candidate for mayor ＿＿＿＿＿＿ unwilling to debate his or
whose, who's

her opponents ＿＿＿＿＿＿ not going to get my vote.
is, its, it's

**10.** ＿＿＿＿＿＿ most recent paper was longer ＿＿＿＿＿＿ more
Your, You're an, and

interesting ＿＿＿＿＿＿ the previous one.
than, then

**EXERCISE 21z** | *Ask someone to dictate each example to you. Then compare what you have written to the original. You could tape record each example, and then write from your own dictation.*

**1.** Losing one of your loved ones can be quite an upsetting experience. It's never easy to accept the loss of someone who's been close to you, whether it's a friend or a relative. The loss can affect your emotions longer than you may expect.

**2.** The brain of an infant needs stimulation in order to reach its full intelligence. Scientists now know that babies whose parents often speak to them and read to them develop more quickly than babies whose parents ignore them for long periods of time. If you're a parent, it's important to talk to and play with your baby often.

**3.** Though many people would like to think that there is an easy, painless way to lose weight, they're fooling themselves. Though the manufacturers of diet pills promise fast and easy weight loss, it is thought that these pills can have a very harmful effect on the body. Doctors advise a sensible diet and moderate exercise if people are serious about losing weight.

**4.** The Mansens thought they were going to have a peaceful, quiet evening. Their plans, however were ruined when the weather changed. A severe storm passd through the area, and heavy rains flooded a river that had already been threatening to overflow its banks. The Mansens were advised to leave their home. They went to an emergency shelter, where thay passed the night, hoping that had not lost their house.

CHAPTER

# 22

# English Idioms for ESL Writers

Learning to speak and write a second language is a great accomplishment, and being bilingual has many advantages. You can already communicate extremely well in English. You are using English at school, at work, and in many other areas of your life.

When speaking or writing, you have probably noticed that a word-for-word translation from your first language into English does not always work. Why not? Each language has its own grammar rules and expressions, its own idioms. **An idiom is a way of putting words together to express a particular meaning.** The meaning of an idiom is not just the translation of each separate word. Although many languages do have similar expressions, each language puts words together differently.

## USING IDIOMS

It would be impossible to list all English idioms in one chapter; it is also impossible to learn idioms well just by studying them in a textbook. To master English idioms, you must do several things. First, read as much as possible in English—newspapers, novels, short stories, magazines. Second, watch some English-language movies and television programs. Third, use new idioms when you speak and write. To help you get started, this section contains some common idioms arranged in categories.

## Idioms Concerning Family and Relationships

| *Idioms* | *Idioms Used in Sentences* |
|---|---|
| to marry (someone)<br>↑<br>no preposition | My father married my mother twenty years ago. |
| to get married to | Maria got married to Tony last year. |
| to end a relationship | I ended my relationship with my boyfriend.<br>↑<br>not *finished* |
| brothers and sisters | I have two sisters and two brothers.<br><small>Since brothers means only males, sisters must be mentioned too.</small> |
| children (any age, even adult) | My parents have three grown children, two sons and one daughter. |
| relatives (people in the extended family) | All my relatives have brown eyes. |
| to be pregnant with (a baby) | I was very happy when I was pregnant with my first child. |
| to take care of (a child) | I told my sister that I would take care of her children while she went to the dentist. |
| to be divorced from | Marilyn was divorced from George last year. |
| to get a divorce from | He wants to get a divorce from his wife. |
| to divorce (someone)<br>↑<br>no preposition | Edna divorced her husband Henry two years ago. |

## Idioms Concerning Times and Dates

| *Idioms* | *Idioms Used in Sentences* |
|---|---|
| on (a specific day) | We will have a test on Monday. |
| | Alex was born on June 2, 1980. |
| in (a month, a year) | He was born in June. |
| | Ann and Jim were married in 1975. |
| at (a time) | My job interview begins at ten A.M. |

**BRIEF PRACTICE 22.1**    *Write a sentence answering each question. The first one is done as an example.*

1. How many children do your parents have?

   *My parents have two children, one daughter and one son.*

2. Choose any relative. What person did that relative marry and when?

3. Do you have any brothers and sisters?

4. On what day were you born?

5. In what month did you graduate from high school?

6. In what year was your best friend born?

## Idioms Concerning Age and Physical Conditions

| *Idioms* | *Idioms Used in Sentences* |
|---|---|
| to be ( ) years old | My brother is six years old. |
| to weigh ( ) pounds | I weigh one hundred and ten pounds. |

| Idioms | Idioms Used in Sentences |
| --- | --- |
| to be (   ) feet tall | She is five feet, three inches tall. |
| to be hungry | He was very hungry all day. |
| to be thirsty | I am very thirsty. |

---

**BRIEF PRACTICE 22.2**    *Write a sentence answering each question. The first is done as an example.*

**1.** How old is your best friend?

*My best friend is twenty-four years old.*

**2.** How old are you?

_____

**3.** How tall are you?

_____

**4.** Were you hungry or thirsty this morning?

_____

---

## Idioms Concerning Emotions

| Idioms | Idioms Used in Sentences |
| --- | --- |
| to be afraid of | I am afraid of snakes. |
| to be angry with (or at) | Your brother will be angry with you if you take his bike. |
| to feel left out (to feel alone and unloved) | All her friends were at a party, and Rosa felt left out. |
| to be tired of doing something | They are tired of working and want to go home. |
|  | I am tired of cooking; let's go out for dinner. |
| to be satisfied with | Some children are not satisfied with what they get. |
| to look up to (to admire) | I really look up to my father. |
| to be confused about | She is confused about her future; she is not sure what major to choose. |

**BRIEF PRACTICE 22.3**   *Write an answer to each question. The first one is done as an example.*

**1.** Are you satisfied with something? What is it?

*I am satisfied with my new job.*

**2.** Are you afraid of something? What is it?

_____

**3.** Are you tired of doing anything? What is it?

_____

**4.** Are you confused about something?

_____

**5.** Do you look up to any special person?

_____

## Idioms Concerning Thinking

| Idioms | Idioms Used in Sentences |
| --- | --- |
| to agree with (someone or something) | I agree with most of your ideas. |
| | I agree with you that voting is important. |
| | I do not agree with you that chess is boring. |
| to be in agreement with | I am in agreement with most of your ideas. |
| to agree to (to accept a plan or a suggestion, to be willing) | The union agreed to the terms of the new contract. |
| | My bank has agreed to give me a loan. |
| to think about (*or* of) | I am thinking about majoring in biology. |
| | I am thinking of asking him to the dance. |
| to think for oneself (to be independent) | You are old enough to think for yourself and to make your own decisions. |
| to think only of oneself (to be selfish) | Those people think only of themselves, never of their neighbors. |
| to be right | I thought it would rain, and I was right. |

| Idioms | Idioms Used in Sentences |
|---|---|
| to be wrong | Edward thought the grocery store was open, but he was wrong. |
| to make a decision | He has to make a very important decision. |

---

**BRIEF PRACTICE 22.4**    *Write an answer to each question. The first one is done as an example.*

**1.** What are you thinking about doing?

*I am thinking about looking for a summer job.*

**2.** Do you agree or disagree with your best friend's ideas?

_____

**3.** I thought it would rain today. Was I right or wrong?

_____

**4.** When did you make an important decision?

_____

---

## Idioms Concerning Behavior and Action

| Idioms | Idioms Used in Sentences |
|---|---|
| to pay attention to (someone or something) | She did not pay attention to my advice |
| | He pays close attention to the instructor. |
| to adjust to | It is not always easy to adjust to a new neighborhood. |
| to attend school | By law, children must attend school until |
| | ↑ no preposition |
| | they are sixteen years old. |
| to let (someone) do something | My parents will not <u>let me go</u> out by myself. |
| to allow (someone) to do something | My parents will not <u>allow me to go</u> out by myself. |
| to spend a vacation | We spent our vacation in Mexico. |
| | ↑ not *passed* |

| *Idioms* | *Idioms Used in Sentences* |
|---|---|
| to stop (doing something) | Please stop talking during the movie. |
| to stop to (do something) | I am very busy, but I always have time to stop to talk to you. |
| to have a (good, bad) time | Did you have a good time at the beach? |

---

**BRIEF PRACTICE 22.5**    *Write an answer to each question. The first one is done as an example.*

1. When did your friend stop smoking?

    *My friend Gloria stopped smoking almost five years ago.*

2. Where did you spend your last vacation?

    _____

3. Do you allow your young children to watch violent shows on television?

    _____

4. Do you let your children watch whatever they want on television?

    _____

5. What school are you attending?

    _____

---

## Idioms Concerning Speaking, Persuasion, Command, and Wishes

| *Idioms* | *Idioms Used in Sentences* |
|---|---|
| to tell (a lie, the truth) | He is telling a lie, but they are telling the truth. |
| to speak (to someone) | I must speak to you immediately. |
| to say (that . . .) | She says that she will be a little late to work today. |
| to tell (someone that . . .) | Nobody told me that the library was closed. |

| Idioms | Idioms Used in Sentences |
|---|---|
| to tell (someone) to do something | Ms. Rios told her children to go to sleep. |
| to invite (someone) to do something | My friend invited me to go with her to the movies. |
| to ask (someone) to do something | Mr. Tan asked us to drive him to the bus station. |
| to remind (someone) to do something | Bill reminded Alex to lock the front door. |
| to convince (someone) to do something | Ms. Smith convinced him to apply for a better job. |
| to want (someone) to do something | My parents want me to study for hours every night. |
| to make (someone) do something | My parents made me study several hours every night. |
| to force (someone) to do something | My parents forced me to study several hours every night. |
| to dream of being (or any *ing* word) | I have always dreamed of being a famous actor. |
| | Many people dream of winning the lottery. |

**BRIEF PRACTICE 22.6**   *Write an answer to each question. The first one is done as an example.*

1. What did your professor remind you to do?

*My professor reminded me to review the class notes every evening.*

2. What did your friend ask you to do?

3. Can you tell if a person is telling a lie or the truth?

4. Did someone convince you to do something? What was it?

5. What does the manager want the clerks to do?

**EXERCISE
22a**

*Write a sentence using each suggested idiom.*

*EXAMPLE*    was tired of

*I was tired of doing the same things every day, so last
week I decided to make some changes in my daily
routine.*

**1.** is ten years old

**2.** I agree with

**3.** were married last year

**4.** ended our relationship

**5.** thinks only of himself

**6.** was thinking about

**7.** not telling the truth

_____

_____

_____


**EXERCISE 22b** | *Write a sentence using each suggested idiom.*

**1.** always agree with her

_____

_____

_____

**2.** were very hungry

_____

_____

_____

**3.** made him quit his job

_____

_____

_____

**4.** allow us to go out

_____

_____

_____

**5.** let us go out

_____

_____

_____

CHAPTER

# 23

# Advice for ESL Writers

Students who are learning English as a second language (ESL) have many strengths. It is a great cultural and intellectual accomplishment to speak and write more than one language. If English is not your native language, however, you may face special challenges in writing standard edited English. Many chapters in this book provide information that is particularly useful to ESL students:

| | |
|---|---|
| articles ("the," "a," and "an") | Chapter 20 |
| confusing words | Chapter 21 |
| "ed" endings | Chapters 15, 16, and 24 |
| idioms | Chapter 22 |
| irregular verbs | Chapter 15 |
| progressive verb forms | Chapter 17 |

This chapter concentrates on the following areas that may be especially useful to ESL writers:

Forming questions

Using adjectives

Dealing with singular and plural amounts

## FORMING QUESTIONS

In English, statements and questions are not formed the same way. In most (but not all) sentences that make a statement, the subject comes before the verb. In most questions, the verb has two or more words, and the subject is placed in between them. Compare the following statements and questions. The subjects are *italicized,* and the verbs are **boldfaced.**

| Statements | Questions |
|---|---|
| *We* **are** late for class. | **Are** *we* late for class? |
| The *flowers* **were** on the table. | **Were** the *flowers* on the table? |
| *Ms. Martinez* **works** downtown. | **Does** *Ms. Martinez* **work** downtown? |
| *He* **closed** the window. | **Did** *he* **close** the window? |
| *You* **were writing** a letter. | **Were** *you* **writing** a letter? |
| *Mr. Jenkins* **has been promoted.** | **Has** *Mr. Jenkins* **been promoted?** |
| That *package* **should have been sent.** | **Should** that *package* **have been sent?** |

**EXERCISE 23a**

*Rewrite each statement so that it is a question.*

*EXAMPLES*   **a.** You know the answer.

*Do you know the answer?*

**b.** Laura has written her sales report.

*Has Laura written her sales report?*

1. The rain is still falling.

_____

_____

2. You are angry at your friend.

_____

_____

3. We washed all the dishes.

_____

_____

4. The baby has been sleeping all afternoon.

_____

_____

5. Ms. George has worked at the nursing home for a long time.

_____

_____

6. The letter should have been mailed this morning.

_____

_____

7. You have been notified of the change in the schedule.

_____

_____

8. This cat will eat any brand of cat food.

_____

_____

9. The tree fell onto the fence.

_____

_____

10. Ms. Carter was working in her garden.

_____

_____

## USING ADJECTIVES

Adjectives are words that describe people, places, things, and ideas. Adjectives answer the question *what kind?* (See Chapters 19 and 27.) English and other languages do not always use adjectives in the same way.

### Regular Adjectives Describing Singular or Plural Nouns

Unlike many other languages, English does not have different forms of adjectives for singular and plural. In the following examples, the adjectives are in **boldface.** In the first example of each pair, the adjective describes a singular noun; in the second example, the adjective describes a plural noun.

A **happy** child is playing in the yard.

Two **happy** children are playing in the yard.

My answer to the third math problem is **different** from yours.

My answers to all the math problems are **different** from yours.

This flower looked **beautiful.**

These flowers looked **beautiful.**

Whether the adjective is describing something singular or plural, the adjective itself does not change.

**BRIEF PRACTICE 23.1**    *Write a sentence using each phrase. Then make the phrase plural and use it in another sentence. The first one is done for you.*

**1.** an interesting book

*I was reading an interesting book last night.*

*interesting books*

*I have read some interesting books this year.*

**2.** a different idea

_____

_____

_____

**3.** an official letter

_____

_____

_____

**4.** a helpful neighbor

_____

_____

_____

## The Difference Between Adjectives Ending in *ing* and *ed*

In English, many verbs can be transformed into adjectives by adding *ing* or *ed* to the base form. Then the new adjective can be used to describe a person, place, or thing. Look at the following examples:

| *Verb* | *Adjective* | *Adjective Used to Describe a Noun* |
|---|---|---|
| to irritate | irritating | I hear a very **irritating** noise. |
| | irritated | The **irritated** man shouted at the noisy children. |

If the person, place, or thing is *performing an action,* choose the *ing* form. If the person, place, or thing is *having an action done to him, her,* or *it,* choose the *ed* form. Look at this example:

The movie is **boring.**

**To bore** is a verb that sometimes means "to put to sleep with dullness." The movie is *doing the action;* it might put people to sleep. Therefore, we choose the *ing* form, *boring,* to describe the movie. The adjective *boring* means "dull, unexciting." Now let's look at another example:

Mary was really **bored** by the movie.

Mary is not doing the action. She is not putting people to sleep. The action is being done to her by the movie, so to describe Mary, we use the *ed* form, *bored.*

In general, the adjective *bored* means "tired, not interested":

Mary was often **bored.**

Now let's consider the difference in meaning when we use the *ing* form, *boring,* to describe Mary:

Mary is **boring.**

The last example is a criticism of Mary; it says that Mary is a dull person with nothing interesting to say. Here are a few more examples of adjectives ending in *ing* and *ed.* Consider the differences in meaning between these two forms:

This is an **exciting** game.

The **excited** fans were shouting at the players.

Yesterday I had a long, **tiring** shift at work.

I was extremely **tired** at the end of the day.

That new roller coaster ride was very **frightening.**

The **frightened** passengers screamed.

**BRIEF PRACTICE 23.2**     *Choose the correct word for each sentence. The first one is done for you.*

1. boring, bored          The mayor gave a very *boring* speech.

2. irritating, irritated     A really _____ thing happened to me at work.

3. terrifying, terrified     After the explosion, _____ people ran from the building.

4. interesting, interested   My young son is really _____ in dinosaurs.

**EXERCISE 23b**     *Write a sentence using each adjective to describe a person, place, thing, or idea.*

EXAMPLE     exhausting     *The ten-hour bus ride to Maine was exhausting.*

exhausted     *Some exhausted passengers slept during the ride.*

1. annoying     _____

_____

annoyed     _____

_____

2. depressing     _____

_____

depressed     _____

_____

**3.** exciting

      excited

**4.** interesting

      interested

**5.** pleasing

      pleased

**6.** trusting

      trusted

**7.** boring

      bored

**8.** satisfying

      satisfied

## Nouns Used as Adjectives

English is a very flexible language that can use one word in many different ways. (See Chapter 19.) Many English expressions use a noun to describe another noun so that the first noun is working as an adjective. Here is a list of some common expressions:

| | |
|---|---|
| baseball cap | marriage ceremony |
| boy scout | library book |
| bus driver | biology professor |
| girl scout | marriage license |
| football player | ticket seller |
| tennis player | apartment building |
| town hall | bank loan |
| insurance policy | tomato juice |
| health insurance | table manners |
| school policy | day-care center |
| life insurance | college courses |
| apple pie | milk carton |
| vegetable garden | water pitcher |
| flower garden | government grant |
| science teacher | brain surgery |
| engagement party | |

Notice that these expressions do not use the possessive 's. In each expression, the first noun does not possess the second noun but has become an adjective to answer the question "what kind?" For example, what kind of surgery? *Brain* surgery. What kind of grant? A *government* grant.

**EXERCISE 23c**

*Write a sentence using each phrase.*

*EXAMPLE*   movie reviewer

*That movie reviewer did not like "Men in Black," but I did.*

**1.** taxi driver

_____

_____

**2.** biology professor

_____

_____

**3.** library book

_____

_____

**4.** sports news

_____

_____

**5.** soccer ball

_____

_____

**6.** history book

_____

_____

**7.** family reunion

_____

_____

**8.** child psychology

_____

_____

**9.** city streets

_____

_____

**10.** weather forecast

_____

_____

## USING AMOUNTS

## Count and Noncount Nouns

In English, many nouns can be counted one at a time and can be added to each other—one book, two books, one thousand books, and so on. These kinds of nouns are called **count nouns.** Count nouns can be singular or plural. Here are some examples:

| Singular Count Nouns | Plural Count Nouns |
| --- | --- |
| pencil | pencils |
| dollar | dollars |
| baby | babies |
| investment | investments |
| idea | ideas |
| chair | chairs |
| necklace | necklaces |
| assignment | assignments |

**Noncount nouns** name things that are general categories and cannot be counted one at a time. Each noncount noun is always singular; it has no plural form. Here are examples of noncount nouns:

| | |
| --- | --- |
| homework | Spanish |
| jewelry | English |
| furniture | luggage |
| wisdom | information |
| advice | patience |

How can you tell if a noun is count or noncount? Ask yourself these questions: Can I have *one* of this thing? Can I have *two* of it? For example, take the word *bracelet.* Can you have *one bracelet* or *two bracelets?* Yes, you can, so the word *bracelet* is a count noun. Now take the word *jewelry.* Can you have *one jewelry* or *two jewelry?* No, you cannot, so *jewelry* is a noncount noun.

**BRIEF PRACTICE 23.3**    *Identify each noun as count or noncount. The first one is done for you.*

1. scientist    *count*

2. jewelry    _____

3. luggage    _____

4. daughter    _____

5. furniture    _____

6. information    _____

## Demonstratives

The words *this, that, these,* and *those* are called demonstratives. These words show (demonstrate) the distance between the speaker and a particular noun. *This* and *these* indicate nouns that are close. *That* and *those* indicate nouns that are not close. **Use *this* or *that* with a singular noun. Use *these* or *those* with a plural noun.** Look at the following examples:

| Demonstratives with Singular Nouns | Demonstratives with Plural Nouns |
| --- | --- |
| this subject | these subjects |
| that book | those books |
| this idea | these ideas |
| that child | those children |
| this page | these pages |
| that apartment | those apartments |

Look at the following examples of demonstratives working in full sentences. Each demonstrative is in **boldface.**

**This** package is much heavier than **that** one.

**These** children are in first grade, and **those** children are in fourth grade.

Please mail **this** letter as soon as possible.

**That** house at the end of the block is for sale.

**BRIEF PRACTICE 23.4**   *If a noun is singular, write the singular demonstratives* this *and* that *in the blanks. If a noun is plural, write the plural demonstratives* these *and* those *in the blanks. The first one is done for you.*

1. *these* computers          *those* computers

2. _____ assignments          _____ assignments

3. _____ house          _____ house

4. _____ building          _____ building

5. _____ words          _____ words

**EXERCISE 23d**   *Write a sentence using each phrase.*

*EXAMPLE*   this money

*I have to return this money because it does not belong to me.*

**1.** several people

_____

**2.** these papers

_____

**3.** a lot of homework

_____

**4.** this newspaper

_____

**5.** beautiful jewelry

_____

_____

**6.** too much furniture

_____

_____

**7.** her knowledge

_____

_____

**8.** that information

_____

_____

**9.** those jobs

_____

_____

**10.** this work

_____

_____

CHAPTER

# 24

# Word Endings

Sometimes writers forget the endings of words. It is easy to see why this happens. People seldom actually pronounce all the letters in a word, especially those at the end. If words are written just as they are pronounced, they may lack word endings. By far the most troublesome endings are the *ed* and the *s*.

The exercises in this chapter will help you spot and identify troublesome word endings. With practice, you will be able to use these word endings correctly in your writing.

## "S" ENDINGS

The endings *s*, *'s*, and *s'* appear at the end of words for different reasons.

1. **Natural spelling:** The word may have a natural *s* ending.

| | | |
|---|---|---|
| sometimes | Gladys | Mr. Peters |
| boss | possess | economics |
| always | perhaps | news |

2. **Plural nouns:** Most (not all) plural nouns end in *s*. (See Chapter 29.)

bridge**s**      idea**s**
babie**s**       wive**s**
building**s**

3. **Possessives:** *'s* and *s'* show ownership or relationship. Use *'s* in most cases.

Jane**'s** brother is a musician.

Mary**'s** friend is coming to visit.

When a word already ends in *s* (as most plural nouns do), you may add just an apostrophe to the end of the word.

Student**s'** opinions are important.

Both boy**s'** uniforms need cleaning.

In some cases where a noun ends in *s*, the possessive may be formed **either** by adding just an apostrophe **or** by adding *'s*.

Jack is Charles**'** best friend.

Jack is Charles**'s** best friend.

In some cases, adding another *s* after the apostrophe is preferable.

Thomas**'s** left arm hurts.

The boss**'s** daughter works here.

4. **Contractions:** *'s* may stand for *is* or *has*.

He**'s** been sick for three days. (He has. . . .)

That**'s** a good idea. (That is. . . .)

What**'s** the matter? (What is. . . .)

5. **Third-person singular verbs:** In the present tense a third-person singular verb ends in *s*. (See Chapter 14.)

he believe**s**      he ha**s**
she trie**s**        she doe**s**

**Note:** Do *not* use the *s* ending with the following helping verbs:

**can**      He *can* type.

**may**      It *may* snow.

| | |
|---|---|
| **ought** | He *ought* to know better. |
| **should** | She *should* be here. |
| **must** | She *must* be here tomorrow. |

In the following exercises, when you identify an *s* ending, give its full name. Don't say just "plural"; say "plural noun." Don't say "singular"; say "singular verb." Using the full name will reinforce the fact that **a noun with an *s* ending is plural, but a verb with an *s* ending is in the singular form.**

One boy run**s**.

Two boy**s** run.

**EXERCISE 24a** | *Circle all s, 's, and s' endings and identify them as natural spelling, plural noun, possessive, contraction, or singular verb.*

*possessive*          *singular verb*    *natural spelling*

EXAMPLE   A person's choice of career affects his whole life.

1. Charles Morel's motorcycle needs new handlebars.

2. It's been raining for six hours.

3. Carlos wants to see his friend's new car.

4. The guard checks those floors three times an hour.

5. It's difficult to drive when it's snowing.

6. The debate begins in fifteen minutes.

7. George always asks if he's late.

8. Mrs. Smith's writing style gets many compliments.

9. A child's bicycle was in Mr. Young's garage.

10. She believes that there are risks in certain tests for heart disease.

**EXERCISE 24b** | *The* s, 's, *and* s' *endings have been left out. Add the right ending wherever one is missing, and identify it as natural spelling, plural noun, possessive, contraction, or singular verb.*

*singular verb     contraction*

*EXAMPLE*   No one think*s* that it*'s* going to rain.

1. Mariela run five time a week.

2. Of all the mammal, the whale the biggest.

3. Bob sometime speak before he think.

4. Mr. Anderson cake look deliciou.

5. A child emotional health can be affected by how she treated.

6. When there a long drought, many crop suffer.

7. Sam cat Fluffy need to be fed.

8. Ruth speak English and Spanish, and she read two other language.

9. Many of Ted problem could be easily solved.

10. There a good restaurant just two block away.

**EXERCISE 24c** | *In the following paragraph circle and identify the* s *endings as natural spelling, plural noun, possessive, contraction, or singular verb.*

Each year for the past ten years, Alice has planted a garden. She's always believed that gardening brings many benefits. It's obvious that saving money on food is one benefit, but it's not the only one. Gardening also provides exercise and a chance to escape from the day's worries.

| **EXERCISE 24d** | *In the following paragraphs,* s *endings have been left out. Add the right endings where necessary and identify each as natural spelling, plural noun, possessive, contraction, or singular verb. Note: There may be spelling changes when the* s *is added.* |

**1.** When a person walk into Nancy house, he see a spotles living room. All the rug are vacuumed, and the furniture gleam. The window are clean, and there not one speck of dust. Nancy a very tidy person, but sometime I think she overdo it.

**2.** A person who exercise four or five time a week receive several benefit. First, exercising strengthen a person heart. Second, it help the lung to function better. Third, it a good way to lose weight. Finally, it refresh a person and give her more energy.

**3.** Year ago, a zoo purpose wa to display animal. Large animal were put in small cage, which did not resemble their natural surroundings. These day, a zoo serve many purpose. It give people a chance to see rare creature, but it also protect many type of animal from becoming extinct.

**4.** New research suggest that a human being brain need a lot of stimulation in the first twelve month of life. It not enough just to feed and wash an infant. When a parent talk and sing to a baby, the child brain develop well. If a parent do not interact with the baby during those first important month, the brain do not develop well.

## PROOFREADING FOR MISSING "S" ENDINGS

Consider the following sentence:

Ten scientists were working on ten projects.

Write the sentence on a separate sheet of paper. Did you spell the words *scientists* and *projects* correctly? If you did, fine! If you misspelled either word, did you have a problem with the final *s?* The plural of *scientist* is *scientists;* the plural of *project* is *projects. Scientists* and *projects* are difficult words to pronounce; you really have to work to articulate the final letter *s* on each word.

Now consider this sentence:

A rebel resists authority.

Write it on a separate sheet of paper. Did you have trouble with the word *resists?* It is the third-person singular form of the verb *to resist.* The singular form is needed in this sentence because it is about **one** rebel—"a rebel."

Remember that the *s* ending on a noun is the sign of the **plural;** the *s* ending on a verb is the sign of the third-person **singular.** Read aloud the following pairs of sentences, and notice where the *s* endings are placed. Then recopy the sentences on a separate sheet of paper and check your spelling.

One scientist persists in his work.

Two scientists persist in their work.

A writer corrects her essay carefully.

Writers correct their essays carefully.

## TRICKY "S" ENDINGS

Watch out for words that end in *sk, sp, ct,* or *st.* They are difficult to pronounce when the letter *s* is added, but words like *desk, mask, fact, ask, risk, lisp,* and so on will need *s* endings at times.

**EXERCISE 24e**

*The following nouns end in* st, sk, *or* ct. *On the line next to each noun, write the plural form, and then use the plural form in a sentence. Read each sentence aloud, pronouncing each word carefully.*

*EXAMPLE* desk  *desks*
*The desks are new.*

1. scientist _____

_____

**2.** addict _____

_____

**3.** test _____

_____

**4.** guest _____

_____

**5.** desk _____

_____

**6.** risk _____

_____

**EXERCISE 24f** | *Change each of the following verbs to its third-person singular form and then use it in a sentence.*

*EXAMPLE*    inject _injects_
_The baby doctor injects his patients with vaccines._

**1.** resist _____

_____

**2.** ask _____

_____

**3.** insist _____

_____

**4.** detect _____

_____

**5.** suspect _____

_____

**6.** lisp _____

_____

## "ED" ENDINGS

The *ed* ending is used in the simple past tense of most verbs. (See Chapter 15 for past tense.)

Marion walk**ed** quickly down the corridor.

He cautiously stepp**ed** over the roller skate.

The *ed* ending is also used to form many past participles. (See Chapter 16.)

She said she had never receiv**ed** your letter.

I should have realiz**ed** how late it was.

He has discover**ed** a new way to cook onions.

The package has been deliver**ed.**

The frighten**ed** cat crept under the sofa.

There are two abandon**ed** buildings on this block.

**EXERCISE 24g** | *Circle the* ed *endings in past tense verbs and past participles. Do you know why each* ed *is necessary? Review Chapters 15 and 16 if necessary.*

1. The experiment you stopped must be continued.

2. An injured man was rushed to the hospital.

3. He was delayed and might have missed the bus.

4. This ruined house will be knocked down soon.

5. She has received an unexpected promotion.

6. By next week, the experiment will have been completed.

7. Irritated by his neighbors, he decided to move.

8. I felt exhausted after a day of concentrated work.

9. The deserted building is supposed to be renovated.

10. Some concerned citizens have planned to write to their legislators.

**EXERCISE
24h**

*In this exercise,* ed *endings have been omitted. Add* d *or* ed *where appropriate to past tense verbs and past participles. Note: You may have to double a consonant or change spelling in some words when you add* ed.

*EXAMPLE*   You  should  have  answer $\overset{ed}{\wedge}$ the  letter.

1. The  highway  was  cover  with  spill  gasoline.

2. He  becomes  irritate  when  he  is  frustrate.

3. This  unaddress  letter  cannot  be  mail.

4. Dissatisfy  with  the  movie,  some  customers  have  demand  their  money  back.

5. The  train  was  suppose  to  have  arrive  an  hour  ago.

6. They  were  shock  that  the  President  propose  new  taxes.

7. He  was  amaze  to  find  that  the  door  wasn't  lock.

8. The  delight  audience  applaud  the  high  school  chorus.

9. He  burn  himself  while  cooking,  and  then  he  drop  the  skillet.

10. Children  may  become  enrage  if  their  questions  are  not  answer.

**EXERCISE
24i**

*Circle the* ed *endings on past tense verbs and past participles.*

1.   A  serious  accident  occurred  last  night  when  two  cars  rushed  through  an  unmarked  intersection  and  collided.  Both  drivers  were  injured,  and  one  car  was  totally  destroyed.  The  accident  could  have  been  avoided  if  the  town  had  installed  a  traffic  light.

2.   Six  people  were  injured  yesterday  in  a  fire  that  apparently  started  in  an  attached  garage  that  stored  crumpled  paper,  rags  covered  with  oil,  and  half-used  cans  of  paint.  The  fire  started  at  3  A.M.,

probably ignited by a lighted cigarette, and raced quickly through the house. Awakened by the fire, all six members of the frightened family escaped, though they were badly affected by smoke inhalation and suffered severe burns.

**EXERCISE 24j**  *In the following paragraphs,* ed *endings have been left off the ends of past tense verbs and past participles. Add the missing* d *or* ed *where necessary.*

1.   The tomb of King Tut was not discover until the twentieth century. When the first explorer enter the tomb, he saw many treasures, jumble together and pile in disorganize heaps. Among the priceless objects were carve vases, beautifully decorate boxes, and polish jewelry.

2.   Should smoking be ban in all public places? Smoke exhale by one person is inhale by people locate nearby. Therefore, even nonsmokers can be harm as well as inconvenience by smoking.

3.   A distinguish man has suggest that people and nations that have not study the mistakes of the past are doom to repeat those mistakes. Not having learn about previous failures, they may be tempt to take ill-consider actions and to make uninform decisions.

## PROOFREADING FOR DIFFICULT "ED" ENDINGS

Consider the following sentence:

Juana finally got used to getting up at 5:30 A.M.

Read the sentence aloud to yourself. Then, without looking back at the book, write it on a separate piece of paper. Now compare what you have written with the sentence in the book.

Did you spell the word *used* correctly? If you did, good! If you didn't, perhaps you left out the *d* for a reason. The word *used* is often misspelled because it is frequently followed by the word *to,* which begins with a *t* sound that seems to swallow up the *d* sound at the end of the word *used*. You really have to work to **articulate** the two sounds. Read the following sentences out loud:

> Jorge **used** to walk his dog every morning at 6:30.

> He said he didn't mind getting up at 6:00 because he was **used** to it.

> His dog, Spot, was also **used** to getting out early.

Did you pronounce the words *used to* clearly? Now rewrite the three sentences on a separate piece of paper. Then check your sentences to make sure they match the sentences in the book.

Another word combination that gives many students trouble is *supposed to*. Look at this sentence:

> Billy is **supposed** to do his homework before he watches television.

Now rewrite the sentence on a separate piece of paper and check your sentence against what is written in the book.

The *d* in the phrase *supposed to* is often forgotten for the same reason that the *d* in the phrase *used to* is forgotten. Ask somebody to read the following sentences to you so that you can write them on a separate piece of paper. Then proofread your three sentences for spelling errors.

> Carol is **supposed** to baby-sit for her little brother today.

> Eddie was **supposed** to call me last night.

> Students are **supposed** to proofread all essays.

---

**BRIEF PRACTICE 24.1**    *Now make up three sentences of your own, using the phrase* supposed to.

1. _____

_____

2. _____

_____

3. _____

_____

From now on, whenever you use the phrase *supposed to* or *used to,* remember the tricky *d* endings.

Be careful, however, not to put a *d* where it does not belong. You do not need a *d* every time you use the words *suppose* or *use.* For example, it is not necessary in the following sentences:

I suppose you have done your work.

Jane will use the car tonight.

In order to proofread correctly, you must be aware of when *ed* endings are required and when they are not. If you have trouble in this area, review Chapters 15 and 16.

## PROOFREADING SUGGESTIONS

Many of the editing strategies discussed in Chapter 7 can be helpful as you proofread for missing *ed* and *s* endings. Review these strategies as needed, and consider the following:

1. Proofread once just for *ed* endings, and then proofread just for *s* endings.

2. Before proofreading, write down on scrap paper the reasons for using an *ed* ending, and review these notes as you proofread for *ed* endings. Use the same strategy when you proofread for *s* endings.

3. You can sharpen your proofreading skills by doing dictation exercises. Ask a friend to read to you from a book or magazine. (A tape recorder can be helpful too.) Write what you heard, and then carefully reread what you have written, proofreading for word endings. Then check your sentences carefully against the original.

**EXERCISE 24k** | *Add* s *and* ed *endings where necessary. Note: spelling changes may be needed.*

*EXAMPLE*    Several tiger*s* had escape*d* from the zoo.

1. It been several year since he has visit his cousins.

2. That state has legalize gambling.

3. Mrs. Moffat son was marry last week.

4. After he had chop the wood, he put all the log in a pile.

5. He suppose to meet me at six.

6. Various kind of pet can provide companionship for mentally disturb people.

7. Kyra is depress because she will miss the track meet if her sprain ankle does not heal.

8. New type of vegetable that can resist many disease are develop every year.

9. Some dog have been train to aid handicap people.

10. Ruth brother get enrage when supper late.

**EXERCISE 24l** | *Ask someone to read the following sentences to you. As each sentence is read, write it down on a separate piece of paper. Then check the spelling of each word in the sentence.*

1. The teacher always asks why the desks have marks on them.

2. A student who ignores facts risks making mistakes.

3. Halloween masks are often made to look like beasts.

4. Two disks glowed in the dark sky.

5. Four scientists worked hard on four different projects.

6. God exists, but ghosts do not exist.

7. Janet has a baby, and she insists on washing her baby's toys every day.

8. Cleo often asks why the tests are always so hard.

**EXERCISE 24m** *Ask someone to read the following sentences to you. As each sentence is read, write it down on a separate piece of paper. Then check the spelling of each word in the sentence.*

1. She was surprised to learn that the abandoned building was supposed to be renovated.

2. Parents are supposed to be involved in their children's activities.

3. Students are supposed to prepare carefully for their classes.

4. The governments of major cities are supposed to provide shelters for the homeless.

5. The Coast Guard told the reporters that the bodies of the drowned sailors could not be recovered.

6. They felt satisfied after eating Kathy's home-cooked dinner.

7. My cousin used to live in Arizona before he got married.

8. Elderly hospital patients may become depressed and feel that their families have abandoned them.

Note that Exercises 24a, 24c, 24g, and 24i can also be used for dictations.

CHAPTER

# 25

# Using Pronouns Correctly

Something is wrong with the following paragraph. Can you see what it is?

Mary is studying to be a doctor. Mary hopes to attend medical school after Mary has completed college. Since Mary's grades are excellent, especially in science, Mary hopes to win a scholarship. Mary's parents are very proud of Mary.

The paragraph above is awkward because no pronouns have been used. Instead, the noun **Mary** or its possessive form **Mary's** has been used over and over again.

**EXERCISE 25a**    *On the lines below, rewrite the paragraph, substituting the pronoun* she *or* her *where appropriate.*

> Mary is studying to be a doctor. Mary hopes to attend medical school after Mary has completed college. Since Mary's grades are excellent, especially in science, Mary hopes to win a scholarship. Mary's parents are very proud of Mary.

_____

_____

_____

_____

_____

_____

You can see that substituting *she* or *her* for *Mary* or *Mary's* improves the paragraph. Obviously pronouns play an important role in writing, so you should learn to use them correctly.

## PRONOUNS AND THEIR ANTECEDENTS

A **pronoun** is a word we use to substitute for a noun. If we analyze the word *pronoun,* we get:

**pro** (for) + **noun.**

So **pronoun** literally means "for a noun."

The word that the pronoun replaces is called the **antecedent.** Look at the following sentences:

antecedent                                              pronoun

James is very reliable. A person can always count on him.

*Him* is the pronoun. It refers to *James,* so *James* is the pronoun's **antecedent.**

**BRIEF PRACTICE 25.1**   *In each of the following sentences, circle the pronoun and draw an arrow from the pronoun to its antecedent. Write the word "pronoun" over the pronoun and "antecedent" over the antecedent. The first one is done for you.*

*antecedent*                                    *pronoun*

1. Television is fine, but people should not watch it all the time.

2. Some thoughtless people do not realize when they are being selfish.

3. The cat kept her kittens very clean.

4. Geometry is a difficult subject, but it can be mastered by most students.

Here is a list of common personal pronouns. Notice that these pronouns are the words used as the subjects of verbs.

| Singular | Plural |
|---|---|
| I | we |
| you | you |
| he, she, it | they |

Other common personal pronouns are the following:

| Singular | Plural |
|---|---|
| me, my | us, our |
| your | your |
| him, her, his, its | them, their |

Another group of pronouns is as follows:

| Singular | Plural |
|---|---|
| myself | ourselves |
| yourself | yourselves |
| herself, himself, itself | themselves |

**Note:  In standard English there are no such words as *hisself, theirself,* and *themself.***

**EXERCISE
25b**

*In the following sentences circle each personal pronoun and draw an arrow from the pronoun to its antecedent.*

*EXAMPLES*   **a.**  Jim was in the crowded room, but I couldn't see (him.)

**b.**  Rick liked the house because (it) was modern.

**c.**  Dr. Anderson telephoned (her) husband.

1.  Soccer is very popular; it is now considered the foremost sport in the world, and millions of people follow its famous international competition, the World Cup Championship.

2.  Soccer gets its name from "assoc.," an abbreviation for "association football."

3.  On a soccer field, most of the players are not permitted to touch the ball with their hands; they usually move the ball by kicking it.

4.  One of the most famous soccer players of all time is Pelé; he did much to promote the popularity of the game by amazing crowds with his skill.

5.  Born in Brazil as Edson Arantes do Nascimento, Pelé played for the Brazilian national team and became its star.

6.  Although Pelé retired from competition in 1974, he returned when the New York Cosmos offered him a three-year contract.

7.  Many young women are becoming interested in soccer as they discover what a wonderful game it is.

8. A promising young girl from a local high school has been playing soccer since she was six years old, and she is now coaching her own team.

9. Whenever this young athlete has a soccer game, her whole family goes to watch her play and to cheer for her and her team.

10. Soccer owes its growing popularity to the energy of its young supporters, to electrifying players like Pelé, and to the excitement of the game itself.

## PRONOUNS REFERRING TO "ING" WORDS

Sometimes a pronoun replaces an *ing* verb form that is being used as a noun. For example:

antecedent                                    ┌── pronoun
   ↓
Swimming is fun, and it is good exercise too.

In the sentence above, the pronoun *it* replaces *swimming,* a verb form that is being used as a noun.

---

**BRIEF PRACTICE 25.2**    *Circle the pronouns and draw arrows connecting them to their antecedents.*

1. Writing is an important skill because it is necessary for many occupations.

2. Physical fitness experts say skiing is good exercise because it tones the body.

3. Rollerblading is popular in most major cities because it provides a quick and exciting way to get around.

## PRONOUN-ANTECEDENT AGREEMENT

When a pronoun replaces a singular noun, the pronoun must be singular. When a pronoun replaces a plural noun, the pronoun must be plural. In other words, **a pronoun must agree with its antecedent.** Look at the example below:

antecedent (plural)

*CORRECT:* The books were overdue, so Fred hurried to the library to return them ←

plural pronoun referring to *books*

Suppose the sentence said:

*INCORRECT:* The books were overdue, so Fred hurried to the library to return it ←

singular pronoun;
does not agree with *books*

Such a sentence would be very confusing because of the agreement error, the mismatch between the pronoun and the antecedent.

Look at the following sentence and explain why it might confuse the reader:

*INCORRECT:* Snowstorms are common in January, so we must be prepared for it.

Can you correct the sentence?

---

**BRIEF PRACTICE 25.3**   *Circle the correct pronoun for each sentence. Then draw a line from the pronoun to its antecedent.*

1. The store went out of business because no one liked (its, their) merchandise.

2. The room looked large because (they, it) had mirrors on two of (its, their) walls.

3. Prescription medicines can be dangerous, so don't misuse (it, them).

## PRONOUN-ANTECEDENT AGREEMENT WITH COMPOUNDS

As we learned when we studied subject-verb agreement, a compound subject is usually considered plural because we are talking of more than one thing. If a pronoun refers to a compound formed with *and,* that pronoun must be plural. For example:

compound antecedent

Danger and hardship are not pleasant to experience, but they make interesting subjects for books.

plural pronoun
referring to two things:
*danger* and *hardship*

Both the country and the city have their attractions.

plural pronoun to agree with
*country* and *city,* compound
antecedent.

The president spoke about ignorance and poverty; he said that we must eliminate them.

plural pronoun to agree with
*ignorance* and *poverty,* compound
antecedent

**BRIEF PRACTICE 25.4**   *In the following sentences, circle the correct pronouns and draw a line from them to their antecedents.*

1. The rutted roads and freezing temperatures made (its, their) contribution to the traffic problems of the city.

2. Both Bob and Allen were at the party, but Karen had not seen (him, them) yet.

3. Love and money can both cause problems, and most people have trouble with (it, them) at some point in their lives.

## PRONOUN-ANTECEDENT AGREEMENT WITH COLLECTIVE NOUNS

Some nouns represent a group of people—for example, *family, team, committee, jury, audience,* and *tribe.* These words are usually treated as singular; therefore, verbs and pronouns that agree with them are singular. Consider the following sentence:

The committee meets every week, and its meetings usually

     ↑       ↑                 ↑

   collective   third-person       singular pronoun to
   noun        singular verb     agree with *committee*

last one hour.

Sometimes a writer wishing to emphasize the individual members of a group may treat a collective noun as a plural.

The team are packing their bags for their trip.

    ↑     ↑         ↑           ↑

  collective  plural        plural pronouns
  noun      verb

In a reference to a group as a whole, American usage favors treating it as a singular. To refer to the individual people in a group, it is better to use the word *members.* Look at the following examples:

The baseball team is having a good season; it has won

           ↑   ↑               ↑

      collective   singular verb     singular pronoun
      noun                to agree with *team*

every game.

The members of the baseball team are very happy because

   ↑                           ↑

  plural subject              plural verb

they have won every game.

↑

plural pronoun to
agree with *members*

When deciding whether to use a singular or plural pronoun, remember to be consistent. If a noun has been treated as a singular in the first part of the sentence, it should continue to be considered singular. Do not switch in the middle of a sentence.

The team is playing well this season, and it (*not* they) hopes to win the pennant.

The verb *is* in the first part of the sentence shows us that *team* is here considered singular. It is one unit, so in the second part of the sentence the singular pronoun *it* must be used.

---

**BRIEF PRACTICE 25.5**    *Circle the correct pronoun and draw a line from the pronoun to its antecedent.*

1. The team has played (its, their) best games recently.

2. Members of the audience rose to (its, their) feet after the performance.

3. The committee presents (its, their) recommendations after each of (its, their) monthly meetings.

---

**EXERCISE 25c**    *Circle the correct pronoun for each sentence and draw a line from the pronoun to its antecedent.*

*EXAMPLE*    Both Mrs. Jones and Mrs. Reed earned (their, her) Master's degrees last year.

1. The jury has reached (its, their) verdict.

2. Regular exercise is good because (it, they) will strengthen the heart.

3. The committee is ready to submit (its, their) report.

4. If you see Frank and Lisa, tell (her, them, him) to make an appointment with Mr. Rivers.

5. The football team looks at videotapes of (its, their) past games.

6. Ms. Ruiz is interested in stamps, so she reads many articles about (it, them).

**7.** The Transportation Commission is going to open (their, its, his) meetings to the public.

**8.** The chairperson of the committee has announced that (it, they) will meet in June.

## GENDER AND PRONOUNS

Gender means sexual identity, that is, whether something is masculine or feminine. When we refer to a male antecedent, we use one of the masculine pronouns: *he, him,* or *his.* When we refer to a female antecedent, we use one of the feminine pronouns: *she* or *her.* In most cases, when we refer to an animal or a thing, we use one of the neuter pronouns: *it* or *its,* although occasionally a masculine or feminine pronoun may be used for an animal (or, rarely, a feminine pronoun for a ship). Notice that in the plural, whether the antecedent of the pronoun is masculine, feminine, or neuter, the third-person pronouns are the same: *they, them,* or *their.*

| Singular | Plural |
|---|---|
| The house had its shutters painted. | The houses had their shutters painted. |
| The man was carrying his briefcase. | The men were carrying their briefcases. |
| The woman was carrying her briefcase. | The women were carrying their briefcases. |
| The cat was caring for her kittens. | The cats were caring for their kittens. |

## Indefinite Singular Pronouns and Gender

The following pronouns are always considered singular:

*anybody* (think: any single body)

*anyone* (emphasize the *one*)

*each* (think: each and every *one*)

*either* (think: either *one*)

*everybody* (think: every single body)

*everyone* (emphasize the *one*)

*neither* (think: neither *one*)

*nobody* (think: not *one* single body)

*no one* (think: not *one*; also note that *no one* is two words)

*somebody* (think: some particular body)

*someone* (emphasize the *one*)

These pronouns often act as the antecedents for other pronouns:

**Everybody** has (his) problems.

**Everyone** has (her) work to do.

In the past it was common practice to use only the masculine pronoun to refer to a word that could be either masculine or feminine, as in this example:

Anybody can succeed if **he** works hard at **his** job.

Nowadays some people object to the custom of using *he, his,* or *him* when gender is unknown. They suggest using *she* or *her* also. For example:

Anybody can succeed if *he* or *she* works hard at *his* or *her* job.

Sometimes this form is awkward, especially when you have to repeat *he or she* or *his or her* many times. For this reason, when people speak, they often use the plural pronouns *they, them,* and *their* to express indefinite gender. For example, many people may say, "Everyone should do their own work," using the plural *their* with the singular *everyone* because *their* is neither masculine nor feminine. Although this usage is allowable in spoken English, it is technically an agreement error because *everyone* is singular and *their* is plural. Written English must be more precise than spoken English. Therefore, even though sentences like "Everyone should do their own work" are permissible in speech, they should be avoided in writing.

## Pronouns for People in General

When you write about people in general, you can find alternatives to words like "everybody" and "anyone" or phrases like "any doctor" or "every student." For example, you can use plural phrases like "most people," "all doctors," "many parents," or "most college students." Look at the following pairs of sentences:

A judge should make his decisions carefully.

All judges should make their decisions carefully.

A parent must feed her children nutritious meals.

Parents must feed their children nutritious meals.

All these sentences are grammatically correct, but in the second sentence of each pair, using the plural allows us to include all people. Not all judges are men, and not all parents are women.

**EXERCISE 25d**    *Circle the correct pronoun or pronouns and draw an arrow to the antecedent.*

*EXAMPLES*    **a.**  All people want a good future for (his or her, (their)) children.

**b.**  Has anybody left (their, (his or her)) car windows open?

1.  Anyone who wants a scholarship must send in (their, his or her) application soon.

2.  Everyone on the girls' soccer team must pick up (her, their) uniform.

3.  Three people started a safety patrol in (his, their) neighborhood.

4. One of the boy scouts has forgotten (his, her, his or her, their) cap.

5. Some players on the girls' basketball team have forgotten (their, her) sneakers.

6. Everyone has (his or her, their) own dreams and ambitions.

7. All people have (his or her, their) own dreams and ambitions.

8. Most people can improve (their, his or her) reading comprehension if (they, he or she) will read a good newspaper every day.

9. Anybody who wants to check out books must present (his or her, their) library card.

10. All employees at the hospital are required to wear (his or her, their) identity badges to work each day.

## DIFFERENT PRONOUNS FOR DIFFERENT USES

When you talk about yourself as a **subject,** you use the pronoun *I.* For example:

**I** will get tickets to the play.

When you talk about yourself as the **object** of a verb or a preposition, you use the pronoun *me.* For example:

Jack told **me** that he will buy tickets for **me.**

All of the students except **me** are going on the trip.

Similarly, the pronouns *we, he, she,* and *they* are used as subjects, but the pronouns *us, him, her,* and *them* are used as objects. The pronoun *you* can be used as either a subject or an object. Look at the following chart with examples:

| *Pronouns Used as Subjects* | | *Pronouns Used as Objects* | |
|---|---|---|---|
| I | **I** am working hard. | me | Believe **me.** Look at **me.** |
| you | **You** are cute. | you | I like **you.** I am crazy about **you.** |
| he | **He** is my friend. | him | I have known **him** for many years. I go everywhere with **him.** |
| she | **She** runs the business. | her | Everyone admires **her.** Everyone looks up to **her.** |
| it | The dog is running. **It** is running. | it | Mark sees **it.** Mark runs after **it.** |
| we | **We** are honest. | us | Everyone trusts **us.** Everyone thinks well of **us.** |
| they | **They** always sit on the porch. | them | We see **them** every day. We pass by **them** on our way to work. |

Straightforward examples like those above do not present problems. But there are a few areas where people make grammatical errors in choosing between the subject pronouns and the object pronouns. We will look at these in the next section.

## USING THE CORRECT PRONOUN WITH A COMPOUND SUBJECT OR OBJECT

Nobody would say, "Me went to the store," or "Ken gave a ride to I," but sometimes people make similar mistakes when they say, for example, "Me and Robert went to the store" or "Ken gave a ride to Mary and I." Look at the sentences corrected below:

Robert and ~~me~~ *I* went to the store.

Use *I* as a subject, and out of courtesy put it second.

Ken invited Mary and ~~I~~ *me* to dinner.

Use *me* as the direct object.

Ken gave a ride to Mary and ~~I~~ *me*.

Use *me* as the object of the preposition *to*.

Just between you and ~~I~~ *me*, I like him.

Use *me* as the object of the preposition *between*.

---

**BRIEF PRACTICE 25.6**   *Choose the correct word.*

1. Hilda and (I, me) like to swim.

2. Just between you and (I, me), her new hat is ugly.

3. Here comes Jane. (She, Her) and Bill have been married for a year.

---

**TIP**

Sometimes it helps to pretend that the pronoun is alone. In other words, drop part of the compound and hear how the sentence sounds. In number 1 above, drop the words **Hilda and**; then ask yourself, should it be **I** or **me like to swim?**

**EXERCISE
25e**    *Circle the correct pronoun. On the line at the left state whether the
pronoun is used as a subject or object.*

EXAMPLES    <u>*subj.*</u>    **a.** Mr. Zola and (me, (I)) were promoted.

           <u>*obj.*</u>    **b.** The owner offered new contracts to Billy and
(I, (me)).

_____    **1.** My brother and (I, me) like to go hiking.

_____    **2.** The man was worried because (he, him) and his wife were lost
in the woods.

_____    **3.** Mr. Sitler sent a memo to Jim and (I, me).

_____    **4.** The Battistas showed (we, us) pictures of their new baby.

_____    **5.** The new editor and (I, me) are working together.

_____    **6.** Some members of the Chess Club invited Rona and (I, me) to an
exhibition.

_____    **7.** They feel superior to (we, us).

_____    **8.** Alice lets Sam and (I, me) do all the cooking.

_____    **9.** My sister and (I, me) play tennis often.

_____    **10.** Jake never talks to Diane and (I, me).

_____    **11.** My mother taught my sister and (I, me) to knit.

_____    **12.** Sally and (he, him) had a party for (we, us).

**EXERCISE 25f**

*The following passage contains pronoun errors. Correct them by changing pronouns or antecedents. The first sentence is done. (Note: When you change a pronoun from plural to singular or vice versa, you may also have to change a verb.)*

                                                 *their*

    Reading is a good way for people to develop ~~his~~ vocabulary. Finding new words and looking it up in the dictionary will help a student when they write their compositions. Reading is a way a person can improve themselves intellectually.

    Reading is also valuable for the pleasure it provides. When a person reads, they can imagine many things and mentally travel many places beyond their ordinary experience. Books and magazines are like cars and trains in a way because it can take a person where they have never been before.

    A teacher can encourage reading in their classes. They can make a chart and have every student in the class put a mark on them whenever they have read a book. The teacher can also have his or her students give reports on interesting books or articles he or she has read. In this way a student can develop the reading habit in their early years.

**EXERCISE 25g**

*Review one of your recent compositions looking for pronouns. Remember that all pronouns (except the indefinite pronouns—see pages 330–331) should have clear antecedents. Circle each pronoun you find and draw an arrow from the pronoun to its antecedent. If you find any pronoun errors, make corrections.*

CHAPTER

# 26

# Avoiding Double Negatives

In standard English a negative clause usually has only **one** negative word. Look at the following examples:

I have **no** money. (I do **not** have any money.)

We **scarcely** ever see each other.

I do**n't** want any of that.

Have**n't** you ever gone bowling?

We **hardly** ever go to the movies.

We **never** see Ken anymore.

Each example has just one negative word (in boldface). Each example expresses a negative idea.

If there are two or more negative words, the meaning of the sentence changes. The negative words cancel each other out. Look at the next examples.

*INCORRECT:*  I do**n't** have **no** money.

*CORRECT:*  I **don't** have any money.

*INCORRECT:*  We do**n't scarcely** ever see each other.

*CORRECT:*  We **scarcely** ever see each other.

*INCORRECT:*  I do**n't** want **none** of that.

*CORRECT:*  I do**n't** want any of that.

*INCORRECT:*  Have**n't** you **never** gone bowling?

*CORRECT:*  Have**n't** you ever gone bowling?

*INCORRECT:*  We do**n't hardly** ever go to the movies.

*CORRECT:*  We **hardly** ever go to the movies.

*INCORRECT:*  We **never** see Ken **no** more.

*CORRECT:*  We **never** see Ken anymore.

If you want a clause to be negative, use just one negative word. Here is a list of some negative words:

| | | |
|---|---|---|
| hardly | no one | rarely |
| never | not (n't) | seldom |
| no | nothing | |
| nobody | nowhere | |
| none | scarcely | |

**BRIEF PRACTICE 26.1**    *Rewrite the following sentences, changing all but one of the negatives. The first two are done for you.*

   1. I don't never go to no dances.

   *I don't ever go to any dances.*

   or *I never go to any dances.*

   2. She doesn't owe nothing to nobody.

   *She doesn't owe anything to anybody.*

   or *She owes nothing to anybody.*

   3. We scarcely never buy clothes.

   _____

   _____

   4. Guy hardly never sees his brothers.

   _____

   _____

   5. They don't know nothing about history.

   _____

   _____

   6. George doesn't have no brothers or sisters.

   _____

   _____

   7. I don't have no time to finish nothing.

   _____

   _____

**EXERCISE 26a** | *Most of the following sentences contain too many negative words. On the line below each incorrect sentence, rewrite the sentence correctly. If the sentence is correct, mark it "c" and leave the line below it blank.*

_____   **1.** He doesn't have nothing to say.

_____   **2.** Mary doesn't need allergy pills no more.

_____   **3.** Henry does not enjoy waiting for nobody.

_____   **4.** Don't you never say that again.

_____   **5.** She says she doesn't get no answers to her questions.

_____   **6.** My strange neighbor scarcely ever leaves his house.

_____   **7.** The child doesn't have no shoes or socks on.

_____   **8.** This bus isn't hardly ever on time.

_____ **9.** The newspaper didn't print nothing about the big fire on Main Street.

_____

_____

_____ **10.** My boss won't listen to no explanations for being late.

_____

_____

_____ **11.** Nobody ever does anything to improve the registration process.

_____

_____

_____ **12.** Ms. Bonilla hardly misses none of her classes.

_____

_____

_____ **13.** The baby was sick, but she has not had a fever in the past two days.

_____

_____

_____ **14.** Some apartment buildings don't allow tenants to keep no pets.

_____

_____

_____ **15.** Mr. Whitfield loves his job, and he says he won't never retire.

_____

_____

CHAPTER

# 27

# Using Modifiers Correctly

A **modifier** is a descriptive word or group of words. To modify means to change. Think of a man. Now think of a **tall** man. *Tall* is a modifier; it describes *man*. It made you change your mental image. Now think of a **tall, thin** man. *Thin* is another modifier. Each time a modifier is added, you have to change, or modify, your idea of the man. Now think of a **tall, thin** man **in a green overcoat.** The words *in a green overcoat* are a phrase used to modify the word *man.* Add another modifier to what we already have: a *tall, thin,* _____ *man in a green overcoat.*

## ADJECTIVES

A modifier that describes a noun or a pronoun is called an **adjective.** (See Chapter 19.) Here are some examples:

Two red cars stopped at the traffic light.

The words *two* and *red* are adjectives modifying *cars.* Remember that an adjective answers the question "how many?" or "what kind?" How many cars? **Two.** What kind of cars? **Red.** The word *traffic,* which is usually a noun, is here used as an adjective. What kind of light? A **traffic** light.

Note: **The words *a, an,* and *the* are adjectives. They modify nouns. Sometimes these three adjectives are called articles. Do not forget them in the following exercises.**

---

**BRIEF PRACTICE 27.1**   *Circle the adjectives in the following sentences and use arrows to show what word each adjective modifies.*

1. For Luis, the cool, quiet library was a refuge from the hot, noisy, crowded streets.

2. By the dusty roadside the discouraged driver stared at the overheated engine of the old car.

3. Mary-Lou Brook had a calm manner and gave sensible advice; she was a great comfort to troubled friends.

---

Sometimes adjectives can be spotted by the way they end. Many adjectives end with the letters *ful—hopeful,* for example. Here are some more adjectives with the *ful* suffix (word ending):

careful          hopeful          restful

Can you think of some more adjectives ending in *ful?*

_____   _____   _____

**SPELLING TIP**

Note the spelling of the *ful* suffix. It has only one *l.*

Other adjectives have the suffix *less:*

careless          hopeless          restless

Note the difference in the meanings of the *ful* and *less* suffixes.

Can you think of some more adjectives ending in *less?*

_____   _____   _____

Another adjective suffix is *able:*

adorable          curable          desirable          lovable

Now add some of your own adjectives ending in *able.*

_____   _____   _____

Another adjective suffix is *ible:*

edible          horrible          legible

Now add some of your own adjectives ending in *ible.*

_____   _____   _____

Many adjectives end in *y:*

fancy          hairy          lazy

Add some of your own adjectives to this list.

_____   _____   _____

There are many other adjective suffixes, such as:

ent (independent)_____

ant (expectant)   _____

ious (envious)   _____

ous (horrendous) _____

ive (suportive)   _____

ish (selfish)   _____

Can you think of at least one other example for each suffix?

Adjectives can be made from verbs. Present participles (*ing* verbs) can be adjectives, and so can past participles (past participles often end in *ed,* but there are many irregular forms; see Chapter 15).

For example, look at the following sentence:

The sleeping child lay on a broken sofa.

*Sleeping* is the **present participle** of the verb *to sleep*. Here it is used as an adjective to modify *child. Broken* is the **past participle** of the verb *to break*. It is being used as an adjective to modify *sofa.*

---

**BRIEF PRACTICE 27.2**   *Make adjectives from the following verbs by adding* ing *and write them in the blanks in the following sentences. The first one is done as an example.*

cry       *crying*                help _____

scream _____          burn _____

sleep     _____

1. The *crying* baby kept everyone awake.

2. We should try to lend a _____ hand.

3. There is an old saying, "Let _____ dogs lie."

4. The _____ siren told us that the fire engine was going to a _____ building.

---

## ADVERBS

A modifier that describes a verb is called an **adverb.** (See Chapter 19.) For example, consider the following sentence:

Henry runs swiftly.

The word *swiftly* is an adverb. It tells how Henry runs. Adverbs often answer the question "how?" Here is another example:

Mr. Kay has probably finished his work.

The word *probably,* an adverb, modifies the verb *has finished.*

Adverbs can also modify other adverbs. Consider this sentence:

Henry runs (very) (swiftly.)

Here the word *very* is an adverb modifying the adverb *swiftly*. How swiftly? *Very* swiftly.

Adverbs can also modify adjectives. Look at this sentence:

Carlos is (very) (intelligent.)

Here the word *very* is an adverb modifying *intelligent*. And *intelligent* is an adjective modifying *Carlos,* a noun. Remember: Adjectives answer the question "what kind?" Adverbs answer the question "how?" What kind of person is Carlos? Intelligent. How intelligent? *Very* intelligent.

The word *too,* like *very,* is a common adverb used to modify an adjective or another adverb.

Bill works (too) (slowly.)

*Slowly* is an adverb modifying the verb *works. Too* is an adverb modifying the adverb *slowly*. How does Bill work? Slowly. How slowly? *Too* slowly.

The soup is (too) (hot.)

*Hot* is an adjective modifying the noun *soup. Too* is an adverb modifying the adjective *hot*. What kind of soup? Hot. How hot? *Too* hot.

---

**BRIEF PRACTICE 27.3**    *Circle the adverbs in the following sentences and draw an arrow from each adverb to the word it modifies. The first one is done as an example.*

1. Karen writes (very) (well.)

2. We thought very carefully about the problem.

3. It was unbearably hot in the room.

4. Ms. Brown speaks very slowly, clearly, and precisely.

Adverbs often end in the suffix *ly*. Many adjectives can be converted to adverbs by adding the *ly* ending, as shown below:

| *Adjective* | *Adverb* |
|---|---|
| clear | clearly |
| graceful | gracefully |
| sincere | sincerely |
| real | really |

Notice how the words are used:

| | | |
|---|---|---|
| Adj. | clear | Mrs. Jones always gives **clear** instructions. |
| Adv. | clearly | Mrs. Jones always gives instructions **clearly.** |
| Adj. | graceful | Viola is a **graceful** dancer. |
| Adv. | gracefully | Viola dances **gracefully.** |
| Adj. | sincere | Susan is a **sincere** person. |
| Adv. | sincerely | Susan always speaks **sincerely.** |
| Adj. | real | Homelessness is a **real** problem. |
| Adv. | really | Homelessness is **really** a serious problem. |

**EXERCISE 27a** | *Change the given adjective to an adverb and then use the adverb in a sentence.*

*EXAMPLE*   Adjective: careful     Sandra is a careful person.
Adverb: __*carefully*__   *Sandra does things carefully.*

1. Adjective: quick        He gave a quick answer.

   Adverb: _____   _____

   _____

2. Adjective: probable     It is probable that the senator will be reelected.

   Adverb: _____   _____

   _____

**3.** Adjective: intense      Bill was intense when he played
                              tennis.

   Adverb: _____      _____

                        _____

**4.** Adjective: sincere      Jeanette sounded sincere when she
                              regretted that she could not attend the
                              party.

   Adverb: _____      _____

                        _____

**5.** Adjective: selfish      Mike was selfish when he gobbled up
                              all of the candy without sharing it.

   Adverb: _____      _____

                        _____

**6.** Adjective: effective      The medicine was effective; it cleared
                              up the rash.

   Adverb: _____      _____

                        _____

## A SPECIAL PROBLEM: "GOOD" AND "WELL"

*Good* is an adjective. It modifies a noun:

   These are good cookies.

   This is a good book.

   He is a good ballplayer.

*Well* is usually an adverb. It usually modifies a verb.

   Roberta sings well.

   I did well on the exam.

   My typewriter works well now.

**Note: Linking verbs such as *feel, taste,* and *seem* connect the subject with an adjective:**

Ice cream tastes **good.**

He feels **good** about helping others.

He feels **bad** about the accident.

Sometimes *well* can be an adjective meaning "healthy":

Mary seems well now; she has made a good recovery.

You look good today. ⎫
You look well today. ⎬ Both statements are gramati-
        ⎭ cally correct, but they have
         slightly different meanings.

---

**BRIEF PRACTICE 27.4** *Use either* good *or* well *to fill in the blanks, and then draw an arrow to the word modified. The first two are done.*

1. The senator speaks _____*well*_____ .

2. He is a ____*good*____ speaker.

3. You did a _____ job on that report.

4. Your _____ work is _____ known.

5. Pelé played soccer very _____ .

6. Dr. Gomez is a _____ psychologist.

7. Apple pie tastes _____ .

**BRIEF PRACTICE 27.5**   *In most of the following examples, the words* good *and* well *have been used incorrectly. Find the errors and correct them. If the sentence is correct, mark it "c." The first two have been done for you.*

*c*   **1.** Brian writes good stories.

                    *well*

      **2.** Doris Lessing writes ~~good~~; she is a good novelist.

      **3.** We all work good together.

      **4.** I did good on the test.

      **5.** Mimi feels good about performing good.

      **6.** That tastes well.

      **7.** Pierre speaks English good now.

      **8.** The new copier is working good.

      **9.** Rice and beans go well together.

      **10.** Rice and beans taste good together.

**EXERCISE 27b**   *In the sentences below, circle the correct modifier and write "adj." or "adv." above it. Then draw a line from the modifier to the word it modifies. Remember:* good *is an adjective;* well *is usually an adverb.*

*EXAMPLES*   **a.** Bert thought that chess was (impossible, *(adv.)* (impossibly)) complex.

      **b.** Escape from the prison was (*(adj.)* (impossible), impossibly).

      **c.** Max will (sure, *(adv.)* (surely)) arrive on time.

      **1.** The bus fare will (probable, probably) increase.

      **2.** Rick does (good, well) in geometry.

3. I felt (certain, certainly) that Mary would win the contest.

4. The play was (enthusiastic, enthusiastically) applauded.

5. The car was (total, totally) destroyed in the accident.

6. Some people talk (endless, endlessly) on the telephone.

7. Mr. Reyes works (quiet, quietly) but (effective, effectively).

8. Leslie did (good, well) on the police exam.

9. The store was (unusual, unusually) busy.

10. You play the clarinet (extreme, extremely) (good, well).

## COMPARATIVE FORMS OF ADJECTIVES

When comparing two things:

| | |
|---|---|
| add *er* to a short adjective: | use the word *more* before a longer adjective: |
| hard $\longrightarrow$ harder | difficult $\longrightarrow$ more difficult |
| The second puzzle is harder than the first. | The second puzzle is more difficult than the first. |

**Note: Use <u>either</u> the *er* suffix (word ending) <u>or</u> the word *more* before the adjective. But <u>never</u> use both together.**

**BRIEF PRACTICE 27.6**   *Write the comparative form of the adjective given, and then use it in a sentence. The first two are done as examples.*

1. funny _funnier_ _Ray thinks that "Laugh It Up" is funnier than any other show._

2. eventful _more eventful_ _This year has been more eventful than last year._

3. nice _____ _____

_____

4. helpful _____ _____

_____

5. beautiful _____ _____

_____

6. early _____ _____

_____

## SUPERLATIVE FORMS OF ADJECTIVES

When comparing three or more things:

add *est* to a short adjective:

young—youngest
    Jean is the **youngest**.
    member of the firm.

pretty—prettiest
    It was the **prettiest**
    picture in the gallery.

use the word *most* before a longer adjective:

youthful—most youthful
    Emma is the **most youthful** member of the senior citizens' club.

beautiful—most beautiful
    It was the **most beautiful** day of summer.

**Note:  Use <u>either</u> the *est* suffix <u>or</u> the word *most* before the adjective. But <u>never</u> use both together.**

**BRIEF PRACTICE 27.7**    *Write the superlative form of the adjective given and then use it in a sentence. The first one is done for you.*

1. terrible *most terrible*    *Hurricane David was the most terrible storm of the season.*

2. sharp _____    _____

_____

3. dark _____    _____

_____

4. intelligent _____    _____

_____

Here is a list of comparative and superlative forms of some common adjectives. Note that the first two are irregular.

| Regular Form | Comparative Form | Superlative Form |
|---|---|---|
| good | better | best |
| bad | worse | worst |
| fine | finer | finest |
| lonely | lonelier | loneliest |
| silly | sillier | silliest |
| remote | more remote | most remote |
| horrible | more horrible | most horrible |
| incredible | more incredible | most incredible |

## COMPARATIVE AND SUPERLATIVE FORMS OF ADVERBS

We add *more* or *most* before most adverbs:

efficiently        more efficiently        most efficiently

Mitchell works efficiently. Karen works **more efficiently.** Vinnie works **most efficiently** of all.

## A SPECIAL CASE: "GOOD, BETTER, BEST" AND "BAD, WORSE, WORST"

As we have learned, *good* is an adjective, but *well* is usually an adverb.

He is a **good** player.

He plays **well.**

The comparative and superlative forms of *good* and *well* are *better* and *best.* Both *better* and *best* can be used as either adjectives or adverbs.

Better (comparative)

Used as an adjective:   Judy is a **better** player than Sam.

Used as an adverb:   Judy plays **better** than Sam.

Best (superlative)

Used as an adjective:   The third product is the **best.**

Used as an adverb:   Karen plays well, George plays better, and Marge plays **best** of all.

The comparative and superlative forms of both the adjective *bad* and the adverb *badly* are *worse* and *worst.* These words can be used as either adjectives or adverbs. It is important to remember that *worse* is comparative; you use it to compare two things. *Worst* is superlative; you use it to compare three or more things.

Worse (comparative)

Used as an adjective:   Sam is a **worse** player than Judy.

Used as an adverb:   Sam plays **worse** than Judy does.

Worst (superlative)

Used as an adjective:   The third product is the **worst.**

Used as an adverb:   Karen plays badly, George plays worse, and Marge plays **worst** of all.

This chart summarizes these forms:

|  | Regular Form | Comparative | Superlative |
|---|---|---|---|
| **Adjectives** | good | better | best |
|  | bad | worse | worst |
| **Adverbs** | well | better | best |
|  | badly | worse | worst |

**Note: Standard English has no such words as *worser*, *worsest*, or *bestest*.**

**EXERCISE 27c**    *Fill in each blank with* worse *or* worst.

*EXAMPLE*    It was the *worst* storm in five years.

1. Alcohol was his _____ enemy.
2. The first movie was bad, the second was _____, and the third was the _____ of all.
3. The _____ part of his speech was at the beginning.
4. *A Tale of Two Cities* begins, "It was the best of times; it was the _____ of times."
5. I thought my singing was bad, but his is _____.
6. Of all the tenors in the chorus, he is the _____.
7. What was the _____ experience of your life?
8. As the days went by, her illness got _____.
9. My problem is _____ than yours.
10. Murder is _____ than theft.
11. The air-conditioning always breaks down at the _____ possible moment.
12. Who was _____, Rasputin or Robespierre?
13. This pie tastes bad, this one is _____, and this one is the _____ of all.

**14.** Which is _____, a flat tire at midnight on a lonely road or a terrible rainstorm during a picnic?

**15.** In high school, history was Raul's _____, subject, but now he excels at it.

**EXERCISE 27d**

*Fill in each blank with* better *or* best.

*EXAMPLE*   Joan had two job offers, so she took the job that paid ___*better*___.

**1.** Marie was _____ prepared for her driving test the second time she took it, so she passed.

**2.** Phil thinks that his college years have been the _____ part of his life.

**3.** Charles Dickens said, "It was the _____ of times; it was the worst of times."

**4.** My cat won a prize as the _____ in the show.

**5.** People often think of youth as the _____ time in a person's life, but some people say that their fifties are

_____ than their twenties were.

**6.** The inexperienced rider asked for the _____ horse in the stable.

**7.** People who are enjoying themselves often say, "Life doesn't get

any _____ than this."

**8.** Of the two plans proposed, the committee decided that Plan A

was _____.

**9.** The developer of Plan B was convinced that his plan was really

the _____ of the two.

**10.** Many people have said that everything gets worse before it gets

_____.

## AVOIDING MISPLACED AND DANGLING MODIFIERS

When using modifiers, be sure that the modifying word or words are clearly connected to the element in the sentence that they modify. Place a modifier as close as possible to what it modifies. If a modifying word is misplaced, the meaning of the sentence may not be clear. For example:

*UNCLEAR:*   Greta only said that she would be back in five minutes.

This sentence is unclear. The reader may wonder: Is this the only thing Greta said, or did she mean that she would return in only five minutes? It would be better to move the modifying word "only" closer to what it modifies:

*IMPROVED:*   Greta said that she would be back in only five minutes.

If a modifier is a group of words, a phrase, make sure that the phrase is placed logically within the sentence. Consider the following:

*UNCLEAR:*   The President wrote his speech while he was riding on a train on the back of an envelope.

The modifying phrase "on the back of an envelope" should be closer to the verb "wrote" because that is what it is supposed to modify.

*IMPROVED:*   The President wrote his speech on the back of an envelope while he was riding on a train.

If a modifier has nothing that it can logically describe in a sentence, it is called a **dangling modifier.**

*CONFUSING:*   After graduating from high school, my family moved to L. A.

dangling modifier

The words *after graduating from high school* have nothing in the sentence to modify. The whole family did not graduate from high school. This sentence can be revised as follows:

*CLEAR:*   After graduating from high school, I moved to L. A. with my family.

OR

*CLEAR:*   After I graduated from high school, my family moved to L. A.

**Hint: Dangling modifiers often occur at the start of a sentence. If your sentence starts with a modifier, make sure that it can logically modify an element in your sentence.**

When a sentence contains a misplaced or dangling modifier, it will confuse the reader because of its lack of logic and clarity. Thus, careful writers avoid this problem in order to maintain sentence coherence (see Chapter 13).

**EXERCISE 27e**  *Most of the following sentences contain misplaced or dangling modifiers. Circle these words or phrases and rewrite the sentences on the lines below. If the sentence is correct, make no changes.*

*EXAMPLE*  (At the age of five,) Richard Wright's father abandoned his family.

*When Richard Wright was five, his father abandoned the family.*

1. For each child who comes to Family Fun Day at the Garden Shop, there will be a package of seeds, accompanied by a parent.

   _____

   _____

2. After searching for an hour, my wallet was found.

   _____

   _____

3. John had finished the most difficult part of the job almost when he felt tired and took a break.

   _____

   _____

4. Recognized as a gifted conductor, Andre Previn has won many awards.

   _____

   _____

**5.** After driving for three hours, a terrible thunderstorm began.

_____

_____

**6.** At the age of ten, Lucy's mother gave her a lovely doll.

_____

_____

**7.** Running down the street, the bus was early and Sam chased it.

_____

_____

**8.** Running down the street, Sam chased the bus, which had come early.

_____

_____

**9.** Recognized as a talented writer, many awards were won by Wright.

_____

_____

**10.** After publishing many fine novels, the Nobel Prize was awarded to Saul Bellow.

_____

_____

CHAPTER

# 28

# Capitalization

Using capital letters in the right places is an important writing convention. If you write your papers by hand, be sure to make your capital letters clear. Here are some basic rules for capitalization.

**1.**

> Capitalize proper nouns, that is, the names of specific people and places. Capitalize initials.
>
> Jack **J.** Jones and Jessica **Q.** Hunter hiked from the **T**appan **Z**ee **B**ridge in **N**ew **Y**ork **S**tate to the **G**olden **G**ate **B**ridge in **C**alifornia.
>
> **K**im **W**oodhall graduated from **C**entral **H**igh **S**chool in **G**len **V**iew, **K**ansas.
>
> BUT
>
> That new student in our class comes from a high school in another state.

**2.**

> Capitalize the first-person singular pronoun *I* wherever it appears in a sentence. (But do not capitalize *me* and other pronouns.)
>
> Doreen told me that **I** had bought the wrong size blouse for her.

**3.**

> Capitalize the first word of each sentence. Do not capitalize after a semicolon (unless another rule applies).
>
> **T**he opening of the new supermarket attracted many people.
>
> **J**ohn is a long-distance runner; he runs fifteen miles a day.
>
> **J**ohn runs distance races; **M**ary runs sprints.

**4.**

> Capitalize titles like doctor or professor when used as part of a name, but not when used in general.
>
> I saw **P**rofessor Adams walking with two other professors.
>
> When I went to see **D**r. Green, he advised me to have an operation, but I want to consult another doctor first.

**5.**

> Capitalize words for family members, such as *Mother* or *Father*, when using them as names of people, but do not capitalize words referring to family members in a general sense.
>
> Karen said, "Really, Mother, I don't know why you won't let me stay out past 11:00 if Father says I may stay out until midnight."
>
> Karen says that her father is more permissive than her mother.

**6.**

> Capitalize adjectives based on the names of places. Capitalize the names of nationalities, races, and religions.
>
> Juana is **P**uerto **R**ican; she is **C**atholic and speaks both **S**panish and **E**nglish.
>
> Hilda is **D**utch; she is **P**rotestant and speaks **D**utch, **G**erman, and **E**nglish.

**7.**

> Capitalize the days of the week, the months of the year, and the names of specific heavenly bodies, except for the earth, the sun, and the moon. Do not capitalize spring, summer, fall, and winter.
>
> Every **M**onday, **W**ednesday, and **F**riday during **N**ovember and **D**ecember, Professor Findley takes his astronomy class to the Wilson Observatory to observe the moon, **V**enus, **M**ars, and several other heavenly bodies.
>
> Joan says that her favorite season of the year is spring; she especially likes the month of **M**ay.

**8.**

> Capitalize specific courses, but not general names of subjects (unless they are the names of languages).
>
> I am studying chemistry, psychology, **E**nglish, astronomy, and math now.
>
> I think that **H**istory 23 must be a very good course because Clyde loves it, and he usually has no interest in history.

**9.**

> Capitalize the names of holidays and historical events and periods.
>
> The **R**enaissance and the **I**ndustrial **R**evolution were periods of rapid change.
>
> The **G**reat **D**epression occurred between **W**orld **W**ar I and **W**orld **W**ar II.
>
> The **B**oston **T**ea **P**arty was one of the events that led to the **A**merican **R**evolution.
>
> **I**ndependence **D**ay, **T**hanksgiving, and **L**abor **D**ay are national holidays in the United States.

**10.**

> Capitalize the *Sabbath,* the *Bible,* the *Koran, God,* the *Lord,* and pronouns referring to *Him.* Do not capitalize the gods of mythology (unless their names are mentioned) or the word *god* in a general sense.
>
> In the **B**ible and the **K**oran we read about **G**od and **H**is works.
>
> Ebenezer Scrooge made money his god.
>
> Edith Hamilton has written about the gods of Roman and Greek mythology such as **J**upiter (**Z**eus), **J**uno (**H**era), and **V**enus (**A**phrodite).

**11.**

> Capitalize the first word, the last word, and all important words in any title. (Do not capitalize articles, prepositions, and conjunctions that are not first or last in the title.) Capitalize any word following a colon (:) in a title.
>
> I am reading *The **O**ld **M**an and the **S**ea.*
>
> For my term paper I am reading a book entitled *Strange* **L**ights: *A **S**tudy of* **F**aulkner's *Novels.*

**12.**

> Capitalize the first word of a sentence in a direct quotation. If a quotation is interrupted in the middle of a sentence, it is not necessary to capitalize the first word in the next part of the sentence.
>
> Martha said, "Cat fur makes me sneeze."
>
> "Cat fur," Martha said, "makes me sneeze."
>
> "Cat fur makes me sneeze," said Martha. "Is there a cat here?"

**13.**

> Capitalize the names of clubs and organizations.
>
> The League of Women Voters often sponsors debates between political candidates.
>
> The Math Club has invited a famous mathematician to speak at the next meeting.

**14.**

> Capitalize names of companies, but not the products they manufacture.
>
> The Nabisco Company makes many products.
>
> The sandwich was made with Arnold's bread, Kraft cheese, and Hellman's mayonnaise.

**Note:** **Avoid unnecessary capitals. Remember that *high school* in a general sense (without the name of a specific school), should not be capitalized. Similarly, do not capitalize names of professions and professionals in a general sense. Although Nurse Smith, a specific person, would be capitalized, the words *nursing* or *nurse* used in a general sense begin with small letters. Seasons of the year also begin with small letters.**

> **After Mary received her high school diploma last spring, she worked as a nurse's aide for the summer. In the fall she went to college, and she hopes to become a registered nurse in a few years.**

**EXERCISE 28a** | *Capitalize where necessary.*

                      *M   L          I*

*EXAMPLE*   mrs. leary lives in ireland.

1. when helen forbes finishes high school, she will attend columbia college.

2. mark twain, whose real name was samuel l. clemens, spent his childhood in hannibal, missouri; he is well-known as the author of *the adventures of tom sawyer* and also *the adventures of huckleberry finn.*

3. atomic bombs were dropped on hiroshima and nagasaki, two japanese cities, in august 1945, hastening the end of world war ii.

4. in 1953 arthur c. clarke published a novel called *childhood's end.*

5. every tuesday, wednesday, and friday, i take a course which is titled african and caribbean history. i like all my history courses, but this one is my favorite.

6. as soon as the diner opened, mr. palmer, a neighbor of mine on warwick street, rushed in to buy a cup of coffee.

7. james, a sophomore at the university of vermont, is taking spanish, physics, and history this semester.

8. we plan to spend thanksgiving with my cousins in atlanta, georgia.

9. in jane austen's novel *persuasion* there are three sisters, whose names are elizabeth, anne, and mary.

10. next friday you have an appointment with ms. vickers, the new president of our college.

**EXERCISE
28b**
*Capitalize where necessary. Mark unnecessary capitals with a slash.*

EXAMPLE    *jane is very interested in Chemistry.*

1. *from this book i learned that general george washington chose General Nathanael greene to fight against the british Troops in north and south carolina.*

2. *Gerry asked, "have you read <u>second Sight,</u> a Book of poems By jonathan aaron?"*

3. *The Border Between canada and the United states is the longest unguarded frontier in the World.*

4. *in our part of the world, the Longest Days of the year are in june, and the Shortest are in december.*

5. *Many christians consider sunday the sabbath, but for the seventh-day adventists, the sabbath is saturday; the jewish people also worship on saturday, and moslems celebrate the sabbath on friday.*

6. *my friend joan is a linguist; she speaks english, spanish, french, italian, german, and two other Languages.*

7. *after eddie called the police, officer thomas arrived and Asked, "what seems to be the trouble?"*

**EXERCISE
28c**

*Rewrite the following paragraphs on separate paper. Capitalize where necessary.*

1.    in bergenfield, a small town in new jersey, many of the streets have the names of flowers; you can find carnation street, magnolia street, lilac street, and tulip street.

2.    california shows the influence of the early spanish settlers in the names of its cities and towns. two of its most famous cities are san francisco and los angeles. other california cities with spanish names are santa rosa, san jose, palo alto, san diego, and santa maria, to name just a few.

3.    many months of the year are named for the gods of roman mythology or for the roman emperors. for example, january gets its name from janus, the god of all doors and thus beginnings. march is the month of mars, the god of war. may is the month of maius jupiter, the great god, while june is named for the goddess juno, who was jupiter's wife. july and august are named for the emperors julius and augustus. do you know where the other months get their names?

4.    "why is the water pressure so low?" asked mr. taylor. "there's practically no water coming out of the faucet."

"the fire department is flushing out the hydrants," replied mrs. taylor. "i spoke to captain fuller, who said that the process will last only a few hours."

CHAPTER

# 29

# Spelling

If you have frequent spelling errors in your essays, you probably want to improve your ability to spell. But like many students, you may think of spelling as a very complicated subject. It is true that there are many exceptions to the basic spelling rules. Nevertheless, if you review the rules and their exceptions carefully, and if you do the exercises in this chapter, you can become a better speller. The following guidelines can help you avoid the most common spelling problems.

## PLURAL FORMATION IN NOUNS

The most common way to make a singular noun plural is to add *s* to it. **No apostrophe is used,** just the noun plus an *s*.

| Singular Noun | + | s | = | Plural Noun |
|---|---|---|---|---|
| (a) girl | + | s | = | (some) girls |
| (one) bridge | + | s | = | (several) bridges |
| (one) highway | + | s | = | (the) highways |
| (one) thing | + | s | = | (many) things |

There are some variations to this plural rule. They are discussed in the following sections.

## The "ies" Variation

If a singular noun has a consonant before a final *y*, change the *y* to *ie* before adding *s*.

| Singular Noun | Plural Noun |
|---|---|
| baby | babies |
| country | countries |
| spy | spies |
| story | stories |

Note that a word with a vowel before a final *y* follows the ordinary rule of adding only *s*.

| Singular Noun | Plural Noun |
|---|---|
| monkey | monkeys |
| highway | highways |
| valley | valleys |
| delay | delays |

## The "es" Variation

Add *es* to words ending in *ch, s, sh, tch,* and *x.*

| Singular Noun | Plural Noun |
|---|---|
| church | churches |
| boss | bosses |
| bush | bushes |
| flash | flashes |
| witch | witches |
| fox | foxes |

## The "f Becomes v" Variation

If a singular noun ends in *f*, we often change the *f* to *v* and add *es*.

| Singular Noun | Plural Noun |
|---|---|
| leaf | leaves |
| shelf | shelves |
| loaf | loaves |
| thief | thieves |

**Note:** **The plural of *self* is *selves*. It forms the pronouns *ourselves*, *yourselves*, and *themselves*.**

If a singular noun ends in *fe*, change the *f* to *v* before adding *s*.

| Singular Noun | Plural Noun |
|---|---|
| wife | wives |
| life | lives |
| knife | knives |

**Note:** **Some nouns ending in "f" simply add "s" to form the plural.**

| *Singular Noun* | *Plural Noun* |
|---|---|
| **belief** | **beliefs** |
| **roof** | **roofs** |

## Other Exceptions

Some nouns make other spelling changes to show the plural.

| Singular Noun | Plural Noun |
|---|---|
| man (and its compounds) | men |
|   policeman |   policemen |
| woman (and its compounds) | women |
|   policewoman |   policewomen |
| child | children |
| mouse | mice |
| foot | feet |
| tooth | teeth |

Some nouns make no change at all in the plural:

| Singular Noun | Plural Noun |
|---|---|
| fish | fish |
| moose | moose |
| sheep | sheep |
| deer | deer |

**Note:  Some nouns are not used in the plural:**

*advice, equipment, furniture, homework, information.*

**Also note that the plural of *person* is usually *people*. Occasionally the word *persons* is used, but this usage is rare and very formal.**

**EXERCISE 29a**

*Fill in the correct form of each noun.*

*EXAMPLES*  **a.** a thief        two    *thieves*

**b.** one brush      several  *brushes*

**c.** two teeth       one    *tooth*

1. a horse        three    _____
2. one tooth      two      _____
3. a baby         two      _____
4. one shelf      five     _____
5. three men      one      _____
6. one sheep      four     _____
7. a monkey       several  _____
8. five children  a        _____
9. one country    ten      _____
10. one woman     some     _____
11. a contest     several  _____
12. one story     two      _____

**13.** one mouse       many     _____

**14.** some spies      a        _____

**15.** one delay       many     _____

**16.** a foot          three    _____

**Note:  The plural of *this* is *these*. For a list of singular and
plural pronouns, see page 323.**

**EXERCISE
29b**

*Rewrite each sentence, changing the underlined words from singular
to plural. Be careful to change verbs and pronouns too when necessary. (Some sentences are started for you.)*

*EXAMPLES*   **a.** A reporter interviewed me yesterday.

*Reporters interviewed me yesterday.*

**b.** This country was admitted to the U.N. in 1960.

*These countries were admitted to the U.N. in 1960.*

**1.** The spy had visited this country many times.

_____

_____

**2.** I enjoy reading a story to the child.

_____

_____

**3.** This woman put the book on the shelf.

*These* _____

_____

**4.** At the farm, my cousin wanted to see the cow, the sheep, and
the duck.

_____

_____

**5.** My <u>tooth</u> <u>hurts</u>, and so <u>does</u> my <u>foot</u>.

_____

_____

**6.** Never leave <u>a</u> <u>knife</u> where your small <u>child</u> could reach <u>it</u>.

_____

_____

**7.** My <u>brother</u> <u>is</u> afraid of <u>a</u> <u>mouse</u>, but I am not.

_____

_____

**8.** The modern <u>dentist</u> <u>tries</u> to avoid pulling <u>a</u> <u>tooth</u>.

_Modern_ _____

_____

**9.** The <u>policeman</u> escorted <u>his</u> <u>wife</u> to the annual ball.

_____

_____

**10.** A <u>child</u> <u>loves</u> to hear <u>a</u> <u>story</u>.

_____

_____

**11.** The <u>city</u> <u>has</u> solved many of <u>its</u> budget problems.

_Cities_ _____

_____

**12.** In the <u>alley</u> next to the movie <u>theater</u> <u>was a mouse</u>.

_____

_____

**13.** <u>Duty</u> must be performed, and <u>responsibility</u> must be fulfilled.

_____

_____

**14.** The <u>girl</u> said <u>she</u> had caught <u>a fish</u> all by <u>herself</u>.

_____

_____

**15.** The <u>fly</u> buzzed around the <u>body</u> of the dead <u>horse</u>.

_____

_____

## CHANGING "Y" TO "I" IN VERBS

Verbs that have a consonant before a final *y* sometimes need to change their spelling when suffixes are added.

Change the *y* to *i* or *ie* before adding *ed* or *s*.

marry + ed = married    marry + s = marries
study + ed = studied    study + s = studies

Don't change the *y* if the addition starts with *i*.

marry + ing = marrying
study + ing = studying

**Note: No changes are made if the word has a vowel before a final *y*.**

| obey | obeying | play | playing |
| | obeyed | | played |
| | obeys | | plays |

**Exceptions: lay—laid, say—said, pay—paid.**

**EXERCISE 29c** | *Write the* s, ing, *and* ed *forms of the verb in the blanks.*

*EXAMPLE*    study    He _studies_ . He is _studying_ .
                        s form              ing form

He _studied_ .
       ed form

1. worry    Cathy _____ .    She is _____ .
                          s form                    ing form

   She _____ .
              ed form

2. play    The baby _____ . He is _____ .
                              s form              ing form

   He _____ .
          ed form

3. tally    The accountant _____ . She is _____ .
                                      s form                    ing form

   She _____ .
              ed form

4. rally    The team _____ . It is _____ .
                              s form            ing form

   It _____ .
          ed form

5. try    She _____ . She is _____ .
                    s form                  ing form

   She _____ .
              ed form

6. pity    He _____ . He is _____ .
                    s form              ing form

   He _____ .
          ed form

7. study    She _____ . She is _____ .
                      s form                  ing form

   She _____ .
              ed form

8. carry    He _____ . He is _____ .
                    s form              ing form

   He _____ .
          ed form

**9.** say      She _____. She is _____.
                   *s* form          *ing* form

         She _____.
                   *ed* form

**10.** hurry   He _____. He is _____.
                   *s* form          *ing* form

         He _____.
                   *ed* form

**11.** pay      She _____. She is _____.
                   *s* form          *ing* form

         She _____.
                   *ed* form

**12.** obey    He _____. He is _____.
                   *s* form          *ing* form

         He _____.
                   *ed* form

**13.** pry      She _____. She is _____.
                   *s* form          *ing* form

         She _____.
                   *ed* form

**14.** apply    She _____. She is _____.
                   *s* form          *ing* form

         She _____.
                   *ed* form

**15.** delay   He _____. He is _____.
                   *s* form          *ing* form

         He _____.
                   *ed* form

## KEEPING OR DROPPING THE FINAL "E"

When you are adding letters to words that end in silent *e*,

1. **Keep** *e* if the addition (suffix) starts with a consonant.

   love + ly      = lovely        hope + less = hopeless

   sincere + ly = sincerely      hope + ful  = hopeful

   (Exceptions: truly, argument, judgment)

2. **Drop** *e* if the addition (suffix) starts with a vowel.

Thus, drop silent *e* before *ing*.

   ridé + ing    = riding        lové + able    = lovable

   writé + ing = writing        believé + able = believable

   (Exception: Keep the *e* before *able* if it follows a soft *c* or *g*: knowled**gea**ble, noti**cea**ble, pea**cea**ble)

**Note: Remember that the letter *y* at the end of a word is a vowel. Thus:**

   **stoné  +  y  =  stony**
   **shiné  +  y  −  shiny**
   **noisé  +  y  =  noisy**
   **nosé  +  y  =  nosy**

**EXERCISE 29d**    *Fill in each blank with the correct spelling of the word indicated. Drop the* e *if necessary.*

*EXAMPLE*    The __*management*__ is concerned about __*saving*__ money.
                     manage + ment                         save + ing

1. We were _____ and _____ sorry for him.
                     true + ly              sincere + ly

2. Your _____ shows _____ , _____
         write + ing          improve + ment   indicate + ing

   that you have been _____.
                              practice + ing

3. _____ will not get us closer to _____ the problem.
   Argue + ing                              solve + ing

**4.** My mood changed from ＿＿＿＿＿ to ＿＿＿＿＿ when I
hope + less    hope + ful

saw that my business was ＿＿＿＿＿.
improve + ing

**5.** We are interested in ＿＿＿＿＿ and ＿＿＿＿＿ good
locate + ing    hire + ing

employees as soon as possible.

**6.** He is ＿＿＿＿＿ convinced that his obvious lies are
absolute + ly

＿＿＿＿＿.
believe + able

**7.** ＿＿＿＿＿ at the winning ticket, he came to the ＿＿＿＿＿
Stare + ing    realize + ation

that he had won the lottery.

**8.** There was a ＿＿＿＿＿ dent on the fender of my ＿＿＿＿＿
notice + able    shine + y

new car.

**9.** The weather is ＿＿＿＿＿ in October.
change + able

**10.** We were ＿＿＿＿＿ along on the ＿＿＿＿＿ trail.
stumble + ing    stone + y

**11.** Our ＿＿＿＿＿ team is ＿＿＿＿＿ of victory this
debate + ing    hope + ful

year because of the ＿＿＿＿＿ of our adviser.
encourage + ment

**12.** ＿＿＿＿＿ high school is an ＿＿＿＿＿ most
Complete + ing    achieve + ment

people are proud of.

**13.** A ＿＿＿＿＿ girl was ＿＿＿＿＿ to be selected for the lead
love + ly    hope + ing

in the play.

**14.** By ＿＿＿＿＿ often, you can improve your ＿＿＿＿＿.
practice + ing    write + ing

## WHEN TO DOUBLE A CONSONANT

When adding endings that begin with vowels, such as *-ed, -ing, -er, -ance, -ence,* or *-en,* double the consonant if:

1.  the root word ends in a **single vowel** followed by a **single consonant,** and

2.  the accent is on the **last syllable** or there is just **one syllable.** For example:

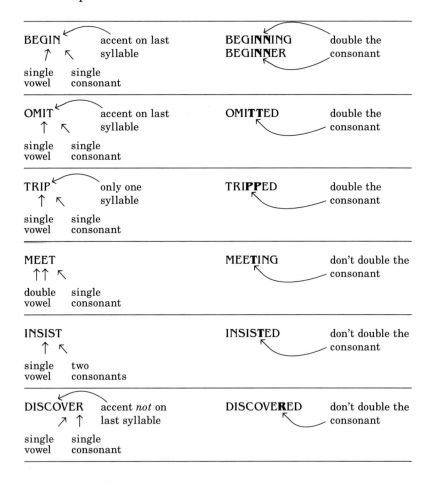

BEGIN — accent on last syllable
single vowel — single consonant
BEGINNING / BEGINNER — double the consonant

OMIT — accent on last syllable
single vowel — single consonant
OMITTED — double the consonant

TRIP — only one syllable
single vowel — single consonant
TRIPPED — double the consonant

MEET
double vowel — single consonant
MEETING — don't double the consonant

INSIST
single vowel — two consonants
INSISTED — don't double the consonant

DISCOVER — accent *not* on last syllable
single vowel — single consonant
DISCOVERED — don't double the consonant

## Pronunciation Note

One reason for doubling the consonant is to keep the pronunciation right. Pronounce these two words:

1. bit     It takes a short time to pronounce *i* in *bit*.
   This is a **short** *i*.
2. bite    It takes a longer time to pronounce *i* in *bite*.
   This is a **long** *i*.

When endings are added to words with short *i*, the doubled consonants keep the *i* short.

BITTEN
short *i*    doubled consonant

WRITTEN
short *i*    doubled consonant

When the sound is **long**, as in *bite*, only a single consonant follows:

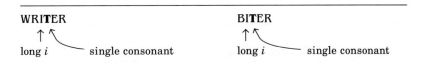

WRITER
long *i*    single consonant

BITER
long *i*    single consonant

This works for *i*, and for other letters too, in many words. For example:

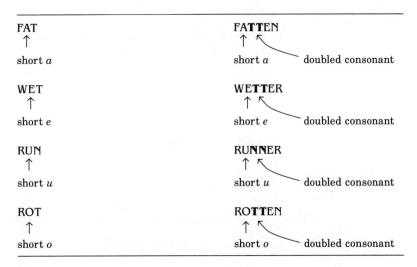

FAT
short *a*

FATTEN
short *a*    doubled consonant

WET
short *e*

WETTER
short *e*    doubled consonant

RUN
short *u*

RUNNER
short *u*    doubled consonant

ROT
short *o*

ROTTEN
short *o*    doubled consonant

---

**BRIEF PRACTICE 29.1**    *Write the* ed *and the* ing *forms of the following verbs. The first one is done as an example.*

1. mop    *mopped*                                  *mopping*
           ed form                                    ing form

2. hop    _____                               _____
           ed form                                    ing form

3. hope   _____                               _____
           ed form                                    ing form

4. mope   _____                               _____
           ed form                                    ing form

---

**EXERCISE 29e**    *Fill in each blank with the correct spelling of the word indicated. Double the final consonant or drop the final* e *where necessary.*

1. Clark is _____ to enjoy his new job.
            begin (*ing* form)

2. Mr. Zorensky has been _____ the annual report.
                          write (*ing* form)

3. When the train _____, everyone was _____
                   stop (*ed* form)              hope (*ing* form)
   that it would soon start again.

4. The movie was _____ to me, but a man _____
                  excite (*ing* form)              sit (*ing* form)
   next to me was _____ all through it.
                   snore (*ing* form)

5. My vacation has been _____.
                         defer (*ed* form)

6. Pete got into trouble for _____ a frog into the public
                              put (*ing* form)
   _____ pool.
    swim (*ing* form)

7. I nearly _____ when I was _____ to as the
             faint (*ed* form)        refer (*ed* form)
   _____ of the contest.
    win + *er*

8. Why do those lobsters keep _____ out of the _____
   pop (*ing* form)    bake (*ing* form)
   dish?

9. The accident _____ at noon.
   occur (*ed* form)

10. He added some _____ onions and _____ carrots
    slice (*ed* form)    chop (*ed* form)
    to the stew that he was _____.
    cook (*ing* form)

11. She _____ up the letter and _____ the pieces
    rip (*ed* form)    drop (*ed* form)
    into the wastepaper basket.

12. The basketball player _____ only one foul.
    commit (*ed* form)

## "I" BEFORE "E," EXCEPT . . .

The combinations *ie* and *ei* are confusing. Most words with these letters follow this rule:

*i* before *e*

except after *c,*

or when sounded like *a*

as in *neighbor* and *weigh.*

**Exceptions:  *either, leisure, neither, seize, their, weird.***

**Note: Some words contain *c* followed by *ie*—for example, *ancient, conscience, deficient, efficient, proficient.* The *ie* does not make the long "ee" sound in these words.**

**EXERCISE 29f**  |  *Fill in each blank with* ie *or* ei.

1. I bel _____ ve that he is dec _____ tful and conc _____ ted.

2. Rec _____ ving a college degree is a fine ach _____ vement.

3. N _____ ther of us has lost w _____ ght this month.

4. A short burglar is called a br _____ f th _____ f.

5. The World Ser _____ s is a major event.

6. Make sure to get a rec _____ pt for that money.

7. We cannot perc _____ ve a difference between the two
p _____ ces of material.

8. Her new n _____ ghbors are w _____ rd!

9. My brother rec _____ ved an ach _____ vement award.

10. A king r _____ gns; a president governs.

11. A d _____ sel engine is very effic _____ nt.

12. Daryl wants to become a profic _____ nt writer.

13. Where Don got that w _____ rd bel _____ f I just cannot
conc _____ ve!

14. A wild boar is a f _____ rce animal.

15. My n _____ ce is named Denise.

16. Sometimes excessive gr _____ f masks a guilty
consc _____ nce.

## COMMONLY MISSPELLED WORDS

You can improve your spelling by learning the words presented
here. You can learn them a few at a time and ask a friend to quiz you
on them.

Put checks next to the words that are special problems for you.
At the end of this list, you can add some more words. This last group
will be your personal spelling list.

| | | |
|---|---|---|
| absence | athletic | consequences |
| accidentally | attendance | criminal |
| accommodate | | criticize |
| acknowledge | because | crowded |
| acquaintance | believe | customary |
| acquire | business | |
| across | career | debt |
| address | chance | defense |
| amateur | changeable | definitely |
| analyze | column | descend |
| argument | conscience | descriptive |

destroy
develop
disappear
disastrous
discipline
discouraged
dissatisfied
drowned

embarrass
environment
exercise

familiar
fascinate
February
financial
foreign
fortunately
forty
fourth

government
governor

handicapped
hindrance

incidentally
individual
intelligent
interesting
involvement
irresistible

jealous

knowledge
knowledgeable

leisure
library
license
listen

marriage
misspelled
mortgage

ninety
ninth
noticeable
nowadays

occasionally
occurrence
often
opinion
opportunity

performance
permission
possession
precede
pregnant
prejudice
prescribe
prescription
privilege
probably
proceed
professor
pronunciation

really
repetitious
resemblance
resistance
responsibility
restaurant
reversible
rhythm

sacrifice
separate
similar
speech
strict
studying
succeed
supposed
surprised
suspension

though
thought
through
tragedy

unanimous
unnecessary
useful
usually

violence

Wednesday
writing

yield

Add your own list of troublesome words. You may find some in your previously corrected essays.

| | | |
|---|---|---|
| _____ | _____ | _____ |
| _____ | _____ | _____ |
| _____ | _____ | _____ |
| _____ | _____ | _____ |
| _____ | _____ | _____ |
| _____ | _____ | _____ |

CHAPTER

# 30

# Punctuation

## THE PERIOD (.)

A period should be put at the end of a statement.

The school bus had a flat tire.

Noise pollution is harmful to your health.

Roger asked if I had ever visited California.

A period is also put at the end of an abbreviation.

| | |
|---|---|
| Mr. Dodd | Jan Karp, Ph.D. |
| A.M. | Dr. Laura M. See |
| P.M. | Ms. Rosa Torres |

## THE QUESTION MARK (?)

A question mark comes at the end of a direct question.

Can you lend me your physics book?

Where are the scissors?

Do you know if the exam schedule is posted?

**Note:  A period, not a question mark, comes after an indirect question.**

**I asked Mary if she had seen Rose.**

**The scientist wondered what the experiment would show.**

## THE EXCLAMATION POINT (!)

A writer may use an exclamation point for emphasis.

"Fire! Clear the building!" shouted the superintendent.

This is a terrible mess!

**Note:  Don't use exclamation points often in formal compositions.**

**EXERCISE 30a**  |  *Put* ⬚ , ⬚ , *or* ⬚ *where necessary.*

*EXAMPLE*    Where is the office of the town clerk *?*

1. How much time is allowed for this exam

2. All these computers have built-in modems

3. A valuable painting was acquired by the museum

4. Which of these trains goes to Iowa City

5. Dr Kelly M Gregory is a surgeon

6. Get away from the fire

7. Spanish and Italian have many similar words

8. Where does the bus stop

9. What do you plan to serve at your dinner party

10. My friend asked me what I planned to serve at my dinner party

11. What a wonderful time we had

12. Dr Jerome asked me when William Blake was born

13. I told him that William Blake was born in 1757

14. Dr Jerome then asked me if I was sure of the date

15. Do you know when John Keats was born

## THE SEMICOLON (;)

The main use of the semicolon is to separate two independent clauses whose subject matter is closely related. (See Chapters 10 and 12.)

Professor Davidson is very popular; his classes are always well attended.

**Note: The semicolon could be replaced by a period.**

**Professor Davidson is very popular. His classes are always well attended.**

There is a simple but good rule for the semicolon: **Use a semicolon only where you could put a period.** There are a few exceptions to this rule, but they are rare.

We didn't have to wait long; the bus was right on time.

It was snowing heavily; the schools had to close early.

**Note: Remember that when two related clauses are combined in one sentence with a connecting adverb such as *however* or *therefore*, or a connecting phrase such as *for example* or *in fact*, a comma alone is not the correct punctuation. Use a semicolon.**

**Reading is a very effective way to improve your writing style; therefore, it is wise to read widely if you wish to write better.**

**Our club's garage sale was a huge success; in fact, it was the most profitable fund-raising event of the year.**

**EXERCISE 30b**  *Separate these run-on sentences with semicolons.*

*EXAMPLE*   Owls are useful birds; they kill mice and snakes.

1. English football is not the same as American football the game the English call football is called soccer in America.

2. Computers are not all alike some are easier to use than others.

3. The trunk of his car leaks he has to bail it out after each rain.

4. The weather may affect people's moods many people feel happier when the sun is shining than when it is raining.

5. Always leave sufficient time for important jobs rushing through a complicated task can be very frustrating.

6. Soccer has always been popular in South America it has not been popular in North America until recently.

7. The cinnamon rolls tasted peculiar the baker had put in cayenne pepper instead of cinnamon.

8. On his vacation Richard likes to travel fast he does not spend much time in any one place.

9. Several people in our town started a recreational softball league they play every Thursday night during the summer.

10. Taking large doses of some vitamins can be harmful ingesting huge amounts of vitamin A can actually be fatal.

## THE COMMA (,)

1.

> If a sentence has two independent clauses linked by a conjunction, put a comma just before the conjunction.
>
> (The cage door was open), (and all the rats were loose.)
> independent                    ↑      ↑            independent
>   clause                    comma conjunction        clause

**2.**

> Use a comma after a subordinate clause at the beginning of a sentence. (See Chapter 10.)
>
> Because the car broke down, I was late to work.
>
> Before we telephoned, Mary had left the house.

**3.**

> Use a comma after a long introductory phrase. With short introductory phrases, use a comma to avoid confusion.
>
> At the end of the semester, Mr. Rollins reviewed all the material.
>
> Upon leaving, Mary was in tears. (A comma is needed after **leaving** in order to avoid confusion.)
>
> At noon we will leave for Washington. (There is no comma because **At noon** is short and does not cause confusion.)

**4.**

> Use a comma after each item in a series of three or more (including the item just before *and*).
>
> Stephanie made Christmas decorations of green, red, yellow, and white felt. (series of adjectives)
>
> Mr. Franley stepped outside, slammed the door, and walked to his car. (series of verb phrases)
>
> The students in his evening class included nurses, engineers, dancers, and accountants. (series of nouns)
>
> We bought dates and walnuts for the cake. (No comma is needed because only two items are mentioned.)

**5.**

> Use a comma to mark off items in an address.
>
> She lives at 438 Tremont Street, Albany, New York.
>
> The address read 61 Andrews Avenue, San Jose, California, U.S.A.

**6.**

> Use commas to set off words not absolutely necessary to the meaning of a sentence.
>
> My mother, **a practicing lawyer,** is a great negotiator.
>
> ↑
>
> This information is interesting, but not crucial, so it is marked off by commas.
>
> Jimmy hates people **who are cruel to animals.**
> ↑
> There is no comma here because this information is absolutely necessary; otherwise, we might think that Jimmy hates **all** people.

**7.**

> Use a comma or commas to mark off interrupting material and certain introductory words. Here is a partial list:
>
> | | | |
> |---|---|---|
> | Moreover, | First, | Consequently, |
> | Therefore, | In fact, | However, |
> | Yes, | Of course, | Thus, |
>
> Therefore, we shall have to change our plans.
>
> Yes, I can tell you the history assignment for tomorrow.
>
> There are, in fact, two solutions to your problem.

**8.**

> Use a comma before a direct quotation, but not before an indirect quotation.
>
> Fred said, "I haven't delivered the package."
>
> Fred said that he hadn't delivered the package.
> ↑
> no comma necessary

**9.**

> Use a comma to set off a noun of direct address, that is, the name of a person being spoken to.
>
> Jimmy, please help with this job.
>
> What time are you leaving, Sue?

**10.**

> Use a comma between the name of a person and an abbreviation that follows the name. Also, use a comma after the abbreviation if that abbreviation is not at the end of the sentence.
>
> The accounting firm in our town has just hired Mary McCloud, Ph.D.
>
> Martin Luther King, Jr., was born in 1929.
>                               ↑
> Note that the comma is placed after the period needed for the abbreviation.

**11.**

> Use a comma to set off contrasting elements in a sentence.
>
> Myrna is six years old, not seven.
>
> Ms. Foy is generous, but not extravagant.

**Note: Don't use unnecessary commas. A comma in the wrong place is often worse than one omitted. When in doubt, leave it out.**

**EXERCISE 30c**

*Put commas where necessary.*

1. The manager of the factory had thought that some people would have to be laid off. However several big orders came in unexpectedly. Therefore nobody was fired.

2. If you look carefully at the map of the city you will notice that there is a shortcut to the football stadium. Although most people think they have to take the turnpike to get there it is not really necessary. If you follow my suggestions Larry you will avoid a lot of traffic.

3. Dr. Kendrick gave up his medical practice sold his house and moved away. His new address is 999 Lemon Street Orangeville Florida.

4. Although Europe uses the metric system the United States still uses the English system of measurement. Europeans are accustomed to measuring length and distance in centimeters meters and kilometers. Americans however usually think in terms of inches feet yards and miles.

## QUOTATION MARKS (" ")

**1.**

> Use quotation marks around direct quotations (a person's actual words).
>
> Richard shouted, "Run, or you'll miss the train!"
>
> "I refuse to believe such a silly story," said Jim.
>
> "I have never seen such a thing," said Jane, "in my life."
>
> (Note that this quotation is interrupted by the words *said Jane*. Only the words she said are quoted.)
>
> Fred told me that he couldn't come to class.
>
> (There are no quotation marks here because these are not his exact words.)

**2.**

> Use quotation marks around titles of essays, articles, poems, short stories, and songs.
>
> Hawthorne wrote a tale called "The Birthmark."
>
> Have you ever read the poem "Harlem"?
>
> Mrs. Nicols's article, "Politics in the Inner City," was published in this morning's newspaper.
>
> E. M. Forster's essay "My Wood" is well-known.
>
> Elvis sang "Don't Be Cruel."

**Note:** **Titles of books, magazines, newspapers, and plays are underlined.**

**We went to see <u>Hamlet</u> at the City Center.**

**Do you like <u>Vogue Magazine</u>?**

**<u>Brave New World</u> is a frightening book.**

**I read <u>The Washington Post</u> every day.**

**3.**

> Use quotation marks around words used as words or around letters discussed as letters.
>
> Many people confuse the words "their," "there," and "they're."
>
> Sometimes the word "achieve" is misspelled by people who forget that "i" usually comes before "e."

**Note:** Do not misuse quotation marks. They should not be placed around a word to emphasize it. (Words may be underlined for emphasis.)

**Note:** When quotation marks are combined with other punctuation, place them as follows:

1. Commas and periods are placed within quotation marks.

   After I read "My Wood," I went to sleep.

   Jim said, "I'll return the book tomorrow."

2. Semicolons and colons are placed after quotation marks.

   I read "My Wood"; then I went to sleep.

   Orwell discusses many ideas in the essay "Politics and the English Language": the relationship between truth and language, the effect of language on behavior, and the need for clear writing.

3. Question marks and exclamation points may be placed within quotation marks or after them, depending on the meaning of the sentence. If the question mark or exclamation point is part of the quotation, place it within the quotation marks. If it expresses the meaning of the sentence as a whole, place it after the quotation marks.

   He asked, "Where is the paper?"

   Did he say "Dinner is served"?

   "Fire!" he yelled. "Clear the building!"

   The teacher called Sam "Sweetie Pie"!

**EXERCISE
30d** | *Put quotation marks where necessary.*

**1.** The reading list for the course in American literature includes two of Hawthorne's stories, The Birthmark and Rappaccini's Daughter. Also listed are two tales by Edgar Allen Poe, The Tell-Tale Heart and King Pest.

**2.** All young people should serve their country for a year, said Ms. Allen.

Not everyone, replied Mr. Flores, would do well in the Army.

Ms. Allen answered, Not everyone should serve in the Army. Some could work in hospitals, schools, or day-care centers.

**3.** Many people are not sure whether the word receive should be spelled with an ei or an ie. One way to remember that it should be ei is to think of the related word reception. The words receive and reception both start with rece.

## THE APOSTROPHE (')

**1.**

> Apostrophes are used in contractions to replace a dropped letter or letters.
>
> He's here. (He is here.)
> ↑
> Put an apostrophe where the letter *i* has been left out.
>
> I'm delighted. (I am delighted.)
> ↑
> The letter *a* has been left out.

**HINT**

Do not use too many contractions in your writing. Writing out words in full can avoid errors.

**2.**

> Use an apostrophe for most possessives. Add s̲ to most words; add ˈ if the word already ends in *s* (or you may add s̲ ).
>
> This is Mary's coat.
>
> Here is Charles's room. OR Here is Charles' room.
>
> I have to clean my daughter's room. (the room belonging to one daughter)
>
> I have to clean my daughters' room. (the room belonging to two or more daughters)
>
> There is a men's clothing store on that block.

**Note:** **Do not use an apostrophe in the possessive *its*. (The word *it's* means *it is* or *it has*.)**

**A nation must live up to *its* ideals. *It's* important.**

**Do not use an apostrophe in the possessives *hers*, *his*, *theirs*, and *whose*.**

**Jenny said the idea was *hers*. Jim said it was *his*.**

**Bob and Carol said it was *theirs*. Nobody knew *whose* idea it really was.**

**Do not use an apostrophe for a noun that is plural but not possessive.**

**Five *girls* and four *boys* were playing softball.**

**Do not use an apostrophe before the *s* in a third-person singular verb.**

**He *runs* fast.**

**EXERCISE 30e**  *Add apostrophes where necessary.*

**1.** The legend of King Arthurs court has been popular for centuries. Its possible that Arthur was a real person, but scholars arent positive. A manuscript thats 1,400 years old describes one of Arthurs battles, but Arthurs name is not mentioned.

**2.** My brothers son Alan and my sisters daughter Diana will be in college next year. However, Dianas choice is a large urban university while Alans small college is in a quiet area far away from the nearest city.

**3.**   The registration committee had its first meeting yesterday. Its trying to find ways to prevent problems during the registration process. Last semester, many students programs were canceled by mistake, an error the committee hopes will not happen again.

**4.**   That store is known for its large boys and girls clothing departments, but its womens and mens clothing departments are small. Ive heard that its planning to expand them.

**5.**   Now that theyre retired, the Smiths plan to spend every winter in Florida because theyre both tired of the cold weather, they dont like driving on icy streets, and they dont like to shovel snow. The Smiths daughter will visit them at the end of every December, but she doesnt intend to move to Florida because her daughters dont want to leave their friends and their home in Massachusetts.

## THE DASH (—)

You may give special emphasis to words by setting them off with a dash at the end or at the beginning of a sentence. A dash may also be used for remarks that interrupt the sentence.

Consideration and sincerity—these are qualities I value in a friend.

She waited eagerly for her birthday—a day she would never forget.

A watched pot—so the saying goes—never boils.

## PARENTHESES (  )

Use parentheses to set off words or figures that give extra information. Do not overuse parentheses, and remember that they come in pairs.

Mahatma Gandhi (1869–1948) helped to win the independence of India.

Jane Austen's novel *Sanditon* (never finished by her) has been completed by a modern author.

## THE COLON (:)

Use a colon after the greeting in a business letter. Use it also between the hour and minute numbers for a time of day.

You may use a colon to introduce a list or in place of a semicolon if the second clause of the sentence explains the first.

Dear Mr. Garvey:

12:40 P.M.

Today the town council will discuss the following things: balancing the budget, improving the parks, and repaving Main Street.

I have learned an important lesson from my experiences as a mother: never force a child to eat.

## THE HYPHEN (-)

Use a hyphen to join some prefixes to the main word or to join two or more words that are working together.

ex-President

a Johnny-come-lately candidate

twentieth-century literature

a well-cooked turkey

**Note: Usually when two words are hyphenated, they come before a noun. In the following examples the hyphen is not needed.**

**the literature of the twentieth century**

**a turkey that is well cooked**

**EXERCISE 30f**  *Add periods, commas, apostrophes, and other punctuation marks where necessary. Underline words as needed.*

1. Mr Nolan was a student at this college now twenty years later he is a biology professor and an assistant dean

2. That little store doesnt open until 10 its elderly owner cant find a manager to open earlier

3. Whenever the principal looked in the classroom was very quiet

4. Were going to a party at Sandras house unfortunately we cant all fit into Bills car so Ill take a taxi

5. There was a small fire in Davids office but luckily no one was hurt

6. I cant decide whether to use a period a comma a semicolon or a question mark

7. The woman sitting at that desk will give you an application form

8. Richard opened the envelope unfolded the letter and shouted for joy

9. Dr Franklin has retired Do you know who will take over her practice

10. No I cant come to your party said Freida I'll be out of town

11. Franks office is closed almost everyone who works there has the flu

12. Mr Jones daughter has one great gift her artistic ability

13. The essay entitled My Wood by E M Forster 1879–1970 is one of my favorites

14. Iris put the following items into her briefcase a notebook a pen and a dictionary

15. Aldous Huxley 1894–1963 wrote Brave New World a novel that presents a frightening picture of a future world that has everything needed for happiness but lacks two important things freedom and love

16. Nineteenth century literature has always interested Lisas sister she intends to become an English professor some day

# PART TWO

## Reader with Study Questions and Vocabulary-Building Exercises

**AESOP**

Very little is known about Aesop, who was a slave, later given his freedom, in the sixth century before Christ. He may have been an African. He told stories designed to teach lessons about human behavior. Each story, called a fable, has a moral.

Aesop's characters are usually animals, as in two of his most famous fables, "The Tortoise and the Hare" and "The Fox and the Crow." Using animals as characters is amusing and at the same time makes it easier to criticize human mistakes. "The Treasure in the Orchard," however, is a fable with human characters, who learn, at the end, a very valuable lesson.

# THE TREASURE IN THE ORCHARD

An old gardener who was dying sent for his two sons to come to his bedside, as he wished to speak to them. They came in answer to his request, and, raising himself on his pillows, the old man pointed through the window towards his orchard.

"You see the orchard?" said he, feebly.

**feebly** (adv.): weakly.

"Yes, Father, we see the orchard."

"For years it has given the best of fruit—golden oranges, amber apricots, and cherries bigger and brighter than rubies!"

**amber** (adj.): a dark orange-yellow.

"To be sure, Father. It has always been a good orchard!"

The old gardener nodded his head, time and time again. He looked at his hands—they were worn with the spade that he had used all his life. Then he looked at the hands of his sons and saw that the nails were polished and the fingers white as those of any fine lady's.

**worn** (adj.): damaged through much use, roughened.

"You have never done a day's work in your lives, you two!" said he. "I doubt if you ever will! But I have hidden a treasure in my orchard for you to find. You will never possess it unless you dig it up. It lies midway between two of the trees, not too near, yet not too far from the trunks. It is yours for the trouble of digging—that is all!"

**midway** (adv.): halfway.

Then he sent them away, and soon afterwards he died. So the orchard became the property of his sons, and, without any delay, they set to work to dig for the treasure that had been promised them.

Well, they dug and they dug, day after day, and week after week, going down the long alleys of fruit trees, never too near yet never too far from the trunks. They dug up all the weeds and picked out all the stones; not because they liked weeding and cleaning, but because it was all part of the hunt for the buried treasure. Winter passed and spring came, and never were there such blossoms as those which hung the orange and apricot and cherry trees with curtains of petals pale as pearls and soft as silk. Then summer threw sunshine over the orchard, and sometimes the clouds bathed it in cool, delicious rain. At last the time of the fruit harvest came. But the two brothers had not yet found the treasure that was hidden among the roots of the trees.

**alleys** (noun): rows.

Then they sent for a merchant from the nearest town to buy the fruit. It hung in great bunches, golden oranges, amber apricots, and cherries bigger and brighter than rubies. The merchant looked at them in open admiration.

**merchant** (noun): trader, seller.
**open** (adj.): obvious.

"This is the finest crop I have yet seen," said he. "I will give you twenty bags of money for it!"

Twenty bags of money was more than the two brothers had ever owned in their life. They struck the bargain in great delight and took the money-bags into the house, while the merchant made arrangements to carry away the fruit.

**struck the bargain** (idiom): made the agreement.

"I will come again next year," said he. "I am always glad to buy a crop like this. *How you must have dug and weeded and worked to get it!*"

He went away, and the brothers sat eyeing each other over the tops of the money-bags. Their hands were rough and toil-worn, just as the old gardener's had been when he died.

**eyeing** (verb): looking at. Note that *eyeing* is an exception to the spelling rule in Chapter 29.
**toil-worn** (adj.): roughened by hard work.

"Golden oranges and amber apples and cherries bigger and brighter than rubies," said one of them, softly. "I believe that that is the treasure we have been digging for all year, the very treasure that our father meant!"

## THINKING ABOUT YOUR READING

### The Main Point

What is the lesson, or moral, of this fable by Aesop?

### Details

1. What did the old gardener grow in the orchard?
2. When the gardener looked at his sons' hands, what did he see?
3. Why did the sons dig so much in the garden?
4. How much money did the merchant give the brothers for their fruit?

### Your Opinion

5. Do you approve of what the old gardener did?
6. Would the sons have listened to their father if he had told them to care for the orchard without promising them a treasure?
7. Did your opinion of the two sons change at the end?

## Topics for Further Discussion and Writing

8.  The title of this fable is "The Treasure in the Orchard." How many different things could the word *treasure* apply to?

9.  Do you agree with the sons at the end that all the beautiful fruit is worth more than rubies?

10. Why does the storyteller emphasize the *hands* of the two brothers, before and after their hard work? Which kind of hands do you respect more? Which kind would you actually want to have yourself?

11. Some people might say that the old man should not have played a trick on his sons. Others might say that it was not really a trick. What is your opinion?

12. In this fable, the old father does not directly tell his sons what he wants them to learn. He lets them find it for themselves, even though it takes a long time. Do you agree or disagree with this method of teaching a lesson?

13. Write a short fable of your own about *one* of the following human faults:

    a. greed

    b. laziness

    c. envy

    End your story with a moral.

## VOCABULARY BUILDING

Here is a list of words from the fable.

eyeing        open
feebly        worn
merchant

**Vocabulary Exercise 1** | *Fill in each blank with the correct word. Use the correct form of the word.*

1. Marcia was _____ the jewelry in Tiffany's window.
   *looking at*

2. The old man walked _____ to the door.
   *weakly*

**3.** That old rug is _____ in several spots.
<br>damaged through much use

**4.** The children looked at the giraffe with _____ surprise.
<br>obvious

**5.** All the _____ had set up booths at the fair.
<br>sellers

## STUDENT RESPONSE

The following student essay was written in response to question 12 on page 405. The first paragraph states the writer's thesis (see Chapter 3), which is then developed in the next two paragraphs (see Chapters 4 and 6). Note that one main-body paragraph uses Aesop's fable as an example while the second main-body paragraph describes a personal experience that supports the thesis. The concluding paragraph restates the thesis and summarizes the writer's two examples.

Martha Perez
English 02-1832

### Experience as Teacher

The best teacher for a person is his own experience. People do not learn because another person has told them about his personal experiences. People learn from their own experiences.

In the selection "The Treasure in the Orchard," the gardener made his sons work as hard as he did himself. He was teaching them the value of the garden. The two sons learned this value by experiencing the hard work with their own two hands. Otherwise, they would not have learned that the garden itself was the treasure that their father was talking about.

People learn from their own experience. I have learned from experience that education is the only way to go if you want to have a better future. That is why I'm back in school, trying to get the education that I took for granted when I was a teenager. My parents told me a lot of times that education pays off in the long run, but I didn't listen, and I dropped out of school at the age of 15. When I tried to get a job, I couldn't because I had no education and no skills. Everywhere I went, it was the same story—no education, no job for you. That is how I learned that my parents were right and that the only way to reach my goals was and still is education.

It is true that nobody learns because other people have given advice. People learn only because of their own experience. The gardener's sons learned the value of the garden by working very hard in it. As soon as they found out that their work in the ground made the garden grow more beautiful fruits than ever, they realized how valuable the garden was. They realized that the garden itself was the treasure that their father was talking about. From my own experience I learned that my parents were right and that the only way to get a better future is by educating myself.

## LOOKING AT THE STUDENT RESPONSE

### Questions

1.  What is the thesis of the essay by Martha Perez?
2.  What examples does she use to support her thesis?
3.  How does Ms. Perez use paragraphing to help the reader follow her argument?

### Comment

The essay you have read is an edited draft. The first draft contained errors that were corrected. Here is an excerpt from the original draft showing corrections that were made. Explain why each correction was needed.

*It is*
⋀ Is true that nobody learn⋀ because other people

*have given advice*
~~have give advises~~. People learn only because of their own

experience. The gardener's sons learned the value of the

garden by working very hard in it. As soon as they found out

that their work in the ground made the garden grow more

*a*
beutiful fruits than ever, they realized how ~~much~~ valuable
⋀

*the garden was*
~~was the garden.~~ They realized that the garden itself was the

treasure that their father was talking about. From my own

experience I learned that my parents were right and that the

only way to get a better future is by educating myself.

## MIGUEL DE CERVANTES SAAVEDRA

Miguel de Cervantes Saavedra (1547–1616) is one of the most famous writers in the history of world literature. Born in Madrid, Spain, Cervantes lived an eventful and active life. He was a soldier, government worker, playwright, poet, and novelist. As a soldier, he had many adventures; he was captured by pirates and held as a slave in Algiers, trying unsuccessfully to escape. Finally he was freed when his family paid ransom money. His life was filled with many other difficulties. Because of legal problems, he had to face poverty and prison. In 1605, when his masterpiece, *Don Quixote de la Mancha*, was published, he won fame and some financial security.

*Don Quixote* is sometimes considered the first modern novel. Written in Spanish, it has been translated into many other languages, and it has influenced English literature. It tells the story of a man who has read so many books on knights and their noble deeds that he decides to imitate them, going forth into the world on a skinny old horse named Rocinante and looking for adventures. Don Quixote's head is so filled with fantasy that he cannot see reality, but he chooses as his companion the very down-to-earth Sancho Panza. The following passage is one of the best known in the book; it tells what happens when Don Quixote mistakes some windmills for evil giants and decides to fight against them.

# *From* DON QUIXOTE

squire (noun): a man who helps a knight.
deprive (verb): to take from.
spoils (noun): property taken from an enemy.
encounter (noun): meeting, clash, battle.
righteous (adj.): good, in the cause of right.
accursed (adj.): terrible, awful.
breed (noun): race, type.
league (noun): a unit of distance.
wings (noun): the blades of a windmill.
millstone (noun): a stone that grinds grain in a mill
engage (verb): to involve.
unequal combat: a fight in which one side has the advantage.
spurs (noun): attachments to riding boots used to urge a horse onward.
steed (noun): horse.
heed (noun): attention.
perceive (verb): see.
vile (adj.): evil.
flourish (verb): wave with dramatic gestures.
Briareus: a hundred-armed creature from Greek mythology.
thereupon (adv.): immediately after this.
commend oneself (idiom): entrust oneself, pray to someone for protection.
Dulcinea: Don Quixote's love.
beseech (verb): beg.
succor (verb): help.
peril (noun): danger.
lance (noun): a long, pointed weapon.
bore down upon: rode against.
fell upon: attacked.

At this point Don Quixote and Sancho Panza caught sight of thirty or forty windmills which were standing on the plain there, and no sooner had Don Quixote laid eyes upon them than he turned to his squire and said, "Fortune is guiding our affairs better than we could have wished; for you see there before you, friend Sancho Panza, some thirty or more lawless giants with whom I mean to do battle. I shall deprive them of their lives, and with the spoils from this encounter we shall begin to enrich ourselves; for this is righteous warfare, and it is a great service to God to remove so accursed a breed from the face of the earth."

"What giants?" said Sancho Panza.

"Those that you see there," replied his master, "those with the long arms some of which are as much as two leagues in length."

"But look, your Grace, those are not giants but windmills, and what appear to be arms are their wings which, when whirled in the breeze, cause the millstone to go."

"It is plain to be seen," said Don Quixote, "that you have little experience in this matter of adventures. If you are afraid, go off to one side and say your prayers while I am engaging them in fierce, unequal combat."

Saying this, he gave spurs to his steed Rocinante, without paying any heed to Sancho's warning that these were truly windmills and not giants that he was riding forth to attack. Nor even when he was close upon them did he perceive what they really were, but shouted at the top of his lungs, "Do not seek to flee, cowards and vile creatures that you are, for it is but a single knight with whom you have to deal!"

At that moment a little wind came up and the big wings began turning.

"Though you flourish as many arms as did the giant Briareus," said Don Quixote when he perceived this, "you still shall have to answer to me."

He thereupon commended himself with all his heart to his lady Dulcinea, beseeching her to succor him in this peril; and being well covered with his shield and his lance at rest, he bore down upon them at a full gallop and fell upon the first mill that stood in his way, giving a thrust at the wing, which was whirling at such a speed that his lance was broken into bits and both horse and horseman went rolling over the plain, very much

thrust (noun): a stab,
  attempt to hit.
battered (adj.): beaten.

battered indeed. Sancho upon his donkey came hurrying to his master's assistance as fast as he could, but when he reached the spot, the knight was unable to move, so great was the shock with which he and Rocinante had hit the ground.

"God help us!" exclaimed Sancho, "did I not tell your Grace to look well, that those were nothing but windmills, a fact which no one could fail to see unless he had other mills of the same sort in his head?"

subject (adj.): having a
  tendency toward,
  liable.
Frestón: Don Quixote
  imagines that he is
  being persecuted by
  an enemy named
  Frestón.

"Be quiet, friend Sancho," said Don Quixote. "Such are the fortunes of war, which more than any other are subject to constant change. What is more, when I come to think of it, I am sure that this must be the work of that magician Frestón . . . who has thus changed the giants into windmills in order to deprive me of the glory of overcoming them. . . ."

## THINKING ABOUT YOUR READING

### The Main Point

Is Don Quixote's mistake simply funny, or does Cervantes want to tell us something indirectly?

### Details

1. Who was Don Quixote's squire?
2. Approximately how many windmills were there?
3. What did Don Quixote think the windmills were?
4. To whom did Don Quixote commend himself before the fight?
5. How did Don Quixote account for his defeat?

### Your Opinion

6. Why did Don Quixote make such a mistake?
7. Who is more sensible, Don Quixote or Sancho Panza?
8. What did Sancho Panza mean when he said that a person who failed to see that the windmills were not giants must have "other mills of the same sort in his head"?

## Topics for Further Discussion and Writing

9.  The popular expression "tilting at windmills" comes from this story. Explain what it means and relate it to what you have read.

10. Don Quixote's love of romantic stories about knights made it impossible for him to see reality. Do you agree that too much time spent on fiction (whether in books, in movies, or on television) can cut a person off from the real world?

11. When Don Quixote was knocked off of his horse, he blamed the "fortunes of war" and Frestón, the magician, but he did not realize that his own error was responsible for his fall. Is this type of attitude common?

12. The word *quixotic* has been derived from the name "Quixote." What does the word mean? How does it apply to this passage?

13. Is there a positive side of what Don Quixote does? Is it sometimes good to be quixotic?

## VOCABULARY BUILDING

Here is a list of words from the reading. Review their meanings if necessary, and then do the vocabulary exercise.

| | | |
|---|---|---|
| battered | flourish | righteous |
| deprive | heed | spoils |
| encounter | lance | subject |
| engage | peril | |

**Vocabulary Exercise 1** | *Fill in each blank with the correct word from the list above. Add verb endings if necessary.*

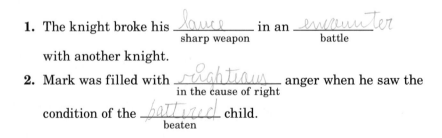

1. The knight broke his _lance_ in an _encounter_
                       sharp weapon         battle
   with another knight.

2. Mark was filled with _righteous_ anger when he saw the
                       in the cause of right
   condition of the _battered_ child.
                      beaten

3. The soldier _~~flourished~~_ his rifle and _~~deprived~~_ an old
waved                        robbed

woman of her money and jewels, calling them the _~~engage~~_ (to be)
loot, property
taken from an
enemy

of war.

4. Some people like to _____ in dangerous sports
be involved

despite their _~~heed~~_ .
danger

5. The reckless driver paid no _~~heed~~_ to the stop sign.
attention

6. Jack was _~~subject~~_ to severe headaches.
liable

## EXPANDING YOUR VOCABULARY: OTHER MEANINGS AND RELATED WORDS

**battered**
**to batter** (verb): to beat, break.    "Let me in, or I'll **batter** down the door,"
                                            yelled the man.

**battery** (noun): beating.              He was charged with assault and **battery.**

**deprive**
**deprivation** (noun):
  1. state of having little.      The child suffered greatly from **deprivation.**
  2. the loss of something.       Clara regretted the **deprivation** of her library
                                            privileges.

**deprived** (adj.): lacking necessities,   That poor little boy is a **deprived** child from a
poor.                                       **deprived** environment.

**engage**
**engaged** (adj.):
  1. busy, occupied.              We cannot see you until next month because
                                            we are **engaged** for the next three
                                            weekends.
                                            I am **engaged** in a new project.
  2. promised in marriage.        Ellen and Bob have just gotten **engaged;** they
                                            plan to marry in May.

**engagement** (noun):
  1. appointment.                 I have an important **engagement** tonight.
  2. plan to marry.               My friends have just announced their
                                            **engagement.**

**heed**
**to heed** (verb): to pay attention.      When you drive, you must **heed** the traffic
                                            signals.

**heedless** (adj.): careless, not attentive.

**Heedless** drivers endanger lives.

**heedlessly** (adv.): carelessly, without paying attention.

He drove **heedlessly** through a red light.

**peril**
**perilous** (adj.): dangerous.

The edge of a cliff is a **perilous** place to stand.

**perilously** (adv.): dangerously.

Paul was standing **perilously** close to the edge of the cliff.

Here is a list of words explained above. If necessary, review the definitions and the examples given, and then do the vocabulary exercise.

| | | |
|---|---|---|
| batter | engaged | heedlessly |
| battery | engagement | perilous |
| deprivation | heed | perilously |
| deprived | heedless | |

**Vocabulary Exercise 2**

*Fill in each blank with the correct word. A word may be used more than once.*

1. The baby was playing _____ close to the edge of the
   dangerously

   swimming pool while his father was _____
   without paying attention

   _____ in conversation with a friend.
   occupied

2. A person who is found guilty of assault and _*battery*_
   beating

   will probably go to prison.

3. For a while David Copperfield was a _____ child who
   lacking necessities

   led a _____ existence in the streets of London.
   dangerous

4. The landlord did not _*heed*_ my request for more
   pay attention to

   heat; if he does not _____ my next request, he will
   pay attention to

   have an _____ with the housing inspector.
   appointment

5. Martha and Ray have been _____ for five years; it is
planning to marry

the longest _____ I have ever heard of.
plan to marry

6. My uncle has led a life of hardship and _____, but he
lack of necessities

is _____ of his own problems and is always _____
not attentive                                           occupied
in helping others.

7. The police had to __*batter*__ down the door when a man
break

committed suicide in his apartment.

8. The drunk driver went __*needless*__ through a stop sign,
carelessly

but he stopped when he hit a truck.

Scene from Romeo and Juliet

## WILLIAM SHAKESPEARE

William Shakespeare (1564–1616) is generally regarded as one of the greatest figures in world literature. He was an English poet and playwright who wrote more than thirty-five plays, among them masterpieces such as *Hamlet, Macbeth, Julius Caesar, King Lear, As You Like It, A Midsummer Night's Dream,* and *Romeo and Juliet,* from which the following selection is taken.

Born in the town of Stratford-upon-Avon in England, Shakespeare attended the local grammar school and then married Anne Hathaway. He moved to London, where he became an actor and a prominent playwright. With others, he founded the well-known Globe Theatre.

Shakespeare is known for his comprehensive understanding of human nature and for his ability to express his ideas in memorable phrases. *Romeo and Juliet,* one of his best-loved plays, depicts the timeless story of young love frustrated by a family feud. The following selection shows the conversation between the lovers, who realize that the quarrel between their families should not be an obstacle to their love. They are supposed to hate each other because of their names—that is, because the Montagues have always hated the Capulets—but Juliet asks a famous question: "What's in a name?"

# *From* ROMEO AND JULIET

wherefore (adv.): why, for what reason.
art thou: are you.
deny (verb): reject, refuse connection with.
thou wilt not: you will not.

Juliet:  O Romeo, Romeo! wherefore art thou Romeo? *where are you*
Deny thy father and refuse thy name!
Or, if thou wilt not, be but sworn my love,
And I'll no longer be a Capulet.

Romeo (aside): Shall I hear more, or shall I speak at this?

Thou art thyself: you are yourself.

Juliet:  'Tis but thy name that is my enemy.
Thou art thyself, though not a Montague.
What's Montague? It is nor hand, nor foot,
Nor arm, nor face, nor any other part
Belonging to a man. O, be some other name!
What's in a name? That which we call a rose
By any other name would smell as sweet.
So Romeo would, were he not Romeo call'd,

Retain (verb): keep.
Retain ... title: Keep all the qualities that he has despite his name. (*Owes* here means *owns*.)
doff (verb): take off, remove.
new baptiz'd: newly named.
Henceforth (adv.): from now on.

Retain that dear perfection which he owes
Without that title. Romeo, doff thy name;
And for that name, which is no part of thee,
Take all myself.

Romeo:  I take thee at thy word.
Call me but love, and I'll be new baptiz'd;
Henceforth I never will be Romeo.

## THINKING ABOUT YOUR READING

### The Main Point

What point does Juliet make about names?

### Details

1. What are the last names of Romeo and Juliet?
   *ROMEO MONTAGUE + JULIET CAPULET*
2. What flower does Juliet mention?
   *A ROSE*

## Your Opinion

3.  Juliet sees "perfection" in Romeo. Is this attitude usual when people are in love? *Yes*

4.  Is Juliet justified in asking Romeo to give up his name?

## Topics for Further Discussion and Writing

5.  Juliet says, "A rose by any other name would smell as sweet." Is she right? If the names of things are changed, do our attitudes toward those things also change?

6.  Why do people choose the names of their children very carefully? Can a name influence a person's character or life? In what way is a name part of a person's identity?

7.  Romeo says that if Juliet loves him, he will give up his old name. It has been the custom for married women to drop their old names and take the names of their husbands. If you are a man, would you be willing to take your wife's name? If you are a woman, would you want your husband to adopt your name?

8.  Romeo and Juliet have just fallen in love, and their ideas are very romantic. Should you get married with a romantic attitude or a realistic attitude? Which will lead to a happier marriage?

9.  Juliet asks Romeo to reject his family for the sake of love. Is this request fair? Would you be willing to cut yourself off from your own family for the sake of love?

## VOCABULARY BUILDING

Here is a list of words from the reading.

| | | |
|---|---|---|
| baptize | doff | retain |
| deny | henceforth | |

BAPTIZE = PUT NAME IN church.
DENY = REJET, REFUSE CONNECTION WITH.
DOFF = TAKE OFF, REMOVE
HENCEFORTH = FROM NOW ON
RETAIN = KEEP

**Vocabulary Exercise 1**

*Fill in each blank with the correct word. Use correct verb forms.*

1. The old-fashioned gentleman ___doffed___ his hat whenever
   <u>took off</u>

   he met a woman.
2. Mr. and Mrs. Anderson's baby will be ___baptize___ next
   <u>named in church</u>

   Sunday.
3. Governor Green ___denied___ the prisoner's request for a
   <u>rejected</u>

   pardon.
4. These dried flowers have ___retained___ all the lovely colors of
   <u>kept</u>

   fresh blooms.
5. The preacher said, "___henceforth___ you will resist all
   <u>From now on</u>

   temptations."

*Read for*
*enjoyment.*

## ELIZABETH CADY STANTON

Elizabeth Cady Stanton (1815–1902) was born in Johnstown, New York. As a young woman, she studied law with her father, since law schools at that time did not admit women. She became a reformer, opposing slavery and supporting women's rights.

In 1848 Stanton, along with Lucretia Mott, organized the first women's rights convention in America. Held in Seneca Falls, New York, the convention issued a "Declaration of Sentiments" based on the American Declaration of Independence. Stanton stated, "All men and women are created equal" and strongly supported the right of women to vote.

As the mother of seven children, Stanton was also very concerned with family life and child care. She lectured and wrote on these subjects. In the following passage from her memoirs, she tells how an experience from her own life taught her that respect for women and respect for the seriousness of child care go hand in hand.

# From "MOTHERHOOD"

. . . Though motherhood is the most important of all the professions—requiring more knowledge than any other department in human affairs—there was no attention given to preparation for this office. If we buy a plant of a horticulturist we ask him many questions as to its needs, whether it thrives best in sunshine or in shade, whether it needs much or little water, what degrees of heat or cold; but when we hold in our arms for the first time a being of infinite possibilities, in whose wisdom may rest the destiny of a nation, we take it for granted that the laws governing its life, health, and happiness are intuitively understood, that there is nothing new to be learned in regard to it. Here is a science to which philosophers have as yet given but little attention. . . . Having gone through the ordeal of bearing a child, I was determined, if possible, to keep him, so I read everything I could find on babies. But the literature on this subject was . . . confusing and unsatisfactory. . . .

*[After giving an example of the dangerous theories written on child care in the nineteenth century, Stanton tells of her conflict with a nurse, who wanted to follow the doctor's orders and wrap the newborn baby tightly, as was the custom. Stanton, however, was firm in refusing to do this.]*

Besides the obstinacy of the nurse, I had the ignorance of physicians to contend with. When the child was four days old we discovered that the collar bone was bent. The physician, wishing to get a pressure on the shoulder, braced the bandage round the wrist. "Leave that," he said, "ten days, and then it will be all right." Soon after he left I noticed that the child's hand was blue, showing that the circulation was impeded. "That will never do," said I; "nurse, take it off." "No, indeed," she answered, "I shall never interfere with the doctor." So I took it off myself, and sent for another doctor, who was said to know more of surgery. He expressed great surprise that the first physician called should have put on so severe a bandage. "That," said he, "would do for a grown man, but ten days of it on a child would make him a cripple." However, he did nearly the same thing, only fastening it round the hand instead of the wrist. I soon saw that the ends of the fingers were all purple, and that to leave

**horticulturist** (noun): person who grows and studies plants.
**thrive** (verb): to grow and do well.

**infinite** (adj.): unlimited, endless.

**intuitively** (adv.): by instinct.

**ordeal** (noun): difficult experience.

**obstinacy** (noun): stubbornness.
**contend** (verb): to fight, oppose.

**impede** (verb): to slow something down.

**severe** (adj.): harshly restricting.

propose (verb): intend.

aghast (adj.): shocked.

brisk (adj.): lively.

arnica (noun): a liquid, derived from herbs, used to treat sprains and bruises.

budding (adj.): beginning to grow.
compress (noun): a folded cloth or a pad applied to a part of the body.
inflammation (noun): redness, soreness, irritation.
subside (verb): to go down, lessen.
sons of Aesculapius: doctors. Aesculapius was a legendary physician, son of the Greek god Apollo.

supreme (adj.): most important, highest.

absolutely (adv.): totally.

dignified (adj.): honored, respected.

lamentable (adj.): regrettable.

that on ten days would be as dangerous as the first. So I took it off.

"What a woman!" exclaimed the nurse. "What do you propose to do?" "Think out something better myself; so brace me up with some pillows and give the baby to me." She looked at me aghast. "Now," I said, talking partly to myself and partly to her, "what we want is a little pressure on that bone; that is what both of those men have aimed at. How can we get it without involving the arm, is the question?" "I am sure I don't know," said she, rubbing her hands and taking two or three brisk turns around the room. "Well, bring me three strips of linen, four double." I then folded one, wet in arnica and water, and laid it on the collar bone, put two other bands, like a pair of suspenders over the shoulder, crossing them both in front and behind, pinning the ends to the diaper, which gave the needed pressure without impeding the circulation anywhere. As I finished she gave me a look of budding confidence, and seemed satisfied that all was well. Several times, night and day, we wet the compress and readjusted the bands, until all appearance of inflammation had subsided.

At the end of ten days the two sons of Aesculapius appeared and made their examination, and said all was right, whereupon I told them how badly their bandages worked, and what I had done myself. They smiled at each other, and one said, "Well, after all, a mother's instinct is better than a man's reason." "Thank you, gentlemen, there was no instinct about it. I did some hard thinking before I saw how I could get pressure on the shoulder without impeding the circulation, as you did." Thus, in the supreme moment of a young mother's life, when I needed tender care and support, the whole responsibility of my child's supervision fell upon me; but though uncertain at every step of my own knowledge, I learned another lesson in self-reliance. I trusted neither men nor books absolutely after this, either in regard to the heavens above or the earth beneath, but continued to use my "mother's instinct," if "reason" is too dignified a term to apply to a woman's thoughts. My advice to every mother is, above all other arts and sciences, study first what relates to babyhood, as there is no department of human action in which there is such lamentable ignorance.

## THINKING ABOUT YOUR READING

### The Main Point

What points is Stanton making about women, motherhood, and child care? *Women should*

### Details

1. What problem did Stanton's baby have? *collar bone was bent,*
2. What treatment did the doctors give the baby?
3. What was wrong with that treatment? *To dangerous.*
4. Why was Stanton's treatment better? *Because she thought*
5. What did the doctors say to Stanton when they examined the baby ten days later?

### Your Opinion

6. What is your opinion of the nurse employed by Mrs. Stanton? Why did the nurse act the way she did?
7. Do you think Mrs. Stanton was right not to trust doctors or books about babies?
8. Why did the doctors smile at each other just before one of them said, "A mother's instinct is better than a man's reason"?
9. Why does the author call the doctors "sons of Aesculapius"? Why doesn't she just call them "the doctors"?

### Topics for Further Discussion and Writing

10. Stanton said that "motherhood is the most important of all the professions." Do you agree?
11. If you are a parent, describe your feelings during the first few weeks after the birth of your first child. Did you have an experience like Stanton's?
12. Many people have written books about babies. Are these books useful? Would you read them *before* your baby was born?

13.   Stanton says she knew how to treat her baby because of "hard thinking," not because of "a mother's instinct." How can taking infant care classes, reading books on child development, and thinking hard about their new responsibilities help prepare people for parenthood?

14.   Stanton says that this experience taught her "a lesson in self-reliance." Describe an experience that taught you to be more independent.

15.   In this passage Stanton discusses not only child care, but also male attitudes toward women. The doctors were expressing the attitude that men think logically whereas women act by instinct. Is this attitude common today? Do you agree or disagree with this attitude?

## VOCABULARY BUILDING

Here is a list of words from the reading. Reread the definitions if necessary and do the following exercise.

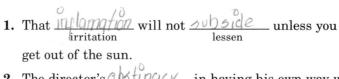

| | | |
|---|---|---|
| absolutely | impede | obstinacy |
| aghast – *shocked* | infinite | ordeal – *dificult experience* |
| brisk – *lively* | inflammation | severe |
| budding – *Begining* | intuitively | subside |
| contend – *to grow* | lamentable | thrive – *to grow & do well* |

**Vocabulary Exercise 1** | *Fill in each blank with the correct word.*

1. That *inflamation* will not *subside* unless you
   ———————         ———————
   irritation            lessen
   get out of the sun.

2. The director's *obstinacy* in having his own way will
   ————————————
   stubbornness
   *impede* progress.
   ——————
   slow down

3. The President was *ag hast* when the Senate voted
   —————————
   shocked
   against his proposal, for he was *absolutely* convinced it
   ————————————
   totally
   was a good one.

4. Does a mother know _intuitively_ or through experience
   <u>by instinct</u>

   what will help her children ___*thrive*___?
   <u>grow and do well</u>

5. Henry thinks it is an ___*ordeal*___ every year when he has
   <u>difficult experience</u>

   to _*contend*_ with the Internal Revenue Service.
   <u>fight</u>

6. She had a ___*budding*___ confidence that she could cope with
   <u>beginning to grow</u>

   an _*infinitive*_ number of situations.
   <u>unlimited</u>

7. It is _*lamentable*_ when parents place harsh, _*severe*_
   <u>regrettable</u>                                        <u>strict</u>

   limits on a child's freedom.

8. A ___*brisk*___ walk will cheer us up.
   <u>lively</u>

## EXPANDING YOUR VOCABULARY: OTHER MEANINGS AND RELATED WORDS

**contend**
**contender** (noun): a person who strives or fights.

He is a **contender** for the heavyweight title.

**contention** (noun):
  1. a point in an argument.

His **contention** is that the town should build a new school.

  2. rivalry.

The two tennis players are in **contention** for the top ranking.

**impede**
**impediment** (noun):
  1. something in the way, a stumbling block.

The minister asked if there were any **impediments** to the marriage.

  2. a problem, difficulty.

He worked hard to overcome his speech **impediment.**

**inflammation**
**inflammatory** (adj.): tending to stir up anger and excitement.

The rebel leader's speech was **inflammatory.**

**intuitively**
**intuition** (noun): instinct.
**intuitive** (adj.): instinctive.

Her **intuition** told her not to accept that job.
He had an **intuitive** understanding of animals.

**lamentable**

**to lament** (verb): to mourn, to regret.

Napoleon **lamented** his defeat at Waterloo.

**lamentation** (noun): grief, mourning.

The king ignored the **lamentations** of his people.

**obstinacy**
**obstinate** (adj.): stubborn.

He is too **obstinate** to change his mind.

**obstinately** (adv.): stubbornly.

She **obstinately** insisted she was right.

**severe**
**severely** (adv.): seriously, harshly.

She was **severely** injured in an accident.

**severity** (noun): harshness.

The **severity** of winter in northern Canada keeps the population low.

Here is a list of words explained above.

| | | |
|---|---|---|
| contender | intuition | obstinate |
| contention | intuitive | obstinately |
| impediment | lament | severely |
| inflammatory | lamentation | severity |

**Vocabulary Exercise 2**

*Fill in each blank with the correct word. Add verb endings if necessary.*

1. The heavyweight __contender__ is very __obstinacy__
   (person who fights)            (stubbornly)
   refusing to train properly.

2. The rebel was __severely__ punished for his
                 (harshly, extremely)
   __inflammatory__ actions.
   (tending to stir up anger)

3. Her __contention__ is that there is no such thing as woman's
      (point in an argument)
   __intuition__.
   (instinct)

4. When Gandhi died, there was a great __lamentation__ in India.
                                          (mourning)

5. An __obstinate__ airplane passenger refused to put on his
      (stubborn)
   seat belt.

6. The __severity__ of the desert climate prevents much
      (harshness)
   agriculture.

7. My daughter __lamented__ the death of her pet turtle.

8. The parents had an *intuitive* ~~instinctive~~ feeling that their son's

   speech *impediment* ~~problem~~ could be cured.

## HENRY DAVID THOREAU

In 1846, Henry Thoreau, who was living by himself in a house he had built in the woods, was arrested and put into jail for refusing to pay his poll tax, a small amount of money that every adult was required to pay annually. Thoreau refused to pay this tax because he wanted to reject the authority of a government that allowed slavery. He was also protesting the Mexican War.

Although Thoreau spent only one night in jail, the essay that he wrote to explain his protest has had far-reaching effects. "Resistance to Civil Government," or "Civil Disobedience," as it is often called, has been read by people all over the world. Mahatma Gandhi used Thoreau's ideas in the struggle for the independence of India. In the United States, Martin Luther King, while still a college student, first read Thoreau and was deeply moved by his ideas. He found Thoreau's idea of a "peaceable revolution" a highly effective weapon in the struggle for equal rights for African Americans. He stated in 1966, "The teachings of Thoreau are alive today."

# *From* "CIVIL DISOBEDIENCE"

**mode** (noun): way, manner.
**situated** (adj.): placed in a certain position.
**distinctly** (adv.): clearly.
**effectual** (adj.): effective, workable.
**indispensablest**: old form of "most indispensable." **Indispensable** (adj.): absolutely necessary.
**deny** (verb): reject.
**civil** (adj.): 1. having to do with government. 2. polite. (Thoreau intends this double meaning as a play on words.)
**parchment** (noun): heavy paper on which laws were written.
**cease** (verb): stop.
**withdraw** (verb): pull out, leave.
**copartnership** (noun): relationship. (here between the individual and the government.)
**therefor** (adv.): for this reason.
**abolition** (noun): ending or stopping something (here, ending slavery).
**desponding** (adj.): despairing, discouraged.
**principles** (noun): rules of conduct or behavior.
**fugitive** (adj.): fleeing, running away.
**abide** (verb): remain, stay, live.
**afflict** (verb): torment, cause pain to.
**eloquently** (adv.): with graceful and persuasive speech.
**merely** (adv.): only.
**conform** (verb): be similar; agree; go along with.
**alternative** (noun): a choice between two possibilities.

I meet this American government, or its representative the state government, directly, and face to face, once a year, no more, in the person of its tax-gatherer; this is the only mode in which a man situated as I am necessarily meets it; and it then says distinctly, Recognize me; and the simplest, the most effectual, and, in the present posture of affairs, the indispensablest mode of treating with it . . . is to deny it then. My civil neighbor, the tax-gatherer, is the very man I have to deal with—for it is, after all, with men and not with parchment that I quarrel. . . .

I know this well, that if one thousand, if one hundred, if ten men whom I could name—if ten *honest* men only—aye, if *one* HONEST man, in this State of Massachusetts, *ceasing to hold slaves,* were actually to withdraw from this copartnership, and he locked up in the county jail therefor, it would be the abolition of slavery in America. For it matters not how small the beginning may seem to be: what is once well done is done for ever. But we love better to talk about it. . . .

Under a government which imprisons any unjustly, the true place for a just man is also a prison. The proper place today, the only place which Massachusetts has provided for her freer and less desponding spirits, is her prisons, to be put out and locked out of the State by her own act, as they have already put themselves out by their principles. It is there that the fugitive slave, and the Mexican prisoner on parole, and the Indian come to plead the wrongs of his race, should find them; on that separate, but more free and honorable ground, where the State places those who are not *with* her but *against* her—the only house in a slave-state in which a free man can abide with honor. If any think that their influence would be lost there, and their voices no longer afflict the ear of the State, that they would not be as an enemy within its walls, they do not know by how much truth is stronger than error, nor how much more eloquently and effectively he can combat injustice who has experienced a little in his own person. Cast your whole vote, not a strip of paper merely, but your whole influence. A minority is powerless while it conforms to the majority; it is not even a minority then; but it is irresistible when it clogs by its whole weight. If the alternative is to keep all just men in prison, or give up war and slavery, the State will not hesitate which to choose. If a thousand men were not to pay their tax-bills this year, that would not be a

revolution (noun): the overthrow of a government or a great change.

violent and bloody measure, as it would be to pay them, and enable the State to commit violence and shed innocent blood. This is, in fact, the definition of a peaceable revolution, if any such is possible. . . .

## THINKING ABOUT YOUR READING

### The Main Point

What is the central idea of this passage? What is "civil disobedience"?

### Details

1. What wrongs was Thoreau protesting in this essay?
2. According to Thoreau, what does the tax collector represent?
3. What advice does Thoreau give those who wish to protest?

### Your Opinion

4. Thoreau says that if *one* honest man were to withdraw from the government, that act "would be the abolition of slavery in America." What do you think Thoreau means by this statement?
5. What does Thoreau mean when he says, "Under a government which imprisons any unjustly, the true place for a just man is also a prison"?
6. Do you agree that "truth is stronger than error"?
7. In the third paragraph Thoreau says that a person can more "eloquently and effectively" fight against injustice when he or she has personally experienced it. Do you agree?

### Topics for Further Discussion and Writing

8. Do you agree with Thoreau that a person must sometimes break a law if he or she feels that the government is unfair? Under what circumstances is civil disobedience justified?

9. Thoreau says that the only way a person in his situation meets the government is by being told to pay taxes. Is this the only way that most people today deal with their government? (You might consider the following: the courts, departments of public assistance, school systems, town meetings, and health-care programs.)

10. Thoreau says that one person who is truly committed to fighting against injustice can make a difference. Do you agree?

11. Thoreau says that a minority of the population is powerless if it does not act, but is irresistible when the people who make up the minority act together to oppose something unfair. Do you agree or disagree? Give examples to support your view.

12. Would you personally be willing to go to prison to protest a law that you considered wrong? If so, under what circumstances?

## VOCABULARY BUILDING

Here is a list of words from "Civil Disobedience."

| | | |
|---|---|---|
| abide — remain | deny | mode — way or maner |
| abolition | distinctly | parchment |
| afflict — torment, affliction | effectual | principles |
| alternative | eloquently | revolution |
| cease stop | fugitive | situated |
| civil | indispensable | withdraw |
| conform | merely | |

**Vocabulary Exercise 1** | *Insert the correct word in each of the blanks below. Use the correct form.*

1. Jack's parents were upset about his ___mode___ of life.
  (way)

2. The senator promised to work for the ___abolition___ of the draft.
  (ending)

3. At Grace's funeral, her cousin sang "___abide___ with Me,"
  (remain)

and her brother _____ gave the eulogy.
  (with graceful speech)

**4.** The army was _____ in a dangerous place.
located

**5.** As the mist cleared, Tom could see the bank of the river

quite _____.
clearly

**6.** Everyone ought to live by his or her _principles_
rules of conduct

**7.** The defeated army had no _alternative_ except to _withdraw_
choice                          pull out

**8.** The widespread use of machine labor began with what is now

called the Industrial _____.
great change

**9.** Some people refuse to _comfort_ to society's rules.
agree, go along with

**10.** A sturdy pair of boots is _____ on a long hike.
absolutely necessary

**11.** In the southern states the American _civil_
relating to government

War is still known as "The War Between the States."

**12.** The Bible tells us that Job refused to _deny_ God's
reject

authority, even though God had _afflict_ him.
tormented

**13.** A will written on an old piece of _parchment_ was
heavy paper

discovered in Mrs. Wilson's attic.

**14.** Writing in a journal is an _effectual_ way to improve
effective

writing skills.

**15.** Juan had no time to study his assignment, so he _mearly_
only

skimmed it.

**16.** The _____ slave was tracked by bloodhounds.
runaway

**17.** "This noise must _cease_ at once," said the teacher.
stop

## EXPANDING YOUR VOCABULARY:
## OTHER MEANINGS AND RELATED WORDS

**abolition**
**to abolish** (verb): to do away with, to end.

Thoreau wanted the government to **abolish** slavery.

**abolitionist** (noun): one who favored the abolition of slavery.

John Brown was a famous **abolitionist.**

You try it: use one of these new words in your own sentence:

_____

_____

**cease**
**cessation** (noun): a halt or stopping.

There was a **cessation** of all work on the project because of a lack of funds.

**unceasing** (adj.): without a stop.

The group got tired of Flora's **unceasing** complaints.

Your sentence: _____

_____

**conform**
**conformist** (noun): one who goes along with or follows others.

Eric was too much of a **conformist** to be very original.

Your sentence: _____

_____

**desponding**
**despondency** (noun): state of being discouraged or depressed.

The failure of his business led Jack into a period of **despondency.**

**despondent** (adj.): discouraged, depressed.

Jennie felt **despondent** after losing the debate.

Your sentence: _____

_____

**distinctly**
**distinct** (adj.): clear.

The cup had left a **distinct** ring on the table.

**distinction** (noun):
  1. difference.

As far as we could see, there was no **distinction** between the cheaper and the more expensive product.

  2. special honor.

Mark graduated from college with **distinction.**

Your sentence: _____

_____

**effectual**

**effectually** (adv.): in an effective manner.

That ointment **effectually** relieves the itching of insect bites.

Your sentence: _____

_____

**eloquently**

**eloquent** (adj.):
1. effective and graceful in speech or writing.
2. gracefully and effectively expressed.

**eloquence** (noun): effective and graceful speech or writing.

Martin Luther King, Jr., was an **eloquent** speaker.

Katy made an **eloquent** speech at the town meeting.

John F. Kennedy was known for his **eloquence.**

Your sentence: _____

_____

## EMILY DICKINSON

Emily Dickinson (1830–1886) is now considered one of the greatest American poets, but she was unknown in her own day. In fact, only seven of her poems were published during her lifetime. She lived a very quiet, secluded life in the small town of Amherst, Massachusetts, and wrote most of her poetry in secret. She hardly ever left Amherst after the age of twenty-five, and in her later years after her parents had died, she seldom left her house and always wore a white dress. Local people considered her very strange and called her "the myth."

After Emily Dickinson's death, her sister Lavinia discovered over 900 of her poems and had them published. Later, others were found, and today we know that she wrote more than 1,770 poems on a wide range of subjects, many of them dealing with very personal feelings and the wish to communicate with God. Her poetry has been translated into many languages, and her life, so very quiet and private, has been the subject of many books and articles. In the following well-known poem, she writes about being a private person as opposed to a public one.

# I'M NOBODY! WHO ARE YOU?

advertise (verb): give
  public notice.

dreary (adj.): dull and
  depressing.
livelong (adj.): whole,
  entire.
bog (noun): wet area,
  small swamp.

I'm Nobody! Who are you?
Are you—Nobody—Too?
Then there's a pair of us?
Don't tell! they'd advertise—you know!

How dreary—to be—Somebody!
How public—like a Frog—
To tell one's name—the livelong June—
To an admiring Bog!

## THINKING ABOUT YOUR READING

### The Main Point

What does the poem say about the difference between being
"somebody" and being "nobody"? Which condition does Emily Dickinson prefer?

### Details

1. What animal is mentioned in the poem?
2. What does it represent?

1R, A FROG—THAT MEANS EVERYONE FOOLISH

### Your Opinion

2R. TO CALL AN ATTENTION.

3. What does it mean to be "nobody"? Is any person really a
   "nobody"? MEANS NOT TO BE KNOWING
4. Look again at line 4: "Don't tell! they'd advertise—you
   know." What does this line mean? Who are "they"?
5. Do you think the poet is glad to discover another "nobody"?

## Topics for Further Discussion and Writing

6.  What are the advantages and disadvantages of being a famous person? Would you like to be famous?

7.  Would you describe yourself as an introvert (a quiet person who likes to be alone) or an extrovert (a very sociable person who enjoys company)?

8.  Consider your friends and relatives. Describe one who is an introvert and one who is an extrovert.

9.  Reread the brief introduction about Emily Dickinson and then look her up in an encyclopedia. Does the information given about her personality and life help to explain why she wrote this poem?

## EXPANDING YOUR VOCABULARY: OTHER MEANINGS AND RELATED WORDS

**advertise**
**advertisement** (noun): public notice or announcement, often to sell a product or give notice of a job opening.

Eddie placed an **advertisement** in the newspaper in order to sell his car.

**bog**
This word can be both a noun, as we have seen, and a verb.
**to bog** (verb): to get stuck, or to make something or someone stuck.

The whole project became **bogged** down in red tape.

**dreary**
**dreariness** (noun): state of being depressed and dull, desolation.

The **dreariness** of the old house depressed Hilda.

**pair**
**Pair** can be both a verb and a noun.
**to pair** (verb): to match, put together.

Mrs. Findmate, a born matchmaker, **paired** Joe with Betty because they are both very tall.

**public**
**publicity** (noun):
1.  notice or attention from the public.

The shy movie star avoided **publicity.**

2.  action to see that notice is attracted.

Her agent, however, employed a full-time director of **publicity** to make sure that the star was in full public view.

**to publicize** (verb): to give publicity to.

**publicly** (adv.): in an open manner, in front of everyone.

**to publish** (verb):
1. to make public, announce.

2. to bring out in printed form, to issue.

The committee worked hard to **publicize** the dance.

The politician **publicly** denounced the mayor, who was his former friend.

The chemist could not wait to **publish** the results of his experiment.

Emily Dickinson **published** only seven poems during her life.

Here is a list of words appearing in the poem or in the "Expanding Your Vocabulary" section. Review their definitions if necessary and do the exercise below.

advertise *give public notice*
advertisement
bog— *wet area, small swamp.*
dreariness *dull and depre-ssing.*

dreary *dull + dyire.*
livelong *wide entire*
pair — *To match put together.*
public *notice of attention*

publicity *action to see*
publicize
publicly *open manner, in front of everyone.*
publish *brought up*

**Vocabulary Exercise 1**

*Use the correct words from the list above to fill in the blanks. You may use a word more than once. Use the correct verb form.*

1. Mr. Martin refused to ___publish___ Mr. Orwell's letters
   *print*

   from Spain.

2. You do not have to ___publish___ the fact that you are
   *give publicity to*

   dieting. That is a ___dreary___ subject.
   *dull and depressing*

3. Marilyn is in charge of ___publicity___ for
   *action to see that notice is attracted*

   the school dance, so she has placed an ___advertisement___ in the
   *announcement*

   student newspaper.

4. Jessica has been ___bog___ down with boring work lately and
   *stuck*

   often complains of the ___dreariness___ of her life.
   *state of being dull and depressing*

5. Although the two movie stars stated ___advertise___ that
   *openly, to the public*

   they were just good friends, they were seen holding hands in

   many ___publicly___ places.
   *open to all*

**6.** Working in a nearby _____*bog*_____, the biologist selected a
<br>small swamp

frog to be _____*pair*_____ for an experiment with one raised in
<br>matched

a laboratory.

**7.** Jane was happy and cheerful the _____*live long*_____ day and never
<br>whole

felt _____*bog*_____ down by her duties as a _____*public part*_____
<br>stuck   relating to people

health nurse.

**8.** It pays to _____*advertized*_____.
<br>give public notice in order to sell a product

## MOHANDAS KARAMCHAND GANDHI

Born in India in 1869, Mohandas Gandhi was educated there and in England. At age twenty-four, he went to South Africa, where he taught school, practiced law, and became involved in the struggle to stop discrimination against Indians, organizing his first campaign of nonviolent resistance to unjust laws. In 1915, he returned to India. For thirty years, he led many nonviolent campaigns against British rule in India, and as a result, he was arrested and imprisoned several times. Gandhi worked not only for the freedom of India but also for unity among its different people, including Hindus and Muslims. In 1948, he was shot and killed by a religious fanatic.

Gandhi was highly respected by all the people of India, who gave him the title of *Mahatma*, meaning "great soul." His ideas of civil disobedience and nonviolence were adopted by proponents of civil rights in the United States and other countries.

The following selection describes a time when Gandhi was a schoolteacher trying to discover the best way to influence children morally and spiritually.

# SPIRITUAL TRAINING

**to be acquainted with:** know, understand.
**elements** (noun): basics.

**Tolstoy Farm:** a school named for Leo Tolstoy, a Russian writer and social philosopher.
**self-realization** (noun): developing one's potential, gaining self-knowledge.
**held:** believed.

**moral** (adj.): relating to ideas of right and wrong.
**impart** (verb): to communicate knowledge of.

**idle** (adj.): useless.
**valiant** (adj.): courageous.
**self-restraint** (noun): self-control.
**object lesson:** a lesson (person or thing) that teaches by example.
**impose** (verb): place.
**wards** (pl. noun): people one is responsible for protecting.
**unruly** (adj.): badly behaved, hard to control.
**exasperated** (adj.): extremely irritated.
**adamant** (adj.): firm, immovable.
**overreach** (verb): get the better of.

The spiritual training of the boys was a much more difficult matter than their physical and mental training. I relied little on religious books for the training of the spirit. Of course I believed that every student should be acquainted with the elements of his own religion and have a general knowledge of his own scriptures and therefore I provided for such knowledge as best I could. But that, to my mind, was part of the intellectual training. Long before I undertook the education of the youngsters of the Tolstoy Farm I had realized that the training of the spirit was a thing by itself. To develop the spirit is to build character and to gain a knowledge of God and to have self-realization. And I held that this was an essential part of the training of the young, and that all other training without culture of the spirit was of no use, and might be even harmful.

How then was this spiritual training to be given? I made the children memorize and recite hymns, and I read to them from books on moral training. But that was far from satisfying me. As I came into closer contact with them I saw that it was not through books that one could impart training of the spirit. Just as physical training was to be imparted through physical exercise, and the intellectual through intellectual exercise, even so the training of the spirit was possible only through the exercise of the spirit. And this depended on the life and character of the teacher. It would be idle for me, if I were a liar, to teach my boys to tell the truth. A coward of a teacher would never succeed in making his boys valiant, and a stranger to self-restraint could never teach his pupils the value of self-restraint. I saw therefore that I must be an eternal object lesson for the boys and girls living with me. They thus became my teachers, and I learned that I must be good and live straight, if only for their sake. I may say that the increasing discipline and restraint I imposed on myself at the Tolstoy Farm was mostly due to those wards of mine.

One of them was wild, unruly, given to lying, and quarrelsome. On one occasion he broke out most violently. I was exasperated. I never punished my boys, but this time I was very angry. I tried to reason with him. But he was adamant, and even tried to overreach me. At last I picked up a ruler lying at hand and delivered a blow on his arm. I trembled as I struck him, and I daresay he noticed it. This was an entirely

novel (adj.): new, never seen or experienced before.

paid me back in the same coin: done the same to me.

stoutly built: physically large and strong.

resource (noun): something one uses.

repent (verb): regret.

exhibit (verb): show.

brute (noun): the cruel, animal side of a person.

corporal (adj.): physical, of the body.

prompt (verb): stimulate or move a person to action.

avail (verb): to be of use.

misconduct (noun): bad behavior.

endeavor (noun): attempt.

novel experience for them all. The boy cried out and begged to be forgiven. He cried not because the beating was painful to him; he could, if he had been so minded, have paid me back in the same coin, being a stoutly built youth of seventeen. But he realized my pain in being driven to this violent resource. Never again after this incident did he disobey me. But I still repent that violence. I am afraid I exhibited before him that day, not the spirit, but the brute in me.

I have always been opposed to corporal punishment. I remember only one occasion on which I physically punished one of my sons. I have therefore never until this day been able to decide whether I was right or wrong in using the ruler. Probably it was improper, for it was prompted by anger and a desire to punish. Had it been an expression only of my distress I should have considered it justified. But the motive in this case was mixed. This incident set me thinking and taught me a better method of correcting students. I do not know how that method would have availed on the occasion in question. The youngster soon forgot the incident and I do not think he ever showed great improvement. But the incident made me understand better the duty of a teacher towards his pupils. Cases of misconduct on the part of the boys often occurred after this, but I never resorted to corporal punishment. Thus in my endeavor to impart spiritual training to the boys and girls under me I came to understand better and better the power of the spirit.

## THINKING ABOUT YOUR READING

### The Main Point

What does Gandhi feel is the best way to teach and influence students?

### Details

1. In the first paragraph, what three kinds of training does Gandhi mention?

2. Did Gandhi rely totally on religious books in order to impart spiritual training?

3. What was the name of the school?

4. What did Gandhi use to hit the boy?

## Your Opinion

5. Why was Gandhi sorry that he had hit the boy?

6. Would you like to have teachers who behave and think as Gandhi did?

7. If you were a teacher, would you follow Gandhi's ideas about teaching?

8. Why do you think Gandhi was dissatisfied with teaching from books on moral training?

## Topics for Further Discussion and Writing

9. Gandhi says that he must be an "object lesson" for his students, meaning that *he* must always behave the way he wants *them* to behave. What is your opinion of this idea? Does this idea apply to other people as well as teachers?

10. Gandhi taught in a school that allowed corporal punishment. What is your opinion of corporal punishment in schools?

11. In some countries, it is against the law for parents to hit their children. What is your opinion of these laws?

12. Gandhi states that a liar cannot teach children to tell the truth and a coward cannot teach them to be brave. Do you agree or disagree with his opinion? Explain your answer with reasons and examples.

13. Gandhi felt that it was a mistake to hit the student, but he also felt that the incident made him think about ways to become a better teacher. Do you think that people can learn from their mistakes? Explain your answer.

14. Gandhi tells about an incident in which he lost his temper and failed to live up to his ideals. He regretted it for years. Is there an incident in your life that you have regretted for years because your behavior did not live up to your ideals?

## VOCABULARY BUILDING

Here is a list of words from the reading. If necessary, go over their meanings. Then do the exercise.

| | | |
|---|---|---|
| adamant _firm, avoi(_ | exhibit | novel |
| availed | impart | prompted |
| brute | imposed | unruly |
| exasperated | moral | valiant |

**Vocabulary Exercise 1**

*Fill in each blank with the correct word.*

1. He did not mean to be a ___brute___ , but he was so
          <u>cruel person</u>
   _____ by the children's _____ behavior that
     <u>extremely irritated</u>              <u>hard to control</u>
   he shouted angrily and really frightened them.

2. The mayor was ___adamant___ in her position that she would
             <u>firm, immovable</u>
   have to raise taxes, and that ___prompted___ her opponent
                <u>stimulated, moved to action</u>
   to say that she was irresponsible.

3. Parents cannot ___impart___ wisdom and kindness to
           <u>communicate knowledge of</u>
   their children unless they themselves ___exhibit___ the same
                     <u>show</u>
   qualities.

4. Gandhi was not sure whether a nonviolent method of dealing
   with the student's misbehavior would have ___availed___ , but
                        <u>been of use</u>
   he also felt that in striking the boy, he himself had not
   behaved in a ___moral___ way.
          <u>relating to ideas of right and wrong</u>

5. The firefighter made a ___valiant___ attempt to save the
             <u>courageous</u>
   children in the burning building.

6. Being considered a role model by younger children was a
   ___novel___ and pleasant experience for Dwayne, but he soon
    <u>new</u>

found that their admiration ~~placed~~ *imposed* responsibilities

and obligations on him.

## EXPANDING YOUR VOCABULARY: OTHER MEANINGS AND RELATED WORDS

**adamant**
We encountered this word as an adjective, but it can also be a noun: an unbreakable or extremely hard substance.
**adamantly** (adverb): firmly, immovably.

Her stubbornness was as hard and unyielding as **adamant.**
The dean is **adamantly** opposed to any changes in the graduation requirements.

**availed**
In the reading, *avail* meant to be of use. The expression to *avail oneself of* means to take advantage of.
**avail** (noun): advantage, use.

She **availed herself of** every opportunity on campus to get tutoring.
He tried to save money, but to no **avail**; in fact, he got further into debt.

**exasperated**
**to exasperate** (verb): to irritate.

**exasperating** (adj.): irritating.

**exasperation** (noun): the state of being irritated.

Her husband's constant lateness really **exasperates** her.
The dog has an **exasperating** habit of begging for food during our dinner.
My **exasperation** got the better of me, and I told my nasty boss exactly what I thought of him.

**idle**
In the reading, *idle* is used as an adjective. It can also be a verb: to spend time doing nothing.
**idleness** (noun): state of doing nothing.
**idler** (noun): a person who is doing nothing.
**idly** (adv.): in a lazy way, uselessly, without purpose.

He **idled** the whole day lying in a hammock.

**Idleness** will not get you a promotion or a raise in salary.
Several **idlers** were standing in front of the coffee shop.
She was **idly** looking through the pages of a magazine.

**impose**
**imposing** (adj.): impressive because of size or a dignified manner.
**imposition** (noun): burden, or the act of placing a burden on someone.

Tourists looked at the **imposing** statue of Abraham Lincoln.

I was very busy, so it was really an **imposition** when Mary asked me to drive her to the airport.

**valiant**
**valiantly** (adv.): heroically,
  courageously.
**valor** (noun): courage, heroism.

The doctors fought **valiantly** to save the
  child's life.
These soldiers received medals for their **valor**
  in battle.

Here is a list of words appearing in the "Expanding Your Vocabulary" section. Review their definitions if necessary and do the following exercise.

| | | |
|---|---|---|
| adamant | exasperating | idly |
| adamantly | exasperation | imposing |
| avail | idle | imposition |
| to avail oneself | idleness | valiantly |
| exasperate | idler | valor |

**Vocabulary Exercise 2** | *Use the correct words from the list above to fill in the blanks.*

1. He tried to cure himself of the ___exasperating___ habit of mouthing
                                            irritating
   the words when he was reading, but all his efforts were of no
   ___avail___.
       use

2. She was ___idle___ looking through the newspaper without
              without purpose
   actually reading it.

3. This scholarship will allow you to ___avail___ yourself of the
                                        take advantage
   opportunity to go to college full time.

4. In Washington, D.C., there are many ___imposing___ monuments.
                                          impressive

5. People tried ___valiantly___ to prevent the river from
                 courageously, heroically
   flooding their town.

6. The judge was known to be as hard as ___adamant___.
                                          hard, unbreakable substance

7. When people ___to avail idle___ their days away, they will
                 spend time doing nothing
   regret it later.

8. My wife _adamant<sub>ly</sub>_ refuses to go see the dentist regularly,
   firmly, immovably

   behavior that fills me with _exasperating_
   state of being irritated

9. The forty-minute delay certainly _exasperate_ all the
   irritated

   commuters on the train.

10. Her constant _idleness_ means that I have to do extra work;
    laziness

    this situation is a real _imposing_ on me.
    burden

11. To show _valor_ does not mean that a person has no fear;
    courage

    it means the person has mastered his or her fear.

12. Joey gives the appearance of being an _idler_, but
    person who does nothing

    in fact he works very hard.

## CARL SANDBURG

Carl Sandburg (1878–1967) was born in Galesburg, Illinois. His parents were poor immigrants, and it was not easy for him to obtain an education. Nevertheless, he became a famous American writer and poet.

He left home as a young man and was a hobo, a day worker, and a soldier before returning to his hometown to attend college. Always interested in helping working people, he supported the efforts of early labor unions and worked for the Social Democratic Party in Wisconsin. Known as "the poet of the people," he is famous for his *Chicago Poems,* which are based on the experiences of everyday Americans.

This interest in the American experience also led Sandburg to write his six-volume biography of Abraham Lincoln, which won a Pulitzer Prize in 1940. The following excerpt from the first volume emphasizes the "wilderness beginnings" and humble background of the man who became the sixteenth President of the United States. It describes how Lincoln was educated by extensive reading and by contact with the plain working people around him.

# *From* ABRAHAM LINCOLN

In December 1816, Tom Lincoln with Nancy, Sarah, Abe, four horses and their most needed household goods, made their breakaway from Kentucky, moving north and crossing the Ohio River into land then Perry County, later Spencer County, Indiana. They traveled a wild raw country, rolling land with trees everywhere, tall oaks and elms, maples, birches, dogwood, underbrush tied down by ever-winding grapevines, thin mist and winter damp rising from the ground as Tom, with Abe perhaps helping, sometimes went ahead with an ax and hacked out a trail. "It was a wild region, with many bears and other wild animals still in the woods," Abe wrote later, where "the panther's scream filled night with fear" and "bears preyed on the swine." A lonesome country, settlers few, "about one human being to each square mile," families two and three miles apart.

They had toiled and hacked their way through wilderness when about 16 miles from the Ohio River they came to a rise of ground somewhat open near Little Pigeon Creek. Here the whole family pitched in and threw together a pole shed or "half-faced camp," at the open side a log fire kept burning night and day. In the next weeks of that winter Tom Lincoln, with help from neighbors and young Abe, now nearly eight, erected a cabin 18 by 20 feet, with a loft. . . .

*[Several years passed. Sandburg describes the hardships of life on the frontier. Abraham Lincoln's mother died, and his father remarried.]*

School kept at Pigeon Creek when a schoolmaster happened to drift in, usually in winter, and school was out when he drifted away. Andrew Crawford taught Abe in 1820, James Swaney two years later, and after a year of no school Abe learned from Azel Dorsey. The schoolmasters were paid by the parents in venison, hams, corn, animal skins and other produce. Four miles from home to school and four miles to home again Abe walked for his learning, saying later that "all his schooling did not amount to one year." . . .

Dennis Hanks made an ink of blackberry briar root and copperas, an "ornery ink," he called it. And Abe with a turkey-buzzard quill would write his name and say, "Denny, look at that, will you? *Abraham Lincoln!* That stands fur me. Don't look

---

**raw** (adj.): undeveloped.

**swine** (noun): pigs.

**toil** (verb): to work.
**rise of ground somewhat open**: a clearing a little higher than the surrounding area.

**loft** (noun): an unfinished upper floor.

**venison** (noun): deer meat.

**Dennis Hanks**: Lincoln's cousin.
**copperas** (noun): copper water, used in making ink.
**ornery** (adj.): difficult.

a blamed bit like me!" And, said Dennis, "He'd stand and study it a spell. 'Peared to mean a heap to Abe."

Having learned to read Abe read all the books he could lay his hands on. Dennis, years later, tried to remember his cousin's reading habits. "I never seen Abe after he was twelve 'at he didn't have a book some'ers 'round. He'd put a book inside his shirt an' fill his pants pockets with corn dodgers, an' go off to plow or hoe. When noon come he'd set down under a tree, an' read an' eat. In the house at night, he'd tilt a cheer by the chimbly, an' set on his backbone an' read. I've seen a feller come in an' look at him, Abe not knowin' anybody was round, an' sneak out agin like a cat, an' say, 'Well, I'll be darned.' It didn't seem natural, nohow, to see a feller read like that. Aunt Sairy's never let the children pester him. She always said Abe was goin' to be a great man some day. An' she wasn't goin' to have him hendered."

They heard Abe saying, "The things I want to know are in books; my best friend is the man who'll git me a book I ain't read." One fall afternoon he walked to see John Pitcher, a lawyer at Rockport, nearly 20 miles away, and borrowed a book he heard Pitcher had. A few days later, with his father and Dennis and John Hanks he shucked corn from early daylight till sundown. Then after supper he read the book till midnight, and next day at noon hardly knew the taste of his corn bread because of the book in front of him. So they told it.

He read many hours in the family Bible, the only book in their cabin. He borrowed and read *Aesop's Fables, Pilgrim's Progress, Robinson Crusoe,* Grimshaw's *History of the United States,* and Weems' *The Life of George Washington, with Curious Anecdotes, Equally Honorable to Himself and Exemplary to His Young Countrymen.* Books lighted lamps in the dark rooms of his gloomy hours. . . .

Education came to the youth Abe by many ways outside of schools and books. As he said later, he "picked up" education. He was the letter writer for the family and for neighbors. As he wrote he read the words out loud. He asked questions, "What do you want to say in the letter? How do you want to say it? Are you sure that's the best way to say it? Or do you think we can fix up a better way to say it?" This was a kind of training in grammar and English composition.

He walked 30 miles to a courthouse to hear lawyers speak and to see how they argued and acted. He heard roaring and ranting political speakers—and mimicked them. He listened to wandering evangelists who flung their arms and tore the air with their voices—and mimicked them. He told droll stories

**corn dodgers** (noun): fried pieces of corn bread.
**tilt a cheer by the chimbly:** dialect for "lean a chair against the chimney."

**Aunt Sairy:** Lincoln's stepmother.

**hendered:** dialect for *hindered* (stopped).

*Aesop's Fables,* etc. See page 402 for one of Aesop's fables and information about his life. The other books were popular in the nineteenth century, and some are still read today.
**anecdotes** (noun): stories.
**exemplary** (adj.): serving as a model or example.

**ranting** (adj.): raving, talking loudly and excitedly.
**mimic** (verb): to copy.
**evangelist** (noun): a preacher.
**droll** (adj.): amusing.

keenly (adv.): sharply, cleverly.
dram (noun): a small portion of liquid.
rollicking (adj.): funny and high-spirited.
bawdy (adj.): coarse, obscene.
earthy (adj.): down-to-earth, not over-refined.

with his face screwed up in different ways. He tried to read people as keenly as he read books. He drank enough drams of whisky to learn he didn't like the taste and it wasn't good for his mind or body. He smoked enough tobacco to learn he wouldn't care for it. He heard rollicking and bawdy verses and songs and kept some of them for their earthy flavor and sometimes meaningful intentions. . . .

## THINKING ABOUT YOUR READING

### The Main Point

What are the most important things Sandburg wants to get across about the young Abe Lincoln?

### Details

1. When did the Lincoln family move from Kentucky?
2. What river did they cross, and where did they settle?
3. How old was Abe Lincoln when he helped his father to build the log cabin?
4. How much classroom schooling did Lincoln have?
5. How many miles did Lincoln have to walk to and from school each day?
6. Who, according to Abe Lincoln, was his best friend?
7. Name some of the books Lincoln read.
8. What were some of the other sources of Lincoln's education?

### Your Opinion

9. In what ways do you feel Lincoln's "wilderness beginnings" shaped his character?
10. Why was it difficult to obtain an education on the American frontier?
11. What evidence is there that Lincoln valued education?
12. What does Sandburg mean when he says that Lincoln "tried to read people as keenly as he read books"?

13. What did Lincoln mean by saying that he "picked up" education?

14. Many of the quotations in this passage contain nonstandard English (dialect). Why do you think Dennis Hanks and even the young Abe Lincoln spoke this way?

## Topics for Further Discussion and Writing

15. Sandburg says of Lincoln, "Books lighted lamps in the dark rooms of his gloomy hours." Explain what this sentence means.

16. By trying whisky and tobacco, Lincoln learned that he did not care for them. Would he have been better off if he had never tried them? Are there some things that are better learned from personal experience and other things that are better learned from the experiences of others?

17. Lincoln learned about grammar and English composition by helping others to write their letters and by asking them what they wanted to say. What other questions did he ask? Try this method with a classmate or a friend. Write a letter for that person, asking the questions that Lincoln asked.

18. Lincoln obtained some of his education from books and some from other sources like watching and listening to people. Learning from life around us is at least as valuable as learning from books. Do you agree or disagree?

19. What do you admire most about Abraham Lincoln?

## VOCABULARY BUILDING

Here are some words found in the reading. If necessary, review their meanings. Then do the exercise.

| | | |
|---|---|---|
| anecdote | exemplary | ranting |
| bawdy | keenly | rollicking |
| droll | loft | toil |
| evangelist | mimic | |

**Vocabulary Exercise 1** | *Fill in each of the blanks below with the correct word. You may use a word more than once.*

1. My uncle amuses the family with his _____droll_____ and
   _____
   amusing
   sometimes _____bawdy_____ stories.
   _____
   coarse, obscene

2. Many comedians _____mimic_____ well-known actors and
   _____
   imitate
   politicians.

3. Chaucer, a medieval writer, is known for his _____jolly kind_____
   _____
   high-spirited
   and _____bawdy_____ tales.
   _____
   coarse

4. The _____evangelist_____ was giving a rousing sermon.
   _____
   preacher

5. Many women _____toil_____ all day in offices and factories, only
   _____
   work hard
   to come home and _____toil_____ some more.
   _____
   work hard

6. The speaker, _____ranting_____, raving, and waving his
   _____
   talking loudly and excitedly
   arms, drew a large crowd.

7. Mr. and Mrs. Brown's new apartment has a sleeping
   _____loft_____.
   _____
   upper portion

8. The _____evangelist_____ studied _____keenly_____ the faces of the
   _____          _____
   preacher             carefully, sharply
   people he was preaching to.

9. A famous _____anecdote_____ about George Washington concerns
   _____
   story
   his father's favorite cherry tree.

10. Ms. Rodriguez's supervisor praised her for her _____exemplary_____
    _____
    model
    work on the job.

Corbis-Bettmann

**ANTOINE DE SAINT-EXUPÉRY**

In his short life, Antoine de Saint-Exupéry (1900–1944) was a novelist, essayist, and pioneer aviator. He is known both for his bravery as a pilot and his skill as a writer.

Born in Lyon, France, Saint-Exupéry was awarded his pilot's license in 1922, and four years later he began working for an airline company. As one of the first to deliver international air mail, Saint-Exupéry found that flying in single-engine planes, often in bad weather, tested his courage and made him feel like "a warrior in danger." He recorded his experiences, sometimes in fictionalized form, in a series of highly regarded books published from the late 1920s until the 1940s. His novel *Night Flight* (1931) earned literary awards in France and was very popular in the United States as well.

Saint-Exupéry worked as a newspaper reporter and test pilot during the 1930s and became a military reconnaissance pilot for France at the start of World War II in 1939. When the French government collapsed after the German invasion in 1940, Saint-Exupéry escaped to the United States, where he enjoyed being a literary celebrity. Nevertheless, he did not remain in America, but joined the allied forces in North Africa and died in 1944 when his plane was shot down during a reconnaissance mission.

One of Saint-Exupéry's last books was *The Little Prince* (1943). It is an imaginative tale about a pilot who, after making a forced landing in the Sahara Desert, meets a very strange child, the ruler of a tiny planet, who has come to earth as part of his interplanetary journey. In the course of their conversations, the aviator and the prince explore many issues, such as beauty, love, friendship, duty, and the ability to know what is truly important in life. This excerpt from the beginning of the book emphasizes the differences between the ideas of grown-ups and the more imaginative worldview of the child.

# *From* THE LITTLE PRINCE

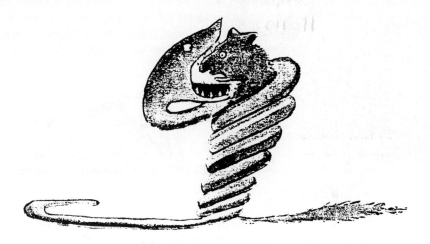

**primeval** (adj.): very ancient.

**boa constrictor** (noun): a type of snake that crushes other animals by wrapping around them and then swallowing them whole.
**prey** (noun): an animal hunted for food.
**ponder** (verb): to think deeply.

Once when I was six years old I saw a magnificent picture in a book, called *True Stories from Nature,* about the primeval forest. It was a picture of a boa constrictor in the act of swallowing an animal. Here is a copy of the drawing.

In the book it said: "Boa constrictors swallow their prey whole, without chewing it. After that they are not able to move, and they sleep through the six months that they need for digestion."

I pondered deeply, then, over the adventures of the jungle. And after some work with a colored pencil I succeeded in making my first drawing. My Drawing Number One. It looked like this:

I showed my masterpiece to the grown-ups, and asked them whether the drawing frightened them.

But they answered: "Frighten? Why should anyone be frightened by a hat?"

My drawing was not a picture of a hat. It was a picture of a boa constrictor digesting an elephant. But since the grown-ups were not able to understand it, I made another drawing: I drew the inside of a boa constrictor, so that the grown-ups could see it clearly. They always need to have things explained. My Drawing Number Two looked like this:

devote (verb): to give entirely; *to devote oneself to something:* to concentrate on something.
disheartened (adj.): discouraged.
tiresome (adj.): boring, troublesome, annoying.

The grown-ups' response, this time, was to advise me to lay aside my drawings of boa constrictors, whether from the inside or the outside, and devote myself instead to geography, history, arithmetic and grammar. That is why, at the age of six, I gave up what might have been a magnificent career as a painter. I had been disheartened by the failure of my Drawing Number One and my Drawing Number Two. Grown-ups never understand anything by themselves, and it is tiresome for children to be always and forever explaining things to them.

So then I chose another profession, and learned to pilot airplanes. I have flown a little over all parts of the world; and it is true that geography has been very useful to me. At a glance I can distinguish China from Arizona. If one gets lost in the night, such knowledge is valuable.

distinguish (verb): mark out, differentiate; to distinguish one thing from another is to tell the difference between them.
matters of consequence: matters of importance.

In the course of this life I have had a great many encounters with a great many people who have been concerned with matters of consequence. I have lived a great deal among grown-ups. I have seen them intimately, close at hand. And that hasn't much improved my opinion of them.

Whenever I met one of them who seemed to me at all clear-sighted, I tried the experiment of showing him my Drawing Number One, which I have always kept. I would try to find out, so, if this was a person of true understanding. But, whoever it was, he, or she, would always say:

"That is a hat."

Then I would never talk to that person about boa constrictors, or primeval forests, or stars. I would bring myself down to his level. I would talk to him about bridge, and golf, and politics, and neckties. And the grown-up would be greatly pleased to have met such a sensible man.

## THINKING ABOUT YOUR READING

### The Main Point

What important difference does Saint-Exupéry see between the viewpoint of the child and the viewpoint of the grownup? What point does he want to make about the minds of children and the way grownups may react to children's ideas?

### Details

1.  What book is mentioned in the first paragraph? What picture in it impressed the young reader?
2.  How old was the child when he saw the book?
3.  What did the child draw after seeing the book?
4.  How was the child's drawing misunderstood by grownups?
5.  When the child drew another picture to clarify his idea, what did the grownups tell him to do?
6.  What was the child's response to being misunderstood by the grownups?
7.  When the child grew up, what profession did he choose? In this profession, which of his courses of study was useful?

### Your Opinion

8.  What do you think of the way the grownups responded to the child's drawings?
9.  The teller of the story says that he always shows clear-sighted people his early drawings. What do you think he means by "clear-sighted" people, and why do you think he shows them his drawings?

10. Why does the narrator refuse to talk to most people about boa constrictors, primeval forests, or stars? Why does he talk about bridge, golf, politics, and neckties instead? Why do people consider him a "sensible person" when he talks about such subjects? Do you agree that people who talk about such subjects are sensible?

## Topics for Further Discussion and Writing

11. This passage from *The Little Prince* shows how grownups often misunderstand what children are trying to express. Why does this misunderstanding occur? Can you think of some examples of this type of misunderstanding occurring in your own experience?

12. This passage seems to suggest that there is a basic opposition between the imaginative and the practical side of a person. Do you agree or disagree with this view?

13. Are children in our society discouraged from being artistic and creative? If so, how and why does this process occur?

14. The narrator of the story says that living intimately with grownups has not improved his opinion of them. Do you think he is being fair?

15. The child's imagination was stimulated by an interesting book. Write an essay explaining why it is important to introduce books to children at an early age.

## EXPANDING YOUR VOCABULARY: OTHER MEANINGS AND RELATED WORDS

**boa constrictor**

**constrict** (verb): to draw together; to bind; to slow or stop.

That tight bandage will **constrict** your circulation.

**constriction** (noun): act of drawing together, closing in, tightness.

The **constriction** in his chest made him fear he was having a heart attack.

**strict** (adj.):
1. sticking closely to the rules.
2. closely enforced.

Mr. Alcock was known as a **strict** teacher.
There was a **strict** rule against eating or drinking in the computer lab.

**strictly** (adv.): closely, in a strict way.

The rule was **strictly** enforced.

**distinguish**
**distinguished** (adj.):
1. marked out for excellence, noted.
2. dignified.

Our French professor is a **distinguished** critic.
Many people like their hair grey because it makes them look **distinguished.**

**prey**
**prey** (verb):
1. to hunt (for food), devour.
2. to take advantage of, to victimize.

Wolves **prey** on deer and sheep.
Con-men sometimes **prey** on elderly people.

**primeval**
**primary** (adj.): first, basic.
**medieval** (adj.): relating to the Middle Ages (about 450 to 1350 A.D.).

My son attends **primary** school.
The museum had a display of **medieval** weapons and armor worn by knights.

Here is a list of words explained above. If necessary, review the definitions and the examples given, and then do Vocabulary Exercise 1.

| constrict | medieval | strict |
| constriction | prey | strictly |
| distinguished | primary | |

**Vocabulary Exercise 1** | *Insert the correct word in each of the blanks below. Use the correct form. You may use a word more than once.*

1. The _distinguished_ art critic was invited to give a lecture on
   _medieval_ art.
   *noted*   *relating to the Middle Ages*

2. Ms. Johnson was known as a very _strict_ teacher in the _primary_ school where she taught.
   *sticking closely to rules*   *first, basic*

3. The thief _prey_ upon the elderly, taking advantage of their inability to run away or fight back.
   *victimized*

4. If you follow your diet _strictly_, you may prevent any further attacks of pain and _constriction_ in your chest.
   *sticking closely to rules*   *tightness*

5. Sometimes street criminals ___prey___ on women who are
   <u>victimize</u>

   very fashionably dressed because they know that the

   ___constriction___ of their clothing and their high heels will prevent
   <u>tightness</u>

   them from running away.

6. Because of his ___distinguished___ appearance, the actor was often
   <u>dignified</u>

   chosen to appear in advertisements for financial companies.

7. Don't wrap that bandage too tightly around your leg, or you will

   ___constrict___ the flow of blood.
   <u>slow or stop</u>

## LANGSTON HUGHES

During his varied life, Langston Hughes (1902–1967) was a schoolteacher, nightclub entertainer, beachcomber, and writer. As an African American, he experienced prejudice and often faced hard times, but he managed to obtain an education and to publish his prize-winning writings.

He attended Columbia University in New York City in 1921 and 1922, and completed his degree at Lincoln University in Pennsylvania in 1929, taking time out from his formal studies to work on a freighter and hold other odd jobs. When not enrolled in college, he often visited the public libraries and read widely on his own. One of his favorite writers was Carl Sandburg (see page 448).

Langston Hughes wrote many types of literature—poetry, plays, short stories, and nonfiction. The purpose of his writing was, in his words, "to explain and illuminate the Negro condition in America." One of his best-known poems, "Harlem," begins:

> What happens to a dream deferred?
>   Does it dry up
>   like a raisin in the sun?

The following selection is taken from his autobiography, *The Big Sea.*

# "SALVATION" *from* THE BIG SEA

revival (noun): prayer
meeting.

I was saved from sin when I was going on thirteen. But not really saved. It happened like this. There was a big revival at my Auntie Reed's church. Every night for weeks there had been much preaching, singing, praying, and shouting, and some very hardened sinners had been brought to Christ, and the membership of the church had grown by leaps and bounds. Then just before the revival ended, they held a special meeting for children, "to bring the young lambs to the fold." My aunt spoke of it for days ahead. That night I was escorted to the front row and placed on the mourners' bench with all the other young sinners, who had not yet been brought to Jesus.

hardened (adj.): tough,
uncaring.
bring the young
lambs to the fold
(idiom): to convince
the young people to
join the others in a
certain belief.
escort (verb): to take,
accompany.
mourners' bench:
front row seats in a
church.

My aunt told me that when you were saved you saw a light, and something happened to you inside! And Jesus came into your life! And God was with you from then on! She said you could see and hear and feel Jesus in your soul. I believed her. I had heard a great many old people say the same thing and it seemed to me they ought to know. So I sat there calmly in the hot, crowded church, waiting for Jesus to come to me.

dire (adj.): severe, ter-
rible, disastrous.

The preacher preached a wonderful rhythmical sermon, all moans and shouts and lonely cries and dire pictures of hell, and then he sang a song about the ninety and nine safe in the fold, but one little lamb was left out in the cold. Then he said: "Won't you come? Won't you come to Jesus? Young lambs, won't you come?" And he held out his arms to all us young sinners there on the mourners' bench. And the little girls cried. And some of them jumped up and went to Jesus right away. But most of us just sat there.

gnarled (adj.): bent,
misshapen.

A great many old people came and knelt around us and prayed, old women, with jet-black faces and braided hair, old men with work-gnarled hands. And the church sang a song about the lower lights are burning, some poor sinners to be saved. And the whole building rocked with prayer and song.

Still I kept waiting to *see* Jesus.

rounder (noun): an
unreliable, morally
loose person.
deacon (noun): an
assistant to the min-
ister in a church.

Finally all the young people had gone to the altar and were saved, but one boy and me. He was a rounder's son named Westley. Westley and I were surrounded by sisters and deacons praying. It was very hot in the church, and getting late now. Finally Westley said to me in a whisper: "God damn! I'm tired o' sitting here. Let's get up and be saved." So he got up and was saved.

swirl (verb): to go
  around and around,
  to whirl.
congregation (noun): a
  gathering of people,
  especially in a
  church.
serenely (adv.): calmly.

Then I was left all alone on the mourners' bench. My aunt came and knelt at my knees and cried, while prayers and songs swirled all around me in the little church. The whole congregation prayed for me alone, in a mighty wail of moans and voices. And I kept waiting serenely for Jesus, waiting, waiting—but he didn't come. I wanted to see him, but nothing happened to me. Nothing! I wanted something to happen to me, but nothing happened.

I heard the songs and the minister saying: "Why don't you come? My dear child, why don't you come to Jesus? Jesus is waiting for you. He wants you. Why don't you come? Sister Reed, what is this child's name?"

"Langston," my aunt sobbed.

"Langston, why don't you come? Why don't you come and be saved? Oh, Lamb of God! Why don't you come?"

Now it was really getting late. I began to be ashamed of myself, holding everything up so long. I began to wonder what God thought about Westley, who certainly hadn't seen Jesus either, but who was now sitting proudly on the platform, swinging his knickerbockered legs and grinning down at me, surrounded by deacons and old women on their knees praying. God had not struck Westley dead for taking his name in vain or for lying in the temple. So I decided that maybe to save further trouble, I'd better lie too, and say that Jesus had come, and get up and be saved.

knickerbockered
  (adj.): wearing
  knickerbockers (old-
  fashioned three-
  quarter length pants).

So I got up.

Suddenly the whole room broke into a sea of shouting, as they saw me rise. Waves of rejoicing swept the place. Women leaped in the air. My aunt threw her arms around me. The minister took me by the hand and led me to the platform.

punctuated (adj.):
  marked, interrupted.
ecstatic (adj.): very
  happy.

When things quieted down, in a hushed silence, punctuated by a few ecstatic "Amens," all the new young lambs were blessed in the name of God. Then joyous singing filled the room.

That night, for the last time in my life but one—for I was a big boy twelve years old—I cried. I cried, in bed alone, and couldn't stop. I buried my head under the quilts, but my aunt heard me. She woke up and told my uncle I was crying because the Holy Ghost had come into my life, and because I had seen Jesus. But I was really crying because I couldn't bear to tell her that I had lied, that I had deceived everybody in the church, that I hadn't seen Jesus, and that now I didn't believe there was a Jesus any more, since he didn't come to help me.

## THINKING ABOUT YOUR READING

### The Main Point

What point does Langston Hughes want to make about the religious education of children?

### Details

1. How old was Langston Hughes when this incident took place?
2. What was happening at his Aunt Reed's church?
3. Where in the church did Hughes and the other children have to sit?
4. What happened after the sermon?
5. Who was left on the bench with Langston Hughes?
6. What happened after Hughes got up?

### Your Opinion

7. Was Westley really "saved" when he went to the altar? If not, why did he go?
8. Was Langston Hughes right in expecting to *see* Jesus? How did he form his ideas about being saved?
9. If Hughes really didn't think he was saved, why did he get up? Was this the right thing for him to do? Did *he* think it was the right thing to do?
10. Why was Langston crying later on that night? Did his aunt guess the reason?

### Topics for Further Discussion and Writing

11. Religion can be very comforting, but it can also create emotional problems for young people, as it did in Langston Hughes's life. Do you think that religion is, in general, helpful or harmful?
12. If you were Langston Hughes's aunt and he told you why he was really crying, what would you say to him?

13. If you are a religious person, describe your place of worship and tell what you like about it.

14. Have you ever had an important religious experience? If so, describe it.

15. Are there ever any times or circumstances in which it would be all right to deceive others? Explain your answer.

16. Do you think that people should rear their children to believe in God and to be religious? Why or why not?

17. Have you ever had an experience like the one Langston Hughes describes in which you let others pressure you into doing something you really did not want to do? Describe this experience.

## VOCABULARY BUILDING

Here are some words from "Salvation." Review the definitions given with the reading if necessary, and then do the exercises.

congregation— _gathe_    gnarled— _bend, misshapen_    revival — _meeting_
dire — _severe, terrible_    hardened — _uncaring_    serenely —
_very_ — ecstatic _overjoyed_    punctuated — _interrupted._    swirl — _go around + around_
_To take company_    escort

**Vocabulary Exercise 1**  |  *Fill in each blank below with the correct word from the list above. Use each word at least once (some may be used more than once). Add verb endings if necessary.*

1. Juveniles who are put into prison with ___hardened___ criminals
   often leave jail worse than they went in.
   <small>tough</small>

2. At the ___revival___ the ___ecstatic___ ___congregation___ prayed
   <small>prayer meeting</small>    <small>very happy</small>    <small>group of people</small>
   and sang.

3. The young man ___escorted___ his mother on a shopping trip.
   <small>accompanied</small>

4. The comedian's act was ___punctuated___ by laughter.
   <small>marked, interrupted</small>

5. The old woman with ___gnarled___ hands gave a
   <u>misshapen, twisted</u>

   ___dire___ warning to Jim when he asked her to tell his
   <u>terrible</u>

   fortune.

6. The smoke ___swirl___ through the room when the
   <u>went around and around</u>

   window was opened a bit, as we sat ___severely___ talking and
   <u>calmly</u>

   listening to music.

7. The old people's bodies were ___gnarled___ and
   <u>misshapen</u>

   ___hardened___ by years of toil.
   <u>toughened</u>

8. The President made a ___dire___ prediction about the
   <u>terrible</u>

   energy crisis.

## EXPANDING YOUR VOCABULARY: OTHER MEANINGS AND RELATED WORDS

**congregation**
**to congregate** (verb): to gather, group together.

The principal told the students not to **congregate** in the halls.

**ecstatic**
**ecstasy** (noun): joy, great happiness and pleasure.
**ecstatically** (adv.): in an ecstatic or very happy way.

Betty was in **ecstasy** when she was told she had won a scholarship to college.
The twins clapped their hands **ecstatically** when their mother promised them a new toy.

**escort**
We encountered this word as a verb, but it can also be a noun: someone who escorts, accompanies, or takes someone someplace.

Ethel thought Fred was the handsomest **escort** she could have wanted.
The defendant, with an **escort** of two policemen, entered the courtroom.

**gnarled**
**to gnarl** (verb): to bend, twist out of shape.

Old age may **gnarl** the body, but it need not dull the mind.

**punctuated**
**to punctuate** (verb):
1. to supply punctuation marks.

2. to interrupt.

**revival**
In addition to a religious meeting, this noun can mean:
1. coming back into use or custom.

2. coming back to life or consciousness.
**to revive** (verb):
1. to bring back into use.
2. to bring back to life or consciousness.

**serenely**
**serene** (adj.): calm.

**serenity** (noun): calmness.

The teacher taught the class how to **punctuate** a compound sentence.
The class **punctuated** the teacher's homework instructions with moans and groans.

There was a great **revival** of learning during the twelfth century.
The **revival** of wood-burning stoves is a result of the energy crisis.
The **revival** of Lazarus, a dead man, is a dramatic story in the Bible.

Hollywood has recently **revived** musical films.
The fireman **revived** the victim of smoke inhalation.

Mrs. Jackson was a **serene** person who rarely got excited.
Everyone enjoyed the peace and **serenity** of the ocean cruise.

Here is a list of words explained above.

| | | |
|---|---|---|
| congregate | gnarl | revive |
| ecstasy | punctuate | serene |
| ecstatically | revival | serenity |
| escort | | |

**Vocabulary Exercise 2** | *Using each of the words from the list above at least once, fill in each blank below. Add verb endings if necessary.*

**1.** The television director hoped that the studio audience would ___punctuate___ the comedy show with laughter.
interrupt, mark

**2.** Arthritis can ___gnarl___ parts of the body.
bend, twist

**3.** Barbara hoped that Dan would be her ___escort___ to the dance.
person who accompanies someone

4. The mayor's car had an ___escort___ of six police cars.
   accompaniment

5. The peace and ___serenity___ of the lake were disturbed by a
   calmness
   motorboat.

6. The police told the people who had ___congreate___ at the scene
   gathered
   of the accident to stand back while they tried to

   ___revive___ one of the victims.
   bring back to consciousness

7. The orphans were in ___ecstacy___ when the firefighters
   state of happiness
   brought them toys on Christmas Eve.

8. Some say there is a religious _____ on college
   reawakening
   campuses all over America.

9. Millions of people visit the Louvre Museum in Paris each year
   to view the ___serenety___ face of the *Mona Lisa*, a famous
   calm
   portrait.

10. Nancy smiled ___ecstacy___ at her new baby.
    very happily

## RICHARD WRIGHT

Richard Wright was born near Natchez, Mississippi, in 1908. Although he had to struggle against poverty and prejudice, he eventually became an award-winning writer, publishing such well-known works as *Uncle Tom's Children,* a collection of short stories, and *Native Son,* a best-selling and critically acclaimed novel, which was made into a film. Having made his mark in the United States, but still feeling the sting of racism, Wright moved to Paris with his wife and daughter and lived there until his death in 1960. He is remembered today as a major literary figure.

In 1945, Wright published his autobiography, *Black Boy: A Record of Childhood and Youth,* which tells of the hardships he faced growing up in the South during the early twentieth century. In the following excerpt from the book, Wright describes the hunger he felt as a five-year-old child after his father left home and the family sank deeper into poverty.

# *From* BLACK BOY: A RECORD OF CHILDHOOD AND YOUTH

gauntly (adv.): with a worn-out, thin appearance; related to *gaunt* (adj.): bony, fleshless.

grim (adj.): stern, harsh.

hostile (adj.): unfriendly, like an enemy.

baffle (verb): confuse, puzzle.

insistent (adj.): determined not to give up; persistent.

clamor (noun): a persistent call for something, a demand.

nudge (verb): push slightly.

Hunger stole upon me so slowly that at first I was not aware of what hunger really meant. Hunger had always been more or less at my elbow when I played, but now I began to wake up at night to find hunger standing at my bedside, staring at me gauntly. The hunger I had known before this had been no grim, hostile stranger; it had been a normal hunger that had made me beg constantly for bread, and when I ate a crust or two I was satisfied. But this new hunger baffled me, scared me, made me angry and insistent. Whenever I begged for food now my mother would pour me a cup of tea which would still the clamor in my stomach for a moment or two; but a little later I would feel hunger nudging my ribs, twisting my empty guts until they ached. I would grow dizzy and my vision would dim. I became less active in my play, and for the first time in my life I had to pause and think of what was happening to me.

"Mamma, I'm hungry," I complained one afternoon.

"Jump up and catch a kungry," she said, trying to make me laugh and forget.

"What's a *kungry?*"

"It's what little boys eat when they get hungry," she said.

"What does it taste like?"

"I don't know."

"Then why do you tell me to catch one?"

"Because you said that you were hungry," she said smiling.

I sensed that she was teasing me and it made me angry.

"But I'm hungry. I want to eat."

"You'll have to wait."

"But I want to eat now."

"But there's nothing to eat," she told me.

"Why?"

"Just because there's none," she explained.

"But I want to eat," I said, beginning to cry.

"You'll just have to wait," she said again.

"But why?"

"For God to send some food."

"When is He going to send it?"

"I don't know."

"But I'm hungry!"

She was ironing and she paused and looked at me with tears in her eyes.

**bewilderment** (noun): state of confusion.

**restriction** (noun): limit, an order limiting behavior.

**whimper** (verb): to cry softly, whine.
**stomp** (verb): to strike one's foot down hard, to stamp.
**pang** (noun): pain, sharp and painful feeling (often from hunger).
**flat** (noun): apartment.

**dispirited** (adj.): depressed, sad.
**despair** (noun): hopelessness.

**solemnly** (adv.): in a very serious way, gravely.
**vague** (adj.): not clear, unfocused.
**dread** (noun): great sense of fear.

"Where's your father?" she asked me.

I stared in bewilderment. Yes, it was true that my father had not come home to sleep for many days now and I could make as much noise as I wanted. Though I had not known why he was absent, I had been glad that he was not there to shout his restrictions at me. But it had never occurred to me that his absence would mean that there would be no food.

"I don't know," I said.

"Who brings food into the house?" my mother asked me.

"Papa," I said. "He always brought food."

"Well, your father isn't here now," she said.

"Where is he?"

"I don't know," she said.

"But I'm hungry," I whimpered, stomping my feet.

"You'll have to wait until I get a job and buy food," she said.

As the days slid past the image of my father became associated with my pangs of hunger, and whenever I felt hunger I thought of him with a deep biological bitterness.

My mother finally went to work as a cook and left me and my brother alone in the flat each day with a loaf of bread and a pot of tea. When she returned at evening she would be tired and dispirited and would cry a lot. Sometimes, when she was in despair, she would call us to her and talk to us for hours, telling us that we now had no father, that our lives would be different from those of other children, that we must learn as soon as possible to take care of ourselves, to dress ourselves, to prepare our own food; that we must take upon ourselves the responsibility of the flat while she worked. Half frightened, we would promise solemnly. We did not understand what had happened between our father and our mother and the most that these long talks did to us was to make us feel a vague dread. Whenever we asked why father had left, she would tell us that we were too young to know.

# THINKING ABOUT YOUR READING

## The Main Point

What point does Wright want to make about his childhood?

## Details

1. Why did Wright begin to wake up at night? What does he say was "standing at my bedside, staring at me gauntly"?

2. How was the hunger Wright felt during this period different from what he had felt before?

3. What had happened to the family that made Wright's situation worse?

4. When Wright first complained to his mother, how did she react? When he again asked for food, what did his mother tell him? When he persisted and wanted to know why there was no food, what did his mother finally tell him?

5. What kind of job did Wright's mother take?

6. When she left for work, what did Wright's mother leave for her sons?

7. What did she tell her sons about the way their lives would be in the future?

8. How did the children react to what Mrs. Wright told them about the future?

## Your Opinion

9. Why do you think Wright's mother tried to joke with her son about his hunger instead of immediately explaining to him what the family's situation was?

10. What kind of relationship had Wright had with his father before this time? How did Wright's feelings change after his father abandoned the family?

11. Do you think that Wright's mother was justified in telling her son that the family's increased poverty and hunger resulted from the desertion of his father? Why do you think she did it?

## Topics for Further Discussion and Writing

12. This passage from Wright's autobiography shows how parents shape the type of life a child leads. Write an essay explaining the relationship between parental behavior and a child's happiness and development.

13. At the present time, as in Wright's day, the issue of parental responsibility for the care and support of children is very important. In your opinion, are mothers more responsible than fathers for the rearing and care of children, or should this responsibility be shared equally?

14. This passage describes what happened in America in 1914. In modern America, would the same thing happen to a child whose father abandoned the family? What kinds of services are provided for impoverished single mothers and their children today? Do these services prevent hunger, or does it still exist? Write an essay discussing these issues, using the library to do some research if necessary.

## VOCABULARY BUILDING

Here is a list of words from the passage. Review their meanings if necessary, and then do Vocabulary Exercise 1.

| | | |
|---|---|---|
| baffle | grim | restriction — limit |
| bewilderment | hostile | solemnly |
| clamor | insistent | stomp |
| dispirited | nudge | vague |
| dread | pang | whimper |

**Vocabulary Exercise 1** | *Insert the correct word in each of the blanks below. Use the correct form. You may use a word more than once.*

1. There were so many _restrictions_ on the hours when the town
   <u>limits</u>

   pool could be used that there was a great _clamours_ for a
   <u>demand</u>

   more open policy.

2. At the supermarket, Robert accidentally _nudge_ the man
   <u>pushed slightly</u>

   in front of him and was _baffle_ by the man's _Hostile_
   <u>puzzled</u>          <u>very unfriendly</u>

   reaction; Robert, who had _nudge_ the other shopper only
   <u>pushed slightly</u>

   by accident, stared in _bewilderment_ as the man began cursing.
   <u>state of confusion</u>

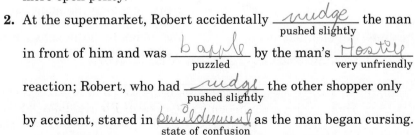

3. The doctor told a _dispirited_ group of researchers some
   sad, depressed

   very _grim_ statistics about AIDS; his report filled
   harsh

   everyone present with _dread_.
   great fear

4. The child would often _whimper_ his feet whenever he did
   stamp

   not get his way, and if that action did not get results, he

   would _whimper_.
   cry softly

5. Jesse did not want to inconvenience his friends by staying

   overnight at their house, but they were _clamor_
   persistent, refusing to give up

   because they felt it was too late at night for him to go home.

6. The judge asked the witness if he _solemnly_ swore to tell
   in a serious way

   the truth.

7. If your doctor's instructions seem _vague_, you must be
   unclear

   _insistent_ in asking for an explanation.
   determined not to give up

8. Infants and children feel hunger _pangs_ much more
   pains

   sharply than adults do.

# EXPANDING YOUR VOCABULARY:
# OTHER MEANINGS AND RELATED WORDS

**bewilderment**
**to bewilder** (verb): to confuse.    The large amount of computer software now available is enough to **bewilder** anyone.

**bewildered** (adj.): confused.    Melissa seemed **bewildered** when she woke in the middle of the night; she did not know where she was.

**bewildering** (adj.) confusing.    The computer store sells a **bewildering** amount of software.

**clamor**
**to clamor** (verb):
    1. to be noisy.
    2. to call for something
       repeatedly.
**clamorous** (adj.):
    1. noisy.

    2. demanding.

The alarm clock **clamored** until I shut it off.
The children **clamored** for the ice cream that they had been promised.

The schoolyard was a **clamorous** place at noon.
Richard could no longer ignore his **clamorous** stomach, which was repeatedly calling for food.

**hostile**
**hostilely** (adv.): in an unfriendly, threatening manner
**hostility** (noun):
    1. state of being an enemy, anger.
    2. opposition to something.

**hostilities** (pl. noun): acts of war.

Martin felt frightened when the stranger stared at him **hostilely.**

After the quarrel the friendship between the men turned to **hostility.**
The committee leader's **hostility** to Ms. Baxter's idea makes it unlikely that it will be accepted.
The diplomats were trying to end the **hostilities** between the nations.

**restriction**
**to restrict** (verb): to limit.

**restrictive** (adj.): limiting.

**restricted** (adj.): limited.

The store always **restricts** the purchase of sale items to three per customer.
Some parents are so **restrictive** that they allow their children to go out only one night a week.
This is a **restricted** area; only authorized personnel are allowed.

Here is a list of words explained above. If necessary, review the definitions and the examples given, and then do Vocabulary Exercise 2.

| | | |
|---|---|---|
| bewilder | clamorous | restrict |
| bewildered | hostilely | restricted |
| bewildering | hostilities | restrictive |
| clamor | hostility | |

**Vocabulary Exercise 2** | *Insert the correct word in each of the blanks below. Use the correct form. You may use a word more than once.*

1. _____ by the _____ children who surrounded
<u>Confused</u>      <u>noisy, demanding</u>

   him and begged for money, the tourist decided that in the future

   he would_____ his walks to well-known areas of the
   <u>limit</u>

   capital city.

2. The reporters were told that the area was _____ because
   <u>limited</u>

   of the outbreak of _____ between warring groups of
   <u>acts of war</u>

   soldiers.

3. The psychiatrist testified that the defendant's uncontrollable

   *hostility* stemmed from a very harsh upbringing by his
   <u>anger</u>

   overly *restricting* parents.
   <u>limiting</u>

4. The people *clamored* for a less *clamorous* government,
   <u>repeatedly called for</u>    <u>limiting</u>

   but the rulers viewed their demonstrations *hostilely*.
   <u>in an unfriendly, threatening way</u>

5. The many choices of goods and services available at a modern

   American shopping mall may seem *confusing* to a visitor
   <u>confusing</u>

   from a third-world nation.

6. At first too many restrictions may simply *confuse* a child,
   <u>confuse</u>

   but in time they may produce a constant state of *hostility*.
   <u>anger</u>

## MAYA ANGELOU

Maya Angelou was born in 1928 in St. Louis, Missouri. A woman of many talents, she has been a dancer, a singer, a political activist, a magazine editor, a professor, and a writer. Her writing includes essays, a number of volumes of poetry, and several autobiographical books. One of her best-known books is *I Know Why the Caged Bird Sings*, which was published in 1970. She read her poem "On the Pulse of Morning" at the 1993 inauguration of President Clinton.

The following selection is taken from her book *Wouldn't Take Nothing for My Journey Now*, a collection of essays on a wide variety of topics, including travel, charity, good manners, decent language, pregnancy, and self-image.

# "PASSPORTS TO UNDERSTANDING"

Human beings are more alike than unalike, and what is true anywhere is true everywhere, yet I encourage travel to as many destinations as possible for the sake of education as well as pleasure.

It is necessary, especially for Americans, to see other lands and experience other cultures. The American, living in this vast country and able to traverse three thousand miles east to west using the same language, needs to hear languages as they collide in Europe, Africa, and Asia.

A tourist, browsing in a Paris shop, eating in an Italian *ristorante,* or idling along a Hong Kong street, will encounter three or four languages as she negotiates the buying of a blouse, the paying of a check, or the choosing of a trinket. I do not mean to suggest that simply overhearing a foreign tongue adds to one's understanding of that language. I do know, however, that being exposed to the existence of other languages increases the perception that the world is populated by people who not only speak differently from oneself but whose cultures and philosophies are other than one's own.

Perhaps travel cannot prevent bigotry, but by demonstrating that all peoples cry, laugh, eat, worry, and die, it can introduce the idea that if we try to understand each other, we may even become friends.

**traverse** (verb): to travel across.
**collide** (verb): to crash into, to run into.
**browsing** (verb): looking casually.
**idling** (verb): moving slowly without purpose.
**encounter** (verb): meet, find, discover.
**negotiates** (verb): arranges, carries on the business of.
**trinket** (noun): a small, inexpensive ornament.

**bigotry** (noun): intolerance, prejudice.
**peoples** (pl. noun): groups of people united by culture, kinship, or belief.

## THINKING ABOUT YOUR READING

### The Main Point

Why does Angelou think that Americans should travel to other countries?

### Details

1.  What continents and cities are mentioned in the reading?
2.  What are some of the tourist activities mentioned by Angelou?

## Your Opinion

3.  Do you agree with Angelou that travel is both pleasurable and educational?

4.  Do you think that, as Angelou states, "Human beings are more alike than unalike"?

## Topics for Further Discussion and Writing

5.  Why is it important to know about cultures and philosophies that are different from our own?

6.  Angelou suggests that when people travel, they may become less prejudiced against others. Do you agree or disagree?

7.  Compare and contrast two cultural groups.

8.  What are some of the advantages of learning another language?

9.  What are some of the important aspects of your own culture?

## VOCABULARY BUILDING

Here is a list of words from the essay.

*[handwritten: prejudice]* bigotry *[handwritten: intolerance,]* encounter *[handwritten: meet]* negotiate *[handwritten: —arranged carefully an]*
browsing *[handwritten: -looking]* idling *[handwritten: find]* trinket *[handwritten: business]*
collide *[handwritten: causally]* *[handwritten: discover]* *[handwritten: small]*
*[handwritten: to crash,]* *[handwritten: Moving slowly]* *[handwritten: inexpensive]*
*[handwritten: to run into]* *[handwritten: without purpose.]* *[handwritten: ornament.]*

**Vocabulary Exercise 1** | *Fill in each blank with the correct word. Use the correct form of the word.*

1.  When two cars ___ *collide* ___ with each other, even at low
    *crash, run into*

    speeds, a lot of damage can result.

2.  People traveling for the first time in a foreign country will

    certainly ___ *encounter* ___ many strange and interesting sights
    *meet, discover, find*

    and situations.

3. In a large cardboard box, the child kept two of her favorite books, some ribbons for her hair, and one or two _____*Trinkets*_____.
<u>small, inexpensive ornaments</u>

4. While I was _____*browsing*_____ in a bookstore, I found an interesting
<u>looking casually</u>
book about ancient cultures of North Africa.

5. People who think that their own beliefs are the only correct ones are showing _____*bigotry*_____.
<u>intolerance, prejudice</u>

6. Representatives from baseball's management and leaders of the players' union were trying to _____*negotiate*_____ a settlement of the
<u>arrange</u>
strike.

7. On warm summer evenings, many people can be found
_____*idling*_____ happily in the park.
<u>moving slowly without purpose</u>

# EXPANDING YOUR VOCABULARY: OTHER MEANINGS AND RELATED WORDS

**bigotry**
**bigot** (noun): a person who shows intolerance for views, races, religions, beliefs that are different from his or her own.

A **bigot** will not vote for anyone of an ethnic group different from his or her own.

**bigoted** (adj.): intolerant.

The mayor said that his opponent was **bigoted.**

**collide**
**collision** (noun): a crash between two or more things.

Two fatalities occurred in the **collision** between a city bus and a taxi.

**encounter**
**encounter** (noun): a meeting.

Yesterday I had an unexpected but pleasant **encounter** with my old girl friend.

**negotiate**
**negotiate** (verb):
1. to arrange or settle, to make a deal.
2. to travel successfully over or through.

A sports agent **negotiates** contracts for the athletes who are his or her clients.
The bus **negotiated** the sharp turn without any trouble.

**negotiable** (adj.):
  1. capable of being arranged or decided.
  2. capable of being traveled on.

The terms of the new contract are **negotiable.**
This road is rough, but it is **negotiable.**

**negotiation** (noun, often used in the plural): bargaining and discussion meant to lead to an agreement.

After lengthy **negotiations,** the strike was settled.

**negotiator** (noun): a person who bargains or controls a discussion.

The **negotiator** for the hospital workers was a friendly, pleasant, but very firm person.

Here is a list of words explained above. If necessary, review the definitions and the examples given, and then do the vocabulary exercise.

| | | |
|---|---|---|
| bigot | encounter | negotiations |
| bigoted | negotiable | negotiator |
| collision | negotiate | |

**Vocabulary Exercise 2** | *Fill in each blank with the correct word. Use the correct form. A word may be used more than once.*

1. The newspaper printed an article about the _negotiating_ (bargaining) between the city and the unions.

2. Although she had not been driving for very long, she _negotiated_ (traveled over) the steep, winding road very well.

3. The roads are not _negotiable_ (capable of being traveled on) because of heavy rains.

4. The two candidates had an angry _encounter_ (meeting) today, each calling the other one a _bigot_ (intolerant person).

5. A _collision_ (crash) does not always have to be physical; two points of views or two cultures can also collide.

6. The Secretary of State needs to be a good _negotiator_ (person who bargains).

7. Because the first *executive* between their two presidents
   meeting

was so ho<u>s</u>tile, the warring nations have canceled further

*negotiations*.
bargaining and discussion

8. The candidate lost the election because many people thought he

was *bigoted*.
intolerant, prejudiced

*bigoted*

## MARTIN LUTHER KING, JR.

Martin Luther King, Jr., (1929–1968) was a famous civil rights leader whose goals were racial equality, justice, and equal economic opportunity for all Americans. He was born in Atlanta, Georgia, and graduated from Morehouse College. He then took advanced degrees at Crozer Theological Seminary and Boston University. As a Baptist minister in Montgomery, Alabama, in 1955, he organized a successful boycott to protest racially segregated seating on public buses.

Dr. King became the first president of a civil rights organization called the Southern Christian Leadership Conference and led many demonstrations to protest segregation and racial discrimination. He was one of the leaders of the famous 1963 civil rights rally in Washington, D.C., where he spoke of his dream of a future in which there could be equality and peace. His efforts led to the passage of landmark legislation against racial discrimination, and in 1964 he was awarded the Nobel Peace Prize.

Although he was often arrested and threatened with violence, he never gave up his struggle for justice or abandoned his belief in peaceful methods. When he was assassinated in 1968, the world mourned the loss of an important leader.

# *From* THE WORLD HOUSE

**interdependent** (adj.): relying on one another for support.
**heir** (noun): one who inherits.
**vast** (adj.): very large.
**eternally** (adv.): always, forever.
**in the red** (idiom): owing (money), in debt.
**beholden** (adj.): obligated to, in debt to.
**interrelated** (adj.): having a shared connection.

**impoverishes** (verb): makes poor.
**inevitably** (adv.): unavoidably, without fail.

All men are interdependent. Every nation is an heir of a vast treasury of ideas and labor to which both the living and the dead of all nations have contributed. Whether we realize it or not, each of us lives eternally "in the red." We are everlasting debtors to known and unknown men and women. When we arise in the morning, we go into the bathroom where we reach for a sponge which is provided for us by a Pacific islander. We reach for soap that is created for us by a European. Then at the table we drink coffee which is provided for us by a South American, or tea by a Chinese or cocoa by a West African. Before we leave for our jobs we are already beholden to more than half of the world.

In a real sense, all life is interrelated. The agony of the poor impoverishes the rich; the betterment of the poor enriches the rich. We are inevitably our brother's keeper because we are our brother's brother. Whatever affects one directly affects all indirectly.

## THINKING ABOUT YOUR READING

### The Main Point

What point does King make about humanity?

*About equal humanity, he wanted to be that everyone has to be equal.*

### Details

1.  What does each nation's "vast treasury" contain?
2.  What areas of the world are mentioned in the passage?
    *West african / Pacific islander, South American, Europe*
3.  Name some of the products we receive from all over the world.
    *Gas, car food, Print, pencil, Clothes, Computer,*

### Your Opinion

4.  What does King mean when he says that each one of us is always "in the red"?

5.  Who are the known and unknown people to whom we owe a debt?

6.  What does it mean to be "our brother's keeper"?

## Topics for Further Discussion and Writing

7.  Look up Martin Luther King, Jr., in an encyclopedia or other reference book and write a report about his life and work.

8.  Every day we use various products from all over the world. Describe some of the things you use daily that come from other countries.

9.  How does the agony of the poor hurt all of us, not just poor people? Why do all people benefit when the condition of poor people improves?

10. King believes that all people are interdependent and therefore should work to help each other build a better world. On the other hand, some people think that human beings are basically selfish and that it is useless to try to change things because we cannot change human nature. Which view do you agree with and why?

## VOCABULARY BUILDING

Here are some words from "The World House." Review the definitions given with the essay, and then do the exercise.

beholden — *obligated*    impoverish — *make poor*    interdependent — *relying*
eternally — *forever*      inevitably — *then*          vast — *large, and and*
heir — *inheriter*                  *inevitable*                           *another*

**Vocabulary Exercise 1** | *Fill in each blank below with the correct word from the list above. Use each word (some may be used more than once). Add verb endings if necessary.*

1.  I am __eternally__ grateful to you for your help.
         forever

2.  Mr. Miller felt __beholden__ to his sister after she paid
                    obligated

    his __vast__ debts.
        very large

3. The death of Martin Luther King, Jr., _impoverish_ all

made poor

people everywhere.

4. The city hospital, the clinics, and the medical school are

_interdependent_ .

relying on each other for support

5. Donald was the only _____ _heir_ _____ to his father's

person who inherits

_vast_ fortune.

very large

6. Anyone who combines working full-time and going to college is

_inevitably_ a very busy person.

unavoidably, without fail


## STUDENT RESPONSE

The following student essay was written in response to question 10 on page 485. Note the clear thesis at the end of the first paragraph (see Chapter 3). The writer's two points about work and action are developed in the two main-body paragraphs (see Chapters 4 and 6). Signal words guide the reader through the essay (see Chapter 5).

Oral Harrison
English 02-1822

Some people believe that working to change the way we human beings live our lives is useless because we cannot change human nature. I believe, however, that if we work towards creating a better world, it can be done.

First of all, working to create a better world is like working to make a living. We go to college for years to learn skills and to build a career. We have to work hard at it and work for long periods of time. We have to devote all our time and say to ourselves, "A better world is what we want, and that is what we are going to create." Nothing comes to us on a silver platter; we have to work to achieve the things we want in life.

Secondly, we have to take action as well. We cannot just say a better world is what we want and expect that everything will go in the right direction from there. We have to take action as Martin Luther King, Jr., did when he fought against unjust laws, or as Abraham Lincoln did when he took action to abolish slavery. Now, if people like Dr. King and Lincoln made a difference and they represent only a small portion of the people, think about what could happen if we all decide to work together to create a better world.

In conclusion, we can create a better world if we all work together. We cannot leave everything to God; we have to try to fix some things for ourselves. I believe, therefore, that we should all work together because nothing can be accomplished if we do not.

## LOOKING AT THE STUDENT RESPONSE

## Questions

1. Oral Harrison did not give his essay a title. Create a title for his essay.
2. What is Oral Harrison's thesis?
3. How many paragraphs does the essay have? What is the function of each paragraph?
4. What signal words are used in the essay?

Dit is een foto, zoals
ik me zou wensen,
altijd zo te zijn.
Dan had ik nog wel
een kans om naar
Holywood te komen.

Anne Frank.
10 Oct. 1942

(translation)
"This is a photo as I would wish
myself to look all the time. Then
I would maybe have a chance to
come to Hollywood."
Anne Frank. 10 Oct. 1942

## ANNE FRANK

Anne Frank was a Jewish schoolgirl who died during the Holocaust. This was a period of persecution and murder conducted by Hitler and the Nazis in the 1930s and 1940s in Germany and the European countries that the Nazis had conquered. Anne was born in Germany in 1929. At the age of four, she left with her family for Holland to escape the Nazis. However, the Nazis conquered Holland, so the Frank family was again in danger. Along with four other Jews, the Franks hid in a secret apartment in the office building of her father's company. While in hiding, Anne kept a diary which describes her daily life and tells of the difficulties of growing up during such terrible times.

In August 1944, after a little more than two years in hiding, the Frank family was captured by the Nazis. Anne was sent to a concentration camp and died in 1945 just before the end of World War II. She was not yet sixteen.

After the war, her father, who was the only survivor of the Frank family, recovered Anne's diary and had it published. It has been translated into many languages and has inspired a play and a movie.

# *From* THE DIARY OF A YOUNG GIRL

*Saturday, 20 June, 1942*

I haven't written for a few days, because I wanted first of all to think about my diary. It's an odd idea for someone like me to keep a diary; not only because I have never done so before, but because it seems to me that neither I—nor for that matter anyone else—will be interested in the unbosomings of a thirteen-year-old schoolgirl. Still, what does that matter? I want to write, but more than that, I want to bring out all kinds of things that lie buried deep in my heart.

**unbosomings** (noun): thoughts, confessions.

There is a saying that "paper is more patient than man"; it came back to me on one of my slightly melancholy days, while I sat chin in hand, feeling too bored and limp even to make up my mind whether to go out or stay at home. Yes, there is no doubt that paper is patient and as I don't intend to show this cardboard-covered notebook, bearing the proud name of "diary," to anyone, unless I find a real friend, boy or girl, probably nobody cares. And now I come to the root of the matter, the reason for my starting a diary: it is that I have no such real friend.

**melancholy** (adj.): sad, seriously thoughtful.
**limp** (adj.): weak, drooping, exhausted.

Let me put it more clearly, since no one will believe that a girl of thirteen feels herself quite alone in the world, nor is it so. I have darling parents and a sister of sixteen. I know about thirty people whom one might call friends. . . . I have relations, aunts and uncles, who are darlings too, a good home, no—I don't seem to lack anything. But it's the same with all my friends, just fun and joking, nothing more. I can never bring myself to talk of anything outside the common round. We don't seem to be able to get any closer, that is the root of the trouble. Perhaps I lack confidence, but anyway, there it is, a stubborn fact and I don't seem to be able to do anything about it.

Hence, this diary. . . .

My father was thirty-six when he married my mother, who was then twenty-five. My sister Margot was born in 1926 in Frankfort-on-Main, I followed on June 12, 1929, and, as we are Jewish, we emigrated to Holland in 1933, where my father was appointed Managing Director of Travies N.V. This firm is in close relationship with the firm of Kolen & Co. in the same building, of which my father is a partner.

**emigrate** (verb): to leave a country.

The rest of our family, however, felt the full impact of Hitler's anti-Jewish laws, so life was filled with anxiety. In

**impact** (noun): effect, result.
**anxiety** (noun): worry.

**pogrom** (noun): organized massacre or killing.
**fled** (verb): past tense of *flee,* go away rapidly.
**capitulation** (noun): surrender. (Anne means the Dutch surrender to Hitler.)
**decrees** (noun): official orders.
**in succession** (idiom): one after the other.
**banned** (adj.—past part. of verb): forbidden.
**trams** (noun): streetcars.
**placard** (noun): poster.
**prohibited** (adj.): forbidden.
**restrictions** (noun): limits.

1938 after the pogroms, my two uncles (my mother's brothers) escaped to the U.S.A. My old grandmother came to us, she was then seventy-three. After May 1940 good times rapidly fled: first the war, then the capitulation, followed by the arrival of the Germans, which is when the sufferings of us Jews really began. Anti-Jewish decrees followed each other in quick succession. Jews must wear a yellow star, Jews must hand in their bicycles, Jews are banned from trams and are forbidden to drive, Jews are only allowed to do their shopping between three and five o'clock and then only in shops which bear the placard "Jewish shop." Jews must be indoors by eight o'clock and cannot even sit in their own gardens after that hour. Jews are forbidden to visit theaters, cinemas, and other places of entertainment. Jews may not take part in public sports. Swimming baths, tennis courts, hockey fields, and other sports grounds are all prohibited to them. Jews may not visit Christians. Jews must go to Jewish schools, and many more restrictions of a similar kind.

So we could not do this and were forbidden to do that. But life went on in spite of it all. Jopie [a friend] used to say to me, "You're scared to do anything, because it may be forbidden." Our freedom was strictly limited. Yet things were still bearable. . . .

*Wednesday, 8 July, 1942*

Years seem to have passed between Sunday and now. So much has happened, it is just as if the whole world had turned upside down. But I am still alive . . . and that is the main thing, Daddy says.

Yes, I'm still alive, indeed, but don't ask where or how. You wouldn't understand a word, so I will begin by telling you what happened on Sunday afternoon.

**veranda** (noun): porch.

At three o'clock . . . someone rang the front doorbell. I was lying lazily reading a book on the veranda in the sunshine, so I didn't hear it. A bit later, Margot appeared at the kitchen door looking very excited. "The S.S. have sent a call-up notice for Daddy," she whispered. "Mummy has gone to see Mr. Van Daan already." (Van Daan is a friend who works with Daddy in the business.) It was a great shock to me, a call-up; everyone knows what that means. I picture concentration camps and lonely cells—should we allow him to be doomed to this? "Of course he won't go," declared Margot, while we waited together. "Mummy has gone to the Van Daans to discuss whether we should move

**S.S.:** Special Nazi forces.

**concentration camps:** guarded areas where Jews, other minorities, and political enemies of the Nazis were imprisoned and killed.

into our hiding place tomorrow. The Van Daans are going with us, so we shall be seven* in all." Silence. We couldn't talk any more, thinking about Daddy. . . .

Each time the bell went, Margot or I had to creep softly down to see if it was Daddy, not opening the door to anyone else.

*[Anne's mother returned with Mr. Van Daan.]*

Margot and I were sent out of the room. Van Daan wanted to talk to Mummy alone. When we were alone together in our bedroom, Margot told me that the call-up was not for Daddy, but for her. I was more frightened than ever and began to cry. Margot is sixteen; would they really take girls of that age away alone? But thank goodness she won't go, Mummy said so herself; that must be what Daddy meant when he talked about us going into hiding.

Into hiding—where would we go, in a town or the country, in a house or a cottage, when, how, where. . . ?

These were questions I was not allowed to ask, but I couldn't get them out of my mind. Margot and I began to pack some of our most vital belongings into a school satchel. The first thing I put in was this diary, then hair curlers, handkerchiefs, schoolbooks, a comb, old letters; I put in the craziest things with the idea that we were going into hiding. But I'm not sorry, memories mean more to me than dresses.

**satchel** (noun): bag.

*[Anne describes how the family hurriedly packed their belongings and left the house for the hiding place that Christian friends had helped to prepare. Margot packed some books and went on ahead with a friend who was helping the Franks.]*

We put on heaps of clothes as if we were going to the North Pole, the sole reason being to take clothes with us. No Jew in our situation would have dreamed of going out with a suitcase full of clothing. I had on two vests, three pairs of pants, a dress, on top of that a skirt, jacket, summer coat, two pairs of stockings, lace-up shoes, woolly cap, scarf, and still more; I was nearly stifled before we started, but no one inquired about that. . . .

**stifled** (adj.): smothered, suffocated.

---

*There would eventually be eight people in the hiding place when the four Franks and the three Van Daans were joined by a Jewish dentist.

*Thursday, 9 July, 1942*

So we walked in the pouring rain, Daddy, Mummy, and I, each with a school satchel and shopping bag filled to the brim with all kinds of things thrown together anyhow.

We got sympathetic looks from people on their way to work. You could see by their faces how sorry they were they couldn't offer us a lift; the gaudy yellow star spoke for itself.

Only when we were on the road did Mummy and Daddy begin to tell me bits and pieces about the plan. For months as many of our goods and chattels and necessities of life as possible had been sent away and they were sufficiently ready for us to have gone into hiding of our own accord on July 16. The plan had had to be speeded up ten days because of the call-up, so our quarters would not be so well organized, but we had to make the best of it. The hiding place itself would be in the building where Daddy has his office. . . .

*[The following excerpt is taken from a later section of her diary. It was written when the family had been in hiding for about six months.]*

*Wednesday, 13 January, 1943*

Everything has upset me again this morning, so I wasn't able to finish a single thing properly.

It is terrible outside. Day and night more of those poor miserable people are being dragged off, with nothing but a rucksack and a little money. On the way they are deprived even of these possessions. Families are torn apart, the men, women, and children all being separated. Children coming home from school find that their parents have disappeared. Women return from shopping to find their homes shut up and their families gone.

The Dutch people are anxious too, their sons are being sent to Germany. Everyone is afraid.

And every night hundreds of planes fly over Holland and go to German towns, where the earth is plowed up by their bombs, and every hour hundreds and thousands of people are killed in Russia and Africa. No one is able to keep out of it, the whole globe is waging war and although it is going better for the Allies, the end is not yet in sight.

And as for us, we are fortunate. Yes, we are luckier than millions of people. It is quiet and safe here. . . . We are even so selfish as to talk about "after the war," brighten up at the

**gaudy** (adj.): overly bright.

**chattels** (noun): belongings.
**sufficiently** (adv.): enough.
**of our own accord** (idiom): willingly.

**rucksack** (noun): backpack.
**deprived** (passive verb): robbed.

**anxious** (adj.): worried.

**Allies:** the United States, Russia, England, France, and other countries fighting the Nazis and Fascists.

thought of having new clothes and new shoes, whereas we really ought to save every penny, to help other people, and save what is left from the wreckage after the war.

clogs (noun): wooden shoes.

stay the pangs (idiom): temporarily stop hunger.

countless (adj.): many.

dejected (adj.): depressed.

The children here run about in just a thin blouse and clogs; no coat, no hat, no stockings, and no one helps them. Their tummies are empty; they chew an old carrot to stay the pangs, go from their cold homes out into the cold street and, when they get to school, find themselves in an even colder classroom. Yes, it has even got so bad in Holland that countless children stop the passers-by and beg for a piece of bread. I could go on for hours about all the suffering the war has brought, but then I would only make myself more dejected. There is nothing we can do but wait as calmly as we can till the misery comes to an end. Jews and Christians wait, the whole earth waits; and there are many who wait for death.

Yours, Anne

*[About a year and a half after Anne wrote this entry, the Frank family was captured by the Nazis. By the end of the war, only Anne's father remained alive.]*

## THINKING ABOUT YOUR READING

### The Main Point

What did you learn about history and human nature from reading these selections from Anne Frank's diary?

### Details

1. How many people were in the Frank family? 4
2. What happened in May 1940 that changed Anne Frank's life?
3. What were some of the anti-Jewish laws that Anne mentions?
4. What was the first thing she packed?
5. How was Anne dressed as she walked to the hiding place?
6. Where was their hiding place?
7. What conditions does Anne describe in Holland during World War II?

## Your Opinion

8. Do you think that keeping a diary helped Anne in any way?

9. What do the anti-Jewish laws tell you about the Nazi government?

10. Why did Anne and her parents wear so many clothes when they went into hiding? Why didn't they pack suitcases?

11. Why didn't anyone offer the family a lift as they walked in the rain?

12. Why did Anne consider herself fortunate?

13. Reread what Anne wrote on January 13, 1943. What does this entry tell you about her character?

## Topics for Further Discussion and Writing

14. What has Anne's diary added to your knowledge of the Holocaust?

15. Could something like the Holocaust happen in the United States?

16. What is the relationship between prejudice and persecution?

17. What can be done to fight prejudice and persecution?

18. How would you react if you and your family were persecuted as the Franks were?

19. What would you have done if you had been a neighbor of the Franks?

20. Have you ever kept a diary? For a week, keep a diary describing your thoughts and feelings.

## VOCABULARY BUILDING

Here is a list of words from the reading. If necessary, go over their meanings. Then do the exercise.

| | | |
|---|---|---|
| anxiety | deprived | limp |
| anxious | emigrate | melancholy |
| banned | gaudy | pogrom |
| capitulation | impact | stifled |
| countless | in succession | sufficiently |
| decrees | | |

**Vocabulary Exercise 1** | *Fill in each blank with the correct word. Use the correct form of the word.*

1. Mrs. Ferris felt a bit _melancholy_ when her youngest
<br>                                        <u>sad, seriously thoughtful</u>
<br>child started school.

2. Tina Jones looked _stifled_ in a huge, _gaudy_
<br>                             <u>smothered</u>             <u>overly bright</u>
<br>overcoat.

3. _Countless_ people were killed in the _pogrom_ .
<br>   <u>Many</u>                                      <u>organized killings</u>

4. The Nazi _decrees_ declared that Jews were _banned_
<br>              <u>official orders</u>                      <u>forbidden</u>
<br>from using public transportation.

5. After losing three games _in succession_, the basketball team
<br>                                      <u>one after the other</u>
<br>felt dejected.

6. The _anxious_ farmer wondered what _impact_
<br>            <u>worried</u>                        <u>effect, result</u>
<br>the drought would have on his crops since he was unable to
<br>irrigate his fields _appropriately_
<br>                                 <u>enough</u>

7. After the _capitulation_ of Holland to Hitler, thousands of
<br>               <u>surrender</u>
<br>people were _deprived_ of their property, their freedom,
<br>                      <u>robbed</u>
<br>and even their lives.

8. The baby's high fever and _limp_ body caused his
<br>                               <u>weak, drooping</u>
<br>parents much _anxiety_ .
<br>              <u>worry</u>

9. Though the Franks _emigrated_ from Germany, they did not
<br>                              <u>moved away</u>
<br>escape the Nazis.

## STUDENT RESPONSE

The following student essay was written in response to question 16 on p. 494. Note that the essay has a clearly stated thesis in the first paragraph (see Chapter 3). The writer's two examples are developed in the two main-body paragraphs, and the thesis is restated in the concluding paragraph (see Chapter 6). Note also the use of signal words (see Chapter 5).

Ruth Rivers
English 02-1823

## Prejudice and Persecution

I believe that there is a direct relationship between prejudice and persecution. Where there is prejudice, there is always the danger of persecution. It is my contention that prejudice is born of ignorance, and ignorance breeds bias.

For example, at the beginning of the Holocaust the Nazis, who believed that they were superior to other people, issued anti-Jewish decrees which isolated the Jews from society. Their freedom was restricted, they were forced to wear a yellow star for identification, forbidden to shop in certain stores, not permitted to use certain forms of transportation, made to adhere to strict curfews, and they were eventually sent to gas chambers and killed.

Similarly, black people have long been in a ceaseless struggle against prejudice in this country. Because of widespread ignorance, they were thought to be inferior and considered to be less than human. They were discriminated against because of the color of their skin and not given a chance for equal participation in the labor market so that they could pull themselves up from the poverty level, where many remain to this day. Black people were not allowed sufficient access to decent housing, and they could not attend the schools of their choice; moreover, history shows that many black people lost their lives in the struggle for human dignity.

Webster's Dictionary defines prejudice as "unreasonable bias, injury or harm resulting as from some judgment or action of another or others." It further states that to persecute is "to afflict or harass constantly so as to injure or distress; oppress cruelly." I conclude that prejudice and persecution usually go hand in hand. Therefore, we as parents and educators alike have a moral obligation to educate our children, to make them aware of the evil consequences of prejudice, especially since prejudice obviously lays the foundation for persecution to follow.

## LOOKING AT THE STUDENT RESPONSE

### Questions

1. How does Ms. Rivers support her thesis that "there is a direct relationship between prejudice and persecution"?

2. What two groups does Ms. Rivers mention who have suffered from persecution? How does her paragraph structure help her to explain these examples?

3. Where in her concluding paragraph does Ms. Rivers restate her thesis? What does she add when she moves beyond restating the thesis? How does this addition strengthen her conclusion and the essay as a whole?

Jerry Bauer

## FRANK McCOURT

Although born in New York, Frank McCourt spent most of his childhood in Ireland because his parents, Irish immigrants, decided to return to their homeland when young Frank was four. After a brief stay in the north of Ireland, the family went south and settled in Limerick, a city on the River Shannon.

The McCourts experienced extreme poverty, which was worsened by the alcoholism of the father, Malachy McCourt. The elder McCourt drank up most of the little money he was able to earn, and he eventually abandoned the family. Although Frank McCourt was an excellent student, he had to leave school for a while at the age of fourteen and take a series of odd jobs in order to earn money to help the family survive. By the time he was nineteen he had saved enough to pay his way back to the United States, where he served in the army and then attended college on the G.I. bill (a government program to provide ex-servicemen with a higher education). After graduating from New York University, McCourt became a teacher. For many years, he taught creative writing at Stuyvesant High School in New York City.

*Angela's Ashes*, the story of McCourt's impoverished childhood, was published in 1996 and was a great success. A bestseller in the United States and abroad, it has also received numerous literary awards, including the Pulitzer Prize.

The following passage tells of an episode that occurred when the McCourts were still in America. Despite the problems created by his father's alcoholism, Frank McCourt here remembers his father as a source of cultural richness and comfort.

# *From* ANGELA'S ASHES

I'm in a playground on Classon Avenue in Brooklyn with my brother, Malachy. He's two, I'm three. We're on the seesaw.

Up, down, up, down.

Malachy goes up.

I get off.

Malachy goes down. Seesaw hits the ground. He screams. His hand is on his mouth and there's blood.

Oh, God. Blood is bad. My mother will kill me.

And here she is, trying to run across the playground. Her big belly slows her.

She says, What did you do? What did you do to the child?

I don't know what to say. I don't know what I did.

She pulls my ear. Go home. Go to bed.

Bed? In the middle of the day?

She pushes me toward the playground gate. Go.

She picks up Malachy and waddles off.

**waddle** (verb): walk clumsily with short, swaying steps.

My father's friend, Mr. MacAdorey, is outside our building. He's standing at the edge of the sidewalk with his wife, Minnie, looking at a dog lying in the gutter. There is blood all around the dog's head. It's the color of the blood from Malachy's mouth.

Malachy has dog blood and the dog has Malachy blood.

I pull Mr. MacAdorey's hand. I tell him Malachy has blood like the dog.

Oh, he does, indeed, Francis. Cats have it, too. And Eskimos. All the same blood.

Minnie says, Stop that, Dan. Stop confusing the wee fellow. She tells me the poor wee dog was hit by a car and he crawled all the way from the middle of the street before he died. Wanted to come home, the poor wee creature.

**wee** (adj.): small.

Mr. MacAdorey says, You'd better go home, Francis. I don't know what you did to your wee brother, but your mother took him off to the hospital. Go home, child.

Will Malachy die like the dog, Mr. MacAdorey?

Minnie says, He bit his tongue. He won't die.

Why did the dog die?

It was his time, Francis.

The apartment is empty and I wander between the two rooms, the bedroom and the kitchen. My father is out looking for a job and my mother is at the hospital with Malachy. I wish I had something to eat but there's nothing in the icebox but cabbage leaves floating in the melted ice. My father said never eat anything floating in water for the rot that might be in it. I fall asleep on my parents' bed and when my mother shakes me it's nearly dark. Your little brother is going to sleep a while. Nearly bit his tongue off. Stitches galore. Go into the other room.

My father is in the kitchen sipping black tea from his big white enamel mug. He lifts me to his lap.

Dad, will you tell me the story about Coo Coo?

Cuchulain. Say it after me, Coo-hoo-lin. I'll tell you the story when you say the name right. Coo-hoo-lin.

I say it right and he tells me the story of Cuchulain, who had a different name when he was a boy, Setanta. He grew up in Ireland where Dad lived when he was a boy in County Antrim. Setanta had a stick and ball and one day he hit the ball and it went into the mouth of a big dog that belonged to Culain and choked him. Oh, Culain was angry and he said, What am I to do now without my big dog to guard my house and my wife and my ten small children as well as numerous pigs, hens, sheep?

Setanta said, I'm sorry. I'll guard your house with my stick and ball and I'll change my name to Cuchulain, the Hound of Culain. He did. He guarded the house and regions beyond and became a great hero, the Hound of Ulster itself. Dad said he was a greater hero than Hercules or Achilles that the Greeks were always bragging about and he could take on King Arthur and all his knights in a fair fight which, of course, you could never get with an Englishman anyway.*

That's my story. Dad can't tell that story to Malachy or any other children down the hall.

He finishes the story and lets me sip his tea. It's bitter, but I'm happy there on his lap.

**Cuchulain** (noun): A legendary Irish hero. One of the Cuchulain stories says that as a small child (named Setanta), he killed a dog. Feeling sorry for the dog's owner (Culain), Setanta promised to stand in as a guard dog himself, thus earning the name the Hound of Culain (in Irish Cu Chulain), or Hound of Ulster, a region of Ireland.

**Hercules:** a hero of Greek and Roman mythology; Hercules was said to be the strongest man on earth.

**Achilles:** a heroic Greek warrior, the hero of the Trojan War.

**King Arthur:** a semi-legendary king who lived in Britain during the sixth century. He is supposed to have gathered the Knights of the Round Table.

*This statement reflects the traditional hostility between the English and the Irish.

## THINKING ABOUT YOUR READING

### The Main Point

The action of this story is shown through the eyes of a very small child. What does this viewpoint reveal about a child's development and understanding of the world?

## Details

1. What is the name of Frank McCourt's brother?

2. How old were the two brothers when the incident on the playground occurred?

3. How did McCourt's younger brother get hurt? Did Frank McCourt realize that he was responsible for the accident?

4. When Frank McCourt went home from the playground, what people did he meet, and what did he see in the gutter?

5. Where did McCourt's mother take his brother for treatment of his injury? What type of injury did he have and how was it treated?

6. Describe the apartment in which the McCourts lived. What did the family have in its icebox?

7. How was Frank McCourt comforted by his father?

## Your Opinion

8. Do you think that McCourt's mother should have allowed him to go home alone while she took care of the younger brother? What would you have done in her place?

9. Why did Minnie MacAdorey tell her husband to "stop confusing the wee fellow" when Mr. MacAdorey tried to explain that many creatures, including humans, have red blood? Do you agree with Mrs. MacAdorey that a three-year-old child would be confused by Mr. MacAdorey's explanation?

10. In your opinion, why did McCourt's father say that Cuchulain was a greater hero than Hercules, Achilles, and King Arthur?

## Topics for Further Discussion and Writing

11. In this passage from *Angela's Ashes,* we see a very young boy who hurts his brother without meaning to because he does not understand the consequences of his act. Tell about a time when you as a child or a child of your acquaintance acted without understanding cause and effect.

12.  The father's story about Cuchulain seems designed to teach his son about Irish cultural heritage. Why is it important for parents to teach their children about their culture?

13.  Despite the difficult experiences of the day, Frank McCourt found comfort in sitting on his father's lap and listening to his story. Write an essay that tells about an experience in your life in which someone close to you comforted you after a difficult day.

14.  If necessary, go to the library or interview a relative to find out about a story that reflects your cultural heritage. Write the story.

# Credits

p. 402  Aesop, "The Treasure in the Orchard," from *Aesop's Fables,* retold by Blanche Winder. Copyright 1965 by Airmont Publishing Company, N.Y. Reprinted by permission of the publisher.

p. 409  Miguel de Cervantes, excerpt from *Don Quixote,* translated by Samuel Putnam. Copyright 1949 by The Viking Press, Inc. Reprinted with the permission of Viking Penguin, a division of Penguin Books USA Inc.

p. 416  *Romeo and Juliet* Copyright © Paramount Pictures. All Right Reserved. Courtesy of Paramount Pictures.

p. 420  Excerpts from *Elizabeth Cady Stanton: As Revealed in Her Letters, Diary and Reminiscences,* edited by Theodore Stanton and Harriet Stanton Blatch. Copyright 1922 by Harper & Row, Publishers, Inc. Reprinted by permission of HarperCollins Publishers.

p. 435  Emily Dickinson, #288 "I'm Nobody! Who are You?" from *The Complete Poems of Emily Dickinson,* edited by Thomas H. Johnson. Copyright 1951, 1955, 1979, 1983 by the President and Fellows of Harvard College. Reprinted with the permission of The Belknap Press of Harvard University Press.

p. 440  Mohandas Gandhi, "Spiritual Training" from *Mahatma Gandhi: His Own Story,* edited by C.F. Andrews (New York: The Macmillian Company, 1930). Reprinted with the permission of HarperCollins Publishers, Ltd.

p. 448  Carl Sandburg, excerpts from *Abraham Lincoln: The Prairie Years and The War Years,* One-Volume Edition. Copyright 1926, 1939 by Harcourt Brace Jovanovich, Inc. and renewed 1953, 1966 by Carl Sandburg, reprinted by permission of Harcourt Brace and Company.

p. 454  Antoine de Saint-Exupéry, excerpt from *The Little Prince,* translated by Katherine Woods. Copyright 1943 and renewed 1971 by Harcourt Brace. Reprinted with the permission of the Harcourt Brace & Company and Heinemann.

p. 461  Langston Hughes, "Salvation" from *The Big Sea.* Copyright 1940 by Langston Hughes. Renewed 1968 by Arna Bontemps and George Houston Bass. Reprinted with the permission of Hill & Wang, a division of Farrar, Straus and Giroux, Inc. and Serpant's Tail, Ltd.

From *The Panther and the Lash: Poems of Our Times,* by Langston Hughes. Copyright 1951 by Langston Hughes. Reprinted by permission of Alfred A. Knopf, Inc.

p. 469  Richard Wright, excerpt from *Black Boy: A Record of Childhood and Youth.* Copyright 1937, 1942, 1944, 1945 by Richard Wright, renewed 1973 by Ellen Wright. Reprinted with the permission of HarperCollins Publishers, Inc. and Jonathan Cape, Ltd.

p. 477  Maya Angelou, "Passports to Understanding" from *Wouldn't Take Nothing for My Journey Now.* Copyright 1993 by Maya Angelou. Reprinted with the permission of Random House, Inc. and Virago Press, Ltd.

p. 483  Martin Luther King, Jr., "The World House" from *Where Do We Go From Here: Chaos or Community?* (New York: Harper Row, 1967). Copyright 1967 by Martin Luther King, Jr. Reprinted with the permission of Writers House, Inc.

p. 488  Anne Frank, excerpt from *Anne Frank: The Diary of a Young Girl.* Copyright 1952 by Otto H. Frank. Reprinted with the permission of Doubleday Dell Publishing Group, Inc.

p. 498  Frank McCourt, excerpt from *Angela's Ashes.* Copyright 1996 by Frank McCourt. Reprinted with the permission of Scribner, a division of Simon & Schuster, Inc. and the Aaron M. Priest Agency.

# Index

Connecting words, summary, 96–97 (*see also* Conjunctions; Connecting adverbs)
Consistency, 328 (*see also* Tense)
Consonants:
  before "a," 254
  before "y," 370
  defined, 253
  doubling, 380–81
Context, 239
Contractions, 308
  agreement with, 159
  avoiding errors in, 159
  examples, 158–59
  negative, 158–59
  subject-verb agreement with, 159
  word endings of, 308 (*see also* Apostrophe)
Contrasting elements, 393
Coordinating conjunctions (*see* Conjunctions)
Coordination, 79–83
Corrected essays, 62 (*see also* Double-correction method)
Correcting essays, 62, 64 (*see also* Double-correction method; Editing)
Crossing out, 64

**D**

Dangling modifier, 358–59
Dash, 398
Declarative sentence (*see* Statement)
Dates:
  capitalization in, 363
  idioms about, 285
Demonstratives, 304 (*see also* Adjectives)
Dependent clause (*see* Subordinate clause)
Description, 6
Descriptive topic, 47, 48 (*see also* Essay)
Descriptive words (*see* Adjectives; Adverbs; Modifiers)
Details, 39, 40, 41
Development:
  defined, 38
  of essay, 46–55
  of paragraph, 35, 38–40
  of thesis, 14, 16–17, 18–19, 20–21, 53–55

Diagram
  of essay, 10–11, 47–50
  mapping of ideas, 32
  notes, 29, 55
Diary (*see* Journal)
Dictation, 319–20
Diction (*see* Confusing words; Parts of speech)
Dictionary, 61, 197
"Did," 207 (*see also* "Do")
Directional thesis, 18
Directions:
  to essay tests, 18
  for neat papers, 64 (*see also* Format)
Direct quotation, 394
Discussion thesis, 18
Distancing, 59
"Do":
  conjugation of, 155
  "do," "does," 155
  as helping verb, 157
Double-correction method, 67–74
Double negatives, 338–39
Double-spacing, 64, 65
Double subject (*see* Compound subject)
Doubling a consonant, 380–81
Draft:
  final, 57, 63, 64
  first (rough), 57, 59
Drafting, 4

**E**

"Ed" endings (*see* Word endings)
Editing, 4, 56–62
  to avoid confusion, 120
  strategies, 57–58, 59–62
  on a word processor, 65 (*see also* Checking an essay)
Editing checklist, 61
"Effect," "affect," 259
Einstein, 30–31, 32–33
English, standard, 337, 356
Erasure, 64
Errors:
  avoiding, 69–72
  correcting, 64, 67–74

## J

Joining words (*see* Conjunctions; Connecting adverbs; Connecting words)
Journal, 6–8

## K

"Know," "no," 268

## L

Language, 3, 283–84 (*see also* Diction)
Legible writing, 63–65 (*see also* Word processing)
Linking verbs, 350 (*see also* Verbs, state of being)
Logic:
  editing for, 56
  in paragraphs, 40
  in sentences, 143, 358–59
  in tense shifts, 227–28, 230
"Loose," "lose," "losing," 266
"Lose," "loss," "lost," 243
"Loss," "lost," 267

## M

Magazines, 394
Main-body paragraphs, 10–11, 47–50, 53–54
Main clauses (*see* Independent clauses)
Main idea (*see* Thesis; Topic statement)
Mapping, 32
Margins, 64–66
Masculine pronouns, 330 (*see also* Gender; Pronouns)
Misspelled words, 384–85
Mistakes (*see* Errors)
Modifiers, 343–60
  dangling, 358–59
  defined, 343
  misplaced, 358
  (*see also* Adjectives; Adverbs)

## N

Neatness, 63–66
Negative contraction (*see* Contractions)
Negatives:
  double, 338–39
  listed, 339
  placement in progressive verbs, 214
Newspapers, 394
"No," "know," 268
Noncount nouns, 303
Note-taking for paper planning, 24–29, 32, 47–50, 55
Nouns, 149, 235–36, 322, 326–29
  as adjective, 301
  count, 303
  of direct address, 392
  noncount, 303
  proper, capitalizing, 361
  (*see also* Collective nouns; Plural nouns)

## O

Objects, pronouns as, 333–35
"Of," confused with "have," 263

## P

Paper, 64, 66
Paragraph:
  coherence, 35, 40–43
    chronological order, 41
    order of importance, 42
    pattern set up by topic sentence, 42
    signal words, 42–43
    spatial order, 41
  creating, 21–34, 46–55
  definition, 25, 35
  development, 35, 38–39
  four-paragraph plan, 47–51
  length, 35
  three-point-thesis plan, 52–55
  unity, 35–38
Parallel structure, 137–38
Parentheses, 398

## Q

Question mark, 388
Questions, 174–75
forming, 294
"Quite," "quiet," 270
Quotation marks, 394–95

## R

Redundancy, avoiding, 145–46
Repetition, avoiding, 145
Run-on sentences, 119–21
ways to correct, 121–27
(*see also* Comma splices)
Run-together sentences (*see* Run-on
sentences; Comma splices)

## S

Semicolon, 389–90
with connecting adverbs, 86–88
to fix run-ons, 122–23, 125–26
to join clauses, 83–84, 96–97
misuse of, 84
"S" endings (*see* Word endings)
Sentence combining, 79–97
Sentence fragment (*see* Fragment)
Sentences:
choppy, 79
inverted, 175–76
passive voice, 202
Sentence structure (*see* Clauses)
Sentence style:
clarity, 141
coherence, 141, 143
grace, 141, 145–46
parallel structure, 137–38
Signal words, 42–43, 56
Singular subjects:
verb agreement with, 149–52, 154–55,
161–62, 164–67, 171, 173
activity nouns, 167–68
collective nouns, 165
indefinite singular pronouns, 164

Spelling, 369–86
changing "y" to "i" in verbs, 375
commonly misspelled words, 385–86
doubling a consonant, 380–81
editing tips, 61, 62
final "e," 378
"ful" suffix, 344
"i" before "e," except . . ., 383
plural formation in nouns, 369–72
Statement, 387
Steps to writing, 4, 23
Subjects:
activity nouns, 166–67
agreement with verbs when difficult to
find, 174–78
in inverted sentences, 175–76
in questions, 174–75
when separated from verb, 177–78
to avoid fragments, 102–103
in clauses, 77
collective nouns, 165
compound, 327
verb agreement with, 169–70
defined, 75
indefinite singular pronouns, 164
nouns as, 149, 165–67, 169–70
pronouns as, 333–35
singular or plural, 171–73
"some," "most," "all," "none," 171
"who," "which," "that," 172–73
subjects and verbs separated, 174,
177–78
Subject-verb agreement (*see* Agreement)
Subject-verb structures (*see* Clauses)
Subordinate clauses:
in building a sentence, 89–94
comma with, 91, 94
defined, 77
fragments, 105
not a complete thought, 77, 105
with relative pronouns, 92–94
showing importance of ideas, 90–91
use of, 89–91 (*see also* Clauses)
Subordinating conjunctions (*see*
Conjunctions)
Subordinating words, 90, 93, 105–106 (*see
also* Conjunctions)